This volume discusses the history of the major Balkan nationalities – the Albanians, Bulgarians, Croats, Greeks, Romanians, Serbs, and Slovenes – in the eighteenth and nineteenth centuries. At the commencement of this period these people lived either under Ottoman or Habsburg rule. The different conditions in the two empires and the experiences of the nationalities are described. The major emphasis, however, is on the national movements, including their programs and the revolutionary activity associated with them. By the end of the nineteenth century, Greece, Romania, and the South Slavic states of Serbia and Montenegro were able to establish independent governments; Bulgaria and Croatia had autonomous regimes. The gradual disintegration of the Ottoman Empire and the national revolutions were major causes of dispute between the great powers. The Eastern Question, a dominant theme in international relations in both centuries, made the Balkans a constant center of international attention and earned it a reputation for instability and unrest. This book thus covers the national movements, their successes and failures to 1900, and the place of these events in the international relations of the day.

D1111294

HISTORY OF THE BALKANS

EIGHTEENTH AND NINETEENTH CENTURIES

VOLUME I

LEARNED SOCIETIES ·
the Joint Committee on Eastern Europe Publication Series
Number 12
THE SOCIAL
THE AMERICAN COUNCIL OF
SCIENCE RESEARCH COUNCIL

HISTORY OF THE BALKANS

Eighteenth and Nineteenth Centuries

VOLUME I

BARBARA JELAVICH

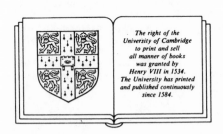

The right of the
University of Cambridge
to print and sell
all manner of books
was granted by
Henry VIII in 1534.
The University has printed
and published continuously
since 1584.

CAMBRIDGE UNIVERSITY PRESS

Cambridge
New York   Port Chester
Melbourne   Sydney

Published by the Press Syndicate of the University of Cambridge
The Pitt Building, Trumpington Street, Cambridge CB2 1RP
40 West 20th Street, New York, NY, 10011
10 Stamford Road, Oakleigh, Melbourne 3166, Australia

First published 1983
Reprinted 1984, 1985, 1987, 1989, 1990

Full term copyright is claimed. Thereafter all portions of this work covered by this copyright
will be in the public domain.
This work has developed under a contract with the U.S. Office of Education, Department of
Health, Education, and Welfare. However, the content does not necessarily reflect the
position or policy of that Agency, and no official endorsement of these materials should be
inferred.

Printed in the United States of America

Library of Congress Cataloging in Publication Data
Jelavich, Barbara Brightfield.
History of the Balkans.
Includes bibliographies and indexes.
Contents: v. 1. Eighteenth and nineteenth centuries – v. 2. Twentieth century
1. Balkan Peninsula – History. I. Title.
DR36.J37   1983   949.6   82–22093

ISBN 0-521-25249-0 (vol. 1) hardback
ISBN 0-521-27458-3 (vol. 1) paperback

Contents

Contents

Maps and illustrations

Maps and Illustrations

Preface

THIS NARRATIVE CONCERNS the history of the people of five modern Balkan states – Albania, Bulgaria, Greece, Romania, and Yugoslavia – over approximately three centuries. Although the Balkan peninsula has played a major role in history, the area has been subject to less intensive study than any other European region. To the outside observer the Balkans often appear to be a puzzle of confusing complexity. A geographic region inhabited by seven major nationalities, speaking different languages, it has usually impinged on the Western consciousness only when it has become the scene of wars or acts of violence. Long characterized as the "powderkeg of Europe," the peninsula has indeed lived up to its reputation. The Crimean War, the major European engagement in the century after 1815, had its origins here; the assassination of Franz Ferdinand in Sarajevo in 1914 was the immediate cause of World War I. After 1944 the Balkan events were a major factor in initiating the Cold War; the Greek civil war was the occasion of the reorientation of American foreign policy with the Truman Doctrine. Although it is certainly true that crises such as these have received thorough study, particularly in their world significance, much less attention has been paid to the study of the area on its own terms. Western historians, hindered by language difficulties and limited access to archival materials, have only recently begun to examine in detail the many aspects of the Balkan experience.

Yet this area, because of both its past contributions and its present importance, certainly deserves a larger place in modern historical studies. Part of former ancient Greek, Roman, Byzantine, Ottoman, and Habsburg lands, and situated at the convergence of Europe, Africa, and Asia, the peninsula has felt the weight of the convergence of alternate imperial drives and competing ideologies. Here at various historical periods major political and cultural borderlines have intersected – for instance, the boundaries between the Eastern (Byzantine) and Western Roman empires, between Islam and Christianity, between Orthodoxy and Catholicism, and today between the military blocs of the North Atlantic Treaty and the Warsaw Pact, alignments representing conflicting social, political, and economic systems. Subject to rival external influences, as well as internal pressures, the area is in a very real sense a testing ground for alternative systems. Thus in the past two centuries the Balkans have been a laboratory in which some of the more elusive aspects of national and liberal forms of political organization and economic development could be observed; at present the socialist regimes offer similar opportunities for investigation. In addition, for both the North and the South American reader, an examination of Balkan history has the added appeal of dealing with the national homeland of millions of emigrants to the New World.

This survey is designed to introduce the reader to the dramatic and fateful history of the Balkan peninsula in the years from the Treaty of Karlowitz (Sremski Karlovci) of 1699 to the beginning of the 1980s. The aim is to present a balanced picture, based on recent research and on the standard histories and monographs, of the development of this region in the modern era. The major theme will be the process by which the Balkan nationalities broke away from imperial control, both Ottoman and Habsburg, established independent national states, and then embarked on the even more arduous road to economic and social modernization. The Treaty of Karlowitz, whose terms were a major permanent setback to Ottoman control, is a convenient landmark at which to begin our story. The subsequent period witnessed the commencement of the movements that were to lead the Balkan people away from the imperial, ecclesiastical organization of the Ottoman government toward the national, secular, state system. The national revolutions, as we shall see, were carried through on an individual basis with comparatively little cooperation among the Balkan nationalities. Nevertheless, the activities of the separate groups shared certain common characteristics. For instance, each national movement was associated with a cultural revival that involved the formulation of a literary language and a renewal of interest in the pre-Ottoman history of the people. Similarly, all of the national leaders organized and carried through armed insurrections, whether successful or not, and they shared a similar vision of the political and economic goals for the future.

The road to political transformation was to be long. The slow pace of the weakening and gradual withdrawal of Ottoman control made the process more difficult. Under the absolute rule of the sultan, internal national and religious rivalries had been muted, and European influences were confined to the periphery of the peninsula. With the increasing inability of the Ottoman government to defend its possessions, the Balkan lands became prizes coveted by other great powers. In the eighteenth century the Russian and Habsburg empires competed both with the Ottoman Empire and against each other for predominance. In the nineteenth century the region moved to the center of the diplomatic stage; the Eastern Question, involving all of the European great powers, became the major continuous diplomatic issue until the commencement of World War I, a conflict whose immediate origins were deeply rooted in Balkan problems. Unfortunately for the Balkan people, during the period of the national liberation movements their lands thus became the focus of international attention. Here the increasingly dynamic imperial drives of Britain, France, and Russia crossed and conflicted. Later the newly united Germany and Italy joined in the battle. By the beginning of the twentieth century the Habsburg Empire, like the Ottoman, was faced with rising national antagonisms within its own boundaries. Nevertheless, this state too attempted to carry through a strong Balkan policy. Although the peninsula declined in significance as a center of diplomatic conflict between the two world wars, its importance as an object of international rivalry revived after 1945, with an altered list of combatants.

Living in a region of international tension, the Balkan people naturally found themselves under constant pressure from abroad. Unwilling to accept the substitution of the rule of other powers for that of the Ottoman Empire, the Balkan national leaderships fought against any outside attempts at annexation or domination. At the same time they were enormously attracted by the material and cultural achievements of the European states. Thus, despite the fact that the national movements were directed toward what was in fact the revival of pre-Ottoman political organizations, their leaderships accepted European political institutions and often justified their actions on the basis of contemporary Western ideologies of liberalism and nationalism. In the nineteenth century the great powers determined the form of government, the person of the ruler, and the boundaries of most of the new Balkan national states. However, their decisions, often based on progressive political concepts, in general reflected the convictions of the majority of the Balkan leaders. In the twentieth century socialist and communist political programs, drawn both from the Soviet Union and from Western Europe, have attracted similar support among some groups.

Until Ottoman control was removed and the national governments were formed, internal political issues and foreign policy received the principal attention of the Balkan leaders. The parallel process of social and economic change went forward at a much slower pace until after 1945, when it became a predominant consideration in Balkan affairs. Until very recent times the bulk of the population has consisted of an impoverished and largely illiterate peasantry living under extremely backward conditions. Although some of its members rose to form the political leadership of the national governments, the greater number witnessed the gradual erosion of their economic and social position under the pressure of the new conditions. Despite their preoccupation with political and diplomatic issues, the Balkan leaders were well aware of the implications of their weak economies, particularly in questions involving general state interests such as national defense. A major aim of all the national governments was thus modernization – including the development of industry, the improvement of agriculture, the introduction of an advanced educational system, and the acquisition of the traits and amenities that were so admired in Western European societies. In this effort, too, the ambivalent attitude toward foreign influences was clearly shown. Although the Balkan states, lacking the necessary capital, resources, expertise, and experience, needed assistance, they feared foreign exploitation or imperial domination.

The theme of the conflicting attraction to and rejection of foreign political, ideological, and economic influence has thus been a constant element in Balkan history. However, although Balkan societies, either willingly or under duress, have accepted much from the outside world, it must be emphasized that even where foreign institutions and ideas were adopted, they were subsequently molded and changed to fit national traditions and prejudices. Certainly, the major element in Balkan life is that drawn from the long historical experience of the people and their own unique reactions to the outside interferences to which the peninsula has been so vulnerable.

This work was prepared as part of a program organized in 1972 by the Joint Committee on Eastern Europe of the American Council of Learned Societies and the Social Science Research Council to provide histories of Eastern Europe. Professor Peter F. Sugar of the University of Washington was the chairman of the special committee that prepared the original proposal; Professor Michael B. Petrovich of the University of Wisconsin became chairman of the supervising committee and was responsible for the subsequent organization. This Balkan history has received generous funding from the Office of Education, including grants that allowed the author the free time necessary to complete the writing and funds to assist in the preparation of the volumes for publication. Dr. Gordon B. Turner, Vice-President of ACLS until 1980, and his successor, Dr. Jason H. Parker, contributed valuable suggestions and assistance. The author is also greatly indebted to Julia A. Petrov of the Office of Education for her advice and support.

As stated in the original project, this book is designed as an introduction to Balkan history; it assumes no prior knowledge. Major European events and political, philosophical, and economic theories necessary to the narrative are also covered. Because of the complexity of the developments being treated, some subjects are touched on in more than one section. This area has played a major role in world affairs. Consequently attention is directed not only to internal Balkan events, but also to the great international conflicts in this period. The book thus covers both Balkan developments and the place of the peninsula in history.

Because of the dual aspect of the text, numerous maps have been included to help clarify both the internal problems and the crises caused by the involvement of the great powers in the region. The illustrations are designed to cover these and other aspects of Balkan history. Almost all are prints prepared in the first half of the nineteenth century. In the eighteenth and nineteenth centuries the Balkans and the Ottoman Empire in general attracted the interest not only of statesmen and generals, but also of writers, poets, and artists, who were drawn to the area by the extreme beauty of the land-scape and by what was to them an exotic and romantic atmosphere. The peninsula itself was little known; there were many misconceptions. As is shown in the map prepared in the early eighteenth century by one of the best British cartographers, Herman Moll, until the middle of the nineteenth century it was generally believed that a lofty and almost impenetrable east–west moun-tain range crossed the entire peninsula. The illustrations make particularly clear the impression left upon the artists by the wild and mountainous nature of the lands.

The narrative has been divided into two volumes, which, with some limi-tations, can be read separately. The first commences with a general introduc-tion on the major historical events through the seventeenth century, but dis-cusses in detail the eighteenth and nineteenth centuries. Here the themes of the nature of Ottoman and Habsburg rule and the subsequent national movements have been emphasized. The volume concludes with the achieve-ment of Greek, Montenegrin, Romanian, and Serbian independence and Bulgarian autonomy and the organization of their new governments. In in-ternational relations Volume I covers the events from the conclusion of the Treaty of Karlowitz in 1699 to the signing of an agreement on the Balkans between Russia and the Habsburg Empire in 1897.

Volume II concerns principally the events of the twentieth century to 1980, although some background on the political developments in the previous decades is included. The major themes are the completion of the territorial unification of the modern states; the great wars and their consequences; and, in particular, the measures taken to meet the enormous political, social, and economic problems faced by these nations in the modern world. The diffi-culties caused by constant outside great-power interference and domination, issues that were very important in the previous centuries, also carry over into the recent period.

The multiplicity of languages and the varieties of spelling used over the past centuries provide certain difficulties for the historian of the area. In this book the attempt has been made to adopt in the spelling of personal names and geographic points the form that is most commonly used and that will be most familiar to the reader. Standard systems of transliteration have been used for Greek and Bulgarian; Serbian words and names appear in their Latin spelling. Complete consistency has not been possible. In addition, names of rulers and Ottoman statesmen and many first names have been anglicized.

Dating also provides some problems, since the Balkan people used three separate calendars until after World War I. The Muslims dated events from the Hegira in A.D. 622. The Orthodox used the Julian, or Old Style, calen-dar, whereas the Catholics and Protestants adopted the Gregorian, or New Style. In the eighteenth century the Julian calendar ran eleven days behind the Gregorian; in the nineteenth century this number increased to twelve; and in the twentieth century it reached thirteen. All dates in this book are in the New Style. The difference in dating produces difficulties principally when a particular day or month is associated with an event. For example, the April Uprising of 1876 in Bulgaria occurred in May under the New Style. When these complications arise, they are explained in the text.

For the most part the footnotes have been limited to identifications of the sources of quotations and of some of the statistical information. The capitalization and spelling of quotations from old sources have been changed to conform to the style of the text. The bibliography is designed to provide the reader with a list of books on various aspects of Balkan history. Books in languages other than English and all articles are excluded, although, of course, these have been used extensively in the preparation of the book.

The author is greatly indebted to her friends and colleagues, specialists in the field, who kindly consented to read the manuscript. Their expert comments and criticisms greatly assisted in the preparation of the final version of the book. All or a major section of the work was read by Professors Richard V. Burks, Wayne State University; Dimitrije Djordjević, University of California, Santa Barbara; Rufus Fears, Indiana University; John V. A. Fine, Jr., University of Michigan; Keith Hitchins, University of Illinois; Halil Inalcik, University of Chicago; John R. Lampe, University of Maryland; Thomas A. Meininger, York University; John A. Petropulos, Amherst College; Michael B. Petrovich, University of Wisconsin; Dennison I. Rusinow, American Universities Field Staff; Traian Stoianovich, Rutgers University; and Peter F. Sugar, University of Washington. In addition, this work is in fact the product of the collaboration of the author with her husband, Charles Jelavich, who contributed not only suggestions and criticisms, but also the results of his own research.

The author would like to thank Debbie Chase, who typed the final copy, and Janis Bolster, whose excellent editorial reading and valuable suggestions added much to the manuscript in its final stages of preparation. She also compiled the index. The maps were prepared by William Jaber.

Introduction

THE LAND

OUR NARRATIVE CONCERNS primarily the history of the peoples of the Balkan peninsula, an area of land surrounded by the Black, Aegean, Ionian, and Adriatic seas. Although the line of the Danube, Sava, and Kupa rivers has often been given as designating the northern perimeter of the region, this account will also be concerned with the fate of lands across the Danube inhabited by Romanian, Croatian, Slovene, and Hungarian populations. From a geographic point of view, the outstanding feature of the area under study is its mountainous character; *Balkan* comes from the Turkish word for a chain of wooded mountains. The great ranges dividing the peninsula and the Carpathians to the north had the effect of separating the peoples from each other; there is no natural center for the region. In order to understand much of subsequent Balkan history the reader should first study Map I, giving particular attention to both the mountains and the river systems.

To the north, in the territory of present-day Romania, the sweep of the Carpathian Mountains dominates the landscape. To the south, Bulgaria is divided by the Balkan Mountains and separated from Greece by the Rhodope chain. Turning to the northwest, a Slovenian and Croatian population is found in the Karawanken and Julian Alps. Continuing southward, the Dinaric Alps form a formidable barrier between the Adriatic coast and the hinterland of Bosnia and Hercegovina. Further south, the Pindus Mountains run the length of Greece.

The major river system of the region is formed by the Danube and its tributaries: the Drava, the Tisza (Theiss), the Sava, the Morava, the Isker, the Sereth, and the Pruth. Throughout history the Danube has been the principal route in this area for military invasion, trade, and travel. This great river highway provided obstacles to communication only at the Iron Gates, a narrow section with rocks and swift currents. The other important rivers – the Vardar, the Struma, and the Maritsa – flow into the Aegean Sea. Because of the mountainous nature of the Adriatic coastline, the rivers emptying into that sea are not of a character to foster waterborne trade or travel. The Ne-

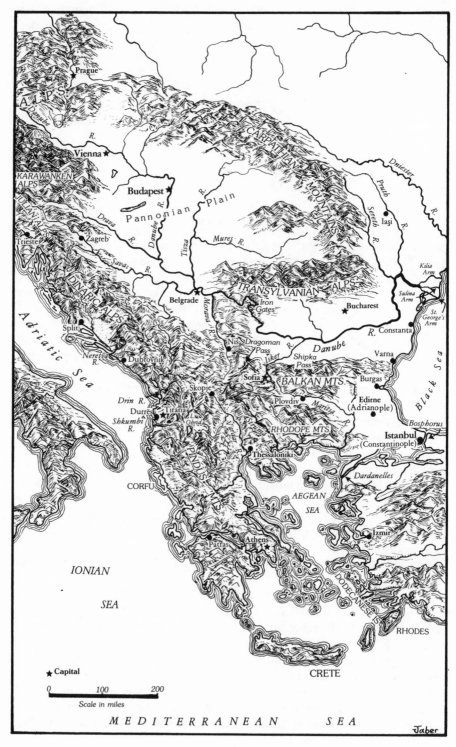

Map 1. Relief map of the Balkans

2

retva, the Drin, and the Shkumbî, nevertheless, played an important part in the development of the adjacent lands.

Dominated by mountains and hills, the region has relatively few areas of rich agricultural land. The exceptions are the Danube River valley, including sections of present-day Romania and two areas of Yugoslavia – Slavonia and the Vojvodina. The Maritsa and Shkumbî river valleys are also valuable agricultural areas. The mountains, with their extensive forests and pastures, of course also provide support for the population. The mineral wealth was exploited in Roman times, but not as much as at the present time.

Situated strategically at the crossroads of Asia, Africa, and Europe, the Balkan peninsula has proved both a tempting object of conquest and a passageway to other regions. Although the mountains contributed to particularism and isolation among the Balkan people, they did not provide a shield against outside invasion. The entire peninsula is cut through by major corridors, which run chiefly through the great river valleys and the mountain passes. Along these relatively few great routes, invading forces could easily enter, whether they were nomadic tribes with their ponies and herds or modern great powers with railroads, cars, trucks, and tanks.

Two principal doorways opened the peninsula to outside penetration. The Danube River valley was historically the major route by which people from the Asian steppelands entered not only the Balkans, but also Central Europe. No natural barriers hindered passage from the lands north of the Black Sea, along the Danube valley, into the Pannonian Plain. Invading tribes could also proceed southward and either cross the Balkan Mountains at one of the convenient passes or follow the coastline. The second roadway commenced at Belgrade at the confluence of the Danube and the Sava and proceded down the Morava valley. At Niš two branches formed, one leading through the Vardar valley to Thessaloniki (Salonika), the great Aegean port, and the other crossing over the Dragoman Pass to Sofia, Plovdiv (Philippopolis), Adrianople (Edirne), and finally Constantinople (Istanbul), the most important city of the Balkans. In Roman times another road, the Via Egnatia, was of principal significance. This major line of communication ran from Durrës (Durazzo) on the Adriatic coast through the Shkumbî valley, by Lake Ohrid, to Thessaloniki, and from there either by sea or through Thrace to Constantinople. Other river valleys were also of significance. The Bulgarian region near the present capital of Sofia is linked with the Danube through the Isker River valley and with the Aegean by the Struma valley. The Neretva River connects the Adriatic seacoast with the Bosnian interior.

The long coastline to the east and south, with its convenient harbors and river outlets, was also conducive to the establishment of influence and control by outside powers; the islands of the Aegean, Ionian, and Adriatic seas were similarly open to attack by sea. Venice, for example, was able to build up an impressive imperial presence in the area because of its commercial and naval supremacy. In more recent times, Britain's naval power enabled that state to exert great influence in the area, in particular in Greece and the entire eastern Mediterranean.

THE HISTORICAL BACKGROUND

Ancient civilizations: Greece and Rome

Although this account commences formally with the last decade of the seventeenth century, a brief survey of the previous period is necessary because of the important role of history in the development of the Balkan national states, the main theme of this book. As will be demonstrated later, at each stage of the formation of the modern governments the leaders repeatedly recalled the past to explain or justify their policies. No attempt will be made here to present a detailed account of Balkan history since the Iron Age; the intention is only to discuss briefly those events and individuals that exerted a direct influence on the later period.

The first inhabitants of the peninsula about whom a body of information is available are the Illyrians, who lived in the region generally west of the Morava valley to the Adriatic, and the Thracians, who settled east of the river in lands stretching from the Aegean to north of the Danube. Both of these peoples, with Iron Age civilizations, had tribal organizations. The Thracians established an organized state in the fifth century B.C. The Dacians, a branch of the Thracians, were to become a basic element in the formation of the Romanian nationality. The Illyrians were the ancestors of the modern Albanians.

The major political and cultural achievements of the ancient period did not, however, take place in the central Balkan region, but to the south in the Greek lands (see Map 2). The shores and islands of the Aegean Sea were to be the site of the first great European civilization, that of the Greeks, who at this time called themselves Hellenes and their land Hellas. An advanced Bronze Age civilization developed in Greece in the period 1600–1200 B.C. Such sites as Mycenae, Tiryns, Pylos, Athens, and Thebes were centers of a palace-based society marked by a relatively complex economic and social organization, literacy, and a refined art and architecture heavily influenced by the non-Hellenic civilization of Minoan Crete. By 1450 B.C. Greeks from the mainland had occupied Crete and Rhodes, and extensive commercial relations existed with the lands of the Near East and Egypt. Records of the Hittite kingdom have been interpreted to indicate the political presence of Greeks on the mainland of Asia Minor. For reasons that are not fully understood, the sophisticated civilization of Bronze Age Greece collapsed in the period after 1200 B.C. The invasion of new groups of Hellenes, speaking the Doric dialect of the Greek language, was accompanied by a marked decline in material civilization on the Greek mainland and by the migration of large numbers of Greeks to the shores of Asia Minor.

4

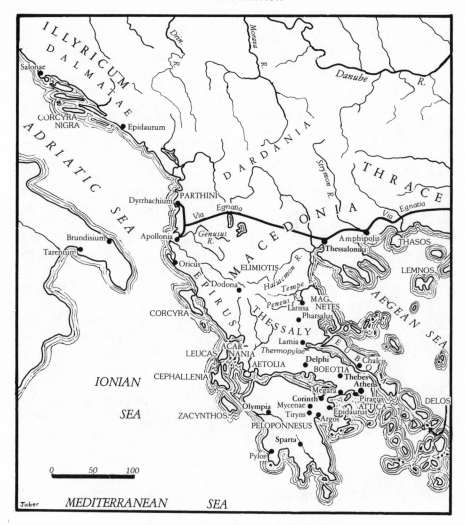

Map 2. Ancient Greece and the Balkans

Greek civilization subsequently developed around the city-states of the mainland, particularly in Attica, the Peloponnesus, and Ionia in western Anatolia. Each was composed of the city with its surrounding territory, the most important being Athens, Sparta, Thebes, Argos, and Corinth. Some, in particular Athens, developed extensive maritime empires. Each had the attributes of a sovereign state; they conducted foreign relations and waged war independently. They were able to cooperate when threatened by the Persian attacks in the fifth century B.C., but they engaged in the suicidal Peloponnesian Wars, which were waged between Athens and Sparta, each supported by its allies. Despite their political divisions and their willingness to war with

Serpent from Tomis (Constanţa), second or third century A.D. (From
V. Canarache, A. Aricescu, V. Barbu, and A. Rădulescu, *Tezaurul de
Sculpturi de la Tomis*. Bucharest: Editura Ştiinţifică, 1963.)

each other, the Greeks were conscious of their cultural unity and shared a
strong feeling of superiority to the "barbarian" outside world.

The great cultural heritage of classical Greece, which so deeply affected
later Western European patterns of thought, is based chiefly on the civilization of the fifth and fourth centuries B.C. in Athens. The architecture of fifth-
century Athens has deeply influenced styles of building, especially of public
offices, to the present. Greek literature – for instance, the plays of Aeschylus,
Sophocles, Euripides, and Aristophanes; the histories of Herodotus and

Thucydides; and the philosophy of Plato and Aristotle – was to become an integral part of the education of the leaders of modern Europe. Moreover, although Greek society was based on slavery, most states developed representative institutions involving the direct participation of free male citizens in the political guidance of the state. The achievements of this age were to remain a unique and brilliant memory for the Greek people and to play a major role in their later national revival.

For Balkan history in general, Greek colonization was most important. The Ionian Greeks of Asia Minor, in particular, were extremely active in founding cities along the seacoasts of the peninsula. Examples of Greek settlement are Istros (Histria), Tomis (Constanţa), Callatis, Odessos (Varna), and Mesembria (Nesebŭr) along the Black Sea coast and Trogurium (Trogir), Epetion (near Split), and Issa (on the island of Vis) on the Adriatic. These cities, primarily commercial centers, reproduced the architecture and modes of life and thought of the Greek parent, and accordingly they had considerable influence on the people living near them. The Greek settlers themselves, however, were content to remain on the periphery of the peninsula. They did not attempt to penetrate into the interior or to make wide territorial conquests.

Although united in language, religion, and culture, the city-states dispersed much of their strength in constant internal quarreling and warfare. They were thus not prepared to meet the challenge of the strong military power that arose in Macedonia beginning with the reign of Philip of Macedon (359–336 B.C.). The Macedonians were probably Illyrian in ethnic background, although by this time the upper class was under the strong cultural influence of Greece. Philip's son, Alexander the Great (336–323 B.C.), perhaps the most famous conqueror of the ancient world, extended his domains as far as India. When he died at a young age, his vast empire fell apart. Macedonia remained an important state, but it could not dominate even the peninsula.

Meanwhile, another imperial power was rising in Italy. Roman forces first moved across the Adriatic in the third century B.C. Their aim was to suppress the pirates who were operating from the eastern coast of the Adriatic, which was subsequently to become the Roman province of Dalmatia. Having defeated Carthage and having become master of the western Mediterranean (201 B.C.), Rome embarked upon a generation of warfare and political activity in the eastern Mediterranean. By 167 B.C., Roman hegemony over the eastern Mediterranean area was an accomplished fact. In the year 148 B.C., after four victorious wars (215–205, 200–197, 171–167, 149–148 B.C.), the Romans acquired the territory of Macedonia and declared it a Roman province. Two years later Roman armies defeated the forces of the Achaean League of Greek cities, destroyed the city of Corinth, and annexed Greece. By the end of the reign of Augustus (27 B.C.–A.D. 14), most of the peninsula south of the Danube had been secured (see Map 3). Unlike the Greek colonists, the

7

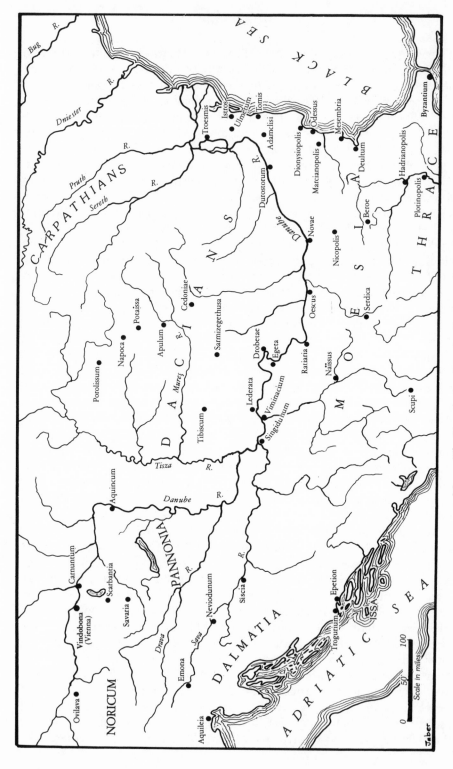

Map 3. The Danube lands under Roman rule

Roman rulers were not content with scattered settlements. They occupied the entire region, and they governed it directly. Intensely concerned with problems of administration and defense, they established a network of military camps and roads. Roman settlements came into being along the great natural highways. Modern Belgrade (Singidunum), Edirne (Hadrianopolis, Adrianople), Niš (Naissus), and Sofia (Serdica), among other cities, were important centers in this period. The Roman cities, like the Greek, resembled their counterparts in the homeland, with temples, forums, baths, and advanced water and sewage systems.

Roman influence was to be profound. Participation in the economic life of a vast empire brought obvious advantages. Agricultural production rose; the gold, silver, iron, and lead mines were exploited. Illyrium, the western section, in particular, enjoyed a period of real prosperity. During the centuries of Roman rule the population became largely Romanized. Some joined the army and the administration; Roman patterns of life, including the language, were accepted. Men born in the Balkans, for instance, the emperors Claudius, Aurelian, Probus, Diocletian, and Maximian, rose to high posts in the state. The entire region also enjoyed the advantages of the Pax Romana; for a long period the population was spared from major outside invasions or disastrous wars.

Defense, nevertheless, was a constant imperial problem. In general, Rome attempted to hold the line of the Danube, but there were some exceptions. Among the barbarian tribes threatening the Roman outposts, a particular danger came from the Dacians. Their king, Burebista (ca. 70–44 B.C.), succeeded in uniting a number of tribes, and he erected a stronghold at Sarmizegetusa in the Carpathian Mountains. Successful expeditions had been sent previously against the Dacians, but in A.D. 101 Trajan (98–117) determined to crush the independent kingdom. In A.D. 106 the Dacians, under their king Decebalus (87–106), were defeated, and their lands were brought directly under imperial rule. For the next 165 years the region was administered by Rome. Soldiers, administrators, and colonists were brought from all over the empire, many of them from other Balkan regions. The native Dacians were also Romanized. This outpost of empire, however, was difficult to defend. In order to shorten the lines of the Roman frontier, Emperor Aurelian (270–275) in 270 ordered the evacuation of the province. The Roman soldiers and administrators, together with part of the population, were then moved across the Danube. What happened to the rest of the inhabitants during the subsequent turbulent centuries was to become a matter of controversy.

From this time the Roman Empire faced increasing difficulties in holding its frontiers and preventing the massive incursion of outside tribes. For the Italian peninsula the chief danger came from the Germanic invaders, particularly the Goths. The Balkan lands suffered a millennium of devastation at the hands of succeeding waves of invading tribes. The Goths of the third, fourth, and fifth centuries and the Huns, also of the fourth and fifth centuries, were followed by the Avars, Slavs, and Bulgars in the sixth and seventh centuries, the Magyars, or Hungarians, in the ninth and tenth, the Pechenegs in the tenth and eleventh, the Cumans in the twelfth and thirteenth, and the Mongols in the thirteenth.

Most of these people had been displaced from their original homelands by stronger tribes; others were attracted by the relative wealth of the Roman lands. In general, they moved with their flocks and families, following the grasslands that were necessary for the subsistence of their horses and livestock. They thus kept to the great highways that have already been described. Movement was necessarily slow; invasion and occupation could last decades. Some of the tribes, such as the Huns and Mongols, came as raiders; they conquered and looted large areas and then passed on. In contrast, the Slavs, Magyars, and Bulgars remained to settle the land. They either conquered and absorbed the resident population or lost their individual identities and amalgamated with the local society. These invasions naturally caused a basic alteration in the ethnic composition of the Balkan people.

Meanwhile, enormous changes had taken place in the organization and the influence of the Roman Empire.

Byzantium

Under increasing pressure from the outside, and facing complex internal problems, the Roman government had to meet the issue of how best to administer its wide domains in a time of adversity. Although maintaining the theory of a united empire, Diocletian (284–305) was forced to create four administrative units. Under Constantine (306–337), a single emperor ruled directly over the entire domain, but the administrative separation was restored after his death. In 395 a final division was made. The line, which was to be of enormous historical significance, ran from the Adriatic coast, along the Drina River, and then to the Sava and the Danube. In the future the boundary between the Catholic and Orthodox churches and the western and eastern cultural zones was to be approximately this frontier.

A language line was in existence, too. Despite the fact that they were the conquering power, the Romans had a deep respect for Greek civilization; they cultivated and preserved Greek art and learning. The Roman Empire was officially bilingual, and Greek as well as Latin was a language of imperial administration and the law courts. Greek was also the chief spoken language in the lands approximately south of Niš in the peninsula and, of course, in all of the areas of Greek settlement in the islands and Asia Minor. The use of Greek as the language of the New Testament is an indication of its importance as a major lingua franca throughout the vast extent of the Roman Empire.

For Balkan history the development of the Eastern Roman Empire was decisive. Its center was to be at the site of the former Greek city of Byzantium, whose name was to become that of the state itself. Here in 330 Constantine founded the city of Constantinople, which was to be the capital of the Byzantine Empire and to carry on the traditions of Rome for over a thousand years. Situated strategically at the crossroads between Asia and Europe, it lay at the junction of the great trade routes running from north to south and east to west. The best natural harbor anywhere in the Balkans and Mediterranean area, the city, surrounded on three sides by water, could be easily defended. Despite repeated attempts at conquest, it was captured only twice, in 1204 and 1453.

The ethnic composition of the empire was complex. In 212 Emperor Caracalla (211–217) granted Roman citizenship to all freemen; the term *Roman* thus no longer represented a geographic or national designation. The citizens of Byzantium called themselves Romans, even if they were of Greek or another background. Moreover, the principal language was Greek. After the division of the entire empire in 395, the position of this language became naturally stronger, since the proportion of Greek speakers to others was increased. Nevertheless, although Greek was the primary language of government, commerce, and the church, the Byzantine citizens did not regard themselves as Greek in nationality in the modern sense of the word. It should be noted also that in this period mainland Greece, the center of the classical civilization, receded drastically in importance; the area became a provincial backwater. Greek life was centered in the Byzantine capital.

Although the basis of the Byzantine government remained the Roman legal and political system, changes in the position of the ruler, influenced by conditions in the neighboring eastern courts, were to be of great significance. An authority has described the emperor as

> transformed into an Oriental, divine, absolute monarch. Diocletian's arrangements completed the transformation. "Proskynesis" or "adoratio" (the eastern ceremony of genuflection addressed to divinity), purple robes, jewelled diadems, belts, and sceptres became permanent parts of the imperial tradition. The emperor, ruler by divine grace, was the sole fount of law. Seclusion of the monarch, an Oriental practice by which the person of the ruler was removed from contact with the profane, was carefully balanced by the splendid official ceremonials, at which his power and glory were displayed to the citizens and courtiers.[1]

This autocratic monarch presided over a large bureaucratic government, whose efficiency and success varied through the centuries. Like every great

---

1 Speros Vyronis, Jr., *Byzantium and Europe* (New York: Harcourt, Brace & World, 1967), pp. 18–19.

empire, Byzantium was beset by constant rivalries between political factions and problems concerning succession to the throne. Moreover, the church and doctrinal disputes played a major and often disturbing part in state life.

After the division of the empire, Constantinople became the center for the Eastern Christian, or Orthodox, church. The conversion of the emperor Constantine began the process by which Christianity became the official religion of the Roman Empire. Constantine's sons prohibited sacrifice to the pagan gods; and in 392 the emperor Theodosius (379–395) forbade pagan worship under penalties of treason and sacrilege. Earlier, in 380, Theodosius had decreed that all his subjects must accept the Christian faith as formulated at the Council of Nicaea in 325. The language of the Byzantine church was Greek, whereas that of the Roman remained Latin. Most of the Balkan people, the Serbs, Romanians, Bulgarians, and Greeks, were to be influenced primarily by the ecclesiastical developments in Constantinople. The Russians were also to be converted from Byzantium and to become part of the Orthodox world. Although the Constantinople hierarchy at first recognized the primacy of Rome, unity proved impossible to maintain. In 1054 the final break occurred, a division that was never to be healed. In doctrine and ceremony the two organizations became increasingly separated. Most important, the relationship between church and state was markedly different in East and West. In the Orthodox system the churches in general supported the power and authority of the secular ruler; they did not directly challenge the state's influence. Thus the political and religious leadership tended to work together against common internal and external enemies. Moreover, the Eastern church did not develop a predominant central institution such as the Papacy in Rome. The Patriarchate of Constantinople had great prestige and influence, but the national patriarchates or archbishoprics that were eventually established in the Balkan states and Russia exerted the prime influence over their members.

As the Italian peninsula was overwhelmed by barbarian invaders and Roman authority in the West was broken, Byzantium became heir to the Roman imperial idea. Like the Greeks and Romans before them, the Byzantine leaders regarded their state as the foremost civilization of the time and the legitimate ruler of the world. The idea of universal empire was shared by the Byzantine enemies. As we shall see, Balkan Christian and Muslim rulers alike attempted to occupy the imperial city and to claim for themselves the prestige and position of the Byzantine emperor. The idea of a single legitimate secular authority and one universal church was extremely beguiling. The Orthodox views also gave support to this conception. As one historian has written:

> The essence of Orthodox belief was that with the confluence at Constantinople of Roman and Christian theories of terrestrial and celestial empire, the world had achieved its final order, of which the Emperor was the symbol. Not only were Orthodox Christians superior

to the rest of mankind; not only was all future improvement or in-
novation impossible; but also error was unthinkable.[2]

At its height Byzantium was the most powerful empire in the Western
world (see Map 4). Its wealth was based on trade and the prosperity of its
lands. Its military commanders adopted the most advanced methods of warfare, and they had the best weapons. The bureaucracy carried out its responsibilities well. In foreign affairs the state followed a system that made "Byzantine diplomacy" proverbial for shrewd, clever, and not too scrupulous
negotiation. Most important, the empire's high level of civilization provided
patterns for government and culture for the Balkan Orthodox states and for
Russia. Balkan rulers wished to be Byzantine autocrats. They copied the court
ceremonial, and they used Byzantine architectural styles for their buildings
and churches. Medieval Balkan civilization was thus in essence Byzantine.

Despite the empire's great achievements, its long history was marked by
many fluctuations of fortune. One of the most notable emperors, Justinian
(527–565), attempted to restore the empire after the devastation of the barbarian invasions of the fourth and fifth centuries. For the future his reign was
of significance for his administrative reforms and his codification of the laws.
He also embarked on an ambitious building program in Constantinople, of
which the great achievement was the construction of Hagia Sophia, the church
of the Holy Wisdom (called Sancta Sophia or St. Sophia in most Western
writing); it was to become the very symbol of Orthodox Christianity. Justinian was not, however, able to find solutions to the great problems that had
previously beset the Roman Empire. Byzantium had great difficulty in defending and administering its wide territories, which were once again faced
with attack in both the Balkan peninsula and Asia Minor.

In the sixth and seventh centuries the chief danger came from the advance
of the Persians and Arabs in Asia and the Avars and Slavs in Europe. The
Persian threat was ended by a military victory in 627. Also in the seventh
century, the empire simultaneously faced its first challenge from a Muslim
people, the Arabs, and attacks from the Avars and Slavs to the north. This
century proved to be a difficult period for Byzantium: Enemies pressed forward on all sides. The Arabian invaders were eventually defeated, but the
Slavic presence in the Balkans was permanently established.

The Slavs: the Bulgarian and Serbian states

The Slavic invasion In the sixth and seventh centuries the Slavs, an Indo-
European people, crossed the Danube frontier and occupied most of the

2 C. M. Woodhouse, *The Story of Modern Greece* (London: Faber & Faber, 1968), p. 30.

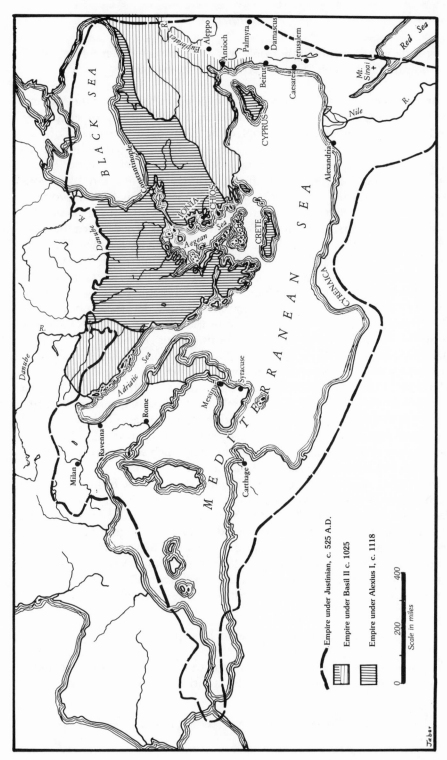

Map 4. The Byzantine Empire

Empire under Justinian, c. 525 A.D.

Empire under Basil II c. 1025

Empire under Alexius I, c. 1118

Scale in miles

0   200   400

Balkan peninsula. At first they were closely associated with the Avars, who apparently held the dominant position in the relationship. The Slavs moved forward in small groups under their own leaders; there was no central organization, although unions were formed among the tribes. Unlike many of the previous invaders, the Slavs settled the land, which they occupied as peasant farmers. The basis was thus laid at this time for the future Bulgarian, Croatian, Serbian, and Slovenian medieval states.

Comparatively little is known about the early history of the Slavic societies; the fate of the indigenous population is also controversial. It is necessary here to deal with events for which there are no written records, so that archeological or anthropological evidence or that gained from the study of language must be used. It is apparent that the Slavic tribes moved throughout the peninsula and penetrated as far south as the Peloponnesus and even the island of Crete. In many areas the original population was forced to retreat to the remote hills and mountains. In the mountainous areas of Greece and Albania a people, known variously as Vlachs, Arumanians, Kutsovlachs, or Tsintsars, have remained until the present. They speak a language related to Latin and close to modern Romanian. In the lands of present-day Greece, Albania, and Romania, the local population absorbed the Slavic settlers, who came to speak the language of the region. Slavic-speaking people were to settle permanently, however, in a wide band of territory stretching from the Adriatic to the Black Sea.

Although the Slavs and Avars reached the gates of Constantinople, they were not able to take the city. After the disasters of the seventh century the Byzantine state recovered and regained some of the lost territory. It now also had to deal with the strong Bulgarian power that had been established on the northern border.

Bulgaria The principal threat to Byzantium from the Balkans was to come in the future from the Bulgarians. Their name was derived from that of the original Bulgars, a Turanian people who had once inhabited an area between the Sea of Azov and Kuban. Defeated by the Khazars, the Bulgars were forced to move. A section under the leadership of Asparukh migrated to an area near the mouth of the Danube. After suffering a defeat, the Byzantine government recognized this group as an independent power in 681, and Pliska became the capital of the first Bulgarian state. Under Khan Krum (803–814) and later, the territory was considerably expanded. The Bulgars had taken possession of land inhabited by Slavs, who considerably outnumbered the conquerors. At first, the two people lived together; the prince and the nobility were Bulgar. Both were pagan and worshiped their own gods. A process of assimilation was accomplished in the ninth century; all of the population became Slavic-speaking and Christian.

Christianity was accepted in 865 by the ruler Boris (852–889). Although he at first briefly recognized the jurisdiction of Rome for political reasons, he subsequently changed the affiliation. The Bulgarian church thus became associated with the Patriarchate at Constantinople and the Orthodox world, but it kept its own ecclesiastical organization. Because of the favorable attitude it adopted toward Christian scholarship, Bulgaria became in fact the first major center of Slavic culture. At this time the Byzantine Empire dispatched the two brothers Cyril and Methodius to the Greater Moravian Kingdom in Central Europe to try to combat the activities of missionaries representing Rome. The brothers had devised a Slavic script, called Glagolitic, and they and their assistants undertook the translation of religious works from Greek into Slavic, using the language spoken near their home in Thessaloniki. Their efforts in Moravia failed; the brothers died. Their disciples, forced to leave Moravia, were welcomed in Bulgaria in 885. Establishing their center in Preslav, which in 893 became the new capital, they continued their task of translating and copying religious texts. Old Bulgarian, or Church Slavic, became the language of the Slavic Orthodox churches and Slavic scholarship for the next centuries. The original Glagolitic alphabet was modified to resemble the Greek more closely, and the subsequent Cyrillic alphabet was adopted by the Orthodox Slavs – the Bulgarians, the Serbs, and the Russians.

The First Bulgarian Empire reached its height in the reign of Simeon (893–927), the second son of Boris. The attraction of Byzantium and Constantinople remained strong for the Bulgarian rulers. Krum had died trying to take the imperial city, and Simeon's prime objective became the capture of the capital and with it the claim to supremacy in the universal empire of the Christian world. In 925, after repeated failures to take the city, he proclaimed himself emperor of the Romans and Bulgars. He also raised the Bulgarian ecclesiastical center at Preslav from an archbishopric to a patriarchate in order to give its head the same title as that held by the Constantinople church leader. The great extent of the Bulgarian lands under Simeon can best be appreciated by examining Map 5. Bulgaria had become the strongest Balkan power.

These conquests had, however, strained the resources of the country. In addition, the Bulgarian rulers faced internal problems. Some nobles challenged the central authority, and a period of religious controversy also ensued. The problem of heresy had always been a major issue for both the Eastern and the Western churches. The Bogomil heresy, which originated in Bulgaria, was to be particularly important. The Bogomils were dualists; they believed that man's soul represented the principle of good, whereas the body and the material world were evil. Neither respecting the rituals nor accepting the sacraments, they leveled strong attacks on the established church. They rejected such religious symbols as the cross, the relics of the saints, and the ikons. Their doctrines were a challenge to both the political and the religious authorities.

At the same time, external threats to the state increased. The major Bul-

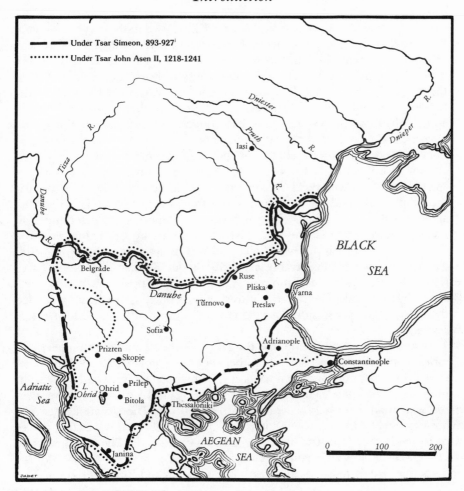

Map 5. Bulgaria in the Middle Ages

garian opponent remained Byzantium, but the new invaders, the Hungarians and the Pechenegs, had to be dealt with. Moreover, the Byzantine Empire was in a period of revival, and the Russians were taking an active part in Balkan events. In 969 the Russian ruler Sviatoslav (964–972) captured Preslav and took the Bulgarian emperor, Boris II (969–972), prisoner. In answer, the Byzantine emperor, John Tzimisces (969–976), sent an army to force the Russians out of Bulgaria. After a military victory, Byzantium took these Bulgarian lands.

A center of resistance, however, remained in the southwest. Here Samuel (991–1014), the son of a district governor, organized a new government with its center at Ohrid, and the struggle with Byzantium continued. Although the Bulgarian forces won some victories, the Byzantine emperor Basil II (963–

17

1025), who was also known as the "Bulgar Killer," was in the end triumphant. In 1014, after a major victory, he took fourteen thousand Bulgarian prisoners. He then had them blinded, leaving one man in every hundred with one eye so that he could lead the defeated army back to its homeland. Samuel died at the sight of this atrocity. In 1018 the Byzantine army took Ohrid, and the region passed into Byzantine possession; there it would remain for a century and a half. Byzantium was now in its strongest position since the Slavic invasions; it was, in fact, the greatest single power in existence at the time.

The Byzantine Empire could not, however, maintain its predominance. Within fifty years of Basil's death the state was again reduced in territory. Internal conflicts weakened the government, and new enemies, in particular the Seljuk Turks and the Hungarians, threatened the borders. This situation allowed a Bulgarian revival. In 1186 two Bulgarian notables, Peter and Ivan Asen, organized a successful revolt. Their action marks the beginning of the Second Bulgarian Empire, whose capital was established at Tŭrnovo. Bulgarian lands were considerably expanded under Kaloian (1197–1207), at a time when the Byzantine Empire was in a desperate position. In 1204 Constantinople was taken by the adventurers of the Fourth Crusade, who divided those Byzantine possessions they conquered into small kingdoms for themselves.

As in the preceding period, the Bulgarian rulers, despite their military victories, had difficulty in controlling their nobles. Kaloian was possibly assassinated by one of his own commanders. The revived empire reached its height in the reign of John Asen II (1218–1241); once again the major Balkan power, the Bulgarian state held a wide block of territory. The situation was not, however, stable. In succeeding reigns the kingdom fell apart; competing nobles controlled the regions that remained in Bulgarian hands. The strongest state in the Balkans was to become Serbia, which took possession of Macedonian lands that had formerly been part of the Bulgarian and Byzantine empires.

Serbia The Serbs, a Slavic people, arrived in the Balkans in the seventh century. They were converted to Christianity in the second half of the ninth century and were subsequently to be Orthodox. From the eighth to the twelfth centuries the majority lived in lands under Bulgarian or Byzantine rule. When, after 1018, the Byzantine Empire destroyed Bulgarian independence, the Serbian leaders were in a better position. Two states were eventually organized: Zeta, in the mountainous area that later became the site of Montenegro, and subsequently Raška, to the east.

The rise of the Serbian kingdom is closely associated with the Nemanja dynasty. The first in this line, Stephen Nemanja I (ca. 1168–1196), became ruler, or grand *župan*, of Raška; his descendants were to hold power for two centuries. Stephen was able to obtain control of Zeta and to expand the Serbian territory to the Adriatic. His son, Stephen II (1196–1227), called the "first-crowned," assumed the title of king. At the same time a separate Serbian archbishopric was established at Žiča under the authority of the youngest son of Stephen I, Sava, who was a monk. Serbia had become a kingdom with an autonomous Orthodox church.

The conquests of the Second Bulgarian Empire were naturally to the detriment of Serbian interests. The state also had to deal with Hungarian advances to the north. The subsequent decline of both Bulgarian and Byzantine power, however, created the opportunity for Serbian expansion. Gains of territory were made in the reigns of Miliutin (1282–1321) and Stephen Dečanski (1321–1331), but the height of the medieval state was reached under Stephen Dušan (1331–1355). With aims of conquest similar to those of the Bulgarian emperors, this ambitious ruler concentrated on the acquisition of lands to the south. His control was to extend over Albanian lands, Macedonia, Epirus, and Thessaly, as well as the Serbian territory, which extended to the Adriatic (see Map 6). In 1346 he had himself crowned emperor of the Serbs and Greeks, and later he added the Bulgars and Albanians to the title. Also in 1346 he raised the Archbishopric of Peć to a Patriarchate. The Serbian political center, too, had shifted southward – from Raš, to Priština, to Prizren, and finally to Skopje (Skoplje, Üsküb). Under Dušan's rule Serbia was the major power in the Balkans, with territory extending from the Adriatic to the Aegean.

Although Dušan was able to assemble this impressive empire, his lands lacked inner cohesion. After his death in 1355, at the age of forty-six, the Serbian kingdom suffered the same fate as the Bulgarian and simply disintegrated. Dušan's son, Stephen Uroš V (1355–1371) succeeded, but he was unable to maintain central control against domestic intrigues and foreign pressure. With his death in 1371 the Nemanja dynasty came to an end. The Serbian lands, like the Bulgarian, were fragmented among competing nobles.

North of the Danube: Hungary, Transylvania, Wallachia, and Moldavia

While the Byzantine, Bulgarian, and Serbian rulers were contending for control of the major part of the Balkan peninsula, important developments were occurring north of the Danube River. After the Roman evacuation of Dacia in 270, that area and the Danube valley faced the full weight of successive invasions; Goths, Avars, Huns, Bulgars, Slavs, and Tartars moved through the region. For the future settlement of the area, the arrival of the Hungarians was to be of lasting significance. Defeated in their attempts to move further westward, these people settled in the Pannonian Plain at the end of the ninth century. Because they were converted to Christianity from Rome, their future religious and political ties were to be with the West. Their greatest medieval ruler was Stephen (997–1038), who was crowned king in 1000 and later canonized. As the patron saint of Hungary, his name was associated

Map 6. Serbia under the Nemanja dynasty

with Hungarian state territory, which came to be referred to regularly as "the lands of the crown of St. Stephen."

In the future the history of Hungary was to be closely associated with that of Croatia and the Romanian principalities, in particular Transylvania. In 1102 the king of Hungary succeeded to the Croatian crown under circumstances that will be described in a subsequent section. In the eleventh century Hungary took possession of Transylvania, a territory that probably had a mixed but basically Romanian population. After the occupation the Hungarian government encouraged immigration in order to strengthen this border region against outside invasion. Most important was the settlement of the Szeklers, who were closely related to the Hungarians, and of the Germans, called Saxons, who came in the twelfth century. In the future the Hungarians, Szeklers, and Saxons were to be the privileged, governing section of the population. Although Transylvania was part of the kingdom of Hungary, it retained wide autonomous privileges.

In the meantime, two Romanian principalities, Wallachia and Moldavia, were in the process of formation. The exact ethnic background of the modern Romanians and the extent of the territory that they occupied at different stages in their history have been a matter of controversy, as have, indeed, similar questions associated with all of the Balkan peoples. The question at issue here is what happened to the population after the withdrawal of Roman administration in 270. Contemporary Romanian historiography emphasizes the continuity in the settlement of present-day Romanian lands, including Transylvania, arguing that the Daco-Roman population remained in occupation of this region and absorbed or repelled the successive invaders. It is, in any case, likely that in the tenth century the majority of the people living to the south and east of the Carpathian Mountains were Romanian: they spoke a Romance language, closely related to Latin, but with a high proportion of Slavic words; they were Christian, although the date of conversion is not clear; they had also accepted the Slavonic religious service and the Cyrillic alphabet, which was used to write Romanian until the nineteenth century. Like the ecclesiastical organizations in the Slavic kingdoms across the Danube, the Romanian church was to remain linked to Constantinople, although with its own national and regional organizations.

Romanian political development was to center around two principalities, Moldavia and Wallachia, which were not to be united until the middle of the nineteenth century. Both states were formed in the fourteenth century when local territorial units under their own lords joined together. In Wallachia the nobility chose as their first prince Basarab (1310–1352). His capital was at Cîmpulung for a time, and then at Argeş. The first prince of an independent Moldavian state was Bogdan I (1359–1365). The early Romanian rulers had constantly to meet the threat of Hungarian conquest; the Polish kingdom and the Mongols were also dangers. The nobility, called *boyars*, were a serious problem for the central authority. Here as elsewhere they formed conspiracies among themselves and carried on intrigues with foreign powers.

Byzantium and the West: Venice and the Fourth Crusade

With the exception of Hungary, the states that have been discussed so far – Bulgaria, Serbia, the Romanian principalities, and, of course, the Byzantine Empire – fell into the orbit of the Eastern Roman Empire and the Orthodox church. Common adherence to the Orthodox creed had certainly not kept these states from warfare. Serbia, Bulgaria, and Byzantium were at different periods responsible for one another's destruction. In addition to the threat offered by the Slavic powers in the Balkans and the Muslim states to the east, the Byzantine government had to meet a challenge from the West that was political and military as well as religious in character.

The attempt of the Byzantine emperors to maintain the claim to the universal authority associated with Rome did not succeed. In 800 the Frankish king, Charlemagne (768–814), was crowned by the pope in Rome with the title of Roman emperor. Despite the implications of this act, the Byzantine government was forced to recognize the action in 812. The title of Roman emperor was to pass finally in the thirteenth century to the German house of Habsburg, whose members were regularly elected to what became in time a hollow dignity. Just as there were two rival empires, there were soon to be two Christian churches with conflicting claims over jurisdiction. At first the Constantinople patriarch had recognized the preeminence of the bishop at Rome. Doctrinal controversies soon, however, clouded the relations between the two capitals. In 1054 the two organizations excommunicated each other. Although the significance of the action was not clear at the time, the breach was never healed despite numerous attempts. It was, in fact, an army representing Western and Catholic interests that was first to break Constantinople's defenses.

The threat to the empire from the east, first from the Persians and then from the Muslim Arabs, has been mentioned previously. In the eleventh century a more formidable Muslim force appeared. At this time Muslim Turks, under the leadership of members of the Seljuk family, became the major danger to the Byzantine state. In 1071 the Byzantine army was defeated in the decisive battle of Manzikert. The Turkish power took over Byzantine possessions in the Near East and, most important, most of Anatolia. A process of Turkish settlement, which was to be carried out over four hundred years, was thus commenced. The region, previously Byzantine and Christian for the most part, became Turkish and Muslim. The change drastically affected the power of the empire, to which this area was important for manpower, food, and taxes.

The conquest of the Holy Lands by a Muslim state led to the organization of crusades in the West. Although under papal sponsorship, these military campaigns were led by unruly, restless, and power-hungry Western knights, who soon proved themselves interested less in religion than in establishing kingdoms for themselves in the East. They certainly were not concerned with restoring to Byzantium its lost lands in Asia Minor.

At this time the Byzantine Empire also came into conflict with Venice. By the twelfth century this enterprising city had built up a great maritime empire based on trade and sea power. It had acquired a chain of islands, ports, and points of settlement throughout the Adriatic, Mediterranean, and Aegean seas. A rival of Constantinople, Venice found the opportunity during the

Fourth Crusade to deal a deadly blow to its opponent. The crusaders, who needed Venetian transport but did not have the money to pay for it, were diverted by Venice to the capture of the Dalmatian city of Zadar (Zara) from the Hungarians. In return, the Venetians offered passage to Egypt. Thereafter, instead of fighting the Muslim Turks, the Venetians and the Christian knights together first proceeded to occupy and then in 1204 to plunder Constantinople. They then elected one of their number, Count Baldwin of Flanders, emperor.

With the capital in their hands, the victors next partitioned the Byzantine lands that they had conquered into small principalities. Some of these lasted but a short time, whereas others, such as the Principality of Achaia (1205–1432), founded by Geoffrey de Villehardouin, and the Duchy of the Archipelago (1207–1566), had long life-spans. Venice too picked up valuable territory, including points on the Dalmatian coast and the Peloponnesus, as well as the island of Crete, which was held until 1669. In the Byzantine Balkans, only the state of Epirus remained in Orthodox possession. The Western knights and Venetians now held lands that were Greek in language and Orthodox in religion. The subsequent policies of the new rulers left a lasting hatred among the people for "the Franks," as the Western Europeans were to be designated. The Catholic church, despite immense efforts, could not win converts.

In 1261 the Byzantine Empire was restored by the Empire of Nicaea, a Greek state established in Anatolia after the fall of Constantinople. Michael VIII Palaeologus became emperor, founding a dynasty that was to last until the final downfall of the empire. Although some Balkan territory was won back, the state was basically weak. The old enemies, of course, remained. The conflicts with the Second Bulgarian Empire and Serbia have already been discussed. Byzantine interests were also affected by the events occurring along the coast of the Adriatic Sea, where Hungary, Venice, Croatia, and Bosnia competed for supremacy.

The Western Balkans and the Adriatic coast: Croatia, Dalmatia, Bosnia, and Albania

After their invasion of the Balkans, the Slovenes and Croatians, both Slavic peoples, settled in the northwest section of the area under study. The Slovenes did not form an independent political entity. In 748 they became part of the Frankish kingdom, and they were to be of solidly Catholic faith. By the end of the fourteenth century the lands they inhabited had passed under the control of the Habsburg Empire. In contrast, the Croats, who lived to the south, in lands north of the Sava and west of the Una, and along the Adriatic coast, did establish an independent state (see Map 7). The first ruler to take the title of king was Tomislav (910–928). The center was Biograd on the Dalmatian coast.

Situated near the line of division between the Eastern and Western em-

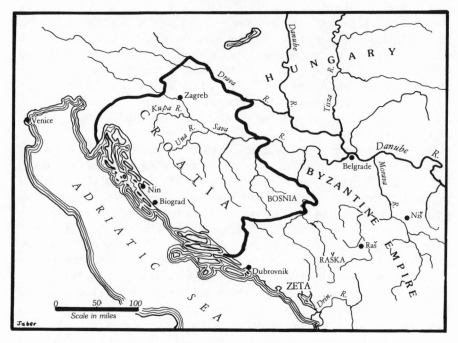

Map 7. Croatia in 1070

pires, and subject to influences from both Rome and Constantinople, Croatia was naturally the scene of religious controversy. Two parties existed, one supporting association with Rome and a Latin liturgy, the other preferring the Slavonic service used in the Orthodox Slavic churches. The choice of Rome was finally accepted in the reign of Zvonimir (1075–1089). After the conversion of the people, the Croatian lands came under Catholic and Western influence.

Croatian independence was not to last much longer. When the death of Zvonimir led to a disputed succession, the crown was claimed by Ladislas I (1077–1095), the king of Hungary. However, the first Hungarian monarch to be crowned king of Croatia was Koloman (1095–1116), a step taken with the consent of the majority of the Croatian nobility. Croatia was thus in 1102 united with Hungary through the person of the king, but the exact nature of this relationship was to be disputed throughout the next centuries. Thereafter, the Croatian leadership was to claim that the union rested on an agreement between equal partners who were joined primarily through the common monarch. Although the Hungarian government did not accept this interpretation of the arrangement, Croatia did thereafter retain a special position within the Hungarian kingdom and did have wide rights of autonomy. Croatia was kept administratively apart from Hungary, and the Croatian assembly of nobles had much authority.

It should be noted that the three areas populated by Croats and associated at times with the medieval Triune Kingdom, that is, Croatia, Dalmatia, and the land between the Sava and Danube known as Slavonia, were henceforth to be governed under separate systems even when they had the same ruler. Only Croatia proper retained a truly autonomous position; Slavonia was soon organized into the Hungarian system of counties, and the subsequent history of Dalmatia was to be turbulent and complicated.

The establishment of the Hungarian Árpád dynasty in Croatia did not settle the fate of Dalmatia. The struggle for possession was waged chiefly between Hungary and Venice, but Serbia and Bosnia also sought a coastline. Although the majority of the inhabitants were Croatian, with a Serbian population concentrated south of Dubrovnik (Ragusa), the cities remained under a strong Italian, primarily Venetian, influence. Most of these had autonomous institutions that were respected by successive occupying powers. The government was in the hands of councils of prominent citizens. The language of trade and administration, which was Latin in Roman times, now became Italian; the Italian language remained preeminent until the recent period. However, this situation did not hinder Croatian literary development, which had its center in fifteenth-century Dalmatia.

The states that vied for dominance over Dalmatian territory also fought to control Bosnia. Situated between the competing Eastern and Western churches, this area was to have a separate religious movement. The Church of the Bosnian Christians, a part of neither the Orthodox nor the Catholic hierarchy, was the object of strong attack from Rome.[3] A Bosnian kingdom was also in existence for a short period (see Map 8). The outstanding leader was Stephen Tvrtko (1353–1391), the first *ban*, or governor, of Bosnia; the land was at that time under Hungarian suzerainty. In 1377 Tvrtko was crowned king of "the Serbs, Bosnia, and the Croats," a title reflecting the considerable amount of territory that he was able to control. He was also able to add Dalmatia to his possessions. After his death, in the familiar pattern we have seen in other Balkan states, his kingdom fell apart under the pressures of domestic conflict and foreign invasion.

The last Balkan region that remains to be discussed, that inhabited by the Albanians, shared in the difficulties found elsewhere. The great prosperity experienced during Roman times came to an end with the invasions. The Slavic advance in particular deeply affected the Albanian lands. The native Illyrian population, however, was not Slavicized. Living in a mountainous area, organized into tribal associations, the people maintained their language and their separate existence. The name ultimately applied to the area and the populations was derived from a tribe called the Albanoi, who lived near Durrës. At this early period the people called themselves Arber or Arbereshe.

---

3 See John V. A. Fine, Jr., *The Bosnian Church: A New Interpretation* (Boulder, Colo.: East European Quarterly, 1975).

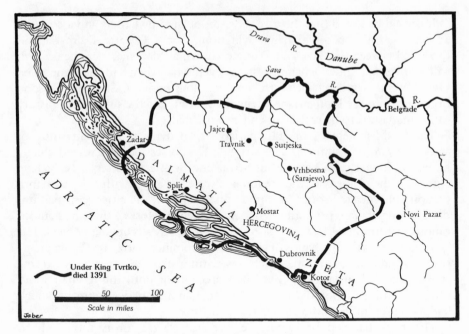

Map 8. Medieval Bosnia

In the twelfth century a principality was organized with its center at Krujë, but it had a short existence. Throughout the medieval period the lands suffered from repeated invasions. Normans, Venetians, and Byzantines raided from the sea; the Bulgarian, Serbian, and Byzantine empires held Albanian-inhabited regions for long periods. Despite this foreign intervention, it should be emphasized that then, as later, it was difficult to control the area. The local notables and clan leaders ran their own districts and fought one another for local preeminence. Because of the difficult internal conditions, a large Albanian migration southward occurred, with groups moving into Thessaly, the Peloponnesus, and the islands. Some islands – for instance, Hydra, Psara, and Spetsai – became primarily Albanian in ethnic character.

The medieval states before the Ottoman conquest

By the end of the fourteenth century the basis had been set for the modern Balkan states, each of which had a counterpart in this period: Romania in Moldavia, Wallachia, and Transylvania; Bulgaria in the medieval empires; Yugoslavia in the Serbian, Croatian, and Bosnian kingdoms; Albania in Illyria; and Greece in the Byzantine Empire. Although there were to be shifts of population within the region and some immigration, there was no subsequent massive intrusion from without comparable to the barbarian invasions. It must be strongly emphasized that none of these early states were *national* in the modern sense. The governments represented primarily alliances of strong nobles around a central leader. There were few autocratic rulers on the Byzantine model. Feudal loyalties rested on the mutual interest of the most powerful men in the state in the protection and extension of its frontiers. When his personal fortunes were better served by opposition to his ruler and alliance with an enemy power, a noble could easily shift his allegiance, as the fate of the Bulgarian and Serbian states well illustrates. The Byzantine government, despite the strong position of the emperor, suffered from similar problems.

This section has been illustrated with numerous maps. The purpose has been not only to demonstrate the size of the successive empires, but to show the overlapping claims and conquests. In the nineteenth century the national leaders, looking back on this period, tended to consider the maximum extension of their medieval kingdoms as the natural historical boundaries for their nations (see Map 9). However, as we have seen, the areas occupied by the states fluctuated radically; there was also no set center of national life – with the exception, of course, of Constantinople for Byzantium. For instance, we have seen the Bulgarian capital shift from Pliska, to Preslav, to Ohrid, and then to Tŭrnovo. The center of Serbia moved southward; Dušan's capital was finally Skopje, although the subsequent movement of Serbian emigration was to be northward. Croatia, with the first center on the Dalmatian coast, was by the sixteenth century to have inland Zagreb (Agram) as its major city. In the future the chief area of conflict was to be Macedonia. Here Albanian, Bulgarian, Serbian, and Byzantine–Greek claims were bound to overlap; all had held the area at some point in their history.

As there were few regions that had not known many rulers, there were also no ethnically "pure" people. On the eve of the Ottoman invasion, a band of Slavic-speaking people separated the Romanians and Hungarians in the north from the Albanian- and Greek-language areas to the south. In each region the population represented a fusion of original inhabitants with subsequent invaders, an amalgamation achieved through military conquest by a stronger group, the absorption of one people by another owing to the weight of numbers, or the acceptance of another language because of the cultural attraction offered by a more advanced civilization. As we have seen, Slavic and Albanian settlers in the southern part of the peninsula adopted the Greek language and culture; in the Albanian lands the Slavs, in contrast, were assimilated. In Bulgaria a fusion took place between the resident Slavs and the conquering Turanian Bulgars. The inhabitants of the Romanian principalities were the descendants of Dacians, Romans, Slavs, and other peoples. Similarly, the Byzantine Empire, with a Greek official language, was mixed in population.

By the end of the medieval period, not only had the foundations for the modern nations been laid, but the area was divided by a long-lasting cultural cleavage, whose boundaries approximated those of the Eastern and Western Roman empires. Basic to this separation was the division between the two

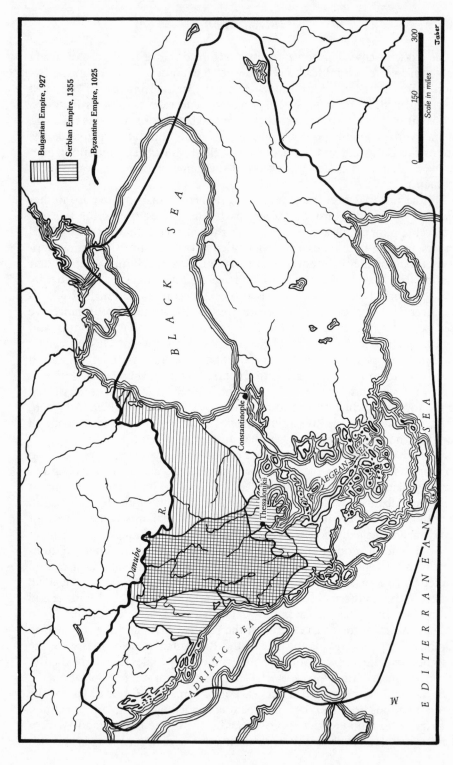

Map 9. Medieval Balkan empires

Bulgarian Empire, 927

Serbian Empire, 1355

Byzantine Empire, 1025

Scale in miles

0   150   300

Jaker

BLACK SEA

Danube R.

Constantinople

Thessaloniki

AEGEAN SEA

ADRIATIC SEA

MEDITERRANEAN SEA

W

Christian churches. The majority of the people, the Bulgars, Greeks, Romanians, Serbs, and many Albanians, became a part of the Orthodox world, with its strong Byzantine influence. The Slavic population used their languages in church services, and Old Slavonic became their common literary language. They wrote in the Cyrillic script. Byzantine patterns were followed in art and architecture. In contrast, Catholic and Western influences predominated in the northwestern Balkans among the Slovenes and Croats, and also among some Albanians and Bosnians. Latin was the language of the church; the Latin script was adopted. Western architectural styles, first romanesque and then gothic, were characteristic of their building.

Of the governments of the time, the Byzantine was obviously the most successful. A series of autocratic rulers in control of a bureaucracy and a strong army was able to establish a great empire that lasted over a thousand years. Even in times of extreme adversity, a nucleus of power was maintained. The Byzantine court, with its magnificent ceremonies, was deeply admired by all the Balkan rulers, who attempted to emulate its practices. Few of these could attain the power of the Byzantine autocrat; the feudal nobility or tribal chieftains could usually join together and effectively challenge the central authority. The ephemeral nature of many of the Balkan political organizations is explained by the fact that political power lay in the hands of the local notables, who were in direct relationship with and had control over the majority of the people.

During the long period that this brief survey has covered, the life and condition of the mass of the people naturally changed considerably. In time of foreign invasion or barbarian attack, the peasant could find himself in a desperate position. Often large areas were depopulated, as their inhabitants were forced to flee or face massacre. However, even in times of peace, life was extremely difficult. The majority of the people supported themselves either by cultivating the land or as herdsmen; livestock raising was always a major occupation. Those living near the sea could become fisherman, sailors, or pirates. The prosperity and happiness of an individual largely depended on the conditions attached to landholding and on the political situation in the region.

The more fortunate peasants were free farmers or shepherds holding their own plots or tending their flocks. In general, they lived in communities where the village held in common the forest, pasture, and water rights, but the individual families controlled their own land. In contrast, conditions might be much worse for those who cultivated the estates of the nobility or the church and were tied to the land under various conditions of bondage.

In its general attributes Balkan serfdom resembled its Western counterpart. Usually the lands of an estate were divided, with one section worked by the peasants for the lord's benefit and the other subdivided into individual plots for village use. As well as cultivating the lord's land, the serf was obligated to pay a percentage of other products of his labor, including such items as wine, honey, and livestock. Similarly enserfed shepherds were expected to deliver part of their flocks. The local noble in most regions had full jurisdiction over his people. He collected taxes for the government, and he had complete administrative and judicial authority in his estate. He kept order, judged criminal cases, and levied fines and punishments. In addition to the payments to the lord, the peasant owed state taxes and labor obligations. He was compelled to work on the roads, bridges, and fortifications. In wartime he was expected not only to fight, but also to provide provisions and transportation.

In contrast to the countryside, most cities enjoyed a wide measure of self-government. They were usually administered by councils of prominent citizens. Situated on the great trade and communication routes, they were the centers for commerce and the crafts. Ports, such as Constantinople, Thessaloniki, and Dubrovnik, played a major role in the life of the region at a time when water transport was far easier than land. The cities were also, of course, the administrative and military centers.

When in the fourteenth century the Balkan peninsula faced the invasion of the Ottoman Turks, certain of the inherent weaknesses in the political and social system were to aid the conquerors. Most important was the lack of unity among the Christian princes. Although sharing a common religion, many Balkan leaders in fact allied with the Muslim power. As far as the peasantry was concerned, the heavy burden of feudalism made them often welcome new rulers who had another land system. The last ruler of Bosnia told the pope that the Turkish authorities had won over the peasants by promises of better conditions.

The Ottoman conquest

After the seventh century, as we have seen, the Byzantine Empire had to meet challenges from Muslim powers, first from the Arabs and then from the Seljuk Turks. At the end of the thirteenth century a Turkish group of warriors established itself in northwest Anatolia, near the Sea of Marmora. The name *Ottoman* which was to be given these people derives from that of the prominent leader Osman or Othman (1290–1326). The expansion of their power was rapid, with the initial great conquests made in the Balkans. Gallipoli, taken in 1354, was the first urban center held by the Ottomans in Europe. The fourteenth century provided certain general conditions favorable to Ottoman interests. At this time the plague spread through Europe; the Black Death decimated large sections of the population and spread terror and panic. From 1338 to 1453 British and French energies were absorbed in the Hundred Years' War. The church at Rome was weakened by internal conflicts. Venice and Genoa, the rival commercial giants, were engaged in mutually destructive conflict. Under these conditions there was little likelihood that the West would be capable of uniting to mount a great crusade to aid the Christian East. The weakness and division in the West were reflected in the Balkans. The feudal states, each with major problems of internal organization, were separated by their jealousies and hatreds. Byzantium, which had stood for centuries as a barrier to invasions from the East, never fully regained its power after the restoration in 1261.

The Ottoman advance was also immensely aided by the leadership of a series of extremely able sultans, each of whom added territory to the state. Murad I (1360–1389) first took Adrianople (1360) and then, after a major victory on the Maritsa River (1371), was able to take control in the Bulgarian, Macedonian, and southern Serbian lands. Sofia was acquired in 1385, Niš in 1386, and Thessaloniki in 1387. During this stage of its advance the Ottoman government left some of the conquered native princes in power, but as vassals they were obligated to pay tribute and render military aid. In the campaigns the sultans thus were supported regularly by Balkan contingents. Other areas and the major urban centers were placed under direct Ottoman rule.

Although the Ottoman victory of the Maritsa was the most decisive engagement for the future of the peninsula, the battle of Kosovo Polje (Field of the Blackbirds) in June 1389 was to be best remembered in legend and epic poetry. Here the Ottoman forces met an army of Serbs, Bosnians, and Albanians. This event was to have a particular significance for Serbia, since it was later commemorated as the symbolic end of the independent Serbian medieval state. Its prince, Lazar (1371–1389), and Sultan Murad both died at Kosovo.

The next sultan, Bayezid the Thunderbolt (1389–1402), continued the pattern of conquest. Tŭrnovo was taken in 1393; the ruler of Wallachia, Mircea the Old (1386–1418), also became a vassal. At this point Western Christendom did make a weak attempt to organize a resistance. Answering a call from Pope Boniface IX (1389–1404), King Sigismund (1387–1437) of Hungary led a crusade in which French, German, and British knights participated. This army was defeated at Nicopolis (Nicop) in 1396 by Bayezid. The victorious Ottoman advance was temporarily halted by the activities of Tamerlane (1369–1405), the last great conqueror to emerge from Asia. The Ottoman forces were crushed at the battle of Ankara in 1402, where Bayezid was taken prisoner.

After the collapse of Tamerlane's empire following his death, and after a civil war in the Ottoman state (1403–1413), Mehmed I (1413–1421) and the next sultan, Murad II (1421–1451), were able to resume the march forward. A new crusade was organized under the leadership of Vladislav (1434–1444), the king of Poland and Hungary, with the support of Wallachia and the Serbian noble, George Branković. The real direction of the undertaking was, however, in the hands of John Hunyadi, known in Romanian historiography as Iancu of Hunadoara, a Romanian in Hungarian service who was the governor of Transylvania. Although the Christian forces won some early successes, they were decisively defeated at Varna in 1444; Vladislav was killed during the fighting. This campaign marked the last united Christian effort to halt the Ottoman conquest of the Balkans.

The next sultan, Mehmed the Conqueror (1444–1446 and 1451–1481), was able to take the single greatest prize on the peninsula. Despite the great Ottoman victories in the Balkans and the loss of Anatolia, Constantinople had been able to remain free. With the Byzantine territories reduced to little more than the city and some surrounding land, the empire urgently needed outside assistance for its defense. The religious division with the West, however, was still in effect. In a desperate situation, the delegates of the Byzantine church at the Council of Florence, held in 1439, agreed to accept most of the Roman terms for reunion, and a temporary union took place. The agreement met with strong resistance throughout the Orthodox world, however, and the empire did not secure Western support. When the Ottoman siege of Constantinople commenced in April 1453, only the king of Naples and some Genoese were willing to send aid.

For two months the Ottoman army invested the city. The advantage was completely on the side of the besieging forces, who greatly outnumbered the defenders. The Byzantine commanders had about nine thousand soldiers, with a city population of around fifty thousand. The Ottoman army, with eighty thousand troops, also had artillery and command of the sea. The city finally fell on May 29. The collapse of the Byzantine state and the taking of the great imperial city was an event of tremendous significance. The chief citadel of Eastern Christianity and the heir to Roman power and splendor was occupied by a Muslim Turkish conqueror. It was now to become the capital of a new empire, which was based on quite different principles.

Mehmed II was also able to extend the Ottoman boundaries in the Balkans. In 1463 Bosnia was taken; neighboring Hercegovina fell in 1482. Most of the Christian areas were subsequently to be governed under a system of administration that will be described in the next chapter. Conditions, however, differed in Bosnia, primarily because of the large-scale conversions to Islam that followed the Ottoman occupation. The subsequent islamization was gradual. The Bosnian towns and the country districts in their vicinity became centers of Islamic culture. A nobility, Muslim in religion but Slavic in language and ethnic background, was in time to control the countryside. There were also conversions among the peasantry and the townspeople. Over the period of Ottoman rule, immigration of Ottoman administrators and military men into the area was, of course, constant. Although the Muslim element did not exceed in numbers the Christian population, its members held the predominant political, social, and economic power.

The Ottoman Empire reached its height during the reign of Suleiman the Magnificent (1520–1566), who is also known as "the Law-Giver." Its territories embraced great expanses of Europe, Asia, and Africa (see Map 10). The rivalry of the European great powers continued to benefit Ottoman interests.

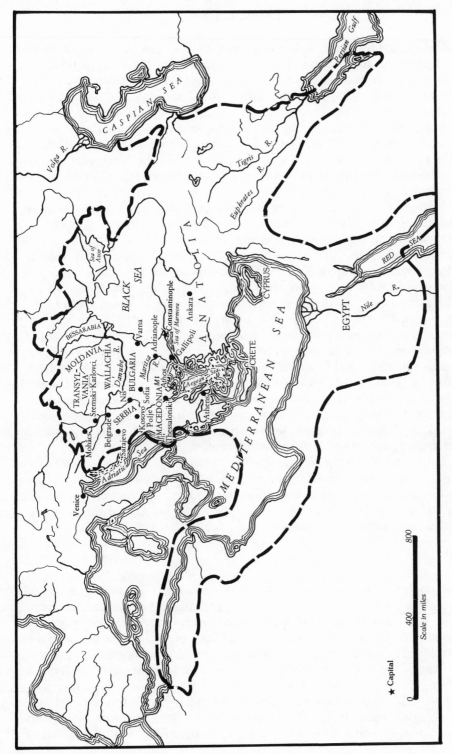

Map 10. The Ottoman Empire in the sixteenth and seventeenth centuries

CASPIAN SEA

Volga R.

Tigris R.

Euphrates R.

Sea of Azov

BLACK SEA

BESSARABIA

MOLDAVIA

TRANSYL-VANIA

WALLACHIA

Danube R.

Sremski Karlovci

Niš

BULGARIA

SERBIA

Belgrade

Sarajevo

Mohács

Kosovo Polje

MACEDONIA

Thessaloniki

Sofia

Maritsa R.

Mt. Athos

Aegean Sea

Adriatic Sea

Venice

Varna

Adrianople

Constantinople

Sea of Marmora

Gallipoli

ANATOLIA

Ankara

CYPRUS

CRETE

Athens

MEDITERRANEAN SEA

RED SEA

Persian Gulf

EGYPT

Nile R.

★ Capital

0   400   800

Scale in miles

33

Although certain states, such as Hungary, Poland, and Venice, had consistently opposed the Ottoman advance, the Christian powers had not been able to organize an effective resistance. Conditions were to become even more favorable for the Ottoman government when the king of France, Francis I (1515–1547), urged Suleiman to attack his Habsburg rival, Charles V (1519–1556). Catholic France thus became one of the first European allies of the Ottoman state. The Reformation in Germany similarly created a diversion that was beneficial to the Ottoman government. The Lutheran princes hesitated to join in a firm front against the Muslim forces, since such an action might aid the papacy and the Catholics.

Under these favorable conditions Suleiman began a series of campaigns in the Balkans. In 1521 he captured the strategically important city of Belgrade. His greatest victory, however, was won in 1526 when he defeated the Hungarian king, Louis II (1516–1526), at the battle of Mohács, which was the Hungarian equivalent of Kosovo. The victory was to lead to major political changes. In subsequent years, after further battles, the greater part of the Hungarian lands, including Transylvania, passed under Ottoman control. The remaining Hungarian possessions, among them some of Croatia and Slavonia, then became a part of the Habsburg Empire. The death of Louis II on the battlefield at Mohács led to a disputed succession. Part of the Hungarian nobility elected Ferdinand, the brother of Charles V, as king, and from this time Habsburg kings ruled the Hungarian lands that were not under Ottoman administration. For its part, the Ottoman government organized most of its Hungarian possessions into administrative districts called *pashaliks*. Transylvania, in contrast, kept a large measure of autonomy and was to act in the future almost as an independent state.

Suleiman's career did not end in complete triumph. Although great victories had been won, the Ottoman armies could not advance further. In 1529, at the first siege of Vienna, they failed to take this important city. Although further conquests were to be made in the north and east of the peninsula under other sultans, the expansion westward had been effectively halted.

Resistance to Ottoman rule

Although the Ottoman Empire was in possession of the Balkans, centers of resistance continued to arise within the peninsula and on its northern frontiers. Because of the extremely complicated nature of these actions, only three are described here: the rebellion of Skenderbeg in Albania, the events in the Danubian Principalities, and the establishment of Montenegro.

One of the major revolts against Ottoman rule commenced in Albania during the reign of Murad II (1421–1451). It was led by George Kastrioti, whose father was an Ottoman vassal. The son had been taken to Constantinople as a hostage; there he converted to Islam, taking the name Skender. In the Ottoman service he rose to the military rank of *beg*, and he is generally known by the name of Skenderbeg, or Scanderbeg. Sent back to his native land as an official, he soon organized a conspiracy. After negotiating for support with both Venice and Hungary, he began his rebellion in 1443. In March 1444 he convened the notables and organized an Albanian League. Each leader kept control of his own district; Skenderbeg had full power in only some regions. The government that was thus created was bound to be unstable. As in the rest of the Balkans, the notables were reluctant to surrender power to one of their number; some cooperated with the Ottoman government. Skenderbeg, who is the Albanian national hero, died in 1468, but resistance continued. Its center was the Albanian highlands, and assistance was given by the Italian states and the papacy. Full Ottoman domination was achieved only in the next century.

The Albanian lands were at this point devastated. Because of the bad internal conditions, thousands of Albanians emigrated. Most important was the settlement of large numbers in the Kingdom of Naples, where they lived in their own villages and retained their language and customs. These Italian Albanians were to play a leading role in the national movement in the future.

The Ottoman Empire also continued to face intrigue and resistance in the Romanian principalities of Wallachia and Moldavia. Although Ottoman suzerainty was first established over Wallachia at the end of the fourteenth century and over Moldavia at the end of the fifteenth, this authority was frequently challenged. The principalities had to meet not only the Ottoman threat, but also the ambitions of neighboring Hungary and Poland. The foremost Romanian princes of the medieval period, Stephen the Great of Moldavia (1457–1504) and Michael the Brave of Wallachia (1593–1601), had to deal with a complex political situation in this part of Europe as well as with the Ottoman overlord. Nevertheless, for a brief period Stephen was able to gain control over both Wallachia and Moldavia; Michael held Wallachia, Moldavia, and Transylvania from 1600 until he was assassinated in 1601. Their actions in joining Romanian lands were to be an inspiration to later nationalist writers and political leaders. The Romanian princes also had difficulty controlling the boyars, who were willing to join with Hungarian, Habsburg, Polish, or Ottoman allies to further their own interests. Like their contemporaries elsewhere, these men feared the concentration of too much power in the hands of one of their peers.

Despite the unstable situation in these regions, the Ottoman Empire did not attempt to incorporate Wallachia, Moldavia, or Transylvania directly into the empire. All three became vassal tributary principalities with their own princes, in theory elected by the local nobility. The chief power remained in the hands of this group, who in turn held full authority over the peasants on their estates. Most of these had been reduced to the status of serfs by the latter half of the sixteenth century.

Despite the fact that control had been established over the peninsula, the Ottoman presence was not felt equally everywhere. Some regions were so remote and poverty-stricken that they were not worth the effort that it would have cost to administer them. An example is shown in the history of Montenegro. The area had been part of the Serbia of Dušan until the breakup of that state. At the time of the Ottoman invasion many of the inhabitants retreated further into the mountains to form a new center with Cetinje as the capital. This city had a monastery, and in 1516 the bishops took over the government. Although Ottoman troops did penetrate into the region and levy a tribute, they had constant problems collecting the money and controlling the actions of vassals who lived in such a wild and inhospitable area as this.

Conclusion

The reign of Suleiman the Magnificent marked the culmination of Ottoman power and prestige. The basic organization of the empire, which will be described in the next chapter, was also set at this time. Although the state was to be hampered by grave internal problems, the boundaries in Europe were held or extended with only some losses. The conflicts and jealousies of the Western governments were to the Ottoman advantage. It was only at the end of the seventeenth century that the situation changed. After that time, European coalitions, of which Russia and the Habsburg Empire were leading members, were able to deal severe blows to Ottoman power.

The long period of Ottoman domination had, as could be expected, a decisive influence on the future course of Balkan history and the development of Balkan society. Except for the minority under Habsburg rule, all of the Balkan people were by this time subject to Ottoman authority. Among the Orthodox Christians, only the Russians were independent. Orthodox Serbs and Romanians in the Austrian state had severe restrictions placed on their activities. For the next centuries the Balkan people under Ottoman rule were to be administered under a system quite different from that in practice in Western Europe, but one that would allow them a great deal of local self-government.

The most obvious immediate effect of the Ottoman occupation on political life was the destruction of the former rulers, Byzantine emperors and Balkan kings alike, and most of the Christian feudal nobility. Only in areas like Bosnia, where the local notables converted to Islam, or the outlying provinces, Moldavia, Wallachia, and Transylvania, did the members of the former ruling class retain their privileges and their estates. It is important to emphasize here, however, that although the secular leadership was thus eliminated, the Orthodox church and its administrative hierarchy remained. In the future the Balkan population was to be directly controlled by the local community, which was left undisturbed, and by the church leadership. As will be explained in detail in Chapter 1, they were to be integrated into the unique Ottoman system of government.

PART I

The eighteenth century

1

Balkan Christians under Ottoman rule

S INCE BALKAN CHRISTIANS LIVED under Ottoman control until the
end of the Balkan Wars in 1913, an understanding of the aims and principles of that government are essential for our narrative. The ideal and
practice of both the Muslim and the Christian institutions are discussed, as
well as their decline in the eighteenth century. The role of the great powers
in Balkan developments and the events in the European provinces and the
Ottoman capital in that century are also treated in this chapter. The period
was one of accelerating internal disintegration from the center and increasing
foreign intervention in the affairs of the Balkan lands. At the same time, local
centers of power, both Christian and Muslim, assumed a stronger position
in the political organization of the state. These events form the background
for the revolutionary movements of the next century.

THE OTTOMAN SYSTEM

The Ottoman government

Although many changes had taken place by the beginning of the eighteenth
century, the Ottoman state as a whole retained much of the structure that it
had attained at its height in the reign of Suleiman the Magnificent. At this
time the empire was governed by a system that contrasted strongly with contemporary European regimes. The Ottoman state had been built up on the
concept of Holy War; the aim was the extension and defense of Islam. The
world was regarded as divided into two spheres, the domain of the faithful,
the *darülislâm*, and the domain of war, the *darülharb*. The duty of the ruler
was to extend the rule of Islam over as wide a territory as possible.

Despite the emphasis on religious war the object was not the destruction
of the darülharb or its peoples, but their conquest and domination in a manner of advantage to Islam. If a city or a region submitted without resistance,
the population could, if it wished, retain its religion and a large measure of
local autonomy; if it resisted, it could be enslaved or massacred, and its property was taken as booty. Conversions to Islam were welcomed, but they were
seldom forced. Conquered people of another religion were allowed a definite
place under the direction of their own ecclesiastical authorities. There was,

however, no question of equality. Non-Muslims paid extra taxes, they were subject to a large number of special restrictions, and they were treated as definitely inferior in status.

The first great division in the state was thus along religious lines. A second separated the people by their social position and function within the community. Here in first place stood the members of the governing class, the *askeri*, the "military," which included those who held high administrative positions, were in the armed forces, or were members of the *ulema*, the religious, educational, and legal authority of the empire. High officials in the Christian society, like the patriarchs of the Orthodox church, also belonged here. Below them were the *reaya*, the subject or "protected flock," the great majority of the population. People in this group, which was both Muslim and non-Muslim, paid the taxes and were subject to restrictions on their mode of life and dress. Ottoman society was organized into a tight pattern of estates. Movement between the levels was difficult.

At the top of the pyramid of state power stood the sultan, an absolute divine-right ruler. Since in theory God gave authority only to him, he was considered the sole source of power and could demand absolute obedience from his subjects; he held complete control over their lives and possessions. He was the owner of the state lands, and he could dispose of them as he chose. Of course, in practice his power had real limitations. Obviously, he had to rule through subordinates, who could control his access to information and his relations with the mass of the people. Moreover, he could not violate religious law or custom; Muslim public opinion, expressed through the ulema, could strongly influence the actions of the sultan. The faith also dictated the duties of a ruler; he had been given his people by God in trust. He was responsible for their care and protection; he was to lead them in the proper direction and to realize the great objectives of Islam.

One of the principal duties of the sultan was the maintenance of religious and civil law. Since social justice and balance were theoretical foundations of the Ottoman system, laws and their enforcement were of prime importance. Two principal bodies of law were in effect. First in importance was the *sheriat*, the religious law of Islam, based on ecclesiastical texts. The Koran, the basic source, was believed to record the word of God. The faithful were convinced that it contained all that an individual needed to know for his own life and his government. The sheriat could apply only to Muslims. To supplement this religious law, which could not cover all of the details of the evolving political life of the state, the sultan could formulate laws, *kanuns*, on his own authority. In practice, these were drawn up by his assistants and then approved by him. They were then issued in the form of an imperial decree, a *firman*. Each sultan upon his accession had to reconfirm the actions of his predecessor.

Holding absolute power from God, the sultan ruled through a governing class, to whom he delegated authority. At the height of Ottoman strength the administration of the country and the principal sections of the army were staffed by members recruited through the *kul*, or slave system. Obviously an absolute ruler had to surround himself with men on whom he could rely with absolute assurance. The allegiance of the soldiers was of particular importance. Previously, Islamic rulers had regularly used slaves for administrative positions, and this system was adopted and extended by the Ottoman sultans. Slaves could be obtained by many means. The ruler was entitled to a fifth of the prisoners of war, who were enslaved. Slaves could also be purchased. The most notable means used, however, was the *devshirme*, meaning "to collect," which was inaugurated sometime around the end of the fourteenth century. It remained in effect until the end of the seventeenth century, but some recruitments were apparently made as late as the eighteenth century. Although conditions varied over this period, in general, every three to seven years Ottoman officials went into the countryside to make their selections. Fathers were expected to present their unmarried male children between the ages of eight and twenty. Muslim families were exempt, since their children could not be enslaved. The children deemed best in both intelligence and appearance were taken and then sent in groups to Constantinople. There they were examined and separated. The most promising were kept in the capital, where they were given an extensive education that was designed to train them to be the future administrators of the state and the trusted members of the sultan's household. The others were sent to live with Turkish farmers in Anatolia, where they learned the language and received religious instruction. Both groups, of course, were converted to Islam. Most of the second section became members of the *janissary* corps, the most effective fighting force anywhere in this period. This body of dedicated converts was responsible for the great victories of the Ottoman armies up to the seventeenth century.

The figures given concerning the number of boys recruited through the devshirme system varies sharply. The number runs from 200,000 to many times that number for the entire period when the practice was in force. Judgments differ widely about the justice of the system. Reports exist of attempts of families to buy their children both out of the collections and into them. The Muslims of Bosnia in particular requested that they be included in the devshirme. In contrast, nationalist Balkan writers often stress the cruelty of taking children by force from their families and converting them to a religion that, by Christian judgment, would lead only to eternal damnation. It must be remembered that the religious issue was of central importance in this time. Nevertheless, although the separation was undoubtedly painful for families, and did perhaps deprive the Balkan communities of their best talent, the children gained the possibility of acquiring the most advanced education available and the opportunity to rise to the top of the Ottoman state system. It should also be emphasized that the status of slave was not necessarily demeaning. To be a slave of the sultan was an honor that conferred high social position and material benefit.

The Ottoman system of government was thus headed by an absolute monarch. His first deputy was the grand vezir, and he was also assisted by an Imperial Council, or *Divan*. This body dealt with all questions of state, but its legal functions were probably the most important. Its members included the grand vezir and the highest officials of the state and of the ulema. Below this body a vast bureaucracy, centralized in Constantinople, ran the empire and collected the taxes that were the source of so much resentment.

Since Holy War was considered a main function of the empire, the military forces were of major importance. The two most effective units were the janissaries, the infantry recruited through the devshirme, and the *sipahis*, the cavalry based on the countryside. The janissaries, as we have seen, were part of the slave system and were directly under the sultan. Forbidden to marry, they were supposed to be ready to go to war at any time. When the country was at peace, they had police duties. The state was also directly served by an artillery corps and a cavalry. The janissary force became particularly significant when the foot soldier carrying firearms proved more effective than the cavalry equipped with sword and spear.

The original great Ottoman victories, however, were largely the accomplishment of the sipahis, who also provided important services in local government. The early Ottoman rulers were faced with the problem of paying their forces. Since the sultan was considered the holder of all of the land, this question was solved by assigning to the members of the cavalry troops the usufruct of a grant of land, called a *ziamet* for a large estate, or a *timar* for the more normal size, from which they could collect certain definite payments. These funds were designed to support the holder, his family, and his retainers, and also to equip him for battle. The sipahi had to belong to the military class. Although a son could not inherit land directly from his father, as a member of the governing class he could apply for and be granted a timar if he qualified. Slaves of the sultan were also eligible to apply. Similar grants of land were sometimes given to pay wages and provide pensions for officials, or awarded to favorites of the sultan or influential men. A timar was usually held by a Muslim, but sometimes in the early period also by a Christian.

When the Ottoman army first occupied a territory, a careful register was made of the population and the resources of the area so that taxes could be properly assessed. At the height of the timar system, the sipahi was entitled only to collect certain specified taxes, usually in kind, and some labor dues. Because these payments were regulated, the peasant was usually better off than he had been under the lords of the previous feudal regimes. Under the policy known as *istimalet*, meaning "to make use of," the Ottoman conquerors attempted to win the peasants' support against their former masters. Most Balkan peasants cultivated the land of a timar, where they held hereditary rights. Their sons could continue to work the land, but this right could not be sold or transferred without permission.

The sipahi usually lived in the village where his lands were located or in a nearby provincial town. He thus was tied to his area, where he had important official duties. He was responsible for the maintenance of order in his district and for the protection of his tenants. He was also the tax collector. Since his support came from his landholding, he was himself principally dependent on the production of his fields, a fact that limited his effectiveness as a fighter. He naturally wished to be home by fall when the crops were gathered in. The normal campaigning season was thus from March to September or October. The sipahi was also entitled to a proportion of the booty obtained by victorious warfare. However, in the period covered by this narrative, the Ottoman troops, deprived of rewarding or spectacular achievements, could not gain much through looting. They fought chiefly, not in new or rich regions, but in the impoverished and depopulated Balkan and Black Sea borderlands, where the best that could perhaps be picked up was someone's stray cow.

In addition to the officials and the military, the ruling class included the members of the ulema. Law, education, and the supervision of the Muslim community's moral and religious life were in their care. Since the basis of the state was religion, their duties gave them prestige and power. They were to apply the sheriat and to further the principles of Islam through their educational and religious institutions. They provided the members of the important state office of judge, or *kadi*. Judges were dispatched throughout the provincial administration to enforce both the sheriat and the sultan's laws. They had jurisdiction over all Muslims and over Christians except in those sectors reserved for the Christian church authorities.

In addition to the kadis, another group, the *muftis*, played an important role in the Ottoman system. They acted as interpreters of both the sheriat and the sultan's decrees, and they were consulted when the meaning of a law was in dispute. At the head of the ulema stood the *seyhülislâm*, who was appointed by the sultan, but who held in fact an independent position. He could issue a *fetva*, which was an opinion or interpretation dealing with the question whether acts performed by the government conformed to Muslim principles. He could not enforce his decisions, but his judgment had an important hold on public opinion. He could and sometimes did determine the fate of a sultan.

The moral basis of this system has been described by numerous authors, both Ottoman and contemporary. Its purpose and ideal has perhaps been best expressed in the "circle of equity" stated in the eight following principles, in which the last leads back to the first:

1 There can be no royal authority without the military.

2 There can be no military without wealth.

3 The *reaya* produce the wealth.

4 The sultan keeps the *reaya* by making justice reign.

5 Justice requires harmony in the world.

6 The world is a garden, its walls are the state.

7 The state's prop is the religious law.

8 There is no support for the religious law without royal authority.[1]

The importance of the concept of justice in this theoretical framework has been emphasized:

> Justice, in this theory of state, means the protection of subjects against abuse from the representatives of authority and in particular against illegal taxation. To ensure this protection was the sovereign's most important duty. The fundamental aim of this policy was to maintain and strengthen the power and authority of the sovereign, since royal authority was regarded as the corner-stone of the whole social structure.[2]

In the Ottoman concept, as we have seen, not only political and religious positions were regarded as fixed, but also social status. Ottoman theory, like medieval European, regarded society as divided into separate estates, each part serving a particular function in a divine order.[3] Movement between classes, or occupations, was not approved because that would ultimately upset a balance ordained by God. As we have seen, the Ottoman scheme placed the "Men of the Sword," the sultan with his bureaucracy and army, and the "Men of the Pen," the religious leaders and the learned men, in the first, or askeri, class. Below them, the reaya were divided into two general categories, first, the merchants and craftsmen, and second, the peasants. This social classification cut across religious lines, although Muslims and Christians were never considered equal at any level.

The aim and ideal was thus that of social justice and balance; everything had its place and purpose as determined by God's will. A good Christian or Muslim fulfilled the role assigned to him. A reaya should not seek to become a general. These restrictions were reinforced by both Muslim and Christian church teachings. Society was static; there was no idea of evolution, progress,

---

1 Norman Itzkowitz, *Ottoman Empire and Islamic Tradition* (New York: Knopf, 1972), p. 88.
2 Halil Inalcik, *The Ottoman Empire: The Classical Age, 1300–1600*, trans. Norman Itzkowitz and Colin Imber (New York: Praeger, 1973), p. 66.
3 See the chart in Kemal Karpat, *An Inquiry into the Social Foundations of Nationalism in the Ottoman State: From Social Estates to Classes, from Millets to Nations*, Research Monograph no. 39 (Princeton, N.J.: Princeton University, Center of International Studies, 1973), p. 22.

or social and individual "betterment" as positive aims to be achieved. In this respect, the assumptions of the Ottoman world were not markedly different from those of the West. The idea of progress was an eighteenth-century Western concept; that of evolution belonged to the nineteenth century.

The emphasis on religion and its political role was also common to both the Ottoman Empire and the European states. When the Ottoman theocratic system was at its height, Europe was entering upon the age of the Reformation, the Counter-Reformation, and the religious wars. Certainly, at this time, in comparison with the excesses of both Catholic and Protestant, the Muslim Ottoman state showed itself as remarkably tolerant. As already noted, except in isolated and exceptional cases conversions were not forced. There was no equivalent of the Inquisition. As we shall see, throughout the long years of Ottoman domination the Christian and Muslim societies lived side by side in relative peace and understanding, although with considerable mutual exclusion.

The breakdown of the system

The previous section described the Ottoman system as it should have functioned. However, no political organization ever attains its stated goals; certainly the Ottoman government, even at its height, never approached the high ideals expressed by its exponents and theoreticians. This intricate, interrelated system was particularly vulnerable. By the beginning of the eighteenth century the empire was in full decline, and the essential elements in the political order either had undergone alterations or had ceased to function. Basic to the success of the empire was a strong, intelligent ruler and a victorious army. In both respects the years after Suleiman's reign witnessed disappointments and disasters.

Obviously, the functioning of the Ottoman government was intimately tied to the abilities of the sultan, who was expected to perform almost superhuman tasks. Not only was he at the head of the government and the religious institutions, but he was also as supreme military commander supposed to lead armies into battle. The first ten sultans were all men of unusual ability; thereafter a swift decline set in. A major problem was the lack of a satisfactory regulation of the succession. On the basis of the assumption that the ultimate choice lay in the hands of God, the requirement for a new sultan was merely that he be an adult male of sound mind and of the royal house. The lack of a clear ruling meant that a murderous competition existed between the eligible princes. The successful candidate usually owed his victory to luck, superior military power, and court intrigue. The extreme rivalry between brothers or others eligible for the throne led to the custom by which the victor sultan executed his potentially dangerous relatives to protect himself. For instance, Mehmed III (1595–1603) had his nineteen brothers and over twenty sisters killed.[4] Changes were also made in the education of the princes. At first the sons of the reigning monarch were sent at the age of twelve to the provinces, where they received administrative training. There they were, of course, in a position to organize political and military centers to support their own interests. To avoid this situation the princes were next confined in the harem in the *kafes* (cage) section. Completely excluded from the life of the country and secluded in a society of court intriguers, women, and eunuchs, these men could never be certain of their ultimate fate. The atmosphere of fear and the lack of employment produced weak and often mentally incompetent rulers. Suleiman II (1687–1691), when informed of his accession, told those who had come to take him from the cage: "If my death has been commanded, say so. Let me perform my prayers, then carry out your order. Since my childhood, I have suffered forty years of imprisonment. It is better to die at once than to die a little every day. What terror we endure for a single breath."[5] Although after Suleiman's reign it became the practice to choose the senior male candidate, no fixed rule of succession was ever set.

With the accession of sultans who were not fit to rule, the power in the state passed to those closest to the throne: the royal household and the ministers. The reigning monarch's mother, the *valide sultan*, became a person of considerable importance, as did the other women in the palace, the eunuchs, and the court servants. Fortunately for the empire, in the second half of the seventeenth century the Albanian Köprülü family provided four extremely able grand vezirs. Coming to office in 1656 at the age of seventy, the first, Mehmed Köprülü, sought to end the extreme corruption and to restore the government to the conditions of the time of Mehmed the Conqueror. In 1661 his son Fazil Ahmed became vezir and continued these policies. His achievements were reflected in the Ottoman military victories at this time.

The Köprülü interlude was an exception. By the end of the seventeenth century the classical administrative system had in fact broken down to a considerable extent. The slave and devshirme organization, in which at least in theory advancement was based on training and merit, had ended. The government and military offices were no longer staffed by dedicated converts but by Muslims and some Christians, who had usually acquired their positions by purchase and who looked upon their privileges as sources primarily of private profit. The collapse at the top was thus reflected right down to the bottom of the centralized bureaucracy. Most dangerous to the state, and typical of the collapse of the system, was the disintegration of the army and the apparent inability of the empire to support a strong military establishment.

Although the entire question of the economic life of the empire will be discussed in a later section, it is important to note here that one of the major

---

4 Stanford J. Shaw and Ezel Kural Shaw, *History of the Ottoman Empire and Modern Turkey*, 2 vols. (Cambridge: Cambridge University Press, 1976, 1977), I, 184.
5 Inalcik, *Ottoman Empire*, p. 60.

causes of the decline of the state was its increasing impoverishment. Most apparent was the high rate of inflation that commenced at the end of the sixteenth century and continued into the seventeenth. With the sharp rise in prices and with the rising costs of the administration and the military forces of the empire, the Ottoman government was forced to increase the rates of taxation and to adopt new methods of collection. The economy also suffered to an extent from the fact that the great trade routes to Asia now shifted to the Atlantic, where the British and Dutch were the main beneficiaries. The relative poverty of the state directly affected its military effectiveness.

As we have seen, the initial great conquests were due primarily to the ability of the sipahi cavalry, which had received its income from the timar and from booty won during the conquests. There had been no question of a cash payment. Unfortunately, this group proved increasingly ineffective against trained infantry armed with guns. The janissaries, equipped with the new weapons, thus became the base of Ottoman fighting strength. These troops, however, had to be paid a salary, and their arms were expensive. The increased costs had to be met at a time when the empire was no longer expanding rapidly, when new sources of booty were not available, and when prices were rising steadily.

The economic problems of the central government were directly reflected in the countryside. Since a cash income was urgently needed, some timar land was brought under the direct control of the treasury and then farmed out for taxes. Courtiers also received land grants as gifts or in return for services. As will be explained later, some land became in fact the private property of the man who held it. With the failure of the empire to acquire new territory by conquest and with the withdrawal of areas from the timar system, the number of sipahis equipped for battle naturally declined. These conditions also affected the peasant population in the provinces. The new controllers of the land imposed harsher conditions, and frequent disorders soon characterized provincial life. Certainly, no "circle of justice" existed. In the seventeenth century the government sent janissaries into the provinces to try to control the situation and, incidentally, to remove some of these unruly elements from the capital. Once assigned to provincial centers, the janissaries tended to make the local conditions even worse. They often joined with the Ottoman officials, the tax collectors, the wealthy local merchants, and landowners and acted against the interests of the peasants who worked the land and were the basic source of the state's tax income.

Although some janissaries settled in the provinces, the center of their power remained Constantinople, where they became an important political force with the ability to depose vezirs and even sultans. Once an elite, dedicated corps, chosen on the basis of ability and carefully trained, the janissaries had by the eighteenth century become something quite different. With the end of the devshirme system the recruits were usually Muslims by birth and not converts. They also had won the right to marry and to enroll their sons in the corps. Once established with homes and families, these soldiers became increasingly reluctant to fight in distant lands in what were seldom victorious campaigns. Moreover, the financial weakness of the government meant that their salaries were often far in arrears. Because of this problem, and also because of the opportunities offered, janissaries entered into trade or crafts. They became an important element in the guild system. Their new status meant that they could not be easily disciplined and they were financially independent. By the end of the eighteenth century they had become a privileged element in the state with a major political role. Their strength as a fighting force was another matter. It has been estimated that of the 400,000 enrolled janissaries, only 20,000 could be called upon in event of war.[6] The fact that members of the military class could so easily pass over into commerce also shows how the system of social classes had weakened.

THE BALKAN CHRISTIANS

The Balkan Christian population was thus living within a system that was rapidly declining at the center. In fact, if we examine the bleak history of the Ottoman state in the eighteenth century, the question immediately arises why the entire structure did not simply collapse from pressures within both the Christian and the Muslim sectors of society. An answer perhaps lies in the basic resilience of the Ottoman administrative system and its ability to isolate its potential opponents. The *Porte* (or Sublime Porte), a term commonly applied to the Ottoman government, did not attempt to deal with the individual citizen directly. It preferred to make use of a chain of intermediaries whom it could control and who in turn could bear much of the blame for disasters. For instance, the Ottoman government did not concern itself with the daily life or the beliefs of its Christian population. The mass of peasantry was controlled on the higher level by the Orthodox church through the *millet* system and on the lower, local basis by village authorities chosen on traditional bases. These two institutions were thus the essential element in the life of the Balkan Christian.

The Orthodox millet

The Balkan peasant, although well aware of the power of the central and provincial administration, was most directly affected by the actions of officials of his own religion, including his ecclesiastical authorities. When the Muslim armies took over new areas during the great period of conquest, they usually found that the former civil administrators had fled, had been killed, or had

---

6 Peter F. Sugar, *Southeastern Europe under Ottoman Rule, 1354–1804*, vol. V of Peter F. Sugar and Donald W. Treadgold, eds., *A History of East Central Europe* (Seattle: University of Washington Press, 1977), p. 193.

to be excluded from office because of their resistance to Ottoman authority. Since the church hierarchy usually remained, the custom of using the leaders of the religious communities for government functions was established early. Although they maintained their superior position, the conquerors were willing to work with people of any monotheistic religion whose leaders submitted to their authority. They respected in particular the Christians and Jews, the "people of the book," that is, with a revealed scripture. The members of the accepted faiths were organized into communities, known as millets. By the eighteenth century there was a Gregorian Armenian, a Catholic, and a Jewish millet, but they were far smaller than the Orthodox. There was also a Muslim millet.

For the Orthodox the most significant step was taken in 1454, immediately after the capture of Constantinople. After the fall of the imperial city, Mehmed the Conqueror considered himself the heir to the Byzantine emperors and the first ruler of the world. He personally was extremely interested in Greek thought and theological doctrine; he held in great respect the civilization that he had subdued. Determined to assure a contented Christian population, he sought a suitable head for the Orthodox church and one with whom he could cooperate. At the time the Orthodox world was torn apart by ecclesiastical disputes, in particular over the question of reunion with the church of Rome. Mehmed chose as the new patriarch a respected scholar, George Scholarios, who as a monk had taken the name Gennadios. He had the advantage of being a firm opponent of union. Together the two men supervised a new church organization, and in 1454 the sultan conferred upon the patriarch his insignia of office.

As head of the Orthodox millet the patriarch of Constantinople assumed heavy duties and responsibilities. Previously, the Byzantine emperors had played a major role in church affairs; like the sultans, they were regarded as God's representatives on earth and responsible to him for the welfare of their subjects. Under the emperors, religious affairs were controlled by the patriarch and the Holy Synod; the patriarch was the highest state official after the emperor. When disputes arose over dogma, the emperor would summon a council of representatives of the five patriarchs – from Constantinople, Antioch, Jerusalem, Alexandria, and Rome before the schism – over which he often presided. With the removal of the emperor and his officials after the conquest, a major portion of their former duties fell under the jurisdiction of the church. Although theoretically the four eastern patriarchs were equal, in practice the Constantinople Patriarchate spoke for the Orthodox and gained a clearly superior position. In fact, by the eighteenth century the other churches had become dependent upon it. Two other autocephalous churches were in existence: in Ohrid for the Bulgars and in Peć for the Serbs. Not only were they not equal to Constantinople, but by the middle of the century they had become so weakened that the Constantinople office was able to obtain their abolition. The Patriarchate then had jurisdiction over the entire Balkan peninsula and the Aegean and Ionian islands. Accordingly, it was the major center for the Balkan Orthodox people.

Although the sultan had agreed that the Orthodox establishment would be run by the patriarch with a Holy Synod composed of his metropolitans, he maintained a strong degree of control. The patriarch was in theory elected by the synod and then confirmed by the sultan. Although they had the power to dictate the choice, the sultans at first rarely interfered in the elections unless state interests were clearly at issue. The patriarchs, in turn, were seldom found in opposition to Ottoman policy. Other high church officials were chosen or dismissed by the action of the patriarch and the synod, but the sultan's approval was necessary. The Patriarchate had full control of the Orthodox churches and their property. The clergy were under the jurisdiction of their own courts, and they were free from taxation. The church was supported by fees, donations, and income from property.

The patriarch's temporal duties and his power had by the eighteenth century become immense. He was the *millet bashi* (head of the millet) and *ethnarch* (secular ruler) of the Orthodox population. Since he was a high official in the Ottoman government and part of the askeri bureaucratic class, he was entitled to a standard with two horsetails (an Ottoman governor or general had three, the sultan six). The patriarch was responsible to his ruler for the behavior and loyalty of his flock. He was also given important duties connected with tax collecting and the maintenance of public order. His judicial functions were particularly significant for the Christian population. The church had full jurisdiction over a wide range of affairs, including matters relating to marriage and the family and, in practice, commercial cases involving only Christians. Although criminal cases, such as murder and theft, were theoretically under the control of the Muslim judicial system, the Orthodox courts often handled these as well, as long as no Muslim was involved. In administering justice the church based its decisions on canon law, Byzantine statutory law, local customs, and church writings and traditions. Ecclesiastical courts could hand out penalties such as imprisonment, fines, and exile, along with the denial of the sacraments and excommunication. The Christian population usually preferred to have recourse to these courts, where they were judged on an equal basis and their testimony had weight and significance.

In integrating Orthodox institutions into their system, the Ottoman government had the advantage of being able to incorporate a complete administrative network. The church had already organized the lands under its jurisdiction into dioceses and subdioceses based on the number of their adherents in an area. A hierarchy from the lowest priest right through the patriarch existed throughout the Balkan lands. Moreover, the church and its officers were accustomed to working with, and not in opposition to, the civil authority.

Since the Patriarchate was so closely associated with the Ottoman state, its institutions were bound to reflect the gradual decline and disintegration of

An Orthodox priest's house on the Bosphorus

the other governmental institutions. This condition was most apparent at the top and in the office of the patriarch itself. Like other high offices, this position came to be awarded to the candidate who could pay the highest price. By the end of the seventeenth century it has been estimated that the cost of an election was about 20,000 piastres, or 3,000 gold pounds, an amount that rose to 5,600 pounds in 1727 and then declined. With this source of revenue it was to the advantage of the Porte for the position to change hands as often as possible. From 1595 to 1695 there were sixty-one separate nominations, but since one man could hold the office many times, only thirty-one individuals were involved. The situation subsequently improved. In the eighteenth century there were only thirty-one appointments, involving twenty-three candidates.[7]

The costs of purchasing the Patriarchate were added to the church budget until 1763. With these expenditures and the enormous losses owing to corruption within the organization, the debt of the Patriarchate reached 1.5 million Turkish piastres by around 1820. Other Orthodox establishments carried similar burdens. Since these charges were passed on down through the hierarchy, the costs ultimately had to be paid by the members of the church on the lowest level, that is, the peasantry, or from profits from ecclesiastical property. On the estates owned by the church this question concerned the dues and obligations of the peasants who worked the lands. In Moldavia and Wallachia the issue was to involve the use of income from local monasteries to support outside institutions.

Nevertheless, despite its close connections with the Ottoman government and the corruption in its operation, the Orthodox church did provide important services for the Christian people. Most significant was the fact that it kept the Christian community almost unchanged in an ideological sense until the age of the national movements. Certainly, the church preserved carefully the idea of Christian exclusiveness. It taught that the Ottoman Empire had been victorious because the sins of the Christians had called down God's punishment. Muslim rule was, however, ephemeral; a new age would soon arrive when the Christian people would again emerge triumphant. Although the Christian was a second-class citizen in the Muslim state, his religious leaders taught him that on a higher moral basis he was infinitely superior to his conquerors. In his personal, daily life the Balkan peasant was surrounded by Christian symbols, by crosses and ikons, and not by reminders of Ottoman domination.

In addition, the civil jurisdiction of the church, particularly its control of family matters, assured that there would be little intermingling of religions or nationalities. All religious organizations forbade intermarriage. Christian girls of Balkan nationalities did indeed often become part of Muslim harems,

7 Steven Runciman, *The Great Church in Captivity* (Cambridge: Cambridge University Press, 1968), pp. 201–203.

but they thereby lost their national and religious identification and joined the Muslim society. There was little chance of conversions from the Muslim community to Christianity, since this action was punishable by death. In general, both Christian and Muslim authorities acted to maintain the religious status quo.

The Patriarchate also preserved Orthodoxy against other sects. During the period of Ottoman domination the major opponent was considered to be the Catholic church. And indeed Catholicism was the main enemy: it was both crusading and intolerant of other beliefs. The Orthodox position was usually that Ottoman rule was preferable to that of a Catholic power. In this matter the interests of the patriarch coincided with those of the Porte, whose main enemies were at first the Catholic Habsburgs and Venice. Although Catholic France was an Ottoman ally, that state did not become a major instrument for Catholic penetration in the Balkans. In the eighteenth century the Orthodox authorities were well aware that in the areas where their followers lived under the jurisdiction of a Catholic state, notably in Transylvania, their position was worse than in the Ottoman Empire.

In one major respect the identification of the foreign interests of Orthodoxy and the Ottoman state was to be modified during the eighteenth century. At that time, Russia, the only Orthodox great power, emerged as the major external threat to the empire. The patriarch and most of the Orthodox Balkan population looked to and expected assistance from this state. Constant Orthodox missions went from Ottoman lands to Russia to seek mainly financial but sometimes military support. It should be strongly emphasized, however, that the Russian government never obtained a dominant influence in the Orthodox hierarchy. The church, like the Orthodox people, expected virtually limitless aid from the northern power, but there was no intention to establish anything like a dependent relationship. During the eighteenth century the church was under one predominant national influence, but it was from the strongest Christian group within the empire.

Greek influence: the Phanariots

Over the centuries of Ottoman rule it could be expected that some Christian nationalities would enjoy better conditions than others. By the eighteenth century certain Greeks had won a privileged status in comparison not only with other Christians, but also with most Muslims. The majority of the Greek people lived much like their Balkan neighbors; their fate will be discussed in a later section. A minority, however, had moved out of the limited, parochial, peasant world and had won wealth and power through commercial ventures, finance, or close association with the Ottoman government.

In comparison with other Balkan people, the Greeks were notable for their dispersion. In antiquity Greek communities were to be found around the shores of the Black Sea and the Mediterranean and in Asia Minor. After the

Ottoman conquest Greeks emigrated in particular to Italy, where the Kingdom of the Two Sicilies and Venice were to harbor large Greek colonies. For the future the Venetian center was to prove most important. With the expansion of European trade, and with the participation of Greeks in it, Greek colonies appeared in the major European cities; London, Vienna, Marseilles, and later Odessa were to prove particularly influential. As at home, the Greek colonies were organized around the local Orthodox church; the members preserved their language and a strong awareness of religious and national identity. These emigrants were not a peasant population. Usually employed as shopkeepers or merchants, they were found at all economic levels. Some became extremely successful; others barely survived. Together they formed a tight, nationally conscious society whose members had opportunities for education and a vision far beyond that of the inhabitant of a Balkan village.

Greek nationals also prospered from their predominance in the commercial life of the empire. In the Balkan peninsula, Greeks formed an important element of the population of the major cities, especially those located on the trade routes. With their connections outside the empire, their strong economic advantages, and their concern for education, they were the most prosperous and successful of the Balkan people.⟩

The really privileged position among the Christians was held, however, not by merchants or even by high church officials, but by another group, the Phanariot oligarchy with its center in Constantinople. Deriving its name from the Phanar, or lighthouse, district, where most of the Orthodox Christians lived and where the Patriarchate was located, this group was largely Greek in nationality, but its members included Hellenized Italian, Romanian, and Albanian families. The influence of the Phanariots was derived mainly from their great wealth, which was gained largely through the high offices they held in the state and the financial rewards that could be extracted from them. They thus profited exceedingly from Ottoman corruption. From the middle of the seventeenth century they enjoyed a unique position in the empire because of both their wealth and their political influence.

As the military power and prestige of the empire declined, and the borders contracted, the Porte was forced to face the fact that it would have to meet the European powers on their terms. Since it could not overpower its adversaries on the battlefield, it would have to learn to deal with them through diplomacy and negotiation. Because Turkish officials did not easily learn other languages, they became dependent on intermediaries in their dealings with foreigners. As the best educated of the Balkan peoples, and the most closely connected with European countries, the Greeks were fully suited to this task. They thus usually filled the post of *dragoman* at all levels. Although this term is translated as "interpreter," a dragoman was in fact an agent or an intermediary, rather than someone simply trained in languages. Through their skill in this occupation, Greeks came to control four major posts in the Ottoman administration: grand dragoman, who became something close to a permanent secretary for foreign affairs; dragoman of the navy, who became the intermediary between the grand admiral of the navy and the Greek islands; and the governorships of the two Romanian provinces of Wallachia and Moldavia. Their role as rulers of the Principalities will be discussed in a following section. Here only the relationship of the Phanariots to the Ottoman government and the Patriarchate is under consideration.

The importance of the Balkan Christian element in Ottoman administration has been emphasized. However, before the seventeenth century, high position in the bureaucracy went almost exclusively to converts. In contrast, the Phanariot officials retained their Christian faith and remained in close touch with the Patriarchate. The first Phanariot to win a high post was Panagiotis Nikousios, whom Ahmed Köprülü made grand dragoman in 1669. With this office came significant privileges, such as growing a beard and riding a horse with attendants, which previously had been accorded only to Muslims. The most famous Phanariot statesman was, however, Alexander Mavrokordatos, who was grand dragoman from 1673 to 1709. Like many Greeks of the time he was educated in Italy at the University of Padua. He then became a doctor. His advancement was rapid; he became grand dragoman in his thirties. He was the chief Ottoman diplomat at the negotiations leading to the Treaty of Karlowitz (Sremski Karlovci); his son Ioannis held a similar position in the discussions relating to the Treaty of Passarowitz (Požarevac). As translators and mediators, the Phanariot diplomats were, of course, able to learn many of the Ottoman state secrets, and they were directly in touch with foreign governments.

The Phanariots at this time were also deeply involved in the affairs of the Patriarchate. Through their financial power, they were able to exert a large measure of control over the church institutions. Always in need of money, the church naturally turned to the wealthy laymen. A great deal of the indebtedness of the Patriarchate was caused by the extreme corruption of the empire and the necessity of purchasing offices and making other payments. In the eighteenth century, for instance, the cost of the Patriarchate was high. Although few candidates had the cash necessary, they could borrow from Phanariot sources at 10 percent. Once a banker had invested in a successful candidate, he had a measure of control over his debtor. The Phanariots also wielded influence by acquiring seats in the synod assigned to laymen and by assuring that vacant positions in the church administration were filled by compliant candidates.

The period of Phanariot control in Orthodox affairs coincided with a shift from a universalist to a Greek national emphasis, particularly in the top church hierarchy. Greek had always been the language of the Patriarchate, but it had not been that of the majority of the Balkan churches. The Slavic churches, the Patriarchate of Peć and the Archbishopric of Ohrid, and the Romanian institutions used primarily Church Slavic. There was also an assumption that the Constantinople office represented Orthodox Christians in general and certainly not Greeks in particular. This emphasis underwent a major shift in the eighteenth century. The most decided action taken was the abolition of the organizations of Peć in 1766 and Ohrid in 1767. Both institutions, which served Slavic peoples, were placed under an exarch appointed by the patriarch. The results of this move were to prove most damaging to the cultural interests of the Bulgarians. Their ecclesiastic and educational institutions were now Greek-dominated. The Serbs had an alternate religious center at Sremski Karlovci in the Habsburg Monarchy.

A Greek hierarchy also was in control in Moldavia and Wallachia. Here Phanariot Greeks ran the political life of the country. In the Balkans only the Montenegrin church, under a hereditary prince-bishop, maintained a position of independence. At the end of the eighteenth century this organization had complete religious autonomy. However, the remoteness, backwardness, and poverty of this area made it a matter of little concern in the general Orthodox world. The center of Orthodox prestige and power remained the Constantinople Patriarchate. Although it did not control the Georgian or Russian churches, neither was a challenge to its position. The Georgian institution was too weak, and Peter the Great abolished the Russian Patriarchate. The Russian church and state were also regarded by the Orthodox as sources of financial assistance and political support.

Although there was much resistance within the church to the penetration of the lay elements represented by the Phanariot interest, the outlook of this group did profoundly influence the attitude of the upper hierarchy of the Orthodox church throughout the empire. Despite the fact that the Phanariots served and cooperated closely with the Ottoman government, their aim was not the welfare or strengthening of the empire. The great Phanariot families felt themselves directly tied to the Byzantine Empire.[8] They took great trouble in trying to discover or fabricate genealogies that would link them to noble Byzantine dynasties. Although these connections could seldom be demonstrated without fraud, individuals did adopt the names and titles of their supposed ancestors. Their ultimate goal, an outlook that embraced the entire Orthodox world, was nothing less than the recreation of a triumphant Byzantine Empire, which they envisioned as a multinational state, governed by a Greek nobility, with Greek as the language of government. The Orthodox church was thus under the strong influence of a class that intended to inherit the Ottoman Empire and replace a Muslim with a Greek Orthodox regime. In the next century this concept was to be the basis of the *Megali Idea* (Great Idea); it would play a major role in shaping the Greek national outlook until 1922. Prominent Phanariots, in particular those who became governors of the Danubian Principalities, adopted what they re-

8 See Cyril Mango, "The Phanariots and the Byzantine Tradition," in Richard Clogg, ed., *The Struggle for Greek Independence: Essays to Mark the 150th Anniversary of the Greek War of Independence* (Hamden, Conn.: Archon Books, 1973), pp. 41–66.

garded as Byzantine styles in their conduct of government and in the luxurious ordering of their lives. Phanariots looked to Russia, the only independent Orthodox state, for assistance.

Thus in the eighteenth century one national group, which had won wealth and high position, did assume a predominant position in the Orthodox millet. This action was particularly significant because the church provided the sole means of education for most Balkan Christians. The Greek imprint on ecclesiastical culture was not acceptable to most of the non-Greek nationalities. Among the first steps in the national movements of the Bulgarians, Serbs, and Romanians was the effort to throw off Greek influence and substitute their own national patterns. This reaction naturally affected the prestige of the Constantinople Patriarchate and limited its effectiveness in influencing all of the Balkan Orthodox people. National movements were to develop apart from, and sometimes in conflict with, the highest religious authority.

Provincial government: village communities

In the preceding sections the emphasis has been on the upper level of Ottoman administration and on the corresponding Christian institutions. The Ottoman government also had a highly developed network of provincial government, which had a Christian counterpart in the village communities with their traditional organization. Many changes were made in the provincial institutions during the entire period of Ottoman rule; this matter will be discussed in greater detail in connection with specific historical issues. For the present it is sufficient to note that the Balkan peninsula, which was regarded as a single administrative unit, was divided into sections that were called at various times *eyalets*, *vilayets*, or *pashaliks*; these in turn had subordinate jursidictions known as *sanjaks* or *livas*, which were further subdivided into *kazas*, then into *nahiyes*. The area was also organized into judicial districts called *kadiliks*; treasury officials, *defterdars*, had a separate administrative system. The local authorities worked in cooperation with the resident sipahis, who had definite duties and obligations. The provincial administration also controlled police forces. Janissaries, who were under the jurisdiction of the central and not the local government, were also supposed to perform police duties. The chief official at the local level, usually titled *pasha*, relied for advice on a council, a divan, in which Christian notables and guild officials might also sit.

The vast majority of Balkan Christians lived in the countryside in small villages organized on traditional and pre-Ottoman bases. Local variations will be discussed subsequently, but it is possible to make some wide generalizations. The villages were usually run by officials known by various titles, according to the local language: *archon*, *knez*, *chorbazhi*, *koca-başi*, or *hodza-bashi*, for example. Some were elected, according to local custom, by the male population of the village, usually from among the more prosperous or braver of the men; others held office simply because they were members of a family or clan that traditionally held the position. They were assisted by, or they governed in cooperation with, the leading men of the community, whom we will refer to as notables or elders. Most communities were controlled by the leading notables. Great decisions, involving the life and fortunes of the inhabitants, were usually discussed by assemblies of all of the male members of the group. Most villages also formed a part of a larger organization; representatives from local communities met at a central location to discuss common problems. Village notables could form part of the local Ottoman official's council, or they could act as unofficial advisers on Christian affairs.

The notables played certain essential roles in the Ottoman administration. Like the church officials they acted as intermediaries between the Ottoman government and the peasant. Their role in tax collecting and in the assessment of what each individual owed was particularly important. In return for their services, they received special privileges, for instance, exemption from the head tax. Over the years the notables won for themselves a generally bad reputation. The corruption of the Ottoman system allowed many to profit at the expense of those under their authority. Some held timars. Others gained wealth through the tax-farming system; that is, they held by agreement with the Ottoman government the right to collect taxes, and they fully exploited the opportunity to enrich themselves. The notable's role in revenue collecting, particularly where it was in kind, enabled him to influence the sale and distribution of local agricultural produce. He could use his advantage to enter into trade in these commodities himself. He often lent money to the local peasants and thus won the traditional stigma attached to usurers in rural societies. Notables were also in a position to buy land, and they could come to control considerable estates. Their wealth naturally allowed them to live in a different manner from that of their poorer neighbors.

Despite the many abuses, the local notables did provide Christian leadership in the countryside. As the central government declined, their importance rose. They were to play a major role in the national movements of the next century. In provincial society they, together with the merchant and the guild members in the trading centers, formed a Christian elite that worked with its Ottoman counterparts. These people together made the Ottoman system work even at times when the central government was in disarray.

At the bottom of the social scale were, of course, the peasants, who farmed the land and paid the taxes. They lived under a variety of conditions. It must be first emphasized that in the eighteenth century the Balkan peninsula was covered by vast forests and great stretches of unused land. In the second half of the century, war, banditry, and disease caused a depopulation of wide areas. The uncertain political situation, together with the existence of more than adequate pastureland, caused the peasant in most areas to rely on animal husbandry as his main occupation. He raised cattle, sheep, and pigs. If local conditions became too bad or taxes were too high, peasant families could move. Serfdom was not prevalent; the Balkan peasant usually was not tied to the soil. Moreover, Ottoman authorities never were able to control the entire peninsula. There were always remote regions of hill and mountain country where the central government could not reach the individual.

For the peasant who earned his living tilling the soil, conditions could differ widely. As previously explained, the agricultural land was regarded as fundamentally belonging to the sultan, who held it from God. All land was divided into three categories: *miri*, or state land; *mülk*, or private property; and *vakif*, which belonged to religious foundations. The timar system rested naturally on miri land. Immediately after the Ottoman conquest, the position of the peasant at least in theory was not bad. Although he had to make certain definite payments, he had important rights. He was regarded as a hereditary tenant or sharecropper, and he could pass on his land to his heirs. Moreover, he could usually farm his holding as he saw fit. There were often no controls on his methods or over what he chose to produce. He could also sell the right to work his plot or transfer it, as long as he obtained permission from the sipahi and found someone who would assume his obligations. The peasant also held some possessions as private property, whether by law or by tradition. In the villages the houses, gardens, and some communal pasture and forest land qualified as such.

Most timar land was devoted to the upkeep of the sipahi. Some estates, however, were preserved for the public treasury and used to compensate high state officials or to support members of the sultan's family or household. The vakif land also became of great significance. It was possible for an individual to assure personal salvation by giving property or money to a Muslim charitable foundation with the intention of having the income used for a pious purpose. Since the Ottoman state did not provide social services, these institutions supported hospitals, orphanages, and similar public services. Although the grants were primarily intended for religious and charitable purposes, they could also serve individual interests. The donor could arrange for the position of supervisor, or *mütevelli*, to be permanently assigned to a member of his family; sometimes the income from the property sufficed only for this person's support. Christian churches enjoyed similar privileges through foundations supported by bequests from their members.

The peasant whose land formed part of a timar or a vakif was obviously closely dependent on the man who held formal control. This situation became more apparent as the central government weakened and proved unable to enforce its edicts in the provinces. Most detrimental to the position of the peasant was to be the gradual conversion of some timar land into estates, called *chiftliks*, which were in operation controlled as the private property of their holders. These arose through various processes. Often a sipahi was able to obtain what were in fact hereditary rights over his territory; sometimes a family or an individual would receive the right of tax farming on a permanent, hereditary basis. On these lands the individual peasant was subject to much heavier obligations than before. On the timar he had had certain definite rights; the state determined his obligations and regulated his relations with the sipahi. The new owners were not similarly controlled, and they had great influence in local government. Although most chiftliks were organized on a sharecrop basis, the peasant had to surrender a much greater proportion of his produce than on the timar. His supplementary payments in kind, money, or labor were higher. In many places he was reduced to the position of an agricultural laborer.

In reviewing the position of peasants in the Balkans in the eighteenth century, it should be emphasized that there was no single uniform system in effect. It is extremely difficult to make wide generalizations because the question has not been studied in detail. Different areas obviously underwent varying developments. However, as far as landholding is concerned, it can be safely said that some peasants lived on timar land. Their obligations depended on the individual situation, but they were in a better position than their counterparts working on chiftlik estates, where payments and obligations were higher. For all peasants the question of the control of the local government was essential. Where the sipahi or chiftlik holder dominated the authorities and the police, the peasant was clearly in a worse position. There were, however, also wide areas where villages paid nothing for the use of the land. Privileged areas and remote villages paid state taxes, when they could be collected, and little else. When conditions became too bad, the peasant had the alternative of fleeing to the mountains, over the border into a neighboring state, or to a large city, such as Thessaloniki or Constantinople.

Since the preceding discussion has applied principally to the Christians, a word should be said about the Muslims, whether of Turkish or Balkan national background. Muslims were, of course, to be found in the towns as government officials, military men, or members of guilds. In the countryside there were Muslim landowners and also peasant villagers. Obviously the sipahi or the chiftlik owner was in a strong position and was part of the ruling establishment. The peasant, in contrast, was usually not in a favorable situation. Some peasants were converts from the Balkan nationalities; others were Turkish colonists brought from Anatolia. Many of the Muslim villages held their land from the state as virtual private property. However, despite the fact that in theory the Muslims held a superior place in Ottoman society, the Muslim peasant, on the bottom of the social ladder, was often little better off than his Christian neighbor. Although excused from some taxes, he still paid a large proportion of his income to the state, and he suffered equally from extortionate local officials and the deprivations of warfare. He was also subject to recruitment into the army, which the Christian was spared.

For all of the citizens of the empire, the single major common complaint concerned the tax system. At issue were not only the amounts demanded, but the methods of collection. The question will be discussed throughout this volume, since it remained the major source of controversy and grievance until the fall of the empire. As the Ottoman government became weaker and local revolt and national feelings grew stronger, resistance to tax payments to an unpopular regime naturally increased. The Christian inhabitant of the empire paid taxes to the state, to whoever held the land he worked, and to his church. The payments could be in kind, in money, or in labor dues. As far as state taxes were concerned, he paid one, the *haraç*, a head tax, that was not levied on Muslims. This payment was regarded as a replacement for the obligation to serve in the army owed by the Muslim population. In addition to the regular taxes, the Christian could be assessed special amounts for particular purposes. Most burdensome once decline set in were the taxes extracted at time of war.

We have seen that the Christian population had on the provincial level its own political organizations under local leaders. There were also Christian armed forces. When it early proved inexpedient or impossible to try to hold all of the lands of the Balkans with its own troops, the Ottoman government assigned either to villages or to groups of Christians the duty of garrisoning important points, such as bridges or passes, or of simply assuring peace and order in their districts. The Christian militia could be appointed by the local Muslim or Christian officials. Members, known usually as *armatoles*, received tax exemptions, land, or other payments. These men were armed and they were trained to fight. In practice, they proved difficult for the central government to control.

Despite its use of local militia, the Porte, especially during the period of decline, was unable to guarantee law and order throughout the Balkans. At all times certain areas were controlled by bands who defied state control. Individual voyagers and merchants had to travel in caravans protected by armed retainers, especially in the mountains. They particularly feared the bandits, known as *klephts*, *haiduks*, or *haiduts*, according to the local language. These outlaws operated in bands of up to a hundred men and often had the full cooperation of the local inhabitants. In good weather they lived in the forests and hills; in winter they retreated to hide in friendly villages. Like the official militia, they were skilled in the use of firearms and in guerilla warfare. Often the link between bandit and armatole was close; they could interchange roles.

Over the years the bandits came to enjoy a high reputation among the Christian peasantry, for some of whom they became a symbol of resistance to political and social repression. They in fact did offer an alternative to the individual who was under severe pressure from his landlord or the state. Although these men were treated as heroes in popular mythology, legend, and song, by the eighteenth century the armed outlaw had become a major problem throughout the Balkans. By that time a floating population of military men, both Christian and Muslim, inflicted continual terror on many parts of the countryside. Some of the bands were formed from deserters from the army or from men who had lost their lands and homes as the Ottoman forces retreated before the Habsburg and Russian attacks. These desperate men, along with the bandits, devastated defenseless villages. The failure to control these groups was another perfectly justified grievance of the Christians against the Ottoman authorities, though the Muslim population, of course, suffered equally.

The city

The major cities of the Balkan peninsula lay along the great military and trade routes to Europe. They were the administrative, military, and judicial centers for the Ottoman government.[9] Here the same separation of people by nationality and religion existed that has been seen in the countryside. The cities were divided into quarters, *mahallas*, each inhabited by a separate group of the population. The national and religious composition could often contrast sharply with that of the countryside. The cities naturally held strong concentrations of the commercial people of the empire, the Jews, the Greeks, the Tsintsars, and the Armenians; the Muslim element, whether composed of administrators, military men, or holders of estates, usually preferred to live in urban centers.

Within the city the activities of the artisans were strictly controlled through the guild system. These organizations could be Christian, Muslim, or mixed in membership. Like their equivalents in the West, their aim was to produce what was needed for the market and to assure a fair division of work and profit for the membership. They exerted a strict control over the price, quality, methods of production, and sources of raw materials for their goods. Since their efforts were directed toward securing a stable market and a product of guaranteed quality, they tended to restrict the activities of their members and to oppose new methods. They were also under strong state supervision. At the head of the guilds stood the masters, followed by the journeymen and apprentices. In addition to their role in the production and distribution of goods, the organizations acted as charitable institutions for their members and cared for the sick, widows, and orphans. Most guilds, representing a conservative and traditional way of life, upheld a strict moral code.

THE WARS OF THE EIGHTEENTH CENTURY

During the eighteenth century the fate of the Christian people was determined not only by the political and social structure of which they formed a part, but by the constant wars that ravaged a large part of the Balkan lands. During this period the military weakness of the empire was demonstrated by repeated defeats; the state was on the defensive in relation to the European great powers (see Map II). The Ottoman disasters had an extremely detri-

9 For the Ottoman city see Sugar, *Southeastern Europe*, pp. 72–92.

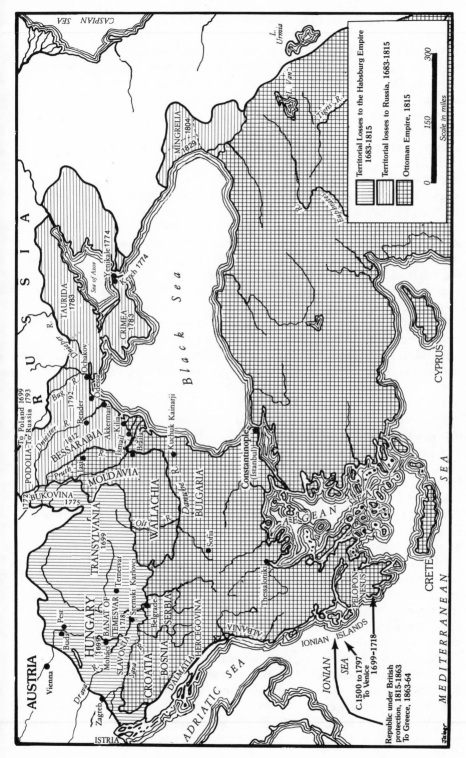

Map II. Ottoman territorial losses, 1683–1815

mental effect on the Balkan lands. The great battles took place deep within the peninsula. Balkan cities and villages were destroyed; populations were scattered. War taxes and army requisitions further impoverished the countryside.

Before the end of the seventeenth century the Ottoman Empire had been in the advantageous position of seeing its potential opponents divided. Beginning with the reign of Francis I, the French government had attempted to bring the Porte into its system of alliances. Along with Sweden and Poland, the empire was to form a part of the Eastern Barrier that France wished to use first against the Habsburg Empire and then against Russia. The rivalry between France and the Habsburg Empire was to prove of benefit right up to the eighteenth century. The great issues of the Reformation, the Counter-Reformation, and the Thirty Years' War similarly distracted the European states. Although Ottoman military power in fact commenced to decline after the reign of Suleiman the Magnificent, the rivalries among the European great powers made it impossible for them to organize a new crusade of Christian states.

Because of this situation the Ottoman Empire was able to continue to make some territorial conquests. Two Venetian possessions, Cyprus and Crete, were taken in 1573 and 1669. Podolia was gained from Poland in 1676; this acquisition marked the furthest extension northward of Ottoman penetration, but also the beginning of what was to be a bitter struggle for control of the land north of the Black Sea. The Ottoman successes were largely due to the wise policies of the one able sultan of the century, Murad IV (1623–1646), and of the Köprülü family of grand vezirs. The first, Mehmed (1656–1661), concentrated on internal reform; his son, Ahmed (1661–1678), recommenced a strong military program with the emphasis on Transylvania and the Ukraine. In 1678 Kara Mustafa Pasha, the brother-in-law of Ahmed, became grand vezir. His great ambition was to inflict a decisive defeat on the major Ottoman opponent, the Habsburg Empire. In 1683, with an army of ninety thousand, of whom perhaps fifteen to twenty thousand were effective troops, he arrived before Vienna, which remained under siege from July to September. Faced by this formidable threat, the Austrian military commander, Charles of Lorraine, withdrew from the city and left it to be defended by a force of under twenty thousand. The siege was lifted in September by an allied force commanded by Charles and King John Sobieski of Poland. The sultan had Kara Mustafa strangled for his failure, and the empire thus lost its most able military commander.

Encouraged by the victory, the Ottoman opponents banded together in a new Holy League, composed of Austria, the papacy, Venice, and Poland, to be joined later by Russia. Assaults were then launched on the major peripheral Ottoman military centers. Buda, the capital of Ottoman Hungary, fell in 1686; Belgrade was taken in 1688. Venice enjoyed similar victories; a campaign was undertaken in the Peloponnesus, and Athens was occupied in 1687. The forward movement of the Western allies, however, was soon halted. A new Köprülü vezir, Mustafa, came to office in 1689 under Sultan Suleiman III (1687–1691). The War of the League of Augsburg with France forced Austria to withdraw troops to that front. In a counteroffensive of 1690 the Ottoman army was able to drive back the Habsburg army. In 1697, by which time Russia had joined the allies, the situation was again reversed. The end of the war in Western Europe released the imperial forces, who under the command of their brilliant general, Eugene of Savoy, were able to inflict a devastating defeat on their enemy at Senta. Faced with disaster, the Porte was forced to make peace. The Treaty of Karlowitz of 1699, concluded with Austria, Venice, and Poland, marks a watershed in Ottoman history and is one of the major peace treaties of modern European history. In this agreement, for the first time, the Ottoman Empire ceded territory permanently to Christian powers. The peace was negotiated through British and Dutch mediation and involved much disagreement among the allies. The Habsburg Empire was most interested in ending the fighting, and it received the principal gains. In the treaty Austria annexed extensive and valuable territories: Transylvania and sections of Hungary, Croatia, and Slavonia that had been under Ottoman control. Venice took the Peloponnesus and most of Dalmatia, and Poland regained Podolia.

In the agreement the Habsburg Empire secured important commercial and religious clauses, which were reconfirmed in later pacts. Article XIV stated: "Let there be free commerce for the subjects of both parties according to earlier sacred treaties in all realms and subject territories of the emperors, so that it may be carried on in useful fashion without fraud and deceit for both parties." Commercial relations were in fact to increase steadily throughout the next century. The provision in favor of the Catholic religion, contained in article XIII, stated that the sultan reconfirmed previous privileges

> so that the adherents of the aforementioned religion can restore and repair their churches and may carry on the customary rituals which have come down from earlier times. And let no one be permitted to establish any kind of vexation or monetary demand on the religious people of any order or condition, against the sacred treaties and against the divine laws, to hinder the practice of that religion, but rather let the adherents of it flourish and rejoice in the customary imperial sense of duty.[10]

Russia, who had not joined in these negotiations, made a separate peace in 1700. The terms included the Russian acquisition of the port of Azov,

---

10 The text of the Treaty of Karlowitz is in Fred L. Israel, ed., *Major Peace Treaties of Modern History, 1648–1967* (New York: Chelsea House, 1967), II, 869–882.

which had been taken in 1696, and the right to send a resident Russian minister to Constantinople.

The Treaty of Karlowitz was a major Habsburg victory; it marked the climax of the monarchy's successful resistance to the repeated Ottoman attacks of the past century. Although some changes were to be made in the Austrian–Ottoman boundary, this frontier was to remain relatively stable until 1878. Only two permanent changes occurred. Austria took the Banat of Temesvar (Timişoara) in 1718 and the province of Bukovina in 1775. Nevertheless, in the course of the next century the Habsburg Empire was to fight three major wars with the Porte. The initiative for these actions, however, would lie more often in St. Petersburg than in Vienna.

The Ottoman Empire at this point found itself perpetually on the defensive on the battlefields. In foreign affairs the most significant development was the emergence of a new strong adversary. As we have seen, in the past the chief opponent had been the Habsburg Empire; France had been a supporter and an ally. In 1682 Peter the Great ascended the Russian throne at the age of ten. He first ruled in conjunction with his half brother, but in 1696, at the latter's death, Peter was free to embark upon active policies. He joined the Holy League and launched an attack on Azov. Although he was involved in campaigns against the Ottoman Empire, his principal attention was directed toward the Baltic and against Sweden. He made peace in 1700 so that he could join in a coalition with Poland, Saxony, and Denmark to attack Sweden, which was ruled by the young king Charles XII. After being defeated decisively at Narva in November 1700, Peter turned to strengthening his military forces and reforming his state.

In 1709 Charles XII, in alliance with the Ukrainian forces of Mazeppa, commenced an invasion of Russia, which was halted at Poltava in July. After their crushing defeat, Charles and Mazeppa fled to Constantinople, where they intrigued to draw the Porte into war against Russia. Their efforts were aided by France and also by the leaders of the Crimean Tartars, who feared Russian encroachment on their lands north of the Black Sea and the Crimea. In 1710 the Ottoman Empire did declare war on Russia.

In the same year Peter embarked upon an ambitious Balkan campaign. For the first time in the modern era Russian armies crossed into Balkan lands and advanced as far as Iaşi (Jassy). Peter then called upon the Balkan Christians to rise in aid of his army. This appeal to the subject population was a new weapon for Russia, although the Habsburg Monarchy had used it during the invasion of Serbian lands. The policy was not a success. Although there was some local action in southern Hercegovina and Montenegro, there was certainly no mass uprising of Orthodox peasants. In the Danubian Principalities, the Moldavian *hospodar* (governor), Dimitrie Cantemir, joined Peter, but Constantine Brîncoveanu in Wallachia refused to act. In July 1711 Peter and his army were surrounded on the Pruth River. In an impossible military position, the tsar signed a treaty surrendering Azov, which he had only recently

Map of the Balkans by Herman Moll, 1717

acquired. Later controversy was to arise over the question whether the Ottoman government should not have used the opportunity to gain much more. It perhaps could even have destroyed the Russian army and taken Peter prisoner. Certainly the Ottoman Empire was never again to have a similar opportunity or to win such a victory over Russia.

Having defeated Russia, the Porte next turned to deal with Venice. In 1715 an army was sent to the Peloponnesus and attacks were made on the Ionian Islands and Dalmatia. In the Greek lands the Ottoman troops were welcomed by the local population, where the Venetian attempts to win converts to Catholicism had aroused much enmity. In 1716 the Habsburg Empire joined Venice. Prince Eugene of Savoy, again back from war against France, demonstrated his great military talents in another sweep through the Balkans. The Treaty of Passarowitz of 1718 gave the monarchy new gains; Austria acquired the Banat of Temesvar, northern Serbia including Belgrade, and Oltenia (Wallachia west of the river Olt). The Ottoman Empire kept the Peloponnesus, but Venice retained the Ionian Islands and Dalmatia.

By 1736 all sides were ready to renew the contest. The Ottoman Empire had just fought an unsuccessful war with Persia, but the Porte was concerned about concurrent developments in Poland, which threatened to fall under Russian control. The French government, with similar apprehensions, also pressed for action. War began between the empire and Russia in 1736; Austria joined the next year. Again a Russian offensive action was undertaken in Moldavia, this time under the leadership of General Münnich. Appeals were addressed once more to the Christian people. The Russian armies took Azov and reached as far as Iaşi in the Principalities. Similar successes were not, however, achieved by the Habsburg forces. The Habsburg government, alarmed at Russia's progress, which could lead it to disproportionate gains, insisted upon peace. In the Treaty of Belgrade of 1739 the monarchy surrendered most of the acquisitions of Passarowitz; the Ottoman Empire thus regained northern Serbia and Oltenia, although the Banat had passed permanently to Austrian control. Forced to make peace also, Russia received Azov and certain commercial privileges in the Black Sea.

Although another unsuccessful war with Persia was fought from 1743 to 1746, the Ottoman Empire was to enjoy almost thirty years of uninterrupted peace in its relations with Europe. The War of Austrian Succession (1740–1748) and the Seven Years' War (1756–1763) absorbed the European energies. At this time European politics were dominated by the figures of three energetic rulers, Frederick the Great of Prussia, Maria Theresa of Austria and Catherine the Great of Russia. Ottoman interests came into conflict chiefly with those of the ambitious and aggressive Russian empress. The true heir of Peter the Great, Catherine embarked on large-scale plans to extend the Russian boundaries southward, to include the Black Sea coast and the Crimea, and westward into Polish lands. The interests of the Ottoman vassals, the Crimean Tartars, were thus directly menaced, as were those of Poland, a state that both the Porte and France wished to maintain.

Russian and Prussian interference in Polish internal affairs resulted in the formation of the Confederation of Bar, an association of Polish nobles who led an uprising against the outside control. Russian troops in pursuit of a group of rebels crossed the Ottoman frontier and burned a town. Urged on by France and the Crimean Tartars, the Ottoman Empire declared war on Russia in 1768. The Porte was soon faced with an enemy offensive on two fronts. A Russian fleet was sent from the Baltic to the eastern Mediterranean, with the aim of destroying the Turkish naval forces and starting a revolt in Greece. The first objective was soon reached. The Russian fleet under the command of Admiral Alexis Orlov successfully engaged the Ottoman navy near the island of Chios and forced it to take shelter in the harbor of Chesme. A fire ship sent into this port destroyed the fleet. The attempt to start a major rebellion in Greece, however, failed. In 1770 Albanian troops crushed the revolt that had broken out. At the same time a Russian army again advanced into the Principalities and took the Ottoman fortresses of Kilia, Akkerman, Ismail, Bender, and Brăila. These Russian victories frightened the other European powers, who feared a complete upset of the balance of power. Frederick the Great thus pressed for a moderate peace with the Ottoman Empire, to be accompanied by a partition of Poland.

The Treaty of Kuchuk Kainarji (Kücük Kajnarca), signed in July 1774, was the equivalent for Russia of the Treaty of Karlowitz for Austria. It was a major military and diplomatic disaster for the Ottoman Empire, since it marked a complete change in the power balance in the Black Sea region. Russia acquired territory formerly belonging to the Khanate of the Crimea, including the fortresses of Kerch and Yenikale, and an area along the Black Sea between the Bug and Dnieper rivers. The Khanate was declared independent, a status that left it open to Russian penetration and eventual annexation. Russia was also granted extensive commercial privileges – most important, the right of free navigation for its merchant ships on the Black Sea and through the Straits. The Black Sea, which had previously been a closed Ottoman lake, was open thereafter to the great northern power. Russia, in addition, received the right to appoint consuls in Ottoman cities and to enjoy the same commercial privileges as had been granted previously to Britain and France. The Porte was also required to pay an indemnity.

For the future the most important provisions were to be those establishing what was to become a Russian foothold inside the empire. First, although Russian troops were evacuated from the Principalities, the Ottoman government gave formal political and religious guarantees to the population, and Russia was expressly allowed the right to intervene with the Porte in their behalf. Second, in two articles of the agreement the Porte gave assurances that were interpreted later by Russian diplomats as giving them the right to speak in behalf of the Orthodox Christian population of the entire empire. Article XIV allowed Russia to build in Constantinople "a public church of the Greek ritual, which shall always be under the protection of the Ministers of that Empire, and secure from all coercion and outrage." Article VII, the most controversial, declared:

> The Sublime Porte promises to protect constantly the Christian religion and its churches, and it also allows the Ministers of the Imperial Court of Russia to make, upon all occasions, representations, as well in favor of the new church at Constantinople, of which mention will be made in Article XIV, as on behalf of its officiating ministers, promising to take such representations into due consideration, as being made by a confidential functionary of a neighboring and sincerely friendly power.[11]

Before the signing of this agreement, in August 1772, Russia, Austria, and Prussia participated in the first partition of Poland, a state that had previously been a major power. In 1774 Austria occupied the Moldavian province of Bukovina, claiming it as a reward for having aided in the achievement of peace. Unable to resist this annexation, the Porte ceded the area formally in 1775.

Despite the gains in the Treaty of Kuchuk Kainarji, Catherine had wider plans embracing nothing less than the destruction of the Ottoman Empire and the partition of its European territories between Russia and Austria. Her most ambitious scheme was the so-called Greek Project, which involved the breakup of the empire and the restoration of a revived Byzantine Empire, with the capital at Constantinople and under Russian protection. The empress had her second grandson named Constantine with this dream in view. Obviously, such a large undertaking could not be accomplished alone, and neither Frederick nor Maria Theresa could be expected to be sympathetic. However, in 1780, at the death of his mother, Joseph II ascended the Austrian throne. Weaker than Maria Theresa in dealing with Catherine, he allowed himself to be drawn into the empress's plans. In a series of letters and in conversations during a visit made by Joseph to Russia, the partition of the Ottoman Empire was arranged. In the division Russia was to obtain the Crimea, lands along the Black Sea to the Dniester River, and territory in the Caucasus. Austria was to receive Oltenia, part of Serbia, Bosnia, Hercegovina, Istria, and Dalmatia. For her surrender of these last two places, Venice was to be compensated by the acquisition of the Peloponnesus, Crete, and Cyprus, territories that she had once held. France would be allowed Syria and Egypt. The remaining Ottoman territory in Europe was to be formed

---

11   The text of the Treaty of Kuchuk Kainarji may be found in Thomas Erskine Holland, *A Lecture on the Treaty Relations of Russia and Turkey from 1774–1853* (London: Macmillan, 1877), pp. 36–55.

into two states, both of which would be under Russian control. The first, composed of Moldavia and Wallachia, was to become the independent nation of Dacia and to be ruled by a Russian prince. The second, a revived Greek-Byzantine Empire, would embrace Bulgaria, Macedonia, and Greece. Constantine would rule, but his throne was never to be united with that of Russia. This arrangement, which gave the major advantages to Russia, was only the first in a series of schemes that the great powers were to discuss among themselves for the partition of Ottoman territories. For states that were in the process of dividing Poland, such a program appeared logical.

With assurances of support in Vienna, Catherine proceeded to move against her initial goal, the Crimea. The Russian government first supported a pretender to the throne; after he gained power and the population arose against this outside interference, Russian troops were ordered to march in on the pretext of "restoring order." The territory was then annexed. The Porte, which had no practical alternative except acquiescence, agreed in 1783, since the Ottoman government could not resist Russia alone. Its single foreign supporter, France, was involved in a conflict with Britain in connection with the American War of Independence. French leaders were also becoming less enthusiastic about the Ottoman connection.

Once in possession of the Black Sea and Crimean lands, Catherine and her ministers, in particular her favorite, Gregory Potemkin, launched a major effort to colonize and develop the newly acquired areas. Russian and German settlers were brought in; efforts were made to encourage the commercial development of the region. Kherson was built up as a naval base, and the foundations were laid for a Black Sea fleet. These developments deeply affected the military balance not only in the Black Sea area, but also in the Balkan peninsula. With a firm hold on the Black Sea coast and with control of the major port cities, the Russian fleet was only two to two and a half days sailing time from Constantinople. The Russian ability to transport by sea an expeditionary force whose aim was the conquest of that capital was recognized and feared by the other powers.

Despite the Ottoman military weakness, war could not be avoided. Russia continued to press forward in the Caucasus. Problems were also encountered in the Principalities; in 1786 the Porte deposed a hospodar in violation of previous agreements. In 1787 the Ottoman Empire declared war on Russia; Austria joined its ally the next year. The Russian war aims were the conquest of the fortresses of Ochakov and Akkerman and the establishment of an independent Dacian state that would serve as a buffer to protect the new Black Sea territories. At first, the Ottoman armies made advances. Russia was distracted by a concurrent war with Sweden, and the Austrian armies also suffered defeats. The situation was then reversed. Russian armies again entered the Principalities, and there the great Russian general Alexander Suvorov won impressive victories. Austrian troops advanced in Bosnia and Serbia.

The Ottoman Empire was to be immensely aided by the problems that

Joseph II was having in internal affairs and by the basic distrust between Austria and Russia. In 1790 Joseph died and was succeeded by the far more cautious Leopold II. Faced with a rising in the Netherlands and fearing what Prussia would do, the new emperor made a separate peace, the Treaty of Sistova, on the basis of the restoration of the status quo before the war. In an additional agreement, Austria also received some territory to be added to the Banat. The Austrian withdrawal was naturally a blow to Russia, whose armies were winning victories. Revolts had also broken out in Greece, and the Ottoman Empire was without allies. Other matters, however, had to be taken into consideration. In 1789 the revolution commenced in France; the international situation was not clear. Russia thus in 1792 concluded with the Porte the Treaty of Jassy. Catherine obtained Ochakov and territory to the Dniester River, but the Principalities were again returned to Ottoman rule. In 1793 and 1795 Russia joined with her neighbors in the final partitions of Poland.

By the last decade of the eighteenth century it was clear that Russia was the predominant European power in the Near East and the principal threat to Ottoman survival. Austria had cooperated in Russian ventures, but its leaders, like Prussia's, feared a rapid Russian advance. The single state that had shown support for the Ottoman government had been France, but that power had never sent military forces to the area. Although concerned about the maintenance of the Eastern Barrier states, the French government had not been able to prevent the division of Poland, the defeat of Sweden, or the continual Russian and Habsburg victories over the Porte.

The French attitude determined at first the position of a power about whom little has yet been said – Great Britain. Principally concerned with its worldwide colonial contest with France, Britain tended to support its rival's adversaries, including Russia, which was seen also as a valuable trading partner. When the Russian Baltic fleet sailed to the Mediterranean in 1769 it took on supplies at British ports, and British officers, notably Lord Elphinstone, accompanied the expedition. However, in the 1770s British opinion began to shift. Catherine's policy of armed neutrality during the American War of Independence was against British interests. Moreover, like Prussia, Britain saw the dangers of too great an increase of Russian power. The stage was thus set for a shift in alliances that would ultimately make Britain the chief supporter of the Ottoman Empire against Russian pressure.

BALKAN PEOPLE UNDER OTTOMAN RULE

The questions discussed in the preceding sections affected all of the Balkan people: the Ottoman government, the Christian ecclesiastical and local administration, and the great wars of the century. It is next necessary to examine in greater detail events in the lands inhabited by the Christian people under direct Ottoman rule: the Greeks, Albanians, Montenegrins, Serbs, and Bulgarians.

Here the general conditions in the areas are considered, as well as the specific effects of the lessening of Ottoman authority and the disastrous wars.

The Greeks

As we have seen, by the eighteenth century the most favorable position among the Christians was held by the Greeks, in particular by the merchants and those who worked with the Ottoman government. However, the peasant population of Greece proper also had wide rights of self-administration. Although a Greek population was to be found scattered throughout the empire, the concentration was in the islands of the Aegean, in the Peloponnesus, in Thessaly, and in Rumeli. Greeks also lived in large numbers in Thrace, Epirus, and Macedonia. An area with only a small percentage of arable land, most of continental Greece was not farmed. Because the land was unsuitable for widespread chiftlik agriculture, these estates were concentrated in certain areas, especially in Thessaly and the Peloponnesus. The inhospitable hill and mountain land was better for animal husbandry, particularly for the raising of sheep and goats. The good agricultural lands were generally part of an estate belonging to a chiftlik, a religious foundation, or members of the sultan's household. In the hill and mountain country agricultural land could be held in what amounted to private property by the cultivators.

Since the Ottoman government did not attempt to control closely areas remote from the major cities and lines of communication, the villages of herdsmen and small farmers in the mountains of continental Greece usually were allowed to run their own affairs as long as they paid their taxes. Some regions, such as Mani in the Peloponnesus, Suli in Epirus, and Agrapha in the Pindus, were in practice almost independent in relation to the central authority. Other areas were granted special privileges in return for services, such as securing a pass or guarding and maintaining a bridge. The people received tax benefits, and they had the right to bear arms.

In the rest of mainland Greece and the islands a vigorous system of local self-government had developed. Since the Ottoman government preferred to deal with organized Christian groups and not directly with individuals, these local systems, which predated the Ottoman conquest, had been supported and encouraged. A network of communal government thus paralleled the Ottoman administrative framework. These institutions took the responsibility for the assessment and collection of taxes, and they assumed regular police duties. The villages were usually under the direction of local notables, chosen from among the prominent men. The most complete system was developed in the Peloponnesus after the Venetian expulsion in 1715. Here the elders of each village formed a council to decide local problems; they also sent representatives to the vilayet council. In turn, this body chose delegates to meet with representatives of other vilayets in the Peloponnesian senate, where matters of administration and taxation were discussed. Two members of this group,

73

The Acropolis of Athens with Ottoman cavalry

together with two Muslims, formed the permanent council of the vezir of the Peloponnesus. The Greeks of the area also had the important privilege of sending two representatives to Constantinople, where they could complain directly to the Porte, over the heads of the local administrators, about conditions or about arbitrary acts of the authorities.

Communal government in Greece was conservative and traditional. It formed a support to Ottoman administration, and it paralleled in spirit and aim the ecclesiastical system. The chief power was in the hands of local notables, called archons, who were also the Christian large landowners or tax farmers. They dominated the assemblies and the Peloponnesian senate. Secure in their privileges, they did not challenge Ottoman rule. As a group, they were to be severely criticized. Frequently unscrupulous and bent on profiting from the system, they often appeared in the role of the oppressors of the poorer and weaker members of their own society. Far from united as a class, they split into family factions that fought for economic and political advantage. This division among the more powerful families and their bitter feuds became clearly apparent in the Greek revolution of the 1820s.

The Greek islands were in an even more favorable position. Since they were usually held by members of the Ottoman royal family, they were under the control of the *kapudan-pasha*, the grand admiral of the Ottoman fleet. By the eighteenth century their actual administration was in the hands of the dragoman of the fleet, who, as we have seen, was a Phanariot Greek. In return for certain services, such as supplying sailors for the Ottoman navy, the islanders were freed from some taxes, and they governed themselves. Notables, chosen by popular assemblies, dominated the political structure as they did on the mainland.

The communal system had an important judicial as well as political function. The local officials together with the church offered a preferred alternative to the Ottoman kadi. The Greek authorities based their decisions on Roman law, the principal source being the Hexabilis of Constantine Armenopoulos of the fourteenth century. Over the years, however, more reliance began to be placed on customary or common law.

The Greek communal organization, like that in other parts of the Balkans, was extremely important for the preservation of local separateness. The local government did not become a center of resistance to Ottoman rule, but it did protect the individual Greek from absorption into a larger unit. It also shielded the individual in what was a lawless and violent environment, particularly when the central government broke down. Then the local authorities with their armed auxiliaries could protect the average citizen. The Greeks, a seagoing people, also suffered from the dangerous conditions on the surrounding waters. Throughout the Ottoman era the population of the islands and the coastal towns faced threats from Muslim and enemy attacks and from the depredations of pirates. Life was often unsafe near the seashores for the peasant population. Just as, in the mountains, the relationship between klepht and armatole was often close, so the pirate was often interchangeable with the sailor, the fisherman, and the commercial shipper.

Because of the mountainous and inaccessible nature of much of the Greek mainland, the Christian armed forces always played an important role in local life. In order to control these areas and to combat the klephts, the Ottoman government organized the remote districts into *armatoliks*, or *kapitanates*. Armatole bands were given jurisdiction over a definite assembly of villages and the responsibility for maintaining law and order and for collecting taxes. They were paid by the district that they were supposed to protect. The leaders were known as *kapitanios*, their followers as *pallikária*. The position of captain could be hereditary in a family, or he could be chosen by the village elders. Although recognized and authorized by the Porte, these bands were closely attached to their areas. There were also police, *kapoi*, hired by the local government or the notables. The activities of the armatoles were greatly admired, and they did indeed act as a protection in times of disorder.

The klephts, whom the armatoles were supposed to be opposing, won even greater fame. Operating in bands of about forty or fifty, they gained the romantic reputation of embodying all the ideals that this mountain society admired. They were known for their "extraordinary imperviousness to fatigue, hunger and thirst"; they were extremely strong and believed to be great athletes. Their shooting ability was legendary. They specialized in guerilla warfare and "in ambushing enemies in the dark."[12] The intense admiration that their activities aroused is reflected in modern Greek historical writing:

> When captured, they displayed great stoicism in the hands of Turkish torturers. It was a question of honor with them to endure all suffering in silence. There is not a single known case of a klepht whose courage failed him or who surrendered his faith in order to save himself from death by torture. The prospect of such a lingering death made them salute their fellows with the words "May the bullet be sure!" If a klepht was so badly wounded that he could not be saved, he implored his comrades – and the request was always honored as though it were sacrosanct – to cut off his head and take it with them so that the enemy could not impale it on a spike and subsequently parade it through the towns and villages.[13]

The Greeks and other inhabitants of the Balkans found that the wars involving the European powers had a deep effect on their own development. Prior to the eighteenth century the influence of Venice, which held Crete,

12 Apostolos E. Vacalopoulos, *The Greek Nation, 1453–1669: The Cultural and Economic Background of Modern Greek Society*, trans. Ian Moles and Phania Moles (New Brunswick, N.J.: Rutgers University Press, 1976), p. 222.

13 Vacalopoulos, *The Greek Nation*, p. 222.

Cyprus, and points in the Peloponnesus and in the islands, had been most directly felt in the Greek lands. During the seventeenth century, however, its power began to wane. Fighting raged over Crete from 1645 to 1669, resulting in the loss of the island to the Ottoman Empire. This extended conflict drained the resources of the merchant city and marked its decline as a Mediterranean power. Despite the fact that Venetian rule represented a European and a Christian control, it did not win the support of the Greek population. The friction was chiefly due to religious conflict. Unlike the Islamic, the Catholic faith was militant and it did seek converts. As we have seen, the chief enemy of the Patriarchate was Catholicism, largely because the main danger to the Orthodox establishment lay in this direction. The principle that "the turban of the prophet is preferable to the cardinal's hat" was to dominate Greek–Venetian relations. In addition, Venetian administration, more efficient than the Ottoman, proved more effective in the collection of taxes and allowed less participation in government by the local Greek population. Venetian merchants were also in competition with Greeks. Although many Greeks did indeed cooperate with the Venetians against Ottoman rule, in the long run little regret was felt when they lost their strongholds in Greek lands.

At the end of the seventeenth century Venetian power in the Aegean had one final period of upsurge. After the formation of the Holy League, the main Ottoman forces were drawn into the northern Balkans to defend the empire against the chief threat, the Habsburg Empire. Venetian forces under Francesco Morosini used the opportunity to launch an expedition in the Peloponnesus. With local support they were able to establish a firm position and to advance as far as Athens in 1687. While attacking the Turkish positions there, they shelled the Parthenon, the most noble monument of the Greek classical past. Although Venetian possession of the Peloponnesus was confirmed in the Treaty of Karlowitz, this acquisition could not be held long. By this time Venice did not have the resources to maintain a great empire. Since it was expensive to fortify, defend, and administer the new territory, the Venetian authorities attempted to raise taxes and to conscript local labor for civil needs and to build fortifications. These actions proved most unpopular. The presence of foreign soldiers and the strong proselytizing activities of the Catholic church caused further deep antagonism. In 1714, when Turkish troops again appeared, they met little resistance among the local population, who apparently preferred a reestablishment of the former regime. In the Treaty of Passarowitz the area was returned to the Ottoman Empire; Venice was reduced to holding the Dalmatian coast and the Ionian Islands, which still left her the strongest power in the Adriatic. Once again in possession of the area, the Ottoman government made an effort to improve conditions in the Peloponnesus and to attract new settlers. As we have seen, Greek local government again assumed great significance.

Although the Ottoman Empire was at war with Austria and Russia in the 1730s, the hostilities did not extend into the Greek lands. Naturally, during the long period of peace following the Treaty of Belgrade of 1739, international problems did not involve the area. However, beginning in the 1760s another external factor began increasingly to influence the Greek position. At this time the Russian interest in the Orthodox church and in general Greek affairs was extended to the mainland. In preparation for war with the Ottoman Empire, agents from the Russian government were sent into Greek territory to attempt to promote an uprising to back the Russian military actions to the north. A Greek captain of the artillery, Grigorios Papadopoulos, was dispatched to Mani, and the organization of a Greek revolt was placed in the hands of the brothers Gregory and Alexis Orlov.

The Russian agents were indeed able to interest some notables in their enterprise; they received promises of men and supplies. However, in return the Greek partisans expected massive Russian assistance – something like ten thousand troops and extensive military equipment. When in 1769 a Russian expedition did indeed arrive, the Greeks were profoundly disappointed to find that it consisted of four ships, a few hundred soldiers, and entirely inadequate supplies of arms and ammunition. Despite the fact that no great Greek uprising occurred and the Russian contribution was totally insufficient, Greek and Russian forces did attempt a campaign; Navarino was taken in April 1770. The Ottoman government, pressed by the necessity of fighting a major war on its northern boundary, called in Albanian troops, who crushed the expedition at Tripolitza (Tripolis). During the campaign the Christian forces had massacred Muslim civilians and destroyed their property; the Albanians now took a fearful revenge. The damage was so extensive and the troops so out of control that in 1779 the Porte finally had to send a Turkish force to suppress the Albanians. The first Greek–Russian endeavor thus proved a total disaster and brought considerable suffering to Greek lands.

Although the Peloponnesian undertaking failed, Russia's victories in the Principalities and in the eastern Mediterranean allowed that government to impose a major peace. In the clauses affecting the Archipelago, the Treaty of Kuchuk Kainarji required the Porte to grant a general amnesty and tax relief and to allow the emigration of those who wished. In addition the treaty stated "that the Christian religion shall not be exposed to the least oppression any more than its churches, and that no obstacle shall be opposed to the erection or repair of them; and also that the officiating ministers shall neither be oppressed nor insulted."[14] In the later Treaty of Ainali Kavak of 1779 the Porte agreed to make payment for Greek lands that had been confiscated during the war.

Interest in Greece continued to mount in Russia after the war, despite the failure in the Peloponnesus. Catherine's Greek Project was no secret. Such plans were discussed in diplomatic circles. Russian agents continued to circulate in Greece, and Greek students were brought to Russia for their edu-

14   Quoted in Holland, *Treaty Relations of Russia and Turkey*, p. 47.

Castle of Parga

cation. When war with the Porte broke out again in 1787, Russian manifestos calling again for Christian rebellion were distributed. Thoroughly discouraged by the failure of the previous action, most Greeks did not move. However, the Christian Albanians of remote Suli took advantage of the situation. They were later defeated by the pasha of Janina (Ioannina), Ali, in an early episode in the career of that remarkable adventurer. Not only did the Christian people not respond to the Russian appeal, but it was not even found possible, as it had been in the previous war, to launch a Russian naval action in the Mediterranean. The declaration of war by Sweden in 1788 confined the Russian navy to the Baltic. The Treaty of Jassy of 1792, ending the conflict, had no specific provisions in regard to Greece.

During the next few years the Russian government retained its interest in the Greek lands and, largely because of the common Orthodox religion, was the most influential foreign power. In the previous peace treaties and in the associated commercial agreements, Russia had gained important rights within the empire. The provision concerning the appointment of consuls was to be particularly significant. These men, usually Greek nationals, had offices in the major cities throughout the Greek provinces. Like the consulates of the other powers, they became centers for intrigue against the Ottoman Empire and for the organization of local Russian partisans. The treaties with the Porte also made the provision that Greek merchant ships could fly the Russian flag and thus enjoy Russia's protection as well as share its commercial privileges. During the wars of the first decade of the nineteenth century, these Greek ships came to dominate Mediterranean trade as French shipping was driven from the seas. The new Russian port of Odessa became a major Greek center with an influential merchant population. The Russian ties with the Constantinople Patriarchate, of course, continued. The church leaders, the Phanariots, and the merchants all expected support from St. Petersburg. Russia was, in fact, the only great power that remained consistently interested in a partition of Ottoman territory.

The Albanians

Although the Albanians shared with the Greeks many of the problems of a people endowed with a rocky, mountainous land, they marked a strong contrast in other respects. Whereas the Greeks had acquired a wealthy, educated merchant and Phanariot class and had won a position of dominance in the Orthodox church organization, the Albanians remained among the most backward people in the Balkans. They also had the largest numbers of conversions to Islam. This second condition was to have perhaps the greatest effect on the course of their history. When the Ottoman armies arrived in Albania, they found the country divided between an Orthodox south and a Catholic north. Although there were at first few conversions, conditions changed in the seventeenth century. Current Albanian historiography ex-

plains this occurrence as chiefly the result of the sharp rise in taxes, in particular in the poll tax paid by the Christian but not the Muslim. In the sixteenth
century the tax, the *djizia*, was 45 akches; in the beginning of the seventeenth
century it was 305 akches, a figure that rose precipitately in the next half
century to 789 akches.[15] Although this rise to an extent reflected the increase
in general prices, the fiscal pressure on the individual made conversion to
Islam a great temptation. In addition, though this was usually not the case
elsewhere, in Albania some measure of force appears to have been used.

The main target was the Catholic population, which declined notably in the
seventeenth century. Like the Orthodox church, the Porte saw the Catholic
church as a major enemy. Catholic Venice was entrenched in the Adriatic Sea;
the Habsburg Empire was a frequent problem. During the war that broke out
with Venice in 1645, Catholic Albanians hoped for a Venetian victory. In 1689,
during the war of the Holy League, they revolted. Most of the forced conversions occurred at this time; many former Catholics were resettled in the Kosovo
area, which thereafter became a center of strong Albanian and Muslim feeling.
Most of the conversions took place in the lowlands around the Shkumbî River,
where direct Ottoman pressure could most easily be exerted.

In the eighteenth century Albania thus presented a complex religious picture. The Catholics, by then the weakest group, were concentrated in an
enclave in the north with Shkodër (Skadar, Scutari) as the center. The Orthodox were to be found principally south of the Shkumbî and in the districts
of Korçë (Koritsa) and Gjirokastër. Muslims lived throughout the country,
but chiefly in the center and in Kosovo. The Catholics looked for support
primarily to the Habsburg Empire, which claimed a right of protection. The
Orthodox were part of the Ohrid Archbishopric until its abolition; thereafter
they were under a strong Greek cultural influence. What education was available to them was in the Greek language, as was the church liturgy.

The Albanian Muslims enjoyed a privileged position not only in their own
lands, but throughout the entire empire. A warlike people, they had many
opportunities to serve the state. The best of the janissaries recruited through
the devshirme system came from the Albanian Christian families. The Albanian sipahis and the mercenary troops were renowned for their effectiveness.
Albanian guards served high officials throughout the Balkans. As Muslims
Albanians had many opportunities to win influential administrative positions. The four Köprülü grand vezirs were the most successful, but it has
been estimated that at least thirty men of Albanian background held this high
post.[16] The Albanian Muslim, who had no reason to dislike the privileges
accorded his faith, was usually one of the strong foundations of the state.

In addition to the three-way division in religion, the Albanians formed

15   Kristo Frasheri, *The History of Albania* (Tirana: n. p., 1964), p. 95.
16   Stavro Skendi, *The Albanian National Awakening, 1878–1912* (Princeton, N.J.: Princeton Uni-
     versity Press, 1967), p. 21.

Albanians at Janina

two other groups, the Ghegs and the Tosks. The Ghegs, inhabiting the rugged northern mountain areas, had developed a self-governing tribal organization similar to that of the neighboring Montenegrins, and one that lasted until recent times. The basic unit was the clan, called a *fis*, which was headed by the oldest male. Associated with the fis was a territorial and political counterpart, called a *bajrak* (standard), which was composed of one or more clans. The position of leader, or *bajraktar* (standard-bearer), was hereditary. The bajrak has been described as "an autonomous state governed by customs and other juridical regulations basically common to all the other bajraks."[17] A tribe was formed of a group of bajraks led by a man from a prominent family. Major matters were settled by assemblies of the male members of the tribe, and judgments were made on the basis of unwritten customary law. Although mountain tribes were supposed to pay taxes, they were very difficult to collect. In fact, the central government could not really control the actions of men living in these inaccessible areas. It repeatedly had to send troops against them.

The Tosks, who had no tribal system, lived in villages under their own elected notables. They were to be found mostly in the southern lowland areas that had early been subject to the timar system. By the eighteenth century large estates, particularly in the central regions, had come under the control of strong families who had both economic and political power. Here the conditions for the peasants were very hard, even though both peasant and landowner might be Muslim. The flat areas of the country were easier for the government to control, but some Tosk Orthodox villages, situated in remote mountain areas, like Suli in Epirus, had won an independent position similar to that of the Gheg tribes. In return for payment of taxes, whose collection was often resisted, the villages were granted an autonomous administration.

Although Albania was not a theater of war in the eighteenth century, conditions were anything but peaceful. Like the other Muslim lands, the Albanian lands contributed many soldiers to the Ottoman campaigns; losses were high. Even worse were the struggles for power among the local Muslim notables. Weighed down with foreign war and internal political problems, the Porte was increasingly unable to control its provincial officials. In Albania the owners of the large estates and the wealthy naturally sought political power, which was to be gained by securing appointments to official positions from the central government. Once in office they could refuse to follow orders unless it suited their personal interests. They were Muslims, and they had bands of armed retainers. These men, known as *beys*, not only were completely out of the control of Constantinople, but fought frequently among themselves for power, position, and extensions of their political jurisdiction. In the mountain areas, similar conflicts raged among the tribal chieftains, each of whom sought to expand the area under his domination. Helpless to

17 Skendi, *Albanian National Awakening*, pp. 14, 15.

83

enforce order directly, the Porte attempted a policy of divide and rule, but that tactic also failed.

As a result of these circumstances, by the end of the eighteenth century two centers of power had emerged. In the north, around the city of Shkodër, the Bushati family gained a dominating position; to the south a second stronghold was established at Janina under Ali Pasha. Ali's career was to influence Ottoman policy until the 1820s; the Bushati family had a shorter period in power. The Bushatis' prime influence in northern Albania was established by Mehmet Pasha in the years between 1757 and 1775. Aided by highland tribes, he was able to extend his area of control, and he received official appointments from the Porte. When he attempted to widen his political jurisdiction further and refused to forward the taxes he had collected, the Ottoman government had him poisoned. Although a conflict over succession followed, his son, Kara Mahmud, took his place. The Porte then unsuccessfully tried to organize a rival coalition of families. The career of Kara Mahmud, who was to exert a major influence on the history of the entire western Balkan area, merges with the progress of events that were simultaneously taking place in neighboring Montenegro.

The Montenegrins

After its conquest in 1499 the Ottoman government made little effort to control the remote mountain land of Montenegro. The timar system was never applied, and in return for the payment of the poll tax, which was not heavy, the region was in general left to itself. The only Ottoman official who appeared was the representative from the central government who attempted, usually in vain, to collect the tax. The Montenegrins, like the armatoles in Greece, were also expected to perform a military function. Because their lands after 1699 were close to Venetian possessions in Dalmatia, they were expected to help defend that frontier, but they were more often found fighting on the opposing side.

The majority of Montenegrins inhabited the mountain areas, where they led a life very much like that of Albanians and Greeks in similar circumstances. Their main occupations were cattle and sheep raising, hunting, and banditry where that proved profitable. The basic social and political unit was the tribe, which in turn was made up of clans. The tribe, held together by ties of family and by the constant quarrels conducted with neighbors, controlled the pasture and woodland communally. Montenegro, together with the adjacent Albanian highlands, was probably the most primitive area in the Balkans, if not in Europe. It has been estimated that in the first half of the nineteenth century the population numbered only about 120,000, from which 20,000 fighting men could be drawn.[18] Nevertheless, as a political unit this country was to play a role far outweighing its poverty, small size, and backward condition.

18 Vladimir Dedijer et al., *History of Yugoslavia*, trans. Kordija Kveder (New York: McGraw-Hill, 1974), p. 291.

Since the land was torn apart by the quarreling tribes, the single element of unity was at first the church. Montenegro was both Serb in nationality and Orthodox in religion. The center was the Cetinje monastery, whose bishops had jurisdiction over the entire territory. They were usually elected by a synod, and before 1766 they were confirmed by the patriarch of Peć. From the eighteenth century the position was always held by a member of the Petrović family from the Njeguš tribe; the first bishop was Danilo (1696–1737). The family came from the district of Katuni, near Mt. Lovčen, the area that was the stronghold of Montenegrin resistance to Ottoman authority and to the invasion of the neighboring Muslim provincial armies. Not only did the church serve as an instrument of unity, but its leaders established relations with other countries. Thus the bishop functioned as a head of state and allowed Montenengro to play at least a small role in international affairs.

The first close relations with an outside state were with neighboring Venice, which made payments to Montenegrin tribal leaders to gain their support. In the war of the Holy League some tribes fought for Venice, an action that led to an occupation by a Turkish force. Uprisings also occurred when Peter the Great called for Christian support for his invasion of the Principalities. Venice, however, remained the most important center of possible assistance. When in the Treaty of Karlowitz Venice extended its possessions to include the whole of Dalmatia, it became a direct neighbor. From 1714 to 1718 Venice was again at war with the Porte. Since it desired Montenegrin assistance, ties between the countries were strengthened. In 1717 the doge of Venice, Cornaro, issued a decree establishing a political officer, called a *guvernadur* (civil governor), for Montenegro. There were now two officials, the bishop and the governor, with political roles. The Venetian appointee at first lived in Kotor, on Venetian territory, on a subsidy. The position was thereafter regularly held by a member of the Radonjić clan, which was also part of the Njeguš tribe. Although both the bishop and the governor were supposed to be elected by an assembly of the heads of the tribes, both positions became in fact hereditary in the two families. Initially the two officials appear to have cooperated well. The first major quarrel came in 1802 over the question of the appointment to the secular office.

After 1718 the link with Venice weakened. Montenegro received no gains in the Treaty of Passarowitz. Although closer relations were sought with Austria, Russia became henceforth the main focus of Montenegrin attention. Already in 1710, it will be remembered, the Montenegrins, supported by tribes in Brda and Hercegovina, had revolted when Peter called for Christian assistance. The uprising had been suppressed with great losses. Thereafter, the major connection was between the church authorities in both countries. In 1716 Danilo went to Russia, where he received gifts of money, books, and equipment for the church. One of the foremost Montenegrin supporters of reliance on Russia was Bishop Vasilije Petrović, who made three visits to St. Petersburg. He hoped that Empress Elizabeth would assume a protectorate over his country.

85

In order to instruct the Russians about his country, he published in Moscow in 1754 a book entitled *History of Montenegro*, in which, needless to say, Montenegrin exploits were not slighted.

Meanwhile, throughout the century, relations with the Porte remained tense. Montenegrin tribes repeatedly raided over their borders, and they were a nuisance and a danger to their neighbors. In 1756 Bosnian troops, aided by Venice, whose subjects were similarly injured by Montenegrin actions, attacked the area. After an Ottoman force invaded their land, the Montenegrins gave assurances that they would pay their taxes and that the raids would cease.

In 1766 a most bizarre episode occurred when an impostor arrived in the country claiming to be Peter III, Catherine the Great's husband, who had actually been murdered in 1762. An educated man of compelling powers, even though of slight stature, this pretender was able to convince many of the primitive and naive tribesmen of his true royalty. He was to rule under the name of Stephen the Small. He could not convince the bishop, Sava, who had received his office in 1735 and had met the real tsar. Nevertheless, Stephen was able to push the bishop aside and assume the power in the state. Despite his dubious background, the new ruler did attempt to introduce some much-needed measures. He tried to establish something like a formal civil government and to end the constant feuding between the rival tribes.

Stephen's actions caused concern to the great powers. Russian subsidies were stopped. Montenegrins also resumed raiding into Turkish and Venetian territory. In 1768 the Porte dispatched an army against Stephen, but could do little since war had also broken out with Russia. Concerned about developments in Montenegro, Catherine sent Prince Iurii Dolgorukii in 1769. Although the envoy recognized that Stephen was an impostor, he did not attempt to secure his removal. On his departure, Dolgorukii left some munitions and money, but Montenegro at this time did nothing to aid Russia in the war. Stephen was finally poisoned in 1773 by a Greek servant in the pay of the Porte.

Relations with Russia then deteriorated. In 1777 a Montenegrin mission was sent to St. Petersburg, but it was not received by Catherine. The Russian government was following a policy of cooperation with Vienna, and it hesitated to interfere in the western Balkans. Montenegro also made approaches to the Habsburg Empire. In 1777 a Montenegrin, Nicholas Marković, offered to form a company to fight for Austria. Nothing was done, since the Austrian government knew little about conditions in Montenegro. In 1781 an Austrian officer, Colonel Paulić, was dispatched to report on the country. His opinion was negative: the hostile factions, Bishop Sava's lack of control over the tribes, and the Venetian and Ottoman opposition to an increase of Habsburg involvement all influenced his judgment.

After Sava's death in 1782, the next leader of importance was Peter I, who became bishop in 1784. He had been part of the unsuccessful mission to

Russia in 1777, but he still wished to be consecrated there. When he was unable to get a passport, he went to Sremski Karlovci instead. Thereafter, he turned to Austria to try to get military supplies and assistance; the governor, Jovan Radonjić, also supported a close Habsburg orientation.

For the rest of the century the main threat to Montenegro came from neighboring Albania and from the wide ambitions of Kara Mahmud, who attempted to set up an autonomous principality in defiance of Constantinople. His first attack on Montenegrin territory took place in 1785. At this time he was able to gain the support of some of the tribes. His victories and his attitude of resistance toward the Porte attracted the attention of both Austria and Russia, who wished to make use of him in their own plans against the empire. It will be remembered that this was the period of Catherine's Greek Project. The Habsburg government was willing to recognize Kara Mahmud as the independent ruler of Albania if he assisted Austria against the Porte. In these circumstances the sultan was forced to offer him a full pardon in return for his allegiance.

Russian policy toward Montenegro also changed, since once again war with the Ottoman Empire was contemplated. When fighting broke out in 1787, the government issued another proclamation calling for the support of the Balkan Christians. Montenegro thus found itself in the pleasant position of being courted by both Austria and Russia, who sent military advisers and gifts. Austrian soldiers and Hercegovinian volunteers began to arrive in the country.

At the same time, the Habsburg government made an effort to make contact with Kara Mahmud, who, it was judged, could be of great assistance in the war. In June 1788 an Austrian delegation went to Shkodër to negotiate with him. The Albanian pasha, influenced by the fact that the Turkish armies were winning at the time, massacred the agents and sent their heads to the sultan. Back in favor in Constantinople, Kara Mahmud was appointed governor of Shkodër. He subsequently fought for the empire in Montenegro and Bosnia.

Although warfare in the region should have ceased when Austria made peace in 1791, the fighting continued in Montenegro. Kara Mahmud, unsatisfied, wished to widen his territorial control; his actions brought on another clash with the Porte, followed by another reconciliation in 1794. In 1796 the pasha thought that he had a fine opportunity to settle his controversies with Montenegro and to gain more land. At this time both Venice and Austria had been defeated in the war that was going on with France. Montenegro was isolated and could not expect outside assistance. Kara Mahmud thus began an invasion. However, at the battle of Krusi he was defeated and beheaded. This event was to be extremely significant in Montenegrin history. It ended for a period the attempts of the Ottoman Empire or its agents to conquer and control the country. Furthermore, Montenegro was able to annex the neighboring region, Brda, which was controlled by the Piperi and

Bjelopavlić tribes, an addition that significantly enlarged its territory. The state at this point had a firm territorial base, and the central government had a stronger position than before against the tribal leadership.

Bosnia and Hercegovina

In Bosnia and Hercegovina, as in Albania, large-scale conversions occurred after the Ottoman occupation; in time many among both the old nobility and the peasants accepted Islam. Moreover, in the subsequent years Bosnia attracted Muslim refugees from the lands that passed under the control of the Christian powers. Peasants, soldiers, craftsmen, and merchants came from Croatia, Slavonia, and Hungary and settled south of the Sava River. Refugees also arrived from Dalmatia. The country thus became a center of strong religious feeling and of local patriotism. The political situation was extremely favorable for the Muslims. The conversions had created a situation in which the political and economic power was held by a Muslim ruling class that was nevertheless of a predominantly local Slavic origin. After the conquest this group had preserved its hold over the land and thereby also over the peasants who worked the estates.

In addition to the native aristocracy, other military elements became a part of Bosnian society. In the eighteenth century sipahis held 144 ziamets (large estates) and 3,617 timars. Usually these men lived on their own lands unless they were away at war. They formed an important element in the Ottoman armed forces. It has been estimated that 1,553 sipahis from Bosnia fought in the battle of the Pruth against Peter the Great.[19] Moreover, large numbers of janissaries settled in the land in the course of the seventeenth and eighteenth centuries. Although many lived in villages, the largest number chose to stay in Sarajevo. Since their pay could be as much as a year in arrears, they were virtually compelled to find alternate occupations. They thus became merchants and craftsmen and played a major role in the guilds. In the eighteenth century they were the most influential political element in the three largest cities, Sarajevo, Mostar, and Travnik.

Among the ruling military there was also an important additional group, the captains, who had functions similar to those of their Christian equivalent in Greece. Since Bosnia was a border province, both with the Habsburg Empire and with Venetian Dalmatia, particular care had to be taken in its defense. The captains were in charge of hereditary military fiefs, the kapitan-ates, of which there were thirty-eight, including sixty-four towns, after the Treaty of Belgrade in 1739. At the end of the century there were about 24,000 soldiers attached to them. The captains' chief duties were to guard the frontiers and the lines of communication, but some were also called to serve outside the country. They and their retainers were sometimes salaried.

19 Branislav Djurdjev, Bogo Grafenauer, and Jorjo Tadić, *Historija Naroda Jugoslavije* [History of the peoples of Yugoslavia], 2 vols. (Zagreb: Skolska Knjiga, 1953, 1959), II, 1321.

The old Slavic nobility holding large estates, together with the high government and military officials, formed the dominant class. This group, known as *beg*s or *bey*s, numbered a few hundred. Below, but still in a privileged position, was a lower nobility called the *aga*s, comprised of smaller landowners, sipahis, and janissaries. This group in the course of the eighteenth century was able to tighten its control of the land. Its political and military power allowed it to infringe on formerly peasant land, exploit the unused or deserted areas, and use the tax-farming system to acquire property. Two types of estates developed. On the *agalik*s the peasants retained their traditional rights concerning the use of the land and the payments required. In contrast, on the *beglik*s the land was regarded as the property of the noble, who either worked the estate himself or let it to tenants. Here the condition of the peasant depended on the arrangements he could make with the owner. Naturally, he was in a much weaker position than the peasant on an agalik, and his payments and labor obligations were higher. The unrest among these peasants, who resented the constantly rising obligations, increased the instability in the country, which was impoverished by the wars of the century.

The social situation in both Bosnia and Hercegovina was made more tense by the fact that although Muslims predominated among the ruling group, they constituted only about 33 percent of the population. The Orthodox had a plurality of about 43 percent, with the Catholics in a minority of 20 percent. On both the begliks and the agaliks a Christian Slavic peasantry was thus likely to be subordinate to Muslim Slavic landlords. As far as their loyalties were concerned, the Muslims naturally favored Ottoman rule, but with strong provincial self-rule, whereas the Orthodox felt drawn to their neighboring Serbs and Montenegrins – a situation that caused difficulties when these people were in conflict with the Porte. The Catholics were attracted to the Habsburg lands and to Catholic Croatia. The monarchy claimed the right of religious protection over them.

As a border province of a steadily weakening empire, Bosnia bore a heavy share of the military burden and was the scene of much fighting. In the Treaty of Karlowitz a border was established that with some readjustments was to last until 1908, but the war left the country in a chaotic state. Not only did Muslim refugees arrive from the lands lost to the Habsburg Empire, but Catholics emigrated from Bosnia, particularly into Slavonia. In 1703 the capital was moved from Sarajevo to Travnik, which became a major craft and trading center as well as a military stronghold. Special attention was given to the question of the defense of the entire province. Guns and munitions were both manufactured locally and imported from Constantinople.

The wars of 1714 to 1718 and 1736 to 1739, involving Austria, Venice, and Russia, were naturally extremely damaging to Bosnian development. Territory was lost to both Venice and the Habsburg Empire in the Treaty of Passarowitz. In addition, Bosnia, like other parts of the empire, suffered severely from the plague and other epidemic diseases. Agriculture was repeatedly disrupted by the Austrian invasions. The Muslims in particular were affected by the wars, since they were called up to fight not only against the European powers, but also against Persia. They had heavy casualties. For instance, of 5,200 men sent to Persia, only 500 returned after peace was made in 1727.

At this time Bosnia had one able administrator, Ali Pasha Hekim Oglu, who was vezir of Bosnia from 1735 to 1740, when he was sent to Egypt. He governed with the assistance of a council composed of the prominent men of the province and representatives of the central government. After his departure, the political situation disintegrated. Although the country did not suffer from an outside invasion for almost five decades, the military elements within turned against each other. A long period of civil turmoil followed, which the Porte could not master.

The struggle for power among the Muslim military involved in particular the captains and the janissaries. The captains used their military strength to acquire chiftlik estates, and they sought political control. The janissaries too became more involved in local affairs. In this situation the provincial administration grew weaker. As the authority of the Bosnian vezir diminished, that of the notables and the captains increased. In 1745 Ali Pasha Hekim Oglu returned, but with the mission from the central government to impose heavy taxes. Opposition from the Bosnian notables caused him to leave the same year. He returned again in 1747 for the same purpose, but since he had alienated his former supporters, he was forced out within a year.

From 1747 to 1756 Bosnia was in a condition of anarchy involving both the cities and the countryside. During this decade the local notables collected the taxes and waged war on each other. Captains fought janissaries, who fought other janissaries. In 1752 another able vezir, Mehmed Pasha Kukavica, was sent to handle the situation. He was able to pacify the province by 1756. He returned for a second term between 1757 and 1760, but he was removed after complaints were made against his administration. Nevertheless, the former disorders did not recur.

The Habsburg Empire, meanwhile, retained its interest in Bosnia. In the discussions between Joseph II and Catherine, this region was designated as part of Austria's share in the division of the Ottoman Empire. Even before war started again, the Austrian government made efforts to increase its influence. Support was expected particularly among the Catholic Croatian population. Bosnian students were brought to study in Zagreb. When war broke out in 1788 the Habsburg government issued proclamations calling upon the Christians to support their armies and the Muslims to remain passive. An army of 51,000, accompanied by some Serbian volunteers, invaded Bosnia. Since the main Ottoman army was engaged elsewhere, only a small force was left to defend the Bosnian frontiers. Local Muslims thus joined to repel the invaders. The conflict is known as the Dubica War, since the main fighting was around the city of Dubica, where the Muslims were defeated. By the Treaty of Sistova some Bosnian land was ceded to Austria.

The Serbs

Although the Serbs lived in wide areas in the western Balkans, the national movement was to have its center in the Smederevo *sanjak*, to become the pashalik of Belgrade. This area, like Bosnia, was a border district, but unlike that province it had no notable Muslim population outside the cities. Moreover, there had been no widespread movement, as there had been in some parts of the Balkans, to transform sipahi and other land into chiftlik estates. The average Serbian peasant retained certain traditional rights over the land he worked. He was technically a sharecropper, and thus usually liable for payments, some of which increased at the end of the eighteenth century, but he had in practice virtually free use of his plot. He could dispose of it more or less as he wished. He could pass it on to his heirs, and he could sell it if he could find someone to assume his liabilities. He could grow what he chose and sell his produce at his convenience. He was not a serf; he was personally a free man. The large landholder could live in the country, but he usually stayed in one of the larger cities.

Like other Balkan people the Serbian peasant had the advantages of a tight local administrative system. The basic unit was the *knežina* (district). The knežinas were composed of villages, which in turn were made up of *zadruga*s (extended family organizations). Each knežina had a council of notables that elected the knez. As elsewhere, this official represented his district before the Ottoman authorities and was responsible for the assessing and collecting of taxes as well as general police duties. The local government also provided judicial services, using customary law as the basis.

The Orthodox church was to play a particularly important role in Serbian history. At the beginning of the eighteenth century the Serbian lands were still under the Patriarchate of Peć, which was an autocephalous organization under the general jurisdiction of the Patriarchate of Constantinople. The church governed itself through the synods and kept in touch with other Orthodox institutions, including those in Russia. The jurisdiction of the Patriarchate extended over a wide range, including the Orthodox of Buda, Arad, Komárom, and Dalmatia, as well as Bosnia, Hercegovina, and lands with a Serbian majority. When Ottoman power was at its height, these territories had, of course, been under one political jurisdiction. The Habsburg and Venetian victories split the area politically, but the ecclesiastical boundaries remained. The majority of the population in the ceded territories was Catholic and not subject to Orthodox authority.

During the period of Ottoman rule the Patriarchate of Peć felt itself the heir to the medieval Serbian kingdom and was well aware of its national mission. The lands under its ecclesiastical jurisdiction were referred to as "Serbian lands" despite their varying religious and ethnic character. The church carried the national idea and kept alive in the minds of the faithful the independent and glorious past. There are in the Serbian church calendar some fifty-eight Serbian saints, including eighteen tsars, kings and queens, princes, and lords, beginning with St. Sava and his father, Nemanja. The cult of Serbian royal saints – "the sacred stock of Nemanja" – constantly reminded the Serbian people, with all of the awesome pomp and artistry of the Byzantine ritual, that the Serbs had once had an independent kingdom, indeed, an empire, blessed by God through His wonder-working saints.[20]

Like the Patriarchate at Constantinople, the Serbian church held fast to the idea that Ottoman domination was a temporary phenomenon and would pass, and it too looked upon the Catholic church as the most serious rival, which undoubtedly it was. The two religions conflicted in Bosnia, and within the Habsburg Empire Catholic pressure on the Orthodox population was constant and strong.

Despite the religious differences, geography dictated cooperation with the Habsburg Empire. The Serbs who subsequently fought with the Austrian troops expected to establish at least an autonomous political unit, not to submit to direct Habsburg rule. During the war of the Holy League, Serbian units participated in the fighting. The most significant action came in 1688, when Habsburg troops had been uniformly successful and were in occupation of Belgrade. At that time the patriarch of Peć, Arsenije III Crnojević, who was in touch with the Habsburg government, called upon his followers to rise against the Ottoman domination. At first, the Austrian army remained victorious; in 1689 Niš, Skopje, Prizren, and Štip were occupied. The next year marked a reversal, however, and the allied forces were pushed back to the former border. Fearing massacre if they remained, Arsenije and some thirty thousand families migrated with the retreating army. This group was joined by others from the Ottoman lands who had compromised themselves by supporting the invader and who feared Ottoman revenge. In Belgrade the Serbian leaders held an assembly and sent an emissary, Bishop Isaija Djaković, to the Habsburg emperor, Leopold I, to discuss their position. They agreed to accept him as their hereditary ruler if he, in exchange, assured them of religious freedom and recognized their autonomous church administration. In 1690 Leopold issued a proclamation in which he called on the Balkan people to rise and support his armies. He promised in return religious liberty, lower taxes, and the free election of the Serbian leaders. With these assurances, a large number of families crossed the border to settle in Habsburg lands.

The emigration created a difficult condition. Both the Habsburg government and the Orthodox authorities expected the situation to be temporary;

---

20 Michael Boro Petrovich, *A History of Modern Serbia, 1804–1918*, 2 vols. (New York: Harcourt Brace Jovanovich, 1976), I, 13.

both awaited a great triumph of Austria over the Ottoman Empire and the return of the Serbs to their former homes. Until then, the Serbian leaders wished to have something like the millet system, which would give the Orthodox church a large measure of political control over its followers, introduced into the Habsburg Monarchy. Although the question caused constant controversy, the Serbs did receive special privileges. A religious and cultural center was established at Sremski Karlovci. The tie with Peć was kept; the metropolitan at Sremski Karlovci swore obedience to the patriarch of Peć and mentioned his name in the liturgy.

The great emigration had unfortunate consequences for the Peć Patriarchate, and it contributed to the alteration of the ethnic composition of the Kosovo area. The movement of Albanians into the region has been mentioned previously; the large emigration of Serbs was to have a lasting effect on the national composition of what had formerly been the heart of the Serbian medieval kingdom. With the departure of the Serbs and the large-scale immigration of Albanians, the region acquired an Albanian majority. The apparent treason of the patriarch naturally affected the attitude of the Porte toward the Peć establishment. Thereafter, it preferred to name Phanariot candidates rather than Serbs. Thus a Greek was chosen to succeed Arsenije, although a Serb held the post next, from 1713 to 1725.

Habsburg incursions into Ottoman territory were renewed in 1716, this time with more success. In the Treaty of Passarowitz of 1718 the monarchy gained control of major Serbian lands. Habsburg administration, although neither particularly popular nor especially successful, was important for the future development of the area. The new arrangements, which were both military and civilian in nature, placed the newly annexed territory, including Oltenia, under a Court Chamber Council with its headquarters at Belgrade and Temesvar. The Serbian section was divided into fifteen districts in which the upper level of administration was in the hands of Habsburg officials, but the lower consisted of a strengthened Serbian local government network. The major unit of administration was the nahije, which was placed under the direction of an official called an *oborknez*. The knežinas headed by the knez remained as before. The duties of the local authorities, as under Ottoman rule, were primarily the collection of taxes, local police functions, and the administration of justice. Belgrade was also affected by the changes. German craftsmen were brought in to replace the Turkish, and the Catholic church made this city the center of its attempts to obtain conversions.

In 1737, it will be remembered, the monarchy was drawn into war through its alliance with Russia. This campaign, which was characterized by inept Austrian military leadership, nevertheless started out on a victorious note. Niš again fell into Habsburg hands. Once more the invading army called for Serbian support. The patriarch of Peć, now Arsenije IV, followed the example of his predecessor and gave assistance. When the Ottoman army reversed the battlefield situation and, recapturing Niš, drove northward, the patriarch and his followers, numbering about two thousand, were forced to withdraw to Belgrade and then across the border. In the disastrous peace that followed, the Habsburg Empire lost its Serbian and Romanian territory, but kept the Banat. A frontier was now established that was to last about a century and a half.

The second treason, in Ottoman eyes, associated with the Patriarchate of Peć was another blow to an organization that was already deeply troubled with maladministration and corruption. After the departure of Arsenije IV, a Greek candidate was chosen, and a swift succession of appointments followed. Since the Habsburg center, Sremski Karlovci, was in a much better economic position than Peć, numerous appeals for financial assistance were directed toward it. Nevertheless, the combination of circumstances, including the pressure of Greek nationalism within the church, its weak financial basis, and its association with the treasonous activities of the two patriarchs, proved too much. In 1766 the Porte abolished the Patriarchate of Peć and transferred its jurisdiction to the Patriarchate of Constantinople. The move had particular significance for the Serbian church. The Metropolitanate at Sremski Karlovci became the main Serbian ecclesiastical center. It was henceforth to have the major cultural and educational influence on the Serbs.

After the conclusion of the peace in 1739, the Turkish administration, together with the sipahis and janissaries, returned to the region. Serbian conditions, however, remained much as before. The Austrian administrative system, which had been based on local tradition, was still used. The village was relatively autonomous, and it was the focus of Serbian life. The Muslim population remained concentrated in Belgrade and the cities. A long period of peace followed. The region was not a scene of battle in the war between Russia and the Porte from 1768 to 1774, but in 1788, when Austria joined Russia in a new conflict, the situation changed and another invasion occurred.

As usual, the Habsburg government commenced the campaign with an appeal for aid from the Balkan Christians. Special Serbian detachments, *Freicorps*, were established, which operated in Serbia, Bosnia, and the Banat. The most important Serbian action, however, was conducted by Koča Andjelković and his followers. In fact, this episode is known in Serbian history as Koča's War. This local leader at the head of a group of about three thousand men endeavored to interrupt the Ottoman lines of communication, particularly in the Šumadija, an area lying between Belgrade and Niš. Despite the fact that they were at first very successful, they could not withstand an attack from the better-organized and more-disciplined Ottoman army.

This war was a disaster not only for the Serbian volunteers, but also for the Habsburg Empire. Although the Austrian army took Belgrade in 1789, it was forced to evacuate the conquered land the next year, owing chiefly to the pressure of events within the monarchy and in the rest of Europe. The Treaty of Sistova of 1791 left the situation much as it had been before the war. The

94

Ottoman Empire promised amnesty for those who had joined the Habsburg army, and about fifty thousand refugees did return. A century of experience of cooperation with Austria had discouraged the Serbian leaders in their hopes of Habsburg assistance. They felt that once more they had been sacrificed and abandoned. The war did have one important consequence: large numbers of Serbs had received experience in fighting in conjunction with the Habsburg army and in their own volunteer bands. The stage was thus set for them to take further action on their own initiative.

Bulgaria, Macedonia, and Thrace

The regions that have been discussed so far – mainland and island Greece, Albania, Montenegro, Bosnia, and Serbia – had the opportunity to control their own local affairs and often to conduct independent policies. The remoteness of their mountain homes gave much independence to some Greeks, Albanians, and Montenegrins. The closeness to the land frontiers and the seas allowed all of these areas to maintain some sort of contact with foreign powers. In contrast, Bulgaria, Thrace, and Macedonia, which will be treated here together, because of their geographical position remained under a tighter control by the Muslim authorities. Nevertheless, they shared many of the experiences of their neighbors. They had the pattern of local administration that has been discussed elsewhere; their village notables collected taxes and had the same opportunity to become wealthy and influential within the Ottoman system. A local judicial system based on customary law existed. However, the area was more affected by the changes in the landholding system. Chiftlik estates arose particularly in the advantageous locations, such as the Maritsa Valley and north of Thessaloniki. Small farms remained common in the hill and mountain regions.

Unlike most of the rest of the Balkans, this area had a large Muslim and Turkish presence. Turkish peasants had emigrated particularly to Thrace and Macedonia, where they lived in conditions not much different from those of their Christian counterparts. The Muslim farmers, however, paid smaller taxes, and they held their land under conditions of virtually private ownership. This area also had one region in which there had been mass conversions. The Pomaks, living mainly in the Rhodope Mountains but also in the Danubian plain north of the Stara Planina, were both Bulgarian and Muslim. They lived apart in their mountain communities and remained a primitive, backward society.

For the Christians, as in other areas, the Orthodox church was the major element of unity. The Bulgarian people were under the jurisdiction of the Archbishopric of Ohrid, whose fate was much like that of Peć. Although it did not blatantly collaborate with an enemy power, it did suffer from the same problems of corruption and debt as did the other Slavic institution. The Greek cultural pressure was also stronger here. When in 1767 the Archbishop-

Pass through the Balkan Mountains, Bulgaria

ric was abolished and the church placed under the jurisdiction of Constantinople, the consequences for the Slavic population were more serious than
they were for the Serbs. The latter always had an alternate authority in Sremski Karlovci, which remained a strong center of Serbian influence. For the
Bulgarians the loss of the Slavic Archbishopric gave rise to a period of Greek
cultural domination. Greek became the language of the services in even solidly Slavic areas. What education was available was also in this language.
When it is considered that Greek was also the language of commerce, the
cultural dominance of the Greek civilization can well be understood.

Although this area was not the scene of major battles in the eighteenth
century, it was not spared from the consequences of war and political anarchy.
Banditry was widespread. A particularly serious problem was the devastation
caused by bands of deserting or returning soldiers. Repeated waves of epidemic diseases and the plague went through the lands. The extra war taxes
also contributed to the general impoverishment. Moreover, as the Ottoman
central authority weakened, Macedonia, like Bosnia and Albania, became the
scene of struggles for power among local officials, military men, and Muslim
notables. The Albanian rivalries involved Macedonia too. The most secure
conditions were to be found in the villages of the Balkan Mountains. The
worst situation arose in the eighteenth century in the area between the Danube and the Balkan Mountains that was depopulated and ravaged by armed
bands, known as *kirdjalis*, and by the supporters of the rebellious pasha, Pasvanoglu.

Despite these unfavorable conditions, the century did witness an increase
in trade, in particular with the Habsburg Empire, and a growth in the size
and prosperity of Thessaloniki, which was the major port for the entire area.
After the signing of the Treaty of Karlowitz, which gave Austria trading
privileges, commerce increased, reaching a height in the last quarter of the
century. The French had been the first to establish themselves in Thessaloniki,
followed by British, Dutch, and Venetian merchants. Regular caravan routes
connected the city with the Balkan trading centers, such as Sofia, Skopje, and
Bitola (Bitolj, Monastir), and ran northward through Belgrade to Austria
and westward toward the Adriatic ports. The carrying trade was in the hands
of Orthodox merchants, especially Greeks.

A survey of conditions in the lands under direct Ottoman rule thus shows
similarities as well as variations in development. All of the regions were affected by the consequences of the wars of the century, both the occupation
by Ottoman and foreign soldiers and the fiscal pressures of the taxation system. In general, the inhabitants were under the dual governorship of the
Ottoman administrative framework and their own village organizations. The
Orthodox church formed a third element not only in the moral and spiritual

life of the Christians, but also in the political control of the region. Some church authorities acted as a support of the system; others, notably some Serbian patriarchs and the Montenegrin bishops, led in the fight to undermine Ottoman rule. In the same manner, some local notables, particularly those who benefited financially from the conditions or who saw no practical alternative, cooperated well with the Ottoman authority; others strongly resisted. It should also be emphasized that even though the Ottoman Empire was in theory a centralized absolutist state, the authorities in Constantinople had little *direct* control over the life of the individual Balkan Christian. They always preferred to govern through intermediaries, either the church or the elected chiefs of the villages. As the eighteenth century progressed they also increasingly lost control over their own provincial authorities.

THE AUTONOMOUS REGIONS: DUBROVNIK MOLDAVIA, AND WALLACHIA

The lands whose histories have just been discussed were regarded as integral parts of the empire. Four other Balkan areas, Transylvania, Moldavia, Wallachia, and the city of Dubrovnik, were linked by special arrangements. Because Transylvania was transferred to Habsburg control in the Treaty of Karlowitz, it will be discussed in another section. A brief comment about Dubrovnik is in order, however, before we proceed to the Danubian Principalities.

Dubrovnik

The city of Dubrovnik, previously a possession of Venice, was placed under Ottoman protection in 1458. A tribute, which was set at 12,500 ducats in 1481, was paid; but aside from this, and the recognition of Ottoman suzerainty, Dubrovnik was for all practical purposes independent. It entered into relations with foreign powers and made treaties with them. Its own flag flew over its ships. The Ottoman vassalage had the important result of giving the city special rights in trade within the empire. It was obviously to Ottoman advantage to have one of its dependents, rather than the Venetians, handle the Adriatic trade. Dubrovnik was in a position to make full use of the privileges that it was given. Its traders received from the Porte special tax exemptions and trading benefits. They were also allowed to set up, in major Ottoman cities, colonies that had extraterritorial rights; that is, the members governed themselves according to their own laws rather than those of the locality. Since this was a Catholic city, religious jurisdiction was also involved.

Like the Italian city-states, Dubrovnik was a republic controlled by its patrician class. The main organ of government was the senate, which represented the interests of this group. The city was both a manufacturing and a trade center and thus had a population of merchants, seamen, and craftsmen.

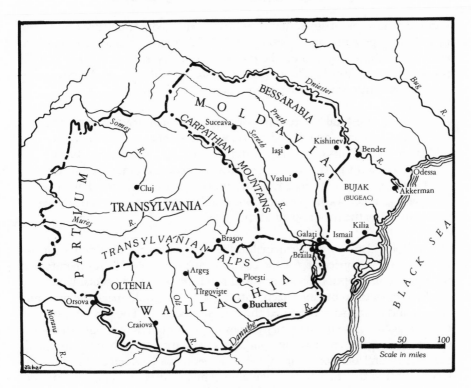

Map 12. Moldavia and Wallachia

The patricians controlled the surrounding agricultural lands. Dubrovnik retained its autonomous position until 1806, when French troops occupied the city.

Moldavia and Wallachia

After Moldavia and Wallachia fell under the control of the Ottoman Empire in the fourteenth and fifteenth centuries, they, like Transylvania, were not incorporated into the imperial system, but became instead autonomous provinces with their own institutions (see Map 12). The native aristocracy, the boyars, was thus left intact and retained its former social and economic, and to a large extent its political, privileges. The relations of the provinces with the Ottoman Empire were determined by a series of treaties whose provisions at first allowed the Principalities a large measure of autonomy. Only in the eighteenth century did this situation change to the great disadvantage of the Romanian population.

The Ottoman Empire did not want to incorporate these lands directly; it needed buffer provinces. Its aim was to assure that the Principalities did not become centers of intrigue, that they formed an adequate defense against the neighboring powers, and that they contributed money and agricultural supplies. The tribute imposed on the provinces was first set at a low level, but it soon rose precipitously. The payments made by Wallachia at the beginning of the eighteenth century have been described as follows:

> In 1709, the total tax receipts of the Wallachian government were 649,000 thalers, and of these, 514,000 were sent in one way or another to the Turks. In 1710, of the total receipts of 547,000 thalers, 430,000 went to the Turks. In terms of gold, this amounted to between 180,000 and 220,000 gold ducats a year for tribute. This was twice as much as the official tribute, and one-third to one-half again as much as the tribute paid in the 1590s.[21]

The Porte also saw the Principalities as a major source of supplies for the military and, in particular, for the city of Constantinople. It thus maintained the right of preemption on agricultural products. Imperial agents, who were chiefly interested in buying sheep, cattle, and grain, could make the first purchases, and they also determined the prices to be paid. The power entrusted to these agents gave them in many cases what amounted to a right of confiscation. Since price and trading conditions were thus severely circumscribed, the agricultural development of the provinces was hampered. In the eighteenth century the chief activity was animal husbandry; grain production was to predominate only in the second half of the next century.

In addition to the tribute and the delivery of food supplies, the Principalities were liable for a long list of other payments, including gifts due at the accession of each new sultan and bribes to maintain the favor of influential officials. The native princes had to make payments, both at their appointment and at periodic intervals during their reigns. In return for these heavy contributions, the provinces enjoyed many privileges not shared by areas directly incorporated into the empire. The council of boyars, which consisted of the richest and most powerful of the native aristocracy, named from among their number the princes, sometimes called hospodars, who then had to be approved by the sultan. Once elected, the prince had important powers, but he ruled in conjunction with the boyars' council. The Turkish troops were confined to the great fortified centers such as Kilia, Akkerman, and Bender. Muslims did not own estates in either principality, nor were there mosques and other Muslim religious establishments.

In practice, the political system did not function smoothly. The power in the country lay in three centers: the prince, the boyars, and the Porte. The fact that the prince was an elected official and not a hereditary ruler made

---

21   Daniel Chirot, *Social Change in a Peripheral Society: The Creation of a Balkan Colony* (New York, Academic Press, 1976), p. 64.

possible innumerable intrigues among the three groups. The Porte also regularly intervened in the elections and named the candidates. Throughout the seventeenth century, the boyars, not the prince, were in the strongest position. Despite these problems both principalities did effectively control the running of their internal administrations, and they had direct relations with foreign governments. As border regions, they were involved in the wars of the suzerain power with its neighbors.

As Ottoman power waned, and as pressure from the outside became stronger, the Romanian princes and boyars were naturally tempted to use the situation to their own advantage. Although they always kept links with both the Habsburg Monarchy and Poland, in the eighteenth century Russia, the great Orthodox power, seemed to offer the best hope of assistance. As that state pressed toward the Black Sea, the temptation to act with the Russian leaders to throw off the Ottoman suzerainty became increasingly stronger. The first practical opportunity for cooperation came from the endeavors of Peter the Great to move southward and his conflicts with Charles XII of Sweden. The Romanian leaders were greatly impressed by the Russian victory over the Swedish king at Poltava in 1709.

Welcoming Romanian support, the Russian government at this time entered into negotiations with Constantine Brîncoveanu, the prince of Wallachia (1688–1714), and Dimitrie Cantemir, the ruler of Moldavia (1710–1711). Although an agreement was also reached with Brîncoveanu, the major Russian achievement was the conclusion of the Treaty of Luck with Cantemir in April 1711. Here the Moldavian prince secured not only advantages for his principality, but also his own personal position. It was agreed that Moldavia would become an independent state under the protection of the tsar. Cantemir was to be prince, and the rule was to be hereditary in his family. In internal affairs the prince was to have more power than the boyars. Unfortunately for Cantemir, the Russian campaign was a disaster; Brîncoveanu took no action. After the Russian army was defeated in July 1711, Cantemir fled to Russia, where he lived a highly productive literary life. As a reward he received from the Russian government fifty villages and fifty thousand serfs, together with two houses in St. Petersburg.[22] Brîncoveanu remained in office until 1714, when he and his four sons were beheaded by the Ottoman authorities on suspicion of treason for their relations with Austria.

The Phanariot regime   The defeat of Peter and the defection of Cantemir had enormous political consequences for the Principalities. After the Treaty of Karlowitz, in which Transylvania had been ceded, the Porte was naturally concerned about the political stability of the frontier provinces. In a period of retreat before the European great powers, it needed princes whom it could trust and who would not conspire with the enemy. The native princes no

22   Nicolae Iorga, *Histoire des relations russo-roumaines* (Iaşi: Neamul Românesc, 1917), p. 128.

longer appeared trustworthy. Since Phanariot Greeks had proven able servants in other areas of administration, their appointment to the highest positions in the Principalities now seemed advisable.

There were already many Greeks in both principalities. The attraction of the Romanian provinces for them was great. In Constantinople they could not display their new wealth and prestige conspicuously. Moreover, other areas did not offer the same opportunities for enrichment. For reasons of personal security, individual preference, and safe investment of funds, so many Greeks entered the Principalities in the seventeenth century that the boyar class felt threatened in its control of landholding, public office, and the ecclesiastical establishments. Despite much opposition, the Greek influence steadily increased. Many wealthy Greeks married into the great boyar families. Some became prosperous merchants, whereas others won many of the high positions within the Orthodox church hierarchy.

The Ottoman appointment of Phanariot princes introduced what is generally regarded as the worst period in modern Romanian history, not only because of the corruption of the system, but also because of the uncontrolled fiscal exactions made by the Porte in the provinces. The choice of Greek princes marked a fundamental change in the political position of the provinces. The new rulers were not representatives of the Principalities, but agents of the Ottoman government sent to guard the interests of the suzerain. They ranked as pashas of two horsetails. From the Ottoman point of view their function was to assure control of the area against foreign intrigue and intervention and to deliver huge sums of money back to the Porte for its military and civilian needs. The securing of food supplies was also necessary, both for the army and for the capital city. It will be noted that the Porte still did not turn the area into a pashalik, nor was it occupied by the Ottoman army. The provinces retained major autonomous rights, but the rulers were under direct Ottoman control.

With the appointment of Phanariot princes, the Ottoman government did succeed in breaking the control of the Romanian boyars over their country. A council of great boyars still took part in the administration; a larger council, which included representatives from all the landowning classes and the church, could be convened on certain occasions. However, the power in the government remained firmly in the hands of the ruler, with his retainers, appointees, and family supporters. The boyars were left with relatively little political influence, although naturally the prince and his Greek contingent could not completely alienate the native aristocracy. The Phanariots had to work with them and through them; they could always find some with whom they could cooperate. Native boyar factions could also intrigue in Constantinople against the prince in office. Despite this loss of political power, the native boyar still maintained his privileged position in relation to the rest of the population, and despite the reforms of the period, his hold over the land and the peasant was not significantly weakened. He also paid few if any taxes.

Nevertheless, throughout the period he remained discontented with the political conditions. Boyar opposition to Phanariot rule was constant; individuals and groups repeatedly sought outside assistance from both Vienna and St. Petersburg.

Certainly the boyar had much to complain about. The prince was now an agent of the Porte. The provinces no longer had anything like an independent or separate stance in regard to foreign powers. The Phanariots did conduct diplomatic negotiations, but as representatives of Constantinople. The provinces had also no independent military forces. The prince had a personal guard, and some troops were available for the maintenance of public order, but the country did not have the corps of armed men that existed even in regions under direct Ottoman administration. Both provinces gave the appearance of being integral parts of the empire, and not self-governing dependencies.

Most important, however, was the fact that the new rulers brought neither order nor prosperity, but instead increasing turmoil and internal anarchy. In the period of Phanariot rule, from 1711 to 1821, eleven families provided candidates for seventy-four different reigns. The average period in office for a prince was 2.5 years. Like the Patriarchates and the other high offices in Constantinople, the Hospodarships in the Principalities were sold to the highest bidder. The competition among the Phanariot families was intense. Most offices were purchased on borrowed money. Once in power, the successful candidate had to assure that he made a profit. He sold lower offices and resorted to measures of outright extortion. The position of Romanian prince was thus expensive, and it was also dangerous. As we have seen, the Porte had a propensity for abrupt execution of those whose policies were displeasing or unsuccessful. The question thus remains why Greek families competed so strongly for what seems a dubious honor. Questions of prestige were, of course, important, but so was the fact that enormous profits could be made from the office. One authority has estimated that around the middle of the eighteenth century the cost of the Moldavian throne was 30,000 gold pounds; that of Wallachia, 45,000. However, the annual tax income of Moldavia was 180,000 gold pounds; that of Wallachia, 300,000.[23] Even after heavy tribute payments to Constantinople, these provinces remained rich sources of private profit.

The Phanariot system was attacked not only for its fiscal and political corruption, but for its style and its Greek coloration. The Phanariot ideal was the Byzantine Empire. The princes could not be Byzantine despots in Constantinople, but they could be in Bucharest and Iaşi. They thus adopted an elaborate court ceremonial, surrounded themselves with articles of great luxury, and treated those beneath them, including often the native boyars, with contempt and indifference in accordance with what they considered an im-

---

23 Runciman, *The Great Church*, pp. 374, 375.

perial manner. They were, nevertheless, always conscious of the instability of their power. A contemporary observer wrote: "What is remarkable about these despots . . . is that all their riches, money, jewels, hordes and furnishings, are always in trunks and traveling coffers, as if they had to leave at any moment."[24]

Although it is possible to overestimate the damage caused by Phanariot rule, it is true that the princes did represent an influence that was foreign to the provinces over which they ruled. The restored Byzantium of the Phanariot dream was indeed Orthodox, but it was not Romanian. What the Phanariot rulers accomplished was the establishment of a Byzantine island within the Ottoman Empire. Greek dominance of the Romanian church has already been mentioned. Phanariots controlled the high offices and the synods. The rulers of the Principalities in the past had always been generous in their donations to Orthodox institutions and causes. The gifts from the Phanariots tended to strengthen Greek influence. Most important was the question of the Dedicated Monasteries. Both Greek and Romanian boyars increasingly gave land to certain monasteries, whose income was devoted to the support of Holy Places, such as the Holy Sepulchre, Mt. Sinai, Mt. Athos, or a Patriarchate. The direction of the establishments was Greek; the heads, or hegumens, were appointed by the Holy Place in question. In time an eleventh of the arable land of the Principalities fell under the control of these establishments, which not only were under foreign domination, but sent their profits out of the country.

The major factor in the Principalities, that which determined the fate of both the government and the individual, was the enormous fiscal pressure of the political regime in power. Having purchased their offices, the rulers had to repay the loans, and they expected to make large personal profits. They had to support a luxurious court and make frequent payments to the right officials in Constantinople to assure that they stayed in favor with the Porte. They also had to give regular contributions, outside of the tribute and private bribes, to the Ottoman government. They recouped their money by selling the offices under their control and by the fraudulent handling of state finances. Huge sums of money thus found their way to Constantinople and into the pockets of the Phanariot supporters.

Aside from the costs of corruption, the Ottoman government was in desperate need of money. Throughout the century pressure was put on the Principalities to increase the money payments and the delivery of food. The chief drain was the military and the high cost of the wars. Moldavia and Wallachia not only paid for war expenses, but, as frontier provinces, suffered exceedingly from the fact that much of the fighting was on their territory. It will be remembered that between 1711 and 1812 the empire was engaged in six wars.

---

24 Quoted in Robert W. Seton-Watson, *A History of the Roumanians from Roman Times to the Completion of Unity* (Cambridge: Cambridge University Press, 1934), p. 130.

Both principalities, in addition to being the scene of combat, had to support the Ottoman or foreign armies while they were on their territory.

Because of the Phanariot regime and the growing weight of financial pressure from the Porte, in every international crisis native Romanian boyars sought assistance in both Russia and Austria. Their goal was separation from the Ottoman Empire and the establishment of an independent or autonomous regime, under the protection of one or both of these states, in which the political power would return to their control. After the defeat of Peter, the Habsburg Empire was in the forefront of the powers in opposition to the Porte. In the war that lasted from 1716 to 1718, some boyars favored incorporation into the monarchy, but with the preservation of Romanian autonomous institutions and a regime dominated by the great boyars.

When in the Treaty of Passarowitz Austria annexed Oltenia, such a regime was indeed inaugurated. However, like Venetian administration in the Peloponnesus, Habsburg rule in the Wallachian region managed to antagonize most of the social classes. Bent on turning the area into a source of food supplies for its army, the Austrian administration introduced fiscal, judicial, and administrative reforms. At first, the monarchy relied on the boyars. Oltenia was governed through a council under the presidency of the *ban* (governor), George Cantacuzino. Two officials were placed at the head of each district. In 1726 any vestige of real autonomy was ended with the abolition of the office of ban. The area remained under the imperial military command. Although the country was more efficiently run, taxation increased and, of course, the power of the local nobility was not restored. The Austrian officials also interfered in the agrarian relationships between the landholders and the peasants. The labor obligations were brought in line with the more severe ones of the rest of the monarchy. The peasant was now subject to fifty-two days of service a year, that is, one day a week, a figure many times higher than that in force in either Moldavia or Wallachia.

In 1736 Russia was again at war with the Porte; Austria joined in 1737. While the Habsburg forces fought in the western Balkans, the Russians in 1739 launched a campaign in the Principalities under the direction of General Münnich. After capturing the stronghold of Khotin, the Russian army entered Iaşi in August. There it was greeted by the boyars, the Orthodox clergy, and all those who hoped for a liberation from both Ottoman and Phanariot rule. In their discussions of war aims, both the Russian and the Austrian governments had indicated their desires in the Principalities. The monarchy had considered an extension of its hold in Oltenia to Brăila; Russia had proposed the maintenance of Ottoman control, but under Russian protection.

All hopes were, however, disappointed. The failure to make decisive military gains, in particular the Austrian setbacks, forced the allies to sign the Peace of Belgrade of September 1739, which reunited Oltenia with Wallachia. The treaty also inaugurated a period of almost thirty years of peace. In this time the Phanariot rulers, in particular Constantine Mavrocordat, made an effort to remedy the grave misfortunes that had descended upon the country as the result of misgovernment and war.

Phanariot reform After the conclusion of the peace both principalities were in a chaotic state. Most desperate was the condition in the countryside, where the mass flight of the peasantry had removed the foundation from under the entire fiscal system. Since direct Ottoman administration had never been established there, Romanian lands had not been assigned as timars. Instead, the land had remained under the control of the native aristocracy. The boyars had retained their estates and political power without having to convert to Islam. A true feudal system was in effect. The peasant, who was usually a serf, was liable to heavy payments both to the state and to the landholder. The entire weight of the corrupt system came to rest on this lowest unit in the social scale. By the middle of the century the burdens had become so overwhelming that large regions were depopulated. Individuals or whole villages found it better to desert to the mountains or to leave the Principalities; they could cross the Carpathians into Transylvania or the Danube to the lands south of the river. They also sometimes emigrated into the territory north of the Black Sea, particularly as it passed into Russian hands. This mass flight of taxpayers ruined the government finances. It has been estimated that in Wallachia 90 percent of the state revenue came from the peasants. Something obviously had to be done to keep them on the land.

The reforms, which were to cover many aspects of life, were primarily the work of Constantine Mavrocordat, the greatest Phanariot prince. Ruling alternatively for ten separate periods, six in Wallachia and four in Moldavia, he supervised the reorganization of the fiscal, social, and administrative systems of the Principalities. His reforms of necessity had to concern more than the outer forms of government and administration; he had to interfere with the traditional relationship of the peasant and the boyar.

The reforms of Mavrocordat had many points in common with similar changes being introduced in the Habsburg Monarchy in the period of enlightened despotism. One problem facing the prince was the reincorporation of Oltenia, whose administration had been fundamentally changed. He accomplished this by in effect transferring much of the system in practice in Oltenia to the rest of the country. Mavrocordat's objective was similar to the aims of the Habsburg government: he wished to centralize the administration and bring it into direct contact with the mass of the population. This action would be at the expense of the power of the boyars and would severely check and diminish their influence. Although the prince was able to accomplish much, he was in a weaker position than the Habsburg rulers, although they had similar problems with their nobility. Mavrocordat had no army behind him, and he could not rely on steady support from Constantinople, although the Porte had an even greater interest in assuring the fiscal stability of the vassal provinces.

The first reform came in 1740 in Wallachia and dealt with the major issue, the collection of taxes. Since the aim was to end the mass flight of the peasants and to increase if possible the state revenues, the taxes had to be kept at a level that would not force the local population to resort to extreme measures such as flight. Efforts had already been made toward tax reform, and there were improvements in the methods of collection in the reigns of Nicolae Mavrocordat in Wallachia (1719–1730) and of Grigore Ghica in Moldavia (1726–1733). Then it was decided that a single fixed tax should be levied four times a year to replace the unregulated, haphazard system that had existed before. War pressures ended this attempt at change. Constantine Mavrocordat's reform provided for the registration of the population so that the state could accurately assess taxes. Previously, some individuals and villages had held a full immunity from taxation even though they did not have boyar status. The census was strongly resisted by the boyars. Not only did it introduce the central authority into the relationship between the lord and peasant, but many boyars had the services of peasants who paid no state taxes and who were thus a better source of profit for their masters. The registration signified that all of the nonnoble population would contribute to the government.

Since most nobles were still free from much of the tax burden, it was to the interest of the central government to regulate and reduce the numbers of boyars. For this purpose a new statute of nobility was issued. Henceforth rank would depend not only on the status and antiquity of the family, but also on the holding of public office. The boyars in both principalities were divided into two categories. The great boyars and their descendants were declared free from all taxation; the small boyars, the *mazili*, were to pay a personal tax, but were largely exempt from other state contributions.

In order to enforce the changes, the central government needed more efficient local administrative control. Two officials, called *ispravnik*s, were assigned to each district. Most important, they were to receive regular salaries; thus the old system where such officials simply collected what they could from the local population was ended. This aspect of the reform soon proved unworkable, and the old abuses returned. When he was hospodar of Wallachia, however, Grigore Ghica sought to reintroduce the payment of civil servants.

Attempts were also made to improve the judicial system. Again, such actions interfered with the previous rights of the boyars and the church. More emphasis was now placed on written court records and on state control of the proceedings. Legal reform was continued in particular in the reign of Alexander Ypsilanti in Wallachia (1774–1782). A Code of Laws was issued in 1780.

In 1741 Constantine Mavrocordat was transferred to Moldavia. He was replaced in Wallachia by Mihai Racoviţă (1741–1744), who reintroduced the old methods of extreme fiscal exploitation. The peasants responded with a resumption of mass emigration from their land. Since its income was affected, the Porte reappointed Mavrocordat for the years 1744 to 1748. In this period social reform measures were introduced, and the state directly intervened in the delicate question of the relations of the boyar and the peasant in regard to the land.

The basic issue – that is, who owned or controlled the land – was not easy to resolve. In the Ottoman Empire, in theory, the sultan held the land from God; it was granted to others in return for state service or for religious purposes. In Wallachia and Moldavia the problem of land ownership and peasant obligations had not been met clearly. The Principalities had a native aristocracy, but its origins and rights were controversial. By the eighteenth century, nevertheless, a situation had developed in which the boyars controlled the land, which was worked by dependent or enserfed peasants from whom the landholders could extract a large number of unregulated payments. Exactly how this situation developed is not clear. However, from the sixteenth century on, the nobles and the monasteries were able to increase their position at the expense of both the central authority and the peasantry. Boyar families gained control over villages by receiving them as gifts from the state or the monasteries. Some villages sold themselves in return for protection or tax exemptions. Noble families could buy into village lands, or seize them, and thus gain a predominant influence. The tax-farming system also was a means of gaining estates.

In the early period the boyars did not usually engage in agricultural work themselves. The control of villages signified the right to collect certain payments; it did not involve the use of the land. If the burden was too heavy, the peasants could desert their plots. Land was plentiful in the Principalities, and animal husbandry, not agriculture, was the principal occupation. Obviously, domination of an area was of no advantage to a landholder unless it contained a working population, so efforts were made to assure that the peasant would not leave. Although serfdom in Wallachia officially dates from the reign of Michael the Brave and measures taken at the end of the sixteenth century, the institution was probably in effect before then. In the subsequent period, the boyars were often able to break the relationship of the serf and his land. They often bought serfs to settle in uncultivated or deserted lands; they could also free the serfs, but keep the plots they worked.

At the time of the reforms there were four categories of peasants. First were the free villagers who held their lands, often in hill or mountain areas, on the basis of traditional rights accepted by the state. Second were the free peasants without land who worked for a noble on an agreed basis. The third group consisted of serfs who were tied to their villages and lands and were under the jurisdiction of a boyar. Fourth, some serfs, *scutelnici*, had no land but served the boyar directly.

The peasantry bore almost the entire burden of the state taxes. They also had to make payments for the use of the land, either to a boyar or to a monastery. In addition, the peasant owed corvée, or labor obligations, called *clacă*. In the eighteenth century the labor dues were not high when compared to those of the neighboring Habsburg Empire. The noble, particularly in Wallachia, seldom was concerned in the actual running of his estate; he wanted an assured income. He thus accepted the conversion of labor dues into payments in kind. The first reforms dealt with this problem of the corvée. In the 1740s it was set at twelve days in Wallachia and twenty-four in Moldavia. Labor obligations were consistently higher in Moldavia because the boyar was more likely to be directly concerned with the working of his estate. Throughout the reform period no attempt was made to define land ownership. The boyar was referred to as "the master of the domain" or "of the village."

In 1746 a boyar assembly was held in Wallachia to deal with the fiscal crisis and the problem of the fleeing peasantry. It was decided that any serf who returned voluntarily to his village would be freed. Since this measure obviously put a premium on flight, the assembly was forced to adopt the next logical step of simply ending serfdom. If the lord did not agree, the peasant was to receive his freedom with the payment of ten thalers. In 1749, when Mavrocordat was again prince of Moldavia, similar measures, but on more stringent conditions, were introduced into Moldavia.

Personal bondage was now ended. The reforms placed in the same category the former serf and the free peasant who had worked land belonging to a boyar on an agreed basis. Both were *clăcaşi*, peasants who made payments for the use of the land. The great weakness of the peasant reform, of course, was the question of enforcement. The boyars controlled the countryside. For reform to work, the central government had to continue to oversee the relations of the lord and peasant and to rely on its own officials. Unfortunately, the Principalities were not to be governed by princes of Mavrocordat's caliber in the future. Moreover, the renewal of a period of protracted warfare forced the Porte to resort to further fiscal pressure. Once again taxes were levied at repeated intervals during the year, and old taxes that had been abolished were reimposed. Mass peasant flights recurred.

The reforms and the state interference remained under attack from the boyars. The native aristocracy saw in these measures just another reason to justify its dislike of Phanariot and Ottoman rule. Where possible, the boyars sought to return to the former system and to increase peasant payments. In 1766 the labor obligations were increased in Moldavia, and a new system of assessing these dues was also introduced. A work quota, the *nart*, was set regulating what a peasant was supposed to accomplish in a day, but it was so high that it could not be fulfilled in that limited a time.

In addition to the payments to the state and to the landholder, the peasant paid taxes on his produce, his animals, and just about everything else he owned or used. An example of the heavy burden thus imposed can be found in the following description of conditions in Wallachia:

By the end of the eighteenth century, the taxes levied on the ordinary villager included: a head tax, levied 4 times a year (but up to 12 times a year when the treasury needed it); a hearth tax, levied twice a year; a tax on cattle, sheep, pigs, vines; a tax on smoke (from the household fireplace), and on cellars; a sales tax on cattle; a tax on pasture grass; a "flag tax" upon the accession to the throne of a new prince, and another tax 3 years later if the same prince was still on the throne (presumably to pay off the bribe debts he owed in order to rule for so long); a tax on soap, on all goods sold in a marketplace, and on bridge tolls; a salt tax; and a tavern tax. Numerous others have not even been recorded because taxes were farmed out and the tax farmers collected what they could without always keeping careful receipts.[25]

The establishment of Russian influence   In 1768 the long period of peace came to an end with the Ottoman declaration of war on Russia. The great Russian victories and the subsequent Treaty of Kuchuk Kainarji were extremely significant for the Romanian lands in that they marked the beginning of a period when, with Russian backing, the provinces were able to gain from the Porte a closer definition of their position and of their obligations in tribute and supplies. At the same time Russia became the power with the principal influence in the area.

Russian intervention in the Principalities had, as we have seen, commenced at the beginning of the century. Russia's interest was first and foremost military and strategic. The provinces were on the road to Constantinople; they were also the gateway for the march of the Ottoman armies into lands of interest to Russia, such as Poland, the Ukraine, and the territory of the Crimean Tatars. As the Russian borders approached those of Moldavia, other problems arose. Agrarian relations were bad in both the Principalities and Russia. Groups of peasants moved in either direction to escape the exactions of their nobility and governments. Fugitives from justice, bandits, and deserting soldiers also formed part of this transient population.

With these considerations in mind, the Russian government was concerned about the political conditions in Bucharest and Iaşi. Because of its geographic position, Moldavia was always of more immediate interest. What would have best served Russian plans at this time would have been the establishment of a buffer state that would cover the Russian conquest and development of the lands north of the Black Sea. This aim could be achieved by the conversion of the Principalities into autonomous regions under Russian protection, even if the area remained technically under Ottoman suzerainty. The direct annexation of the country could not so easily be accomplished. In

25   Chirot, *Social Change*, p. 65.

1774 all of the great powers were opposed to a peace that would radically alter the balance of power in southeastern Europe. The Russian government thus concentrated on gaining from the Porte concessions that would strengthen both the autonomous position of the Principalities and the Russian influence over their development.

Support for the Russian position could always be found within the provinces. Throughout the century the native boyars continued to appeal to both Austria and Russia against the Ottoman and Phanariot rule. They too wanted an autonomous system under some sort of foreign protection, and one that would return the political power to their hands. The Russian government, of course, was also on good terms with the Phanariots, who were Orthodox and conservative and who held influential offices. In turn, the Phanariot circles expected much from St. Petersburg. The goal of the reestablishment of Byzantium could only be reached through Russian military victories.

The Treaty of Kuchuk Kainarji contained important provisions concerning the Principalities and Russia's relations with them. Article XVI, which consisted of ten points, was devoted to the provinces. Here the Russian right of intervention was given concrete recognition: "The Porte likewise permits that, according as the circumstances of these two Principalities may require, the Ministers of the Imperial Court of Russia resident at Constantinople may remonstrate in their favor; and promises to listen to them with all the attention which is due to friendly and respected powers."[26]

In other sections of the treaty the Principalities were given tax relief and allowed to send official representatives to Constantinople to speak for their interests. In the same year the Ottoman government issued a decree regulating the amount that the provinces were to pay. They still were subject to the tribute, to certain gifts, and to assessments whenever a new prince took office, but some taxes were suppressed. It was also agreed that the Porte would pay the market price for supplies obtained in the Principalities. Turkish officials and merchants were to enter the country only with special permission and with official firmans. Muslims were forbidden to buy estates or establish permanent residence. In the years between 1783 and 1802 the Porte made further concessions. The exact amount of the payments was set, and the deliveries of supplies were specified. The prince was not to be deposed unless he committed a crime, and then only with the consent of Russia.

These arrangements naturally greatly increased Russian influence. Russia's position became even stronger with the appointment of consuls, a matter also provided for by the treaty. In 1782, after strong Ottoman resistance, the first consul, S. L. Lashkarev, arrived in Bucharest. Vice-consuls were subsequently sent to Iaşi and Kilia. As in Greece, the offices became centers of political intrigue. In 1783 the Habsburg Empire established a similar consu-

---

26 Quoted in Holland, *Treaty Relations of Russia and Turkey*, p. 47.

late, as did the French in 1796 and the British in 1803. Thereafter the Molda-vian and Wallachian capitals reflected the conflicts among the great powers in Constantinople.

Meanwhile, Catherine the Great and Joseph II were corresponding on their extensive proposals for the partition of the Ottoman Empire, plans that in-cluded the establishment of a Romanian buffer state of Dacia, presumably under Russian primary influence. Already, in 1775, Austria had compelled the Porte to recognize its annexation of Bukovina, which was an integral part of Moldavia. In September 1787 Russia was again at war with the Porte; Austria joined in the following February. For the fourth time in the century, Russian troops appeared in the Principalities, this time at the behest of Catherine's favorite, Prince G. Potemkin, who apparently considered himself a possible candidate for the office of prince of Dacia. Russian aims, as defined at the beginning of the war, called for the establishment of a buffer state with its boundary on the Dniester River. The principal Russian objective was, how-ever, the annexation of the lands between the Bug and Dniester rivers.

Under the leadership of the brilliant general Alexander Suvorov, Russian troops won significant victories, but the international situation was not fa-vorable to Russian interests. Sweden's declaration of war made an expedition to the Mediterranean by the Baltic fleet impossible. Austria was forced to withdraw from the war in 1791. Faced with these problems, Russia concluded the Treaty of Jassy in 1792. Here the principal gain was the acquisition of lands to the Dniester; Russia became the immediate neighbor of Moldavia. In Article IV the Porte declared that it would abide by the previous arrange-ments concerning the Principalities.

In the 1790s both provinces, like all of the powers, were increasingly af-fected by the repercussions of the revolution in France. Henceforth, until after the Congress of Vienna in 1815, Balkan problems were to remain subor-dinate to the great issue of the domination of the European continent. By this time, however, the Principalities had at least begun to advance along the road of internal reform and national autonomy. The Phanariot regime re-mained, but the reforms of Mavrocordat, even if some were later reversed or changed, marked at least the recognition of the major social and political problems. Russian predominance was to stay, in fact to increase, over the next years. The intervention of this government had forced the Porte to fix the Romanian payments and obligations and to give assurances concerning the tenure of the princes. Whether these would be honored depended on the future evolution of events, not only in Europe but in the Ottoman capital.

THE OTTOMAN EMPIRE: POLITICAL
EVOLUTION IN THE EIGHTEENTH CENTURY

Reform and revolution

In the previous pages a century of Ottoman history has been discussed from the viewpoint of the Balkan provinces. It was characterized, as we have seen, by a succession of military defeats that resulted in Ottoman territorial losses, principally in the lands north of the Danube and the Black Sea. This weakness was reflected in the internal situation and the discontent with rising taxes and ineffective government. Conditions of local anarchy arose with the failure of the authorities to keep order and the existence of bands of robbers or of disgruntled and unpaid soldiers. The breakdown of the central authority was paralleled by the rise in prestige and power of local authorities who gained effective control of their regions and removed themselves from the supervision of the center. The situation was to deteriorate even further at the end of the century. Since the central government proved ineffective, the local population turned increasingly to its own leaders and its military bands, both Christian and Muslim, which offered a better source of protection and guidance. The existence of strong provincial authorities naturally deprived the central government of much of its income. Taxes collected locally remained in the hands of these officials. A circle of difficulties was thus created. Without money the government could not maintain a strong military establishment; the result was continuing defeat in war, which in turn led to an increase in the prestige and position of the local authorities, who in turn kept their hands on the public revenues that should have gone to Constantinople to provide for the army and other public needs.

The sultan and his advisers were well aware of the problem, but it was difficult to decide what should be done about it. Severe limitations hampered the efforts of the Ottoman leaders to meet the situation. A principal hindrance throughout both the eighteenth and the nineteenth centuries was the strength of conservative religious tradition and the political influence of the ulema. Unfortunately for those who saw the necessity of radical reform, the Ottoman Empire had enjoyed a glorious past history. It was difficult for many to believe that there was anything fundamentally wrong with the basic principles on which their government rested. The fact that these were derived from a strong and living religious tradition complicated the matter further. To be acceptable, reform had to be based on the conception that the new measures were in fact a return to an older and purer society. Only in that manner could a sufficient number of people be convinced of their necessity. Reform also ran against entrenched interests. Many in power saw no reason to alter the existing institutions, which gave them power and wealth, and feared any change that threatened their personal interests.

The clear and obvious need throughout the century was military reform.

The ambitious plans of other states for the partition of the empire were known in Constantinople. It was apparent that an improvement in the military was a question of life or death for the state. Moreover, something had to be done about the empire's financial condition. Without increased sources of income, a radical improvement in the army would not be possible. Basic to a change here was a reform of the tax-collecting system; administrative reorganization was thus also essential. In the eighteenth century, although the military issue was met, few attempts were made to improve the tax and administrative structure. The sultans and vezirs continued to raise money by their old methods of increasing taxes, adding new ones, and debasing the coinage. Inefficient and oppressive tax-farming systems continued to be employed. The corruption in the administration resulted in the diversion of tax income into private hands, rather than its employment to strengthen the country.

The major military problem was the janissary corps, the former basis of Ottoman power. As we have seen, its members, dispersed throughout the empire, had become an element of political disorder and intrigue. They were the most effectively organized and armed group in Constantinople and in the provincial cities, but they did not show a corresponding ability to defeat invading armies. Closely tied to the guilds and the ulema, they did not prove a firm support of the central authority. Throughout the eighteenth century, in fact until their disbanding in 1826, they were a major cause of political instability; they repeatedly demonstrated their ability to control or overthrow successive sultans and vezirs.

It was, in fact, a janissary rebellion in Adrianople in 1703 that led to the accession to power of Ahmed III, who was to enjoy a relatively long reign, until 1730. His army was able to defeat Peter the Great at the battle of the Pruth, but subsequent unsuccessful campaigns against the Habsburg Empire forced him to sign the highly unfavorable Treaty of Passarowitz. During a large part of his reign he was served by an able vezir, Damad Ibrahim Pasha, who was in office from 1718 to 1730. Both the sultan and his advisers showed a keen interest in concurrent developments in Europe. Representatives were sent to Vienna and Paris to study Western ways and to select those that would be of use to the empire.

Ahmed's reign covered the Tulip Period in Ottoman culture, a time characterized not only by the fad of acquiring and growing these flowers, but also by the adoption of Western, in particular French, styles. French decor, furniture, and gardens were copied. Living in an era of extravagance and luxury, the wealthy devoted much attention to architecture; new palaces, pavilions, mosques, fountains, and elaborate formal gardens were a result of this enthusiasm. The era was characterized by an emphasis on pleasure and a great interest in poetry. As far as achievements in the cultural field are concerned, the introduction of printing in the Turkish language was perhaps the most significant. Previously, Armenian, Greek, Jewish, and Latin books had been printed, but not Turkish. The man responsible for the new development was

Ibrahim Müteferrika, a Hungarian born in Cluj. Taken prisoner of war and sold as a slave, he converted to Islam. He was able to gain the agreement of the seyhülislâm to print in Turkish as long as he did not handle religious works. The first book appeared in 1728. By the time of Müteferrika's death in 1745, his press had produced sixteen books.

The extravagant spending of the Tulip Period produced an inevitable reaction. The luxurious living had to be paid for, and the basis remained the impoverished countryside. The contrast between the opulence at the top and the misery at the bottom intensified. As vezir, Ibrahim made some attempt to introduce measures for a more efficient government and a better collection of taxes, but basically the system remained unchanged. A period of inflation, famine, plague, and rural unrest was inevitable. The unsuccessful and controversial campaigns in Persia further inflamed the situation until finally a major revolt broke out.

Under these circumstances the city of Constantinople seethed with discontent. The problem of the unpaid soldiers was even more serious in the capital than in the provinces. Moreover, Constantinople, like other major cities in the empire, was suffering from a mass influx of the rural population, which was trying to escape the intolerable conditions in the countryside. Anarchy and banditry led many to abandon their lands and flee into cities, which seemed a relative haven of security. Among these newcomers were many artisans who sought to continue their trades, an attempt that brought them into conflict with the local guild organizations. The guilds themselves had ample reason to be extremely discontented with the entire economic situation in the empire, including the tax system, the extra war payments, the debasement of the currency, and the lack of civic stability. The unrest was shown by, among other signs, the increasing number of fires in Constantinople resulting from arson. In 1729 a conflagration destroyed approximately 4,000 houses and 130 mosques with a great loss of life.[27] Repeated outbreaks of plague and cholera in the 1720s made the situation even worse.

The rebellion involved first the lower social classes and was initiated by guild members disgruntled with conditions arising from the commencement of a campaign against Persia. The leader was Patrona Halil, "an ex-second hand clothes dealer and masseur in a Turkish bath"; others prominent in the revolt were "junk dealers, sellers of vegetables, and coffeehouse attendants."[28] The movement, however, soon won the cooperation of, and was in fact taken over by, members of the governing class who were in opposition to Ibrahim and his supporters. Many of these were members of the ulema and discontented janissaries and other military men. The sultan and his vezir were in Üsküdar with the army when the revolt broke out in September 1730. The

27 Robert W. Olson, *The Siege of Mosul and Ottoman-Persian Relations, 1718–1743* (Bloomington: Indiana University publications, 1975), p. 71.
28 Olson, *Siege of Mosul*, pp. 56, 77.

city was soon in the hands of the revolutionaries; the sultan was compelled to surrender Ibrahim, who was executed along with two of his nephews. Ahmed was then forced to abdicate in favor of his nephew, Mahmud I (1730–1754).

Although the new sultan had to promise the revolutionaries what they wanted, he was able to gain control of the situation. At the end of November Patrona Halil, the leader of the lower-class forces, was murdered. In the end the government was reestablished on much the old basis. All of those who had participated in the original movement were hunted down and executed. The revolt, however, had shown not only the unrest among the poorer elements of society, but also the discontent of the conservatives in the ulema and the military with the Tulip Period and French cultural influence.

During the reign of Mahmud I some effort at military reform was made. The use of foreign advisers, particularly French, characterized the further attempts to modernize the army. The chief figure at this time was Claude Alexander, Count of Bonneval, an officer who had served both with Louis XIV and with Eugene of Savoy. He arrived in Constantinople in 1729 and converted to Islam. Since sipahi and janissary opposition made changes in these organizations impossible, he concentrated on the bombardier corps, which he trained according to Austrian and French methods. He established a training center, which the janissaries closed promptly after his death in 1747. Bonneval was also concerned with military technology, and he constructed cannon, powder, and musket factories. There was always less resistance in the empire to the introduction of superior European military equipment then to attempts at military reorganization or interference with profits or traditional privileges.

Although the war waged between 1736 and 1739 was concluded by a favorable peace that returned northern Serbia and Oltenia to the empire, the conflict contributed to the intensification of the difficulties in the countryside. The concentration of military force against the foreign invader left the central government weaker in its relations with the provincial authorities. Conditions were bad in the Balkans, but worse elsewhere. The empire lost practical control over Egypt, Syria, Iraq, and North Africa. The period of peace that followed, which covered the reigns of two sultans, Osman III (1754–1757) and Mustafa III (1757–1774), was not used as an opportunity to reform the government or strengthen the state. The old abuses flourished. The sultans and vezirs kept control by the regular method of maintaining the balance of power between rival factions and pitting strong individuals against each other. Bribery, nepotism, and the sale of offices remained constant attributes of the system.

In 1774 Abdul Hamid I came to the throne. The same year saw the signing of the Treaty of Kuchuk Kainarji, which not only marked a great defeat but identified Russia as the most formidable foreign adversary. The absolute necessity of military reform was clearly demonstrated. The empire had suffered a military disaster, and, worse, provinces under local military leaders were in the process of detaching themselves from the state. Since it was a situation of crisis, even the conservative elements could be convinced of the necessity for change. Foreign military advisers were still needed. Of the powers, France continued to be the main supporter of reforms that would prevent the collapse of its Ottoman ally. Britain and Holland, with large commercial stakes in the area, had similar interests. In contrast, Russia and Austria, both of which sought a partition of the empire, opposed any measures to strengthen their intended victim.

Among the vezirs of Abdul Hamid I, one, Halil Hamid, stands out as a reformer despite his short period in office (1781–1785). He too used French experts, and he devoted much attention to strengthening the Ottoman border fortifications. Recognizing that the great weakness in the military was still the janissary corps, he dismissed a large number of members and raised the pay of those who were left in an attempt to improve the quality of the organization. He also wished the army to be trained by new methods with modern weapons. His reforms, however, caused too much opposition, and he was executed in 1785.

Among the foreign advisers, Baron de Tott was particularly influential. A Hungarian noble, he first went to France and then in 1755 arrived in Constantinople. Unlike previous advisers, he did not convert to Islam. His work was chiefly with the artillery and the engineers. Naval reform was also undertaken, under the direction principally of Gazi Hasan Pasha. The Ottoman fleet had been totally destroyed at Chesme in 1770; since a completely new force was necessary, there was less opposition to change than might otherwise have been expected. Hasan too used French assistance, and he took as his model the French and British navies. By 1784 the Ottoman Empire had an entirely reconstructed navy. Hasan was also concerned about the training of the officers and men, but here he could not make any fundamental changes; officer ranks were still purchased.

The great reformer of the century was the next sultan, Selim III, who reigned from 1789 to 1807. Involved in yet another war with Russia, he was at first not free to devote his attention to domestic problems. The final loss of the Crimea in 1783, with its population of 2 million Muslims, had been a particularly bitter blow to Muslim pride, as had been similar cessions involving Caucasian lands and areas north of the Black Sea. There was now general agreement that radical measures would have to be taken, but again the direction and methods could not be agreed upon. After 1792 Selim had a period of peace before the empire was again involved in war in 1798. In dealing with the question of administrative reform, he used only traditional means. His aim was simply to improve the existing structure and to eliminate the most flagrant abuses. He had no group on which he could count for support for radical measures dealing with the government itself, and there were thus no fundamental administrative changes.

The sultan was, however, freer in dealing with military matters, although he still could not move decisively against either the sipahis or the janissaries. Since he could not reform the old corps, he attempted instead to create an entirely new unit, call *Nizam-i Cedid*, or New Model, which was set up apart from the regular military forces and trained by European methods under the direction of European advisers. This organization was formed primarily of Turkish peasant boys from Anatolia, and by 1806 it contained 22,685 men and 1,590 officers.[29] A major role was again taken by French advisers, except for the years from 1798 to 1802, when the Porte was at war with France. Some naval reforms were also undertaken.

Selim's reign covered the period of the French Revolution and the rise of Napoleon, which was a time of intense activity in international relations. The French preeminence in Constantinople was at this time challenged by both Russia and Britain. The Ottoman government, too, became more concerned with its relationship with the European powers. Regular embassies, newly established in Vienna, Berlin, and Paris, sent back reports on the events in these capitals. The Porte was at war during two periods, with France from 1798 to 1802 and with Russia from 1806 to 1812. At the same time, the government had to deal with the problem of internal anarchy and the insubordination of the provincial pashas. The foreign situation formed an extremely unfavorable background for any attempts at reform. Of necessity, the war involvements dominated the concerns of the government.

The wars of Napoleon

From the invasion of Egypt by Napoleon's armies in 1798 until the signing of the Treaty of Bucharest with Russia in 1812, the Ottoman lands felt the full effects of the great struggle being waged between France and most of the powers of the Continent. Although the major battles were fought in Central Europe or in Russia, the Mediterranean played an important role in the plans of the warring states. Of the Ottoman territories, Egypt, Syria, the Dalmatian coast, and the Danubian Principalities were primarily affected by the fighting. These conflicts not only placed a great burden on Ottoman resources, but also formed the background for the rise of the most powerful of the provincial notables, Ali Pasha of Janina and Pasvanoglu Osman Pasha of Vidin, who were able to challenge the Ottoman state directly.

In the eighteenth century, as we have seen, France remained the European power with the closest relations with the Porte. Since the Ottoman Empire was part of its Eastern Barrier system, which included Sweden and Poland, the French government had every interest in preserving and defending Ottoman territorial integrity. France also supported reforms that might make the Porte better able to resist foreign encroachments. At the end of the cen-

29 Shaw, *History of the Ottoman Empire*, p. 262.

tury, however, France for a short period adopted the unaccustomed role of providing the chief threat to Ottoman domains. In 1797 Napoleon undertook an aggressive campaign in the Mediterranean. In May the French navy occupied the Venetian-owned Ionian Islands. At the same time agents were sent into Greek lands to promote French influence and prepare the way for a revolt in support of France. In October the Habsburg government, after major military defeats, was forced to sign the Treaty of Campo Formio. In this agreement the Venetian possessions were divided between the two states. France annexed the Ionian Islands, including the associated coastal towns of Parga and Prevesa, an action that brought the French boundaries adjacent to those of the Ottoman Empire. Austria, for its share, took possession of the city of Venice and its lands in Istria and Dalmatia. The former Ottoman adversary, Venice, was thus destroyed, but a greater danger had arisen instead. The real shock to the Porte was Napoleon's occupation of Egypt in July 1798. Although Egypt under the Mamluke leaders had acted independently in the past, the country was technically under Ottoman suzerainty. Constantinople was also dependent on Egypt for food supplies. The Porte thus declared war on France.

The alliance pattern in the Near East at this point underwent a radical change. The Ottoman Empire was in agreement not only with Britain, but also with the former opponent, Russia. Catherine the Great had died in 1796 and had been succeeded by her son Paul. A strong critic of his mother's aggressive policies, in particular of her aims at Ottoman partition, the new tsar wished to maintain good relations with the Porte. He also became involved in the affairs of the Catholic religious order of St. John of Jerusalem, which had its headquarters in Malta, and felt personally affronted when the French picked up the island on their way to Egypt. After the war started, the Russian government thus responded to Ottoman and British approaches. In September 1798 a Russian Black Sea fleet for the first time passed through the Straits and into the Mediterranean. A formal alliance, to which Britain adhered, was signed in January 1799; it included a secret article allowing the Russian ships to pass freely in and out of the Straits.

In the next year the British, Russian, and Ottoman fleets cooperated in actions in the Mediterranean. Already in August 1798, at the battle of the Nile, the British had destroyed the French fleet, and thus the French forces were cut off from their homeland. Deprived of needed supplies and reinforcements, the campaign in Egypt soon collapsed. Napoleon himself abandoned his army in August 1799. Alexandria fell to the British expeditionary force in 1801, and the French troops soon surrendered. Although the Russian and Turkish fleets did not participate in this action, they did launch a joint operation to take control of the Ionian Islands. These were occupied in 1799 and subsequently organized as the Septinsular Republic, whose government was modeled on that of Dubrovnik. The islands were placed under Ottoman sovereignty, but Russian protection.

The tsar, however, had become most unhappy with the actions of his allies. Russia was part of the second coalition against Napoleon and thus fought alongside Austria, Naples, and Britain on the Continent. In October 1799, angered by what he considered an Austrian betrayal in the campaign in Switzerland, Paul withdrew his troops from the battlefield and recalled his Mediterranean fleet. He subsequently indicated his intention of reestablishing relations with France. In March 1801 he was assassinated and succeeded by his son, Alexander I. The new tsar, determined to maintain a policy of neutrality, made a peace with France; Britain and the Ottoman Empire concluded similar agreements in 1802.

The general peace lasted scarcely a year. France and Britain resumed fighting in May 1803. By 1805 the third coalition including Britain, Russia, and Austria had been formed. Once again a Russian fleet, this time under Admiral D. N. Seniavin, was active in the Mediterranean; Russian forces were also sent to Naples. Although the Porte was not at war, its support was vital to both sides. To try to gain assistance, the French government, desiring particularly the closure of the Straits to Russian warships, sent an extremely clever diplomat, General Horace Sebastiani, to Constantinople. At the same time French consuls and agents were active in the western Balkans and Greece. The Ottoman attitude was to be chiefly influenced by the apparently irresistible French military power and the great victories at Ulm and Austerlitz.

The battle of the great powers for supremacy in the Mediterranean had direct effects on Ottoman lands adjacent to the Adriatic Sea and on the Danubian Principalities. Although the main Russian attention centered on the Ionian Islands and the Italian peninsula, the occupation of the islands and the interest shown in French actions in Dalmatia inevitably involved Russia in the affairs of Montenegro, Albania, and northern Greece. Both Russia and France competed for influence in the Greek lands and with the leading provincial notable, Ali Pasha of Janina. France, like Russia, was also concerned with events in Montenegro.

In Cetinje Bishop Peter, despite his uneven relationship with Russia in the past, still wished to win the support of that power because he feared the possible encroachment of his ambitious neighbors, in particular Ali Pasha. He thus made continual efforts to gain assistance from St. Petersburg. In 1799 Paul sent assurances that the Russian fleet would protect the Christians in the area and offered a subsidy of three thousand rubles. Peter also had territorial objectives. He wished to acquire a seaport, in particular Kotor, which had an Orthodox population. When the Habsburg Empire gained the area in 1797, he was extremely disappointed. A political realist, Peter maintained contact with French agents as well as with St. Petersburg.

In 1801, in an effort to maintain good relations and to assure a continuation of the subsidy, Peter sent a representative, Vukotić, to Russia to greet the tsar. Once there, Vukotić instead denounced the bishop. The Russian synod and the government condemned Peter and dispatched a Serbian in Russian service, Colonel Marko Ivelić, to Montenegro. He joined in a plot to remove Peter and to replace him with a member of Vukotić's family. Peter was, nevertheless, able to rally a sufficient number of supporters to keep his position. A declaration was sent to Russia that the country was not under the jurisdiction of the Russian church. Despite this episode, good relations were subsequently restored, because the Russian government and the Montenegrins needed each other's support.

In 1805 in the Treaty of Pressburg the Habsburg Monarchy ceded to France the Dalmatian coast. In October 1805 Russia, it will be remembered, was back at war with France and had a fleet operating in the Adriatic. Both the French and Russian forces at this time moved to seize strategic points. In May 1806 a French unit was able to occupy Dubrovnik, a Catholic city that did not offer much resistance. Russian and Montenegrin troops then laid siege to the city and bombarded it heavily, but they were not able to oust the French garrison. Russian troops, however, did hold Kotor and the surrounding area, and the Russian fleet also took the islands of Hvar and Brač. During the war the Montenegrins made use of the ports of Kotor and Budva. This period marked the height of Russian–Montenegrin collaboration. Peter sent Alexander I a letter proposing the establishment of a large state, including Montenegro, Hercegovina, Dalmatia, a part of Albania, and Dubrovnik, which would be the capital. Peter would be the prince, with Russia the protecting power.

Although the Russian government was happy to make use of Montenegrin fighters, the fate of the country weighed little against general Russian interests in the wider European field. In 1807 Russia made an agreement with France, the Treaty of Tilsit, in which Kotor was assigned to the Western power; the Montenegrins were told to evacuate the area. In the next years the small state continued its perpetual conflicts with its Albanian and Ottoman neighbors. In 1813, with British assistance, Montenegrin troops again occupied Kotor. At the end of the war there was hope that the port might be kept, but Russia supported the Habsburg claims. By this time the Russian government had also stopped the subsidies and had sent no arms. Thus, despite almost continual fighting, Montenegro made no further gains beyond those acquired in 1796. The Russian friendship had won no concrete advantages.

Not only the Adriatic coastal areas, but also the Principalities felt the effects of the Russian–French–Ottoman entanglements. Here, however, Russia was clearly dominant. After the peace of 1792 Russian agents returned to the two provinces, but Iași rather than Bucharest became the principal center of Russian activities. In the years before her death in 1796, Catherine showed a renewed interest in acquiring the Principalities. Paul, however, on his accession, preferred to follow a policy of cooperation with the Porte and of maintaining its territorial integrity. He had nevertheless no intention of surrendering the Russian prime influence in the Principalities. Alexander I continued this policy, but his government did use pressure on the Porte to gain some concessions. At this time Wallachia was suffering from the devastation wrought by the provincial notable Pasvanoglu, who from his center in Vidin and northern Bulgaria launched repeated raids into the Romanian lands. In 1802, in an official act, the Ottoman government set the terms of the hospodars at seven years; they were not to be removed except for proven crimes. This decree considerably increased Russian influence by specifying that the Russian government had the right to approve the Ottoman candidates for prince. This measure gave St. Petersburg a weapon that could be used against the Porte and also to control the princes. Two Russian candidates, Constantine Ypsilanti and Alexander Moruzzi, then held office. In this period the Russian representatives continued to involve themselves in the internal affairs of the Principalities and to build up their own party among the boyars. Meanwhile, French influence was increasing in Constantinople, a change that was reflected in the Principalities. In August 1806, on French urging, the Porte deposed the two princes without consulting Russia. Although it soon changed its mind and reinstated the former rulers, the action was in violation of the agreement of 1802. In November Russian troops occupied the Principalities; the Porte declared war in December.

This conflict was in the interest of neither power. Russia could not afford to send a large military force into the area; France was the major concern. The Ottoman Empire was in an even weaker position. In 1804 an uprising had commenced in Serbia that had not yet been suppressed; all over the empire the provincial authorities were asserting their independence. War with Russia also involved Russia's ally, Britain. In February 1807 a British fleet entered the Dardanelles and sailed within eight miles of Constantinople before it withdrew. British forces were at that point firmly entrenched in Egypt.

The greatest blow to the Ottoman interests was the reconciliation of Russia and France in the Treaty of Tilsit in July 1807. Meeting together, the two rulers, Napoleon and Alexander I, settled the affairs of Europe. In addition to regulating their Continental differences, they prepared for a possible partition of the Ottoman Empire. It was agreed that France would attempt to mediate a peace between Russia and the Porte. Should these efforts fail, then a division of Ottoman territory would be made. The details were never made clear, and the suspicion and distrust between the partners was strong. Napoleon under no circumstances would allow Russia the possession of Constantinople and the Straits. At the next meeting of the tsar and the French emperor, at Erfurt in September 1808, the question of partition was abandoned. Previously, at Tilsit, Russia had agreed that France could take Dalmatia and the Ionian Islands. Now Moldavia and Wallachia were assigned to Russia. The rest of the Ottoman lands remained intact.

Although the Porte and Russia were still at war, neither could mount a major offensive. The Ottoman Empire was undergoing another internal crisis. Both the negotiations and the fighting dragged on. In 1809 Britain made peace with the Ottoman Empire, and the two powers in a joint naval expedition took the Ionian Islands from France. Meanwhile, relations between Russia and France declined. The Russian government thus had a pressing need to conclude the conflict in the Balkans. The main obstacle to peace was the question of the Ottoman cession of Moldavia and Wallachia. In an effort to facilitate the negotiations, Russia limited its claim to Moldavia. When the tension with France became stronger, the Russian government further retreated and agreed to draw the boundary at the Pruth rather than the Sereth River. Peace could be made on this basis. In the Treaty of Bucharest of 1812 the major Russian gain was the acquisition of the area to be known as Bessarabia, with the boundary at the Pruth River and with the inclusion of the Kilia canal of the Danube. Russia thus became a Danubian as well as a Black Sea power. Having concluded the conflict with the Ottoman Empire, Russia could direct its full attention to defeating the invading French army. The Ottoman government, although it, too, desperately needed peace, was not satisfied with the terms. The negotiators were subsequently beheaded.

The threat of the provincial notables: the fall of Selim III

Not only did the years from 1798 to 1812 bring external dangers to the empire, but, more important, the central government was faced with the constant resistance of its Muslim and Christian subjects. The Montenegrin actions have been discussed, and as noted previously, the Serbs rose in a major revolt in 1804. What was particularly dangerous for the empire, however, was the inability of the central government to deal with Muslim notables, who often both defied the Porte and oppressed the people under their jurisdiction, Christian and Muslim alike. This situation arose in various regions of the empire, but the events in Asia Minor and North Africa are out of the scope of this discussion. The existence of strong local centers has been noted previously. The tendency of local notables, called *ayans*, to defy the central authority became stronger toward the end of the century, when the wars with Russia left the Porte with no spare troops to deal with internal subversion. The empire attempted to meet the problem by playing one ayan against another. Since these men were also in competition with each other and often quarreled over the control of an area, this policy often proved successful.

The local notables were able to win and hold power not only because they could muster sufficient military force, but also because they did fulfill a real need in many areas. With the disruption of the authority of the central government and its inability to control the countryside, many areas were taken over by bandit groups. These fought with each other, but cooperated against outside interference. The strong leaders, such as Kara Mahmud and Ali Pasha, could at least assure a maintainance of basic order in their region, and they could provide certain governmental services, like police protection and some sort of a judicial system. They also took care of tax collection and could serve as a protection against unjust exactions from the central government. Some were outright tyrants, whereas others were seen as a shield between the people and the bandits, on the one hand, and rapacious officials, on the other. Of course, the notables often worked in cooperation with the bandits, the officials, or other elements. They kept their power because of their military support, an important part of which often came from local janissaries.

Since the Porte could not defeat the janissaries by military force, other means had to be used. Unable to deprive them of their positions, the Ottoman government was often compelled to give them official appointments as the heads of their districts. The policy of divide and rule was also attempted: one notable was incited against another, and efforts were made to win away their followers. Some notables, for example, Ali Pasha of Janina, alternated between serving the government in official capacities and openly defying its commands. Others, like Pasvanoglu, simply refused to recognize the control of Constantinople in any form. A good example of the activities of these men has already been shown in the career of Kara Mahmud Bushati. For later Balkan events the actions of Pasvanoglu and Ali Pasha were most influential.

Pasvanoglu became one of the most destructive of the strong local leaders. He had an adventurous youth. When his father was executed by the Porte, he fled and joined a group of bandits. Subsequently, however, from 1787 to 1792, he served in the Ottoman army. He then returned to an outlaw life. From his center at Vidin, he was able to organize the bands of renegades and bandits who infested the area, and turbulent janissary contingents also joined him. In particular, he established ties with a group of janissaries who desired to take control of Belgrade. In 1795 he declared himself independent of the Porte. His men cooperated with lawless Serbian janissaries and with Bosnian beys who similarly resisted control from Constantinople, and his forces raided deep into Serbian and Romanian territory. The expeditions into Wallachia frightened many residents into fleeing to Transylvania. Pasvanoglu was able to control completely the stretch of Bulgarian territory between the Danube and the Balkan Mountains. Although at times he declared his loyalty to the sultan, he never in fact submitted to his authority.

The raids of these outlaws caused tremendous damage and loss of life. In an effort to defeat him, the Porte called on Ali Pasha, who did succeed in driving him back to his fortress at Vidin. The outbreak of war with France, however, forced Selim III to make peace with the notables so that he could defend his lands against the foreign invasion. Pasvanoglu remained a defiant element in the state; he continued his attacks on Wallachian and Serbian territory, and he was in touch with French agents. His activities ended only with his death in 1807.

Ali Pasha had an even longer and more successful career. Like Pasvanoglu he spent part of his youth as a bandit, although he was a member of a prominent Albanian family. He alternated between legal and illegal activities until 1799, when he became governor of Rumelia, the highest Balkan post.

Throughout this period he was guided by pure self-interest. When it suited his purposes, he cooperated with Constantinople; when it was to his advantage to defy the central authority, he acted independently. His aim was to construct a kingdom from Albanian and Greek land that would be under his personal rule. The instability of the political situation along the Adriatic coast and in Albania gave him the opportunity to realize a great part of his ambitions. He did establish himself as an independent authority at Janina, and he entered into relations with foreign powers. The Ottoman government could not move against him in a serious and determined manner until 1820.

Although some of the unruly Muslim leaders won strong local support, their activities were a threat to the lives and possessions of much of the Ottoman population. We have already seen the effects in some places. The attacks of Kara Mahmud, for instance, forced the Montenegrin tribesmen to limit their internal feuding and delegate at least some authority to one leader. They also appealed to outside powers: Russia, France, and Austria. The Romanian reaction was similar. The raids of Pasvanoglu into Wallachia caused one hospodar, Constantine Ypsilanti, to call on Russia to send in an occupying army. The strongest reaction to janissary unrest and bandit oppression occurred in the pashalik of Belgrade. The Serbian revolt, the first of the major national liberation movements, will be discussed in detail later. Here it is sufficient to say that the Serbs, caught between a powerless central government and rebellious military groups, particularly the janissaries, rose in 1804 not against the Ottoman government itself, but against the control of the local military regime, which had links with Pasvanoglu and the Bosnian beys. At first, the rebels sought only a restoration of order and the rule of law, not an independent or autonomous political organization.

As the Balkan provinces fell into anarchy and civil war, the situation in Constantinople similarly worsened. Selim's reforms, conservative and limited as they were, raised considerable opposition. The policy of cooperation with France and defiance of Russia, adopted in 1806, had been unsuccessful. The familiar problems of economic distress and military failure were again present. In May 1807 the conservative coalition of janissaries, ulema, and students again formed, and Selim was forced to abdicate. The new ruler, Mustafa IV, did not have a firm base of support. Selim's adherents and others who were against the new regime gathered around a provincial notable, Mustafa Bayraktar Pasha, whose center was Ruse (Ruschuk). Although a representative of the ayan class that was causing such havoc in the empire, Mustafa Bayraktar was a supporter of reform, and he did have an army at his command. The group that backed him was known as the Ruschuk Friends. The Ottoman position became more dangerous when the Treaty of Tilsit was signed and the Porte lost French support. It found itself at war with both Russia and Britain. In July 1808 Mustafa Bayraktar moved his forces against Constantinople. In the ensuing struggle Selim III was killed, but his nephew Mahmud II escaped to join the rebels. Once Mustafa took control of the city, Mahmud was placed on the throne. As grand vezir in the new regime, Mustafa sought to strengthen the central government, control the defiant notables, and revive military reform.

Once more the opposition was too strong. The janissaries and their friends gathered their forces and in November 1808 defeated the vezir and the Ruschuk Friends. Mahmud II, however, remained sultan. He was to prove a strong ruler. In order to limit possible intrigues, he had Mustafa IV, who had ruled only a short time, killed. It was clear to Mahmud II that military reform was essential; the janissaries in particular were a mortal danger to the state both in the capital and in the provinces. Although the sultan had to wait many years before he could deal with his internal problems, he did succeed in negotiating a peace. Bessarabia was lost, but this region had been a part of Moldavia, which was already under Russian influence. Moreover, the end of the war allowed the Ottoman government to turn its attention to Serbia and to suppress the revolt there.

Nevertheless, despite the accession of a capable ruler, conditions within the empire, particularly the continuing relative weakness of the central government, set the stage for the national revolts of the century. The imperial administration was to face increasing difficulties in maintaining control over the provinces and in resisting the intrusion of the great powers. One of these, the Habsburg Empire, was to be involved in Ottoman affairs, not only as a neighboring state, but also because many of its inhabitants shared a common national background with some of the Ottoman-ruled Balkan people.

2

Balkan nationalities under Habsburg rule

IN THE PREVIOUS CHAPTER the political problems of the Ottoman Empire were discussed. At its height the state was a centralized, divine-right monarchy that was served by a bureaucracy and a military establishment without being limited by checks from any competing local or provincial authorities. Taxes were levied and soldiers were recruited directly by the state. Whether the soldier was paid by timar land grants or by a salary, he was under the control of Constantinople. In the seventeenth and eighteenth centuries this situation was modified. A series of weak rulers after Suleiman, combined with defeats in war, allowed provincial centers to escape from the central authority. By the end of the eighteenth century, in many regions the local ayans had organized their own military forces and had usurped the tax-gathering functions for their own benefit.

The Habsburg government, in contrast, evolved along another path. This empire was a collection of disparate lands united principally through the house of Habsburg. The local nobility, not the ruler, had direct control over the mass of the population. The power to levy taxes and recruit soldiers was in the hands of the provincial estates. The aim of the government in the eighteenth century was to establish a system of royal absolutism that would bring the average citizen under the direct jurisdiction of the ruler and his bureaucracy. The central state authority was to extend to all the community.

The difference in development between the Ottoman and Habsburg empires can be largely explained by their contrasting past histories. The Ottoman lands had been collected by victorious sultans at the head of conquering armies. It had not been necessary to make concessions to the local nobility; they were annihilated unless they surrendered and converted to Islam. They were then the subjects of the sultan. In contrast, the Habsburg territories were assembled primarily through alliances and marriages; guarantees often had to be given to the local estates that their historic rights and individuality would be protected. Although the original lands of the Habsburg family were in Switzerland, the Upper Rhine, and Alsace, the core Austrian provinces were Upper and Lower Austria, Styria, Carinthia, Carniola, Tirol, and Vorarlberg. Dynastic alliances brought in the vast territories of Spain and her overseas empire, the Netherlands, and part of Italy. At the death of the Hungarian King Louis II at the battle of Mohács in 1526, the Bohemian and Hungarian inheritance was acquired.

Even though the empire was subsequently divided, with Spain and other regions assigned to another member of the Habsburg family, the differences among the provinces under the control of Vienna was great enough to make the application of any uniform system difficult to contemplate. In the seventeenth century the Habsburg Austrian lands consisted of Upper and Lower Austria, Styria, Salzburg, Carinthia, Tirol, Vorarlberg, Carniola, the Netherlands, Bohemia, Moravia, and Silesia, together with the possessions of the Hungarian crown not under Ottoman occupation. In the Treaty of Karlowitz, Transylvania, Slavonia, and additional Croatian territory were annexed. The Banat was added in 1718. These acquisitions added to the ethnic and political complexity of the monarchy.

In the Ottoman Empire relations between church and state did not become a major problem from a theoretical standpoint. The sultan was the religious as well as the political leader of the state, despite the conflicts with the ulema that we have seen. Similarly, the Orthodox church combined spiritual and secular duties. Moreover, the Christian and Muslim establishments had come to an understanding; they did not wage outright religious war against each other. Orthodox hatred was usually directed outward against Catholic encroachment rather than inward against the Muslims. In contrast, religion was a divisive influence in the Habsburg Empire despite the fact that Catholicism was the state religion. At the top there was perpetual tension between church and state authorities over their areas of jurisdiction, a conflict that worsened in the eighteenth century. Even more difficult was the rivalry among the major churches, the Catholic, the Protestant, and the Orthodox, particularly in the eastern lands of the monarchy. The Reformation had achieved major successes in the former Hungarian regions, including Transylvania. After the reconquest of these areas the Catholic church, with continuing Counter-Reformation zeal, tried to win back the population. The Orthodox Romanians and Serbs also became targets for conversion. Religion thus did not contribute to state strength or the union of the people.

Not only was the Habsburg Empire an assemblage of political units of varying character, but it also had an unfortunate geographic position. Until the failure of the second siege of Vienna, the Austrian rulers had to fear the activities of two expansionist powers, France and the Ottoman Empire, who were often cooperating. Thereafter, France remained a probable opponent. The Habsburg monarchs were also drawn deeply into German affairs. The Austrian rulers, in addition to their other titles, also held that of Holy Roman Emperor. This designation, which, it will be remembered, had its origins in the crowning of Charlemagne by the pope in 800, signified that the holder was the chief temporal ruler of Western Christendom. By the eighteenth century it meant little more than that the emperor was the first German prince. Vague as this position was, Habsburg interests until at least 1871 were involved primarily in Western and Central Europe, including Italy. Once the major Ottoman thrust had been blunted and that empire forced on the defensive, Austrian interest in the Eastern borderlands became secondary. The wars of the eighteenth century in the area were embarked upon with considerable reluctance. The government wished an equilibrium in the Balkans, rather than the acquisition of further territory.

POLITICAL AND SOCIAL CONDITIONS IN THE EMPIRE

During the seventeenth century the major South Slavic populations of the Habsburg Monarchy were the Croats and Slovenes. As a result of the wars at the end of the century and, in particular, of the Treaty of Karlowitz, their number was considerably increased by the addition of the non-Slavic Romanians and of the Croats and Serbs of Slavonia. In 1718, with the annexation of the Banat, more Romanians and Serbs were added. In addition, refugee Serbs who fled in the course of the wars, including those who left with Arsenije III, and Croatian Catholics, principally from Bosnia and Dalmatia, had settled in the empire. All of the new territories had formerly been a part of the Kingdom of Hungary. They were now incorporated into an empire with a political and social system which offered the population certain advantages, but in which the position of some sections of society, particularly the enserfed peasant, might in fact be worse than in the Ottoman lands.

In the eighteenth century the Habsburg Empire was ruled by four able monarchs: Charles VI (1711–1740), Maria Theresa (1740–1780), Joseph II (1780–1790), and Leopold II (1790–1792). All attempted with varying degrees of success to deal with what was to be the major problem of their state until its demise in 1918: establishing and maintaining the central power in the government and finding a basis on which to unite the diverse lands and people. This task was to prove difficult. Whereas, at least at the height of the empire, the Ottoman sultan in theory held absolute power from God over the land and the people of his domains, the Habsburg rulers had to deal with a nobility with strong traditional rights, who in turn dominated the rest of the population, which was largely an enserfed peasantry. The nobility thus undertook the tasks handled in the Ottoman Empire by the imperial bureaucracy, the Orthodox millet, and the village communities. They dominated local administration and justice, and they collected the taxes. The central government's field of activity was chiefly matters connected with foreign policy, the armed forces, and the collection of a certain number of clearly defined state taxes. The goal of the monarchs of the eighteenth century, particularly Maria Theresa and Joseph II, was to widen the powers of the central administration and to intervene directly in the affairs of the lower social classes, especially the peasantry. The attempt to establish a type of royal absolutism, similar to that of France and Prussia, was to fail largely because of the strength of the local estates, particularly in Hungary. Since most of the people with whom we are concerned, that is, the Croats, the Serbs, and the Romanians, lived in lands that belonged to the Hungarian crown, this resistance was especially significant.

Although limited in the control of internal affairs, the Habsburg monarchs had complete authority in foreign policy, including commercial relations with other countries. The emperor had full charge of negotiations with other nations: he appointed and received ambassadors; he declared war, made peace, and concluded alliances. These powers, of course, did not prevent enemy states from attempting to ally with opposition elements to subvert his rule. Other governments, for instance, France, the Ottoman Empire, and Prussia, at different times were in touch with Hungarian rebels or the noble opposition. The emperor was also supreme commander of the armed forces, although here his effectiveness was checked by the fact that he had to depend on the local estates for war taxes and recruits, in particular in the Hungarian lands, including Transylvania and Croatia. Dominated by the local nobility, these bodies attempted to keep their contributions as low as possible and to demand favors in return.

The limitations placed on the collection of taxes severely hampered the activities of the central government. The Habsburg monarchs had the use of their family fortune and the income from the Habsburg lands. They could also collect certain taxes, such as customs dues. In times of national crisis or war, however, this income was entirely inadequate. The lack of a sufficient financial base for a modern government was a major incentive for reform.

At the beginning of the eighteenth century, political power lay in the hands of the provincial nobility. In a direct relationship with the mass of the people and in complete control of the unfree peasantry, this group, when united, could effectively defy the central government. Moreover, members of the nobility held the high offices in both the state and the church. They formed the officer corps of the army. They paid either no taxes at all or a very low rate. Their legal position was separate; they could be tried only by their peers. Although in theory they were subject to the laws of the land, they had a definite advantage in court if their interests came in conflict with those of a peasant or a city dweller. They also had no set military duties, although they were under some undefined obligations of service and loyalty to the emperor. Their landholding, unlike that of the sipahis, was not tied to state service. Their real power lay in the fact that they were in effect the owners of the land, certainly in the areas with which we are concerned.

At the local level the noble completely dominated the administration. There was no equivalent to the Ottoman communal system, where elected village elders effectively took charge of their own affairs, except in the few instances that will be discussed later. Instead, the lord of the manor was the local government for the people on his land. In his territory he was responsible for the collection of taxes, the administration of justice, the maintenance of law and order, and the selection of recruits for the army. Along with the church authorities, he provided what health, educational, and general social benefits were available.

In the provinces the nobility exerted their authority through the diets. Here the largest landowners, the magnates, usually held the predominant power, although in the Hungarian diet, the control lay in the hands of the gentry. Expressing their opinions through these assemblies, the nobility considered themselves the political nation. They made decisions concerning the major affairs of their province, and they determined the relationship with the central government. The membership was composed of representatives not only of the nobility, but also of the church and sometimes of the free cities and the professions.

Those who held noble rank, a small minority of the total population, were themselves divided both by their wealth and possessions and by the origins of their titles. At the top of the scale stood the great landowners, some of whom, like the Esterházy family of Hungary, might hold millions of acres; at the other end, some who enjoyed the rank could in fact be little better than free peasants or hold no land at all. At the same time the noble who belonged to an ancient family, to the historic aristocracy, felt superior to those who had been given their titles in return for state service, or who had bought their positions. Although the central government was to an extent able to exploit these differences, the nobility, great and small, ancient or *parvenu*, tended to close ranks when their basic privileges, such as their control over the peasantry or their exemption from taxation, were brought into question.

In general, the nobility, especially the Hungarian, had only a weak conception of loyalty to the empire except where their interests were directly involved. Their prime allegiance, certainly in the regions studied here, was to their provincial centers, the Croatian, Hungarian, and Transylvanian diets, and to their "nation" understood not as an ethnic unit, but as the privileged, noble section of their society. Both the Croatian Triune Kingdom and the Hungarian kingdom predated the association with the Austrian royal house, and they held far more attractive, mystical associations for the nobles who liked to trace their origins to those more glorious times. With these feelings, the nobility naturally opposed attempts at centralization or at subordinating the "nation" to a common concept. This attitude hampered the general development of the empire both in foreign and in domestic policies. It also weakened Austria in the competition with neighboring centralized monarchies, such as France, Prussia, and Russia.

As institutions, both the Catholic and the Protestant churches identified their interests with those of the nobility of their region. Although the Habsburgs were a Catholic dynasty and did give support to that faith, the higher clergy in the provinces usually stood with the estates. The high offices were almost always held by members of aristocratic families, who naturally felt closest to the local gentry. Since the churches were also large landowners, with immense estates worked by serf labor, they too wished to preserve the basis of their wealth, which was similar to that of the nobility.

Under these circumstances the Catholic and Protestant churches were a strong force for the preservation of the status quo and the authority of the estates. They, of course, played an important role in providing education and public services, such as maintaining hospitals, orphanages, and similar charitable establishments. They were seldom, however, a force for social reform. Two other religious organizations, the Orthodox and the Uniate, were to have different attitudes, although they too never became truly revolutionary. Representing a Romanian and Serbian population, which did not have a native nobility or a representation on the diets, they were more sympathetic to change and more willing to rely on the central government.

Between the upper level of society, represented by the nobility, and the base of the dependent peasantry lay the middle ground of free peasants, artisans, merchants, officials, teachers, and others of the professional classes. The entire question of city life, commerce, and industry is considered in a further section, and the status of the free peasantry is covered in subsequent portions of this chapter. Here it will suffice to say that the development of an educated and articulate middle class is a major consideration in tracing the rise of national sentiment in all of the areas with which we are concerned.

At the bottom of the social scale lay the great mass of the population, consisting of either enserfed peasants or those with equal political and economic disabilities. Upon this group weighed the major, in fact almost the entire, burden of state and church taxation. These people also made heavy payments for the use of the land. The dependent peasant population can be divided into two groups. The first, the serfs, were not personally free. Tied to the land, they owed the landholder various payments in kind and in services, and their lives were subject to his close control. The second, who farmed the lands as tenants, were free to change their place of residence, to marry as they pleased, and to take up another occupation, choices all denied to the serf. The weakness of the tenants' position was that they held the land by agreement with the lord, who could evict them at will. The serf, in contrast, was at least assured of his plot for himself and his heirs. Of course, given the control of the nobility over local administration, both groups were subject to the desires of the predominant class.

Manorial land fell into two categories: alodial, or domenical, and urbarial, or rustical. The first was held by the lord as his full property; he could farm it himself or lease it to tenants. The labor could be provided by the serfs through their labor, or corvée, obligations, which were called *robot* in the empire, or by farm laborers paid in kind or in money. Urbarial land, in contrast, was that assigned to the peasant for his own use. These lands were subject to a heavy tax burden. Payments could be made in kind, in labor, or in money. In addition to these, the peasant owed the lord a multitude of other dues similar to those of the peasant on an estate in the Principalities, which had a similar system. The worst abuses in the Habsburg Empire appear to have been associated with the labor obligations.

In return for the payments and services, the noble in theory owed certain obligations to those under him. He should have administered local affairs and the court system justly; he was supposed to provide protection both by maintaining a police force at home and by serving himself as an officer in foreign wars. Acting with the church, he should have provided at least minimum social services. Much, of course, depended on the character of the individual noble and the attitude held toward the peasants in a given locality; conditions differed radically throughout the empire. In any event, the enserfed peasant was dependent on the ability and the good will of the landlord.

As in the Ottoman Empire, the social divisions were accepted as part of the natural order ordained by God. Church and state both taught the message that a good life is that spent in fulfilling as well as possible the function to which one is assigned. Crossing social lines was extremely difficult in both societies. This view was accepted by the peasant as well as by the lord. Peasant rebellion at first was directed not toward obtaining new rights, but against lords who were not carrying out their part of this tacit bargain and were instead encroaching on peasant prerogatives.

HABSBURG FOREIGN RELATIONS IN THE EIGHTEENTH CENTURY

Throughout the eighteenth century the hindrances and limitations placed on Habsburg state power in the international field by this social and political system were clearly apparent. The government had constant difficulties in raising money for the recurrent wars and in paying and recruiting soldiers. Austrian participation in wars with the Ottoman empire has already been discussed; the declining Ottoman state was immensely aided by the relative military weakness of its neighbor. Nevertheless, in the East the monarchy could hold its own, and in fact it did win lands at the expense of the Porte. The danger came from the other direction, from France and Prussia. At crucial periods Habsburg armies had to be removed from the Eastern battlefields to meet challenges in the West. The one long period of peace enjoyed by the Porte, from 1739 to 1768, resulted from the fact that the European powers were tied down by two great wars, the War of Austrian Succession (1740–1748) and the Seven Years' War (1756–1763). Both of these conflicts involved the question of the possession of Habsburg territories, in particular Silesia.

After his succession in 1711 Charles VI had to deal with the problem that he had no male heirs. In 1713, in order to preserve the unity of the lands of the empire and the Habsburg family interests, he promulgated the Pragmatic Sanction, which provided that the succession should go to the female line and that the empire's territorial integrity should be preserved. This change in the rules of inheritance needed the approval of the various diets and the support of the major foreign powers. Through concessions on other matters, Charles VI was able to win over the diets and to gain the support of the neighboring powers, France, Spain, Saxony, and Prussia. These governments, however, consulted together on how they could best profit from the situation.

In 1740 Charles's daughter, Maria Theresa, came to the throne. She was immediately faced with the necessity of defending her inheritance, because Frederick the Great invaded Silesia. In the general European war that followed, Austria was supported by Britain, which contributed mainly subsidies, by Holland, by some German states, and eventually by Russia. In opposition was a strong coalition including Prussia, France, Bavaria, Spain, and Saxony, all of which hoped to gain by the defeat and dismemberment of the monarchy. In the peace concluded in 1748, Austria was compelled to surrender Silesia, but otherwise the Pragmatic Sanction was upheld. Although the integrity of the empire was preserved with this one exception, Habsburg bitterness toward Prussia became extreme.

Maria Theresa at this time enjoyed the services of one of the most able diplomats of the century, Count Wenzel von Kaunitz. Judging Prussia to be the most dangerous enemy of the state, he attempted to form a diplomatic front against that power. To do this he sought to reverse the diplomatic combinations of the past and to come to an agreement with the traditional foe, France. Such a radical shift in alignments was difficult for both powers, but in May 1756 a defensive alliance was concluded. Well aware of the negotiations directed against him, Frederick II in August 1756 invaded Saxony. In this second war of the mid-century, Austria, France, and Russia, with some German states, were allied against Prussia, which was supported by Britain and other German principalities. Although the position of Prussia was often precarious, Frederick was immensely aided by the death of Empress Elizabeth of Russia and the accession of Peter III. An admirer of the Prussian king, the new tsar simply reversed the Russian alignment and joined Frederick. In 1763 the Treaty of Hubertusberg was concluded, which, as far as the Habsburg Empire was concerned, simply confirmed the loss of Silesia. Although the monarchy had thus suffered no irreparable damage, the wars had demonstrated the weakness of the state and the need for radical reform in order to face the future.

THE REFORM PERIOD: MARIA THERESA AND JOSEPH II

Until his death in 1765 Maria Theresa's husband, Francis Stephen of Lorraine, had been both co-regent and Holy Roman Emperor. After his death, his eldest son, Joseph II, held these positions and became closely associated in the formulation and implementation of the reforms. In 1780, on the death of his mother, Joseph became the sole ruler. Both Maria Theresa and Joseph were influenced by the ideas and atmosphere of the Enlightenment. The effect of these doctrines on the national movements will be examined in subsequent sections. For now the importance of these new ideas is that they directly affected the attitude of a group of rulers known as enlightened despots, which included Catherine the Great and Frederick the Great as well as the Habsburg monarchs. Although they differed on many matters, they all were convinced that it was their duty to devote their reigns to the betterment of their subjects' lives and to strengthening their states. Believing that state power should be used to achieve social progress, they favored the intervention of its agents and institutions in many phases of national life. In the Habsburg Empire their attitude was revolutionary in that they wanted to insert the authority of the central government between the feudal nobility and the great mass of the tax-burdened unfree peasantry. The state would thus stand as moderator and judge between two social classes. In no sense were the enlightened despots democratic; they did not consider lord and peasant equals. Autocratic by conviction, they were determined that the government should be controlled by themselves or their representatives. They were firm upholders of the principle of everything for the people, but nothing by the people.

Reforms were carried out both during the joint regency of Maria Theresa and Joseph and when Joseph reigned alone, although the aims and methods of the two rulers differed. Her experiences at the beginning of her reign had shown the empress that reform was a political necessity; the empire had to be strengthened so that it could meet the Prussian challenge. The military establishment had to be made stronger and its tax base widened and made more secure. The reforms were also directed at shifting the real power in the state from the local aristocracy to the central government and at creating a situation in which the agents of the monarch, an appointed bureaucracy, would be in effective control of local government. Representatives of the central government would thus replace agents of the provincial estates and diets. The nobility as a class would still have a special position in the state, but the nobles would serve the central government rather than local institutions representing their own caste. On this basis, they could also join the bureaucracy.

The reforms covered many aspects of national life: administration, justice, religion, education, economic policy, and the relationship of lord and peasant. For the Croats, Romanians, Serbs, and Slovenes of the empire, the measures concerning the peasantry, the regulation of the churches, and the steps taken to improve education were to have the most significance. These reforms are discussed here, first, as they applied to the entire empire (see Map 13), and second, as they affected the areas with which we are principally concerned.

The difficult situation of the peasantry was bound to be the first concern of a reforming government aiming at an increase of state power. The peasantry was the main source of tax income and of recruits for the army. The

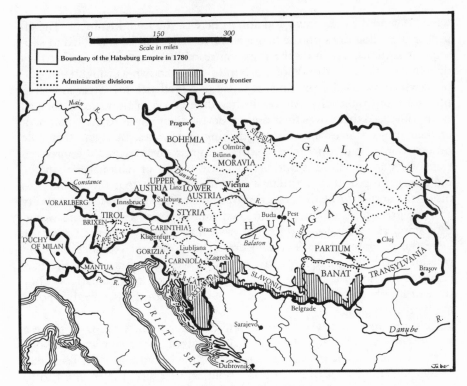

Map 13. The Habsburg Empire in 1780

central authority could not afford to see this section of the population decay. Certain measures had to be taken to assure that it could continue to play its assigned part in state life. Since noble land usually could not be taxed, it was important that the portion assigned to peasant use not be taken over by the lord. It was similarly essential that the peasant have enough land to take care of himself and his family and also to pay the state taxes. He also could not function if he were overburdened with corvée obligations and payments to the landlord, which would affect his ability to contribute to the state. The first reforms were thus directed toward establishing a uniform system and registering peasant obligations and rights. A clear division was to be made between alodial and urbarial land. The new measures were to be enforced by the central bureaucracy, responsible not to the local authorities, but to Vienna. As far as the enserfed peasant was concerned, Maria Theresa would have been willing to allow all of the peasants a free status, but she did not proceed this far. Like the other monarchs of Europe, she did not believe in equality, but accepted the divisions of society as part of a natural order. Her aim was simply to preserve the health of the lowest level and to keep for it the rights that belonged to its station.

Far more doctrinaire than his mother, Joseph II favored more radical measures. Unlike Maria Theresa, who was basically practical and conservative, he gained from his education many of the essential ideas of the Enlightenment, including the conviction that men have inherent natural rights. Although never a proponent of representative government, he did want to make all of the people of his empire, noble and peasant alike, equal citizens before the law and equally responsible to the central government. He had also traveled throughout the empire incognito, so he was aware of peasant problems, in particular, from firsthand observation. He was thus determined to strengthen the central authority and to use his power and that of the imperial bureaucracy for social and political change. His attitude made him an outspoken opponent of the nobility and their historic privileges exercised through the diets; he also criticized their freedom from taxation and their hold over the peasantry.

Soon after his mother's death, when he was freer to follow his own ideas, Joseph II moved to introduce more radical reforms, first the abolition of serfdom. This step was taken in 1785 in the Hungarian kingdom. The serf was given the rights of the tenant: he could marry at his choice, learn a trade, and leave the land if he found a replacement. The major problem, however, was not solved, since he was not given land. He still worked on his portion of the manor, and he continued to have to make high payments in kind, money, or labor obligations to hold it. In 1789 Joseph made a proposal that was intended to ease the heavy burden of taxation on this class. He wished to convert the obligations to the government and the landlord into a cash payment that would be the equivalent of about 30 percent of the peasant's income. This measure was detested not only by the nobles, but also by the peasants, who often were not in a position to face a conversion of payments in kind to those in cash.

The peasant reforms naturally antagonized the nobility; the Catholic church, whose interests as a landowner were similarly affected, objected also to other aspects of the program. Until this time it had been the major influence on education and it had not been subject to state taxation. The attempt to set up a system of state schools and to tax ecclesiastical property aroused bitter opposition. Maria Theresa was herself a devout Catholic; her desire was to extend rather than to limit the spiritual influence of the church. Nevertheless, her reign marked the establishment of a secular system of elementary schools and the founding of institutions of higher education. The new bureaucrats in the strengthened central government obviously needed a secular training. Like other enlightened despots, she had a great faith in education as a means of social and political improvement. She did not wish to damage the church, but she did regard these questions as properly under state supervision.

Her son was far more extreme in ecclesiastical matters. He sought to block completely the power of the Catholic church in areas where it came into competition with the state. His great measure here was the Toleration Patent of October 1781, which gave to Lutherans, Calvinists, and Orthodox the right to practice their religion and to construct church buildings without hindrance throughout the empire. Many of the restrictions on the Jews were also removed. This action, which did not cover religious denominations other than those mentioned, aided Protestants and Orthodox at the expense of Catholic interests. Joseph also moved against the numerous monasteries, many of whom he felt were not performing their true function of providing social services. Between 1782 and 1786 he dissolved around 700 monasteries; all of the purely contemplative orders were eliminated. In place of the monasteries, he founded new state hospitals and institutions to serve the poor, the sick, and the otherwise unfortunate.

As part of his plan to reform the administrative system of the empire, Joseph II attempted to introduce German as the language of government. This measure, whose aim was simply to make government procedures more orderly and rational, stirred up a strong reaction, particularly in the Hungarian crownlands, where Latin was normally used. Although German was the logical choice if one language were to be taken for all of the imperial lands, the issue remained a point of controversy and bitterness among all the nationalities until the dissolution of the empire.

Joseph II thus struck at two of the basic institutions of the monarchy: the provincial nobility, whose strength lay in their domination of local government and the peasantry; and the Catholic church, the most powerful ecclesiastical organization. Unfortunately, the emperor had no large segment of the population that was in a position to give him effective support. The great section of society that he hoped to benefit, the peasantry, had no political organization or experience. In fact, they tended as a group to be suspicious of change. It was soon apparent that Joseph had tried to do too much too quickly. A wave of reaction against the reforms, together with the rise of renewed difficulties abroad, forced the emperor in January 1790 to withdraw most of the changes, particularly in Hungary, but not those regarding serfdom, the Edict of Toleration, and the abolition of the monasteries. These were, of course, very important measures whose enactment had a fundamental influence on lives of the Balkan people in the empire. Joseph died soon after his forced retreat on other issues.

After his accession to the throne in 1790, Leopold II, Joseph's brother, could not devote his major attention to internal reform. The French Revolution had begun, the war with the Ottoman Empire was in progress, and within the empire both Hungary and the Netherlands were in revolt against Joseph's innovations. Leopold was not conservative himself – he had been an enlightened ruler when he was at the head of the administration of Lombardy – but he was compelled to come to terms with the opposition. In 1791 he arranged a compromise with the Hungarian diet that restored its damaged prestige and privileges. In the same year he concluded the Treaty of Sistova with the Ottoman Empire and then moved against the uprising in the Netherlands. His short reign marked the transition to a new period when Austrian concerns would be dominated by the fear of revolutionary France and when essentially conservative policies would be followed.

THE REFORMS IN PRACTICE: THE BALKAN NATIONALITIES IN THE EIGHTEENTH CENTURY

The events just recounted affected directly or indirectly all of the regions in the empire. As we have seen, the majority of the Croats, Romanians, and Habsburg Serbs lived in lands belonging to the crown of St. Stephen. Their fate was thus closely connected with that of the Hungarians and with the decisions reached in the Hungarian, Croatian, and Transylvanian diets. A large number also lived in the Military Frontier, a band of territory stretching along the border with the Ottoman Empire, which was under the direct administration of Vienna. They were affected not only by the reforming policies of the central government, but by the wars of the century with the Ottoman Empire.

Hungary, Croatia, and Slavonia

Throughout the long period of Ottoman domination, the majority of the lands inhabited by an ethnically Hungarian population were organized into a pashalik with its center at Buda. After the expulsion of the Ottoman army and administration at the end of the seventeenth century, the Hungarian nobility was determined to reestablish its control over all of the lands associated with the crown of St. Stephen and to reaffirm its predominant political position. The Hungarian strength lay not with the great landowners, the magnates, but with the lower nobility, the gentry, and their control of the counties, the basic administrative units. The counties had their own assemblies, which ran the local government and chose representatives to the diet. In 1687 this body, meeting at Pozsony (Bratislava), accepted the Habsburg emperor, Leopold I, as the hereditary king of Hungary, but only upon the assurance that historic rights and privileges would be maintained. It will be noted that the title of the Habsburg ruler in this part of his domains was *king*; the designation *emperor* applied to the territories included in the Holy Roman Empire, of which Hungary was not a part.

Thereafter, the Hungarian diet remained in opposition to centralizing pressure from Vienna. This assembly, which could be summoned by the king or the palatine, the king's representative, was divided into two chambers, the first representing the interests of the great landowners and the second representing those of the gentry. The first chamber met under the chairmanship of the palatine and was composed not only of great landowners, but also of

139

church dignitaries, headed by the Catholic primate, the archbishop of Esztergom, and the leading officials of the kingdom, including the ban of Croatia. The lower house contained the representatives chosen by the county assemblies, some delegates from the royal towns, and lower church and judicial officials. In principle, legislation had to originate in the lower chamber, but both houses had to agree on measures before they could be adopted. For the Habsburg government, which handled Hungarian affairs through the offices of the Hungarian Court Chancellery in Vienna, the control held by the diet over the levying of taxes, particularly the extra revenues needed in wartime, and over the recruitment of soldiers was extremely frustrating.

Despite the assent of the diet, the establishment of Habsburg rule in the Hungarian kingdom was a difficult process. Religious differences caused much friction. Most Hungarian nobles had joined the ranks of the Reformation; they were thus Calvinists or Unitarians, and they opposed the diligent efforts of the Catholics in the areas won back from Ottoman control. The terrible conditions caused in the countryside by the wars led to much peasant unrest. This situation, together with the continued opposition of some Hungarian nobles, led to the outbreak of a major revolt against Habsburg rule in 1703. Under the leadership of Ferenc Rákoczy, the movement combined the apparently contradictory issues of the resistance of the nobility to Vienna and the desire of the peasantry for an improvement of their status and, if possible, an end to serfdom. Noble and peasant were thus united against Habsburg rule. The situation was dangerous to the empire because both Louis XIV and Peter the Great gave their support, in order to deal a blow to a competing power. Although the Habsburg army was able to defeat the rebel forces, Charles VI in 1711 in the Peace of Szatmár was forced to accept what was in fact a compromise solution. In return for the recognition of Habsburg rule, he had to confirm again the privileges of the nobles and agree to the large measure of autonomy that the Hungarian lands held. Later the Hungarian diet accepted the Pragmatic Sanction, but only when the king recognized the indivisibility of the lands of St. Stephen; a possible Croatian or Transylvanian secession was thus blocked.

In the Treaty of Karlowitz, Slavonia and a section of Croatian territory came under Habsburg rule; Dalmatia, which had been part of the former Triune Kingdom, became a possession of Venice. The Habsburg government took the full responsibility of organizing the newly won territory despite the fact that it had belonged to the Hungarian crown before the Ottoman conquest. About half of the territory of Croatia and Slavonia was joined to the Military Frontier, under the direct administration of Vienna. The rest, known as Civil Croatia and Civil Slavonia, became two political units separated by a section of the Military Frontier. The center of Croatian political life was Civil Croatia, with its diet in Zagreb. Here the chief influence was in the hands of a middle and small nobility that was Croatian in nationality and Catholic in religion. The large landowners were both Croatian and Hungarian. As in Hungary proper, the strength of the nobility lay in their control of the counties. The Croatian nobles faced a difficult situation. They opposed domination by either Vienna or the Hungarian diet, but they wished to maintain intact their feudal privileges over their lands and serfs. The Catholic church also had a strong position in Croatia, a condition that was to have a decisive influence on relations with the Serbs.

The government of Civil Croatia was headed by the ban, or governor, who was appointed by the crown and was usually a Hungarian. The unicameral chamber, the *sabor*, was composed of the great landowners, the representatives of the lesser nobility elected on the country level, the Catholic prelates, delegates from the free towns, and some others. This body sent representatives to the Hungarian diet. Three went to the lower house, where they were seated apart, and one to the upper chamber. On the country level, as in Hungary, the highest official was nominated by the king from among the large landholders, but his deputy and other officials were selected by the county assemblies, who also chose representatives to send to the diet in Zagreb and were responsible for local administration.

The difficulty of maintaining an existence apart from Hungarian and Austrian direct control remained a major Croatian problem at all times. Unfortunately, the Croatian nobility failed to produce an outstanding national leader. In 1671, after the defeat of a conspiracy in which Ottoman assistance was sought, Fran Krsto Frankopan and Peter Zrinski were beheaded, so that the influence of two leading Croatian–Hungarian families was brought to an end. Throughout the eighteenth century the Croatian nobles, in an effort to maintain their internal autonomy and their special privileges, generally took a middle position in the quarrels between Vienna and the Hungarian opposition. During the Rákoczy revolt they supported the Habsburgs. The Croatian diet also accepted the Pragmatic Sanction, but only in return for assurances that their special rights would be protected. At this time a strong declaration on the nature of the relationship with Hungary was made: it was an equal personal union through the king, who was, of course, the Habsburg emperor:

> According to law we are a land affiliated with Hungary, and in no way a subject people of Hungary. At one time we had our own national non-Hungarian kings. No force or slavery made us subordinate to Hungary, but we through our own free will became subjects not of the Hungarian Kingdom, but of the Hungarian King. We are free and not slaves.[1]

---

1 Quoted in Elinor Murray Despalatović, *Ljudevit Gaj and the Illyrian Movement* (Boulder, Colo.: East European Quarterly, 1975), p. 11.

Despite such declarations, Charles VI, in his promise to the Hungarian diet that he recognized the integrity of the lands of St. Stephen, gave assurance that royal support would not be given to a Croatian withdrawal from the union.

The reforms of Maria Theresa and Joseph II changed aspects of the Croatian administration. In 1767 the empress introduced a new system as part of her reorganization of the empire. A Royal Council, headed by the ban, took the place of the diet as the chief office of government. Its major lasting contribution was the reorganization of the school system, including the establishment of a Royal Academy that later became the University of Zagreb. The Council, which was disliked by the nobility, was abolished in 1779, and both Civil Croatia and Civil Slavonia were placed under the Hungarian Regency Council. With this change both the ban and the Croatian sabor lost authority.

The most radical measures came in the reign of Joseph II. He abolished the county organization of the Hungarian kingdom and divided it into districts headed by officials chosen by the crown. The county assemblies ceased to function. This extreme interference in what they regarded as their legal and historical rights united the Croatian and Hungarian nobility. The landholders, large and small, strongly opposed the abolition of serfdom and the limitation of their traditional freedom from taxation; the attacks on the Catholic privileges and the monasteries aroused Croatian anger. Both the Hungarians and the Croatians opposed the substitution of German for the traditional Latin as the language of administration.

The emphasis on the protection of their class privileges explains many of the actions of the Croatian nobles in 1790. Strongly opposed to Joseph's reforms and to Austrian centralism, they surrendered much of their autonomy to the Hungarian diet. They agreed that the Croatian lands would be under a general Hungarian administrative authority and that the power of the ban and the sabor would be limited. The major political decisions were henceforth to be made, not in the Zagreb assembly alone, but in joint sessions held with the Hungarian diet. In the next years Croatian autonomy was gradually eroded; Croatian laws were made in Hungary. The chief function of the Zagreb diet was to chose representatives to the Hungarian assembly and to discuss the decisions made there. After 1790 much of the old system was reintroduced throughout the Habsburg Empire, but the shift of power in Croatia remained permanent.

Joseph's attempt to make German the language of administration had a particular significance in the Hungarian kingdom. The entire issue of the language of administration was to become a hornets' nest for the next century. Croats and Hungarians joined to oppose German, but then their interests parted. Once the question had been raised, Hungarian representatives wanted their language to be used in the kingdom. This solution would have been extremely unfavorable for the Croats, few of whom knew Magyar, and would naturally have limited their participation in the Hungarian diet and their holding of state offices. The joint diet of 1791 kept Latin, but agreed that Hungarian would be a required subject in the schools of Hungary proper and an elective in Croatia and Slavonia.

The situation in Civil Slavonia differed in many respects from that in Civil Croatia, which enjoyed more privileges and rights of autonomous rule. After the termination of the Ottoman domination the Slavonian lands were devastated and depopulated. Until 1745 they were under a dual military–civilian government that devoted great efforts to resettling the province and restoring its prosperity and productivity. In seeking to develop the area the Habsburg government gave or sold large estates to nobles, government officials, merchants, and others – men who were usually German or Hungarian. Some lands were granted to German settlers who had the status of free peasants. Other peasants moved in from other Croatian lands or from across the Ottoman border. The basic difference between Civil Croatia and Civil Slavonia can be seen in the fact that there were approximately 9,000 nobles in Croatia, but only 314 in Slavonia. A land of large estates and a small noble class of a mixed national background, Slavonia nevertheless shared many of the problems of neighboring Croatia. In 1745, with the establishment of a purely civilian administration, some territory was assigned to the Military Frontier and to Hungary, but the greater part was divided into three counties. As elsewhere, these were the basic units of local government; their assemblies sent delegates to both the Croatian and the Hungarian diets. Despite this organization, the Slavonian status in the empire was in fact hazy; the province certainly did not claim the same position as Croatia.

Most of the inhabitants of Croatia and Slavonia were, of course, peasants who had the same problems as those of their status in other parts of the Hungarian kingdom. Although conditions on the estates differed widely, in general, the serf or tenant was under the obligations that have been discussed elsewhere. He paid dues and labor services to his landlord, the state, and the church. For the use of a plot sufficient to support himself and his family, he surrendered from a tenth to a fourth of his produce; he was also obligated to work at least one or two days a week on the lord's land and to perform transport services with his cart and oxen if he had any. He owed, in addition, the many other taxes and payments common to the time. His landlord controlled not only the land, but the local administration, including the police and the judicial system. The lord of the manor, in the role of judge, could hand out sentences, including fines and corporal punishment. He also, before the administrative reforms, collected the state taxes. The abuses possible in such a system are obvious.

An attempt at peasant reform was made by Charles VI, who, however, was discouraged by strong noble opposition. The first major measure was the regulation of 1756, known as an urbarium, which came into effect in Slavonia in 1762. Its provisions give an excellent picture of the conditions under which the peasant labored. They have been described as follows:

> The basic obligations of the serfs in Slavonia were the payment of a tithe of three florins and the rendering of 24 days of *corvée* with a team of draft animals, or 48 days of manual *corvée*, per homestead. *Corvée* with a team of draft animals and manual *corvée* could, under certain circumstances, be paid in money, with a standard wage of 20 kreutzers for the former and 10 kreutzers for the latter per day. If the landlord needed additional labor, he paid the serfs a standard wage (24 and 12 kreutzers per day, respectively) . . . Agricultural workers without land, but owning a house, paid a tithe of one florin annually and rendered 12 days of manual *corvée*.[2]

A homestead, or basic plot of land, was defined as approximately thirty-four, forty-six, or fifty-seven acres (twenty-four, thirty-two, or forty yokes), depending on the quality of the soil.

Under this regulation the landlords retained important rights, including those of hunting and fishing and of maintaining taverns and butcher shops. They were responsible for the police and justice; they could punish their serfs "by imposition of various fees, beatings, and irons, and sometimes even capital punishment."[3] The peasant was also liable to labor services on public works, as well as his payments to church and state. The provisions dealing with payments for land usage were to remain in effect until 1848 with only some changes.

An urbarium for Croatia was issued in 1780, but its conditions were more stringent for the peasant:

> A full homestead in Croatia amounted to between 14 and 24 yokes of arable land and 6 to 8 yokes of meadows, depending on the quality of the soil. The *corvée* amounted to 52 days annually with a team of draft animals or 104 days of manual work per full homestead, of which 45½ days had to be actually rendered, while the remainder could be paid in money. Serfs with smaller farms had to render proportionately smaller amounts of *corvée*. The tithe in money in Croatia was only one florin per homestead, but the serfs in Croatia, unlike those in Slavonia, had to deliver to the landlord a tithe in produce – a ninth of all crops, wine and livestock. There was also a special tax on houses. If the landlord and the serf agreed, both *corvée* and the

2 Jozo Tomasevich, *Peasants, Politics, and Economic Change in Yugoslavia* (Stanford, Calif.: Stanford University Press, 1955), pp. 71–72.
3 Tomasevich, *Peasants, Politics, and Economic Change*, p. 72.

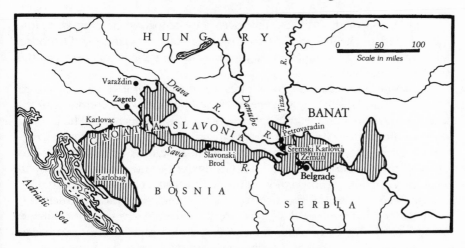

Map 14. The Habsburg Military Frontier

tithe in produce could be paid in money. Furthermore, the serfs were obligated to render to the landlords a couple of capons, a couple of chickens, a dozen eggs, and a quantity of butter per full homestead annually. They were also obligated to render transportation services to the landlord.[4]

Individual serfs in both Slavonia and Croatia could leave their lands if they fulfilled their obligations and if the lord agreed.

The reforms of Joseph II, including the emancipation of the serfs of 1785 and the unsuccessful attempts to limit the peasant payments to around 30 percent of their income, also affected Croatia and Slavonia. After his death, peasant reform languished. The next major changes were not to be made until the revolution of 1848.

The Military Frontier

By the end of the seventeenth century the Habsburg Empire had acquired a large Serbian population concentrated in the Banat and southern Hungary, but also in the lands of the Military Frontier (see Map 14). During the long period when the Habsburg and Ottoman empires shared a common frontier there was constant movement across the borders. The largest single migration occurred with the immigration of Arsenije III and his followers, but individuals and groups were always able to enter the monarchy with relative ease. Although the majority were Serbs, some were Croats, principally from Bosnia. Serbian merchants and craftsmen formed a strong element in the cities, but the majority of refugees were peasants, many of whom constituted

---

4 Tomasevich, *Peasants, Politics, and Economic Change*, pp. 72–73.

the population of the Military Frontier. The occupation of large areas formerly a part of the Triune Kingdom by a Serbian population of Orthodox faith was to have a lasting effect on the area and on the relations between the Croats and the Serbs.

The border between the two empires was difficult for each to hold and to garrison. The Habsburg government, as we have seen, had continual problems raising money and recruiting soldiers for war. An open area, the frontier region suffered from frequent raids organized on both sides. Ottoman irregulars led periodic expeditions to seize the inhabitants to sell as slaves or to carry off their livestock and produce. Groups of bandits, operating freely in a lawless environment, preyed on both the Ottoman and the Habsburg population. The problem of maintaining peaceful conditions was extremely difficult. Neither empire could afford to keep the area under constant military occupation. In the early sixteenth century the Habsburg government began to make use of the transient, unruly population. In return for a guarantee of the free exercise of the Orthodox religion and the use of a plot of land, some of these men agreed to settle as military colonists. They protected the frontier region, but they supported themselves. The state also erected a line of fortified villages and outposts that were manned by these settlers and a few professional soldiers. The colonists elected their own military commanders (*vojvodas*) and their village elders (knezes). Two administrative centers were established: Karlovac for the Croatian Military Frontier and Varaždin for the Slavonian. In the sixteenth century the frontier was extended to the Adriatic, with Karlobag as the headquarters. The expenses of the border defense, such as the provision of guns and ammunition, were carried by the Inner Austrian authorities. Karlovac was under Carinthia and Carniola; Varaždin under Styria.

In 1630 the Habsburg government issued a charter, called the Statuta Valachorum (Vlach Statutes), which formally established the conditions for the area. The Military Frontier was put directly under the control of the emperor; the land thus remained in the possession of the state. It was granted in return for military service, not to individuals but to household communities, zadrugas, which were considered the best basic unit of organization in a difficult and dangerous time. Each zadruga was expected to provide one soldier, and they were collectively responsible for the obligations to the state. The zadrugas were joined in villages, which elected their own leaders, the vojvodas and the knezes; these, along with the Habsburg officials, were responsible for local administration. The members of the border communities thus enjoyed much self-government. The similarities with the political organization within the Ottoman Empire are obvious. The Habsburg government also gave assurances to the Serbian population in regard to the Orthodox church.

The Military Frontier was advantageous to the state in that it provided a cheap source of manpower to garrison the border. The frontier soldier was not paid a salary, but was supported by his family. For the settlers the conditions were much superior to those in the adjoining provinces, where the peasants also usually wanted to join the frontier. The soldier was not a serf; he was a free man living in a self-administering community, and he was proud of his status.

The frontier organization, nevertheless, caused problems of its own. The chief source of friction was the constant conflict with the Croatian diet. As the Austrian border moved forward into former Ottoman lands, the Croatian nobility naturally expected to gain control of them and to reimpose the feudal order of preconquest days. Instead, the Habsburg government took possession of the territory and organized it for its own profit. Although a border area was set up under the ban of Croatia, it did not function as well as or have the significance of the frontier under direct imperial control. Problems were also caused by the Catholic church, which constantly opposed the special status given to the Orthodox. The Inner Austrian administration, which was supposed to provide support, proved reluctant to assume any heavy expenses.

Although conditions on the land within the military confines were better than those outside, there was certainly no economic prosperity, despite some Habsburg efforts to improve conditions. The region remained one of the poorest of the empire. Problems of corruption and inefficiency plagued the military establishment. In addition, as a soldier the frontier peasant was difficult to control and discipline. At first he had been able to collect booty, and he continued to plunder even friendly territories. Frontier bands were also subject to frequent mutiny and desertion.

Reforms introduced during the reign of Maria Theresa were designed to subject this border population to more discipline and control. The soldiers were organized into regiments attached to definite districts. Restrictions were imposed on their right to elect officials, and a tighter organization was introduced. In 1754 a series of regulations was introduced, which further limited self-government. The only settlers to be allowed in the region were to be the peasant soldiers and those directly connected with the frontier organization. The land remained the property of the government; the zadrugas received allotments to support one or more soldiers. Officers, but not regular soldiers, were paid. Some military communities, such as Petrovaradin (Peterwardein), Zemun (Semlin), Slavonski Brod, and Sremski Karlovci, had populations that included merchants and artisans; they paid their obligations to the state in money and were excused from military service.

The Military Frontier was by this time expected to provide men to fight all over Europe and not just on the border. In time of peace the frontier peasant also had to provide services. He was subject to labor obligations on the fortifications, and he was expected to help in the suppression of bandits. One of his important duties was the maintenance of the quarantine. Because of the prevalence of the plague and other dangerous, communicable diseases in the Ottoman Empire, the Habsburg government kept a strict quarantine along the frontiers. Travelers entering the monarchy were forced to remain in seclusion for up to three weeks, and all letters and goods were disinfected by the primitive means of the time.

Throughout the eighteenth century pressure continued from both the Croatian and the Hungarian diets to gain control of the region. Discontent and unrest was also apparent among the frontier soldiers. Because of the resentment arising out of the fact that most of the officers were German, a regulation issued in 1754 provided that two-thirds of the commissions were to go to military colonists, with the preference given to Catholics or Uniates. An officer class thus was created from the Slavic population. Despite the many criticisms, both from the Croatian diet and from within the colonies, the frontier remained intact until 1881. The area contained approximately half the territory and over 40 percent of the population of the historic provinces of Croatia and Slavonia, and was linked with similar frontier organizations in the Banat and Transylvania.

As we have seen, the center of Croatian political life was Civil Croatia, an area where the local administration was in the hands of a Croatian nobility. At the end of the eighteenth century this group voluntarily surrendered most of its autonomy to the Hungarian diet, which was dominated by the Hungarian gentry. The move was a result of fear that centralizing reforms from Vienna would deprive the privileged classes of their special position, including their immunity from taxation and their control over the peasantry. The Catholic church gave support to this attitude and fought bitterly against measures such as Joseph II's Toleration Edict. The Military Frontier caused further friction. The Croatian diet continually opposed the fact that the central government administered territories that had historically been associated with the Triune Kingdom and that were vitally important to the Croatian national position. The settlement of large numbers of Serbs was an issue at this time only in regard to their Orthodox faith. The predominant influence in Croatia was intensely conservative, both in politics and in religion, throughout the period.

The Serbs

The Serbian population of the empire lived in circumstances quite different from those of the majority of the inhabitants of the Habsburg Empire. They controlled no definite portion of territory, and they were of the Orthodox religion, which was under attack in other parts of the monarchy. Nevertheless, they had certain privileges that set them apart and put them in a better position than some of the peasant populations of other ethnic origins. Their relatively favorable status rested on the special privileges granted by Leopold I in 1690 at the time of the migration of Arsenije III and his adherents. It will be remembered that the Serbian refugees were promised freedom of religion and an autonomous church administration. The situation that subsequently developed showed many similarities with the millet system in the Ottoman Empire. The Serbian Orthodox citizens enjoyed their privileges wherever they settled; their rights were not dependent on a territorial base. As in the Ottoman Empire, the church dignitaries became in practice the leaders of a kind of Serbian secular government, with a Serbian metropolitan, established at Sremski Karlovci, at its head. The regular meetings of the councils came to resemble national assemblies. They were held primarily to choose bishops and the heads of monasteries, but they also discussed general problems and matters of interest to the Serbian community. They could hear complaints and make protests. The strong lay element that we have seen in the church under Ottoman rule was also present here; representation in the assemblies reflected the entire Serbian community. After 1749 the membership included the bishops, twenty-five representatives from the clergy, twenty-five from the Military Frontier, and twenty-five from other territories and towns with a Serbian population.[5]

With the suppression of Peć, Sremski Karlovci became the foremost Serbian Orthodox ecclesiastical and educational center. This Metropolitanate was in a far stronger financial position than the other Slavic Orthodox institutions in either the Ottoman Empire or the Habsburg Monarchy. The city acquired impressive buildings in the baroque style, and the first Serbian schools of higher education were established there. Since great reliance was placed on theologians sent from Kiev, Russian influence was strong. The literary language at this time was the so-called Slavo-Serbian, an artificial creation close to Church Slavic, but not to the speech of the common people. As within the Ottoman Empire, the church kept alive the memory of the medieval Serbian empire; its past history was idealized and made glorious. Church painting and literature similarly recalled the past. The cultural activities of the Metropolitanate were backed by the work done in the monasteries of the Fruška Gora.

Despite the advantages that it enjoyed, the Serbian church was naturally not satisfied with what was a secondary status in a state that was predominantly Catholic; the political situation was also unsatisfactory. When Arsenije and his followers left the Serbian lands, they had expected their stay in the Habsburg Empire to be of short duration. They hoped to return with the victorious Austrian army. As years passed and the frontier stabilized, it was to be expected that the Serbian population would press for a special territory and a recognized secular administration. The question of a national area was almost impossible to settle. It could only have been carved out of Hungarian or Croatian lands and accomplished at the expense of these people. The recognition of a civil government brought up similar problems. Despite these differences, in general the Serbian population preferred to cooperate with the

5   Vladimir Dedijer et al., *History of Yugoslavia*, trans. Kordija Kveder (New York: McGraw-Hill, 1975), p. 237.

central authority. Serbian privileges depended upon the protection of Vienna. When this was not given, the Orthodox Serbs could not withstand Catholic Croatian and Hungarian pressure.

By the end of the eighteenth century Serbian colonies were present not only in the countryside, but in the cities. Like the Greek merchants, Serbian traders had by this time become an important element in the commerce of the monarchy. Although they often succeeded in gaining wealth, their Orthodox faith proved a definite hindrance to their activities. They were usually not eligible to buy property or to become full members of the city community. The prohibition on acquiring property held for the Orthodox in both Civil Croatia and Civil Slavonia, as well as in other regions.

Nevertheless, the Serbian population of the monarchy, organized under the Orthodox church and in possession of definite privileges, by the end of the century had established a strong position and had a community of different social levels. The merchants, the Orthodox clergy, the teachers, and the officers of the Military Frontier formed an upper class. The peasant-soldier of the Military Frontier was not only a free man, but one who had gained considerable experience in fighting. The Orthodox church was more than a religious institution. It formed a substitute for secular leadership, and it preserved the memory of Serbian statehood.

Transylvania

Political conditions   After the Ottoman conquest in the sixteenth century, Transylvania was given wide autonomous rights, surpassing in practice those of Wallachia and Moldavia, which had a similar status within the empire. The Transylvanian princes often conducted an independent foreign policy. They waged war and were in direct contact with other governments through their representatives. In governing the province the prince was assisted by a council of twelve and the diet. By the end of the sixteenth century there were three recognized "nations," the Hungarians, the Szeklers, and the Saxons, and four religions, Catholic, Lutheran, Calvinist, and Unitarian. The Hungarians, as we have seen, had arrived in Transylvania in the tenth century, and the area became part of the Kingdom of Hungary. The Szeklers, who were closely related to the Hungarians and spoke their language, followed later; they were at first border guards and free landholders. The Saxons were German immigrants from the Rhineland who had come in the twelfth century. Both the Szeklers and the Saxons had received charters from the king of Hungary confirming their privileges and granting them self-government in the areas where they settled. The Szeklers were to be found primarily in the eastern Carpathians; the Saxons in the area between the cities of Braşov (Kronstadt) and Sibiu (Hermannstadt), with another center around Bistriţa (Bistritz) (see

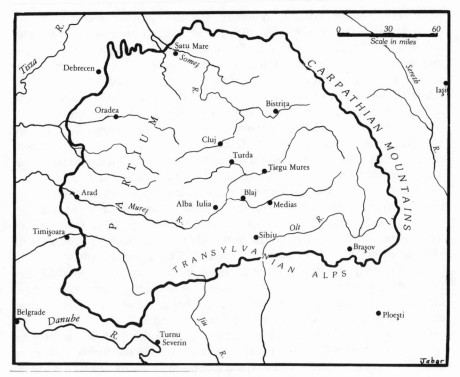

Map 15. Transylvania

Map 15). Cluj (Kolozsvár, Klausenburg), the largest city of Transylvania, was largely Hungarian by the eighteenth century.

The religious divisions in the province were also significant. The Reformation made considerable progress among the Hungarian nobility, who saw it as a movement directed against the Habsburgs. It was also accepted by the Saxons, who became Lutherans. The Hungarians were henceforth both Calvinist and Lutheran; the Szeklers, Catholic, Lutheran, and Unitarian. By the end of the sixteenth century the Protestant churches had an equal status in the province with the Catholics and representation on the diet. The four recognized, or received, religions were thus the Catholic, Lutheran, Calvinist, and Unitarian. The clergy of these faiths all enjoyed the position and privileges of the nobility.

In general, the province was organized much as the other lands of the Hungarian crown. The nobility through their county organizations and their position on the diet dominated the political life of the country and held control over an enserfed peasantry. The Saxon territory, known as the *Fundus Regius*, or *Königsboden* (Royal Land), had certain special institutions. It was governed by a count and an assembly known as the *Nationsuniversität*. This body chose the candidate to be count, but the nomination had to be approved by the king. Recognizing that they were but a small minority in Transylvania, the Saxons were extremely jealous of their autonomy. Hungarians and Romanians were not allowed to hold property in their territory, nor could they marry Saxons. The privileged group consisted not only of the noble landowners, but also of the peasant farmers and the city inhabitants. The Saxon cities, in particular Braşov, were major commercial centers.

The political and religious organization left completely out of the picture the Romanian population and the Orthodox church, that is, the majority of the people in Transylvania in the eighteenth century. Occupying no particular area, Romanians were to be found in all of the regions controlled by the privileged nations. The weakness of the Romanian position lay primarily in the fact that the population consisted almost entirely of enserfed peasants who worked on Hungarian, Szekler, or German estates. A Romanian nobility, representing scarcely 1 percent of this class, tended to cooperate with its Hungarian equals. In no part of the empire did a serf population play a political role. In Transylvania the term *nation* referred to the political "nation" of the privileged orders; it was not an ethnic designation. Hungarian, German, and Szekler peasants were scarcely better off than their Romanian counterparts, except that they belonged to accepted religions.

Certainly the Romanians' adherence to the Orthodox faith was to prove a handicap to their political and social position. Unlike the Serbs, with their cultural center of Sremski Karlovci, the Romanians had not received a special charter or guaranteed privileges. A Metropolitanate was established at Alba Iulia, which was under the jurisdiction of the metropolitan of Ungro-Valachia in Bucharest. It could, however, offer little practical support to its members.

As an autonomous principality under Ottoman sovereignty, Transylvania had been subject to a tribute, which had at first been ten thousand florins and then had been raised, and to a number of other payments. However, it had never been reduced to a pashalik, nor had the Ottoman land system been applied. As in Moldavia and Wallachia, the native nobility remained in control, and it was highly sensitive about its rights and privileges. In 1688, after the defeat of the Ottoman armies, the diet declared an end to Ottoman rule. As elsewhere, the transition to Habsburg rule was not easy. The nobility feared that the existing political system would be disturbed. In 1691 Leopold I issued a charter confirming the continuation of the system of government based on the three nations and the four religions; the old laws and institutions were thus preserved intact. A regular contribution to the empire was agreed upon, but any supplementary taxes would need the approval of the diet. Similar arrangements were made concerning the military. Henceforth, Transylvania was considered one of the Hungarian crownlands, although it preserved its autonomous position.

Transylvania thus entered the Habsburg Empire with assurances that its unique organization would be kept. At the head of the province stood the institution of the *gubernium*, consisting of a president and twelve councilors, whose members were drawn equally from the recognized nations and religions. The diet was composed of a single chamber, which included representatives from the Saxon, Hungarian, and Szekler districts; the high officials of the church and state; and delegates nominated by the crown. These last appointments enabled the central government to exert influence within the province. Since voting was done by estates, each measure had to have the approval of all three nations. In Vienna, the Transylvanian Aulic Council supervised the affairs of the principality.

The Uniate and Orthodox churches   In governing Transylvania the Habsburg government soon faced difficulties similar to those in other lands of the Hungarian crown. However, the existence of the mass of Orthodox peasants, without political or religious rights, offered the central authorities certain welcome opportunities to attempt to strengthen their position. The major opposition to Habsburg control of Transylvania came from the local Hungarian nobility, which was largely Protestant. In the Transylvanian diet the majority was also Protestant. It would obviously be to the advantage of the state should there appear a large group of new converts to Catholicism who would be dependent on Vienna and in opposition to the Hungarian nobility. Moreover, many responsible Habsburg statesmen agreed with the premise popular at the time of the Reformation that it was preferable for a people to have the same religion as their ruler. The missionary zeal of the Catholic church supported this idea. The Jesuit order was back in Transylvania in 1693.

The only obvious large group that might be converted was the Orthodox Romanian. The situation of the Orthodox church was extremely dangerous. Deprived of an adequate source of income, since they could not levy a tithe, the local clergy were dependent on the fees they could collect for services and donations from a congregation that already was forced to pay a tax to the recognized church with jurisdiction in their region. The priest often had to earn his living by working as a serf or tenant on the land of a noble. The Protestant organizations had previously and unsuccessfully tried to make converts here. They had, however, made the mistake of attacking those forms of religion, such as the veneration of ikons, the fasts, and the observance of numerous holidays, that were close to the heart of the Orthodox peasant. Moreover, conversion to a Protestant church offered no social or political advantages. The Romanian, whether he abandoned his faith or not, would remain without political rights or representation.

In seeking converts at the end of the seventeenth century, the Catholics used more subtle methods. They concentrated on winning converts not to Catholicism, but to the Uniate, or Greek Catholic, church. The conditions for membership were simple; very little change in doctrine was required for the Orthodox. The convert had only to agree to the four articles of the Council of Florence of 1439, which had been called to attempt to reunite the two great branches of the Christian religion. These included the recognition of the pope as the head of the church, the acceptance of the descent of the Holy Spirit from both the Father and the Son, and belief in the existence of purgatory.[6] The Orthodox could thus keep much of their faith; the liturgy and canon law were left untouched. The Uniate church made a great effort to win over in particular the Orthodox clergy, whose position was indeed difficult and humiliating. Its members were offered at least a chance of gaining the position held by their equivalents in the recognized institutions.

The attractions of the new church proved overwhelming to a majority of the Orthodox clergy, who accepted it in the hope of bettering their personal situations and of winning at least a semblance of equality with the Catholics. The union was accepted in 1697 in a synod held at Alba Iulia under Metropolitan Teofil. After his death, his successor, Atanasie Anghel, completed the negotiations. In return for the acceptance of the Act of Union of 1698 by the former Orthodox clergy, Leopold I issued a decree, the Diploma of 1699, which made the union legal and gave to the Uniate clergy the rights and privileges of the Catholics. The priests were freed from labor services and tithes. In 1700 a general synod of the church accepted the articles of Florence. Leopold I then issued a second decree in which he renewed his previous assurances. Atanasie was placed at the head of the Uniate organization. Despite their expectations and Leopold's decrees, the Uniate clergy did not obtain a position of equality with representatives of the recognized religions. Their activities were carefully watched, and an official was assigned to supervise them.

The Uniate church became in fact a target for attack from all sides. The privileged nations and religions understood the Habsburg motives in encouraging the conversion. Moreover, the move did have the potential of upsetting the balance of political life in Transylvania. Should the Romanians be in a position to claim equality on the basis of religion, the dominance of the three recognized nations would be threatened. It must be remembered that the Romanians were in the majority throughout the entire province.

Strong opposition also came from the Orthodox establishments both within and without the empire. The metropolitan at Sremski Karlovci, the major Orthodox center of the monarchy, denounced the Uniate church. The patriarchs of Jerusalem and Constantinople, the metropolitan in Bucharest, the Romanian princes, and the Russian clerics all attacked its actions. What was decisive, however, was the fact that the mass of Orthodox peasantry preferred to remain with their old faith. Even though the Habsburg government actively aided the Uniates – in fact, acted as if all the Romanian Orthodox had shifted – the movement did not command widespread enthusiastic support. Some joined simply for convenience, but kept their basic Orthodox loyalties.

---

6 For a discussion of the Council of Florence see Runciman, *The Great Church*, pp. 103–111.

In practice, the two churches had some conflicts, but they also cooperated. Both the Orthodox and the Uniate churches had as the majority of their members peasants to whom differences of doctrine were unintelligible or who were indifferent to these issues.

The basic reason for the weakness of the Uniate movement was probably the failure of the recognized religions to accept this church as an equal. The Hungarian clergy, as has been mentioned, identified their interests with those of the Hungarian nobility, who opposed an increase of Habsburg or Romanian influence. The movement did have, nevertheless, certain unexpected, positive results for the Romanians. The Habsburg officials offered encouragement to the Uniates' educational efforts, since they felt such endeavors would increase the influence of the organization. As a result, the Uniate church became the center of a Romanian intellectual revival that had a profound effect not only on Transylvania, but also within the Principalities. The Romanian national ideology for the next century was shaped by the work of what came to be known as the Transylvanian School. It enunciated and propagated the idea of Romanian national equality, which was justified on a historical basis. The work was begun by an extremely able bishop of the Uniate church, Ioan Inochentie Clain (Klein, Micu), who was in office from 1729 to 1751. His objective was to achieve an equal position in the province for both the clergy and the lay members of his church. He felt that the best method by which to achieve this goal was the acceptance of the conditions of union and the fulfillment of Leopold's decrees. He also believed in working through and cooperating with the central government. Between 1730 and 1744 he sent twenty-four petitions to Vienna.

Clain's program is important both for the goals that he sought to achieve and the arguments that he used. He worked for political rights, that is, the recognition of the Romanians as a fourth nation with an equal position in the diet, and also for peasant reforms. He supported a radical modification in the position of the serfs, claiming that they should be allowed freedom of movement and that they should be able to acquire an education or learn a trade. The corvée, he contended, should be set at two days a week. His ideas were thus similar to those of the reforming monarchs. To justify his demands, Clain argued not only that the Romanians were the majority in the province, the group who paid the most taxes, but also that they had lived continuously in Transylvania longer than the Hungarians or the Saxons. The doctrine of historical continuity was to be the intellectual basis of future national programs and was to cause much controversy between Romanian and Hungarian historians and propagandists.

The ideas expressed by Clain were thus of extreme importance for the future national conflicts. In his writing he claimed that the Romanians of Transylvania were the direct descendants of the Roman settlers, and thus the heirs of ancient Rome. He argued that the Roman legions had completely annihilated the Dacians, the previous inhabitants, and had then settled the area with colonists from Rome and Italy. In 270, when the Roman armies had been forced to withdraw, only the soldiers and administrators had moved across the Danube; the farmers had remained. During the long period of turmoil that followed, this Roman population retreated to the hills and mountains, only to return in more tranquil times. When the Hungarians conquered Transylvania, they found a Romanian government under the leadership of Duke Gelu. After he was killed, the Romanians chose the Hungarian leader, Tuhutum, as their ruler. The union was, nevertheless, on an equal basis. The Romanian position declined only later, when the people were illegally deprived of rights that had been previously guaranteed. As can be seen, Clain's arguments rested not only on the idea of the prior occupancy of the area, but also on the pure Roman stock of the colonists. It will be remembered that, in fact, the Roman settlers came principally from the Balkan lands, and the Romans did intermarry with Dacians, who were not destroyed. Nevertheless, despite certain misconceptions in it, Clain's doctrine served an important national purpose in that it gave the Romanians an ancestry that could be considered superior to that of the Hungarians, Slavs, and Germans. In an age when historic rights and lineage were of prime significance, this argument was very effective.

Not only did the Uniate leaders support programs in the Romanian interest, but their church made great efforts to improve the education available to their supporters. Blaj became the center of Romanian cultural activities. A printing press was established, which produced its first book in 1753, and a secondary school was opened in 1754. Aided by Catholic institutions outside the province, Romanian students were able to go to Rome or Vienna to study. This group of educated clergy, although small in number, supplied the Romanian population with an articulate, active group of intellectuals who were to play a major part in the subsequent national movement in Transylvania. The doctrines they supported and publicized were to be the national program both in their own province and in Moldavia and Wallachia.

The reforms in Transylvania   As in the areas previously discussed, the reforms introduced by Maria Theresa and Joseph II in Transylvania affected chiefly the status of the peasantry, the organization of the administration, and the churches. The peasant question is of principal importance to our account because the Romanians formed the major component of the serf population. In all of Transylvania in the eighteenth century, the nobility constituted a small percentage of the inhabitants, 4.4 percent at the beginning of the century and 6.7 percent by 1867. Of the peasantry, the majority, 73.2 percent, were serfs, and 20.5 percent were free peasants. Among the remainder, a large percentage were migrant workers.[7] Like others in their category in other parts

---

7 Constantin Daicoviciu and Miron Constantinescu, eds., *Brève histoire de la Transylvanie* (Bucharest: Editions de l'académie, 1965), p. 143.

of the empire, the serfs were subject to high payments to the state, the church, and their landholders. In addition, the Orthodox were compelled to contribute to religious institutions of which they were not members. As elsewhere, the corvée obligations caused the most discontent. In 1714 the diet set the rate at the high level of four days a week for all members of a serf family. It will be noted that the feudal burdens were higher in Transylvania than in Wallachia or Moldavia. In 1769 an urbarium issued for Transylvania, known as Certa Puncta, placed the limit at four days, or three if the peasant provided his own animals. The reforms, which paralleled those in other parts of the monarchy, suffered from the disadvantage of being easy for a nobility who controlled the local administration to disobey.

The land question was further affected by the measures taken by the central government to extend the Military Frontier into Transylvania in 1762. The move was made from political rather than military considerations. The frontier zone would give the imperial government a firm base from which to control the local nobility; advantages were also expected in that the area would be the source of taxes and soldiers. The establishment of the frontier, however, was not easy. The Slavonian and Croatian zones had been set up on lands that had been devastated and depopulated; there was also a clear need to defend the area from the danger of attack from across the border, if only from lawless bands. In contrast, the border zones of Transylvania were heavily populated, particularly the Saxon lands; there was no fear of an attack from the Principalities. Nevertheless, despite the strong objections of the local aristocracy, two Romanian and three Szekler regiments were formed and settled in villages running along the frontier with the Danubian Principalities.

As in the other border areas, the conditions for the peasant soldiers were considerably better than those for the serfs and tenants on the neighboring estates. The local peasants pressed to join the frontier settlements. The Romanians, in particular, found themselves in a better situation. At first, the Habsburg authorities sought to settle only Uniates, but they soon also tolerated Orthodox soldiers. In the military colonies the Romanians were on an equal level with the other nationalities, and they were not subject to the dues and labor obligations that were at such a high level in Transylvania.

Although there were repeated small-scale actions of resistance among the enserfed peasantry throughout the century, the largest uprising originated in connection with the Military Frontier. Catherine the Great and Joseph II, it will be remembered, in the 1780s formulated ambitious plans for the partition of the Ottoman Empire. In preparation for war a decree was issued in 1784 registering villages in the frontier zone. Since the peasants thought that this measure applied to the entire country, large numbers of villages attempted to join the frontier establishment. As soldiers the peasants would escape serfdom and be freed of labor dues. When the local nobility attempted to stop the movement, the peasants organized and prepared to resist.

A major revolt in which the peasant participants expressed centuries of bitter grievance broke out under the leadership of three men named Horea, Cloşca, and Crişan. As in all such uprisings, atrocities were committed on both sides. Manor houses were burned, and there were high casualties. At first, the revolt was extremely successful; the rebels gained control of a wide area of Transylvania, and the nobility were thoroughly terrified. Emphasizing their loyalty to the emperor, the rebels declared that the uprising was directed against the Transylvanian estates. Their program was extremely radical for the time; it called not only for the end of serfdom and the establishment of social equality, but also for the division of the lands of the estates. Despite the declarations of loyalty, the Habsburg government had to take action. Since it was at first unable to suppress the movement by force, it undertook negotiations with the rebel leaders. The army was then sent against the peasant forces, which were completely crushed. Two of the leaders, Horea and Cloşca, were publicly executed by quartering as an example to their former followers.

Although the revolt was suppressed with great severity, Joseph II had a complete investigation made of the affair. The emperor was himself well aware of the bad conditions in Transylvania, since he had traveled there incognito in 1773, 1783, and 1786. His commission of inquiry placed the blame for the uprising on the exploitation of the peasantry. In 1785 he issued a decree ending serfdom and, as in other areas, granting the peasant personal freedom and allowing him to move if he had fulfilled his obligations. The burning question, a limitation of labor dues, was not settled. In 1791 and 1792 the diet recognized the abolition of serfdom, but the peasant had to give five months' notice before leaving the estate and he had to find a replacement.

Joseph's radical reforms had perhaps greater significance for Transylvania than for the other regions that have been discussed. Both his peasant measures and his attacks on the political and religious privileges of the entrenched estates shook the entire system. His attitude on religious tolerance was a great benefit to the Orthodox church. The first of the recognized nations to be dealt a real blow was the Saxons. In 1781 Joseph issued a decree on *Concivilität*, or equality of citizenship, which ended the exclusive rights of the Germans and granted an equal position to all of the inhabitants of the Saxon territory. Romanians and Hungarians, like Germans, could now acquire property and enter guilds. The action, which struck at the roots of German privilege, showed that the emperor was no German nationalist despite his desire to introduce German as the language of administration.

In 1784 Joseph II proceeded to a radical reorganization of the Transylvanian political structure. As elsewhere, he eliminated the counties, which were the base of noble power, and substituted new divisions headed by officials who were chosen by and responsible to Vienna. The administrative boundaries were drawn without reference to historic or national considerations. All were to be equal in the province, but German was to be the language of government.

The Edict of Toleration, issued in 1781, was to have a particularly beneficial effect on the Orthodox church. The act allowed freedom of worship in private homes and the building of churches and schools where more than a hundred families subscribed to a faith. The Orthodox were now in a much better legal position; they could set up more churches and act more freely than before. Moreover, the Habsburg government gave up the attempt to treat all Romanians as Uniates. Moves were initiated to choose a new head for the Orthodox of Transylvania, who had not had a bishop since 1698, when Atanasie and his followers had joined the rival institution. Thereafter, the Romanian Orthodox had had to look to the Serbian organization at Sremski Karlovci, although they were not covered by Leopold I's assurances. Now, however, they would again have their own bishop. The metropolitan at Sremski Karlovci was asked to submit three names to Joseph II; he chose Ghedeon Nichitici, a Serb, who assumed office in 1784. His church remained dependent on Sremski Karlovci in matters of doctrine. In 1810 the Romanian Orthodox were given the right to name their own bishops. Sibiu became the Orthodox center, as Alba Iulia was that of the Uniates and Sremski Karlovci that of the Serbian Orthodox.

Although the new measures of toleration strengthened the Orthodox position, they naturally gained Joseph II more enemies. One of the reasons that had led the government to favor the appointment of an Orthodox bishop was its dislike of the influence on Transylvanian Romanians of Orthodox organizations outside the country, particularly in Bucharest. Other consequences of the action also caused great disquiet, particularly among the Catholics. A mass return to the Orthodox church occurred at the expense of the Uniates. Even Joseph was forced to agree to measures that would make such actions difficult.

With Joseph's death the major administrative changes in Transylvania were revoked. The province returned to the system of rule by the three recognized nations and the four religions. Nevertheless, the retention of the provisions abolishing serfdom and the lessening of the limitations on the Orthodox did benefit the Romanian people. Moreover, by the end of the century they had a small intellectual class who could effectively argue for an improvement in the Romanian position. In 1791 some members of this group composed a petition, known as the Supplex Libellus Valachorum, which was sent to Leopold II. Its arguments were very similar to those first expressed by Bishop Clain. The memorandum restated the thesis of the Roman origin of the Romanian people and the assertion that they and the Orthodox church had been on an equal level with the Hungarians and the Saxons until the fifteenth century. The document thus called not for the granting of new rights, but for the restoration of those which had been in existence previously. The petitioners desired that the Romanians be given proportional representation on the Transylvanian administrative bodies and share the privileges of the dominating nations. They also wanted to hold a national assembly similar to those convened by the Serbian Orthodox.

After Leopold II had read the petition, he sent it on to the Transylvanian diet. There, as could be expected, it was firmly rejected. Once back in control, the Hungarian, Szekler, and Saxon aristocracy had no intention of making concessions. Having successfully defied the attempts of Joseph II to impose a centralized administration, they were certainly not going to surrender to a movement that had even more dangerous implications to both their political power and their social position.

The Banat

In addition to the regions discussed thus far, three other areas of the Habsburg Empire are of importance to this narrative. Two of these, Bukovina and the Slovene lands, are discussed in greater detail later. Bukovina became a part of the monarchy only in 1775 and was then administered together with the newly acquired Polish province of Galicia. The Slovenes, who inhabited all of Carniola and part of Styria, Carinthia, Istria, Gorizia, and Gradisca, shared in the history of the events of the German Austrian part of the empire. Since this area had never been the scene of devastating wars or great movements of population, it was more prosperous than the lands previously discussed. A separate Slovene movement did not commence until the next century.

In comparison, the Banat had a turbulent and destructive past. Because it had been under direct Ottoman rule, both the administrative and the land systems of that empire had been in effect. As a border area and the scene of constant fighting, the territory had been largely depopulated except for some centers around fortified points. The peasants raised livestock, which could easily be moved in troubled times. After the Habsburg government acquired the province in 1718, the question of its political future arose. Despite pressure from Hungary, which expected to acquire it, the province was first made a crownland and placed under a military administration. It was divided into eleven districts; the villages remained under the administration of the local knezes according to the system in effect in the Ottoman territories and the Military Frontier. The Habsburg government had full control of the disposal of the land, which was now state property. The aim was to make the region a strong bulwark against the Ottoman Empire and an economically prosperous area that would yield high returns in taxation. An active policy of colonization was thus embarked upon.

At this time, the Banat was a transition area where the Romanian- and Serbian-speaking people merged. Although it originally was primarily Romanian, a large Serbian immigration over a long period had occurred. The population was mostly peasant, but it also included artisans and merchants. After the Habsburg annexation, the authorities made great efforts to attract German settlers, because it was believed that they could develop the land most efficiently. The new immigrants were given the status of free peasants and excused from taxes for a period. Better farming methods were indeed introduced, and new crops such as rice and cotton developed. The government discouraged Hungarian immigration for obvious political reasons.

The Habsburg authorities also handed out large tracts of land as rewards for service or to those with sufficient influence to obtain the grants. Both the Catholic and Orthodox churches held estates. Because all of these were worked by serf or tenant labor, they had the same problems as the neighboring lands and were similarly affected by the reforms. The majority of the population was Orthodox, but the Serbs were in a better position than the Romanians. Nevertheless, the Romanian population did enjoy some of the same privileges, since they formed part of the Serbian congregation. A part of the Banat territory was organized as a Military Frontier similar to that in Croatia and Slavonia. Until the last decade of the eighteenth century the Banat was under the administration of the central authorities in Vienna. After a period of indecision, they joined the region to Hungary, but as a distinct province. It remained thereafter under Hungarian control.

THE FRENCH REVOLUTION AND NAPOLEON

From the accession of Leopold II in 1790 until the conclusion of the Congress of Vienna in 1815, the main concern of the Habsburg government was its relations with France. Leopold's forces were soon to be crushed by the armies of this revolutionary power. In this period France represented a deadly threat because of both its military might and its conquering ideology. The fate of the French monarchs was a shock to conservative Europe. In 1792 Leopold saw his sister, Marie Antoinette, and his brother-in-law, Louis XVI, imprisoned; in 1793 they were guillotined. European rulers also realized that many of the conditions that had brought about the revolution in France were present elsewhere. Within the Habsburg Monarchy the peasants, still burdened with heavy obligations, were a restless element. Sections of the nobility, especially in Hungary, had used the vocabulary of the Enlightenment to justify the maintenance of their national and feudal privileges. Under these circumstances the Austrian government could afford no more experiments such as those in the time of Joseph II. The abolition of serfdom and the Toleration Edict remained, but no further major advances were to occur until 1848.

The next emperor, Francis II (1792–1835), thus brought the era of enlightened despotism to an end. A practical man of little imagination, he introduced a new conservative spirit into the direction of the state. The French Revolution had shaken all of those in privileged positions, and the nobility needed the support of the monarchy against the larger threat. Those who had previously stood for provincial and historic rights found grounds for cooperating with the proponents of a strong central authority. The main enemy of both was French aggression and the associated revolutionary ideology. The struggle was to be carried on not only on the battlefield, but also at home. Various measures of internal control were introduced, including a spy system, increased police surveillance, and a censorship that examined works printed in the country and imported from abroad. Education came to emphasize loyalty and good citizenship; religion was favored as an instrument of assuring and enforcing support for the established regime.

Despite the fears aroused by the revolutionary movement, the question of Hungarian separatism remained acute for Vienna. The landowning nobility had remained prosperous during the Napoleonic Wars, which were not fought in their lands. The wars brought high prices for the products of their estates, and they as a class were free from taxation. Nevertheless, they continued to fight the special war taxes necessary to defend the empire and the recruitment for the army that took peasant labor from their profitable estates. In this period there was also continuing pressure for the introduction of Hungarian as the language of administration and higher education.

The Habsburg conflicts with France resulted in a long series of depressing defeats and unfavorable peace treaties. Almost all of these brought about a loss of Habsburg territory, usually involving the southwestern frontier. From 1792 to 1797 Austria fought in the War of the First Coalition in alliance with Prussia, Britain, Holland, and Spain. In the Treaty of Campo Formio the empire ceded its Belgian lands and in return received Venice, Istria, and Dalmatia. The War of the Second Coalition, from 1798 to 1801, in which Austria fought with Russia, Britain, Naples, Portugal, and the Ottoman Empire, ended with the Treaty of Lunéville, which brought about major changes in central Europe but allowed the monarchy to keep the former Venetian territories. The War of the Third Coalition, commencing in 1805, brought further defeats, in particular the disaster at Austerlitz in 1805, and was concluded by the Treaty of Pressburg. Here the empire ceded the Venetian lands to the new Kingdom of Italy and lost more German territory. In 1809, after a major attempt at national revival, the Austrian army, under the command of Archduke Charles, made a great effort to defeat Napoleon, who at the time was involved in Spain. Further shattering losses forced the monarchy to conclude yet another severe peace. In the Treaty of Schönbrunn Galicia and more German lands were surrendered, along with territory that Napoleon was subsequently to incorporate into a new political entity called the Illyrian Provinces.

For a short period after 1805 the French government controlled important South Slav lands. In 1809 Dalmatia, some Slovene lands, parts of the Croatian Military Frontier, and Civil Croatia were joined together to form the Illyrian Provinces, an area that was incorporated directly into France. Through the creation of this Balkan dependency, the French government aimed to establish a strong political base in the region to protect its position in Italy and to put pressure on the Habsburg Empire. The new boundaries also gave France direct access to Ottoman territory. In setting up the new government, the French officials did not take into consideration the local customs, which they regarded as primitive and barbarous, and they proceded to introduce the French administrative system intact. The country was divided into departments, and it received the legal, administrative, and fiscal institutions of France.

The Napoleonic domination resulted in the application of many revolutionary principles. Since French military power was overwhelming, little care had to be taken of local or conservative sensibilities. The changes went far beyond the most extreme ideas of Josephism. The manorial system was ended; the peasants were to receive all of the land they worked. The labor dues for the landowners and the tithe for the church were abolished without compensation. The Code Napoléon was applied, and all men were declared equal before the law. Taxation, however, remained. Much discontent was aroused by the continuation, or even increase, of the high state taxes and the use of the corvée on public works, such as the building of the roads necessary for French military needs. The local population also did not like being conscripted into the French army.

In the few years that France held the Illyrian Provinces, not all the reforms could be completed. French attention was focused primarily on other and more important sections of Europe. No attempt was made to apply the new institutions to the tribal areas of southern Dalmatia. French military officers admired much in the organization of the Military Frontier; there were few changes there. Moreover, with Britain in control of the seas, little could be done to promote the prosperity of the Dalmatian coastal towns.

Nevertheless, the French occupation had certain lasting influences. First, the old order was completely overturned, and the population was exposed to new ideas and at least the plan for a more efficient administrative system. Local languages were also more widely in use. Although this problem was to have more significance in the future, the difficulty of choosing and adopting one literary language was clearly evident. The Illyrian Provinces were inhabited chiefly by two peoples: the Croats in Dalmatia and Croatia, who spoke dialects of the same language, and the Slovenes, whose Slavic language was distinct from that of the Croats. The Napoleonic rule thus brought together South Slav people under one government, but it did little more than bring out what was to be a major problem hindering Yugoslav unity in the future.

The Habsburg military fortunes remained low until after 1812, when Napoleon launched his ill-advised attack on Russia. Thereafter, the Habsburg government, under the direction of Prince Clemens von Metternich, was one of the leaders of the coalition that brought Napoleon to defeat. In March 1814 the allied troops entered Paris. In the subsequent peace negotiations, which were held in Vienna in 1814 and 1815, few problems arose in connection with the regions with which we are concerned. The great controversy in the peace negotiations concerned the fate of the Polish lands. The chief alteration from the conditions that had prevailed on the Habsburg southeastern border before the long period of war was the definite incorporation of the former Venetian lands into the monarchy. Istria and Dalmatia were annexed; northern Italy was organized into the Kingdom of Lombardy-Venetia, which was placed under a Habsburg archduke. The Treaty of Bucharest of 1812, of course, had already settled the problems with which the Ottoman Empire was directly concerned. The Porte did not participate in the Congress of Vienna, and Balkan problems were not discussed.

The Treaty of Vienna was to have great significance for the Habsburg Empire. Despite its continual defeats in war, the peace settlement left the empire the predominant power in the Italian peninsula and among the German states. Throughout the next fifty-five years, until the defeat by Prussia in 1866, the monarchy was to concentrate on the maintenance of its influence in these areas. Balkan and Eastern questions were secondary. The Habsburg government, which had every interest in preserving this favorable situation, thus joined with Prussia and Russia in the Holy Alliance, whose principal aim was to maintain the status quo and the conservative political order that had been established.

3

Balkan people under Ottoman and Habsburg rule: a comparison

IN THE PRECEDING PAGES we have examined the position of the Balkan people in two great empires, the Ottoman and the Habsburg. Their fortunes were determined not only by the economic, political, and social structure of the state in which they lived, but also by the domestic and foreign issues in dispute at the time. In some respects the problems of the two governments were similar; in others they differed sharply. Certainly for both the Ottoman and Habsburg leaders the chief political question in the eighteenth century was the relative power balance between the central and the provincial authorities. They, however, approached the question from different directions. The Habsburg Monarchy sought to gain a control over feudal estates that it had never possessed previously; the Ottoman sultans, in contrast, attempted to reassert an authority that they had once held. The resistance to Austrian centralism and absolutism came from a historic nobility whose lineage might rival that of the Habsburg family. The Porte was challenged by a motley array of ayans, beys, Christian and Muslim military leaders, and outright bandits – groups that did not have centuries-old traditions of political power.

For both states military defeat, or the threat thereof, played a major role in bringing about reform. The Ottoman situation was comparatively more dangerous, since foreign states did contemplate the dismemberment of the empire. The Porte faced threats from Austria, Russia, and Persia; the monarchy's chief adversary was first France and then, in the middle of the nineteenth century, Prussia. Internal reform thus had to be undertaken in order to put the state in a better condition to face its enemies. The Ottoman attempts at reform were limited; the aim was purely pragmatic. The military had to be improved or the central government would fall before foreign aggression and internal subversion. The Austrian efforts were far more sophisticated. An effort was made to alter the political structure of the empire in a fashion that would enable the central government to collect more taxes and have a better access to the population for the direct recruitment of soldiers. Moreover, the purposes of the changes were more than military. On the basis of the political ideology of the Enlightenment, the reforming monarchs held a definite conception of their role as responsible leaders of all of their people. There was no similar attitude in Constantinople, where reforms were justified as a return to old traditions, and they were not based on a new conception of the duties of a ruler.

It is not easy to make a judgment about the relative positions of the Balkan people in each empire or to compare their experiences under two differing regimes. In the Ottoman lands the Christian people were openly designated as second-class citizens. Nevertheless, they enjoyed a large degree of self-government. Not only the millet system but also the village communities were important. On the local level, the Ottoman Christian was usually directly governed by men from his own locality, who might be chosen by the vote of the male population and who were, at least, from important native families. Justice, the collection of taxes, and the police could be under direct local control. The Christian notable, in turn, dealt with the Muslim provincial authorities or the representatives of the central government. Moreover, the very lawlessness in some areas guaranteed a certain amount of freedom. There were always the vast forests, the inaccessible mountains, and the seas to which overburdened families or individuals could escape. The Ottoman Empire never had a firm control over its territories or the surrounding seas.

The situation in the Habsburg lands was quite different. A manorial system was in effect; everywhere the nobility dominated the local government and held the majority of the peasant population in a condition of servitude. Status depended on social class more than on religion or nationality. Of the Balkan people, only the Croats had a nobility of significance; the Serbs, the Slovenes, and the Romanians did not. As peasants, they therefore had no political rights and no recognized institutions of self-government. Such matters as justice and tax collecting were in the hands of the lord of the manor. The exceptions were primarily in the areas where the Habsburg government had adopted what were in fact Ottoman institutions. In the Military Frontier a system of village government similar to that in Ottoman regions was set up; the immigrant Serbs were allowed an organization in the monarchy that had many features in common with the millet system.

Although the two empires shared many similar problems, to the outside observer at the time the differences were profound. Most obvious were the outward forms of two contrasting civilizations. In the eyes of educated Europeans the Ottoman Empire was a backward, even barbarous, state. Observers of this sort were extremely shocked at the ease with which the government executed, usually by strangling or beheading immediately, officials or generals who failed or who aroused the sultan's displeasure. The Porte also had the habit, after declaring war, of imprisoning the ambassadors and representatives of the enemy powers under extremely unfavorable conditions. The custom of collecting heads and of staking out bodies and heads in public places revolted citizens of countries where such activities belonged to the past. Moreover, Ottoman cities were dirty, congested, and primitive in comparison with those of the West. Conspicuous display of wealth could be dangerous; luxury and wealth were confined to the homes, where they could not be viewed by foreign eyes.

In comparison, in questions of style the Habsburg Empire was one of the great centers of Europe. In an age of baroque culture, Habsburg civilization was splendid. The nobility could afford to maintain magnificent residences and to endow the arts. There was also a comfortable middle class. Law and order were assured; bands of robbers did not roam at will. Public officials were supposed to uphold certain standards. Although corruption exists in all societies, the Austrian service was relatively honest and efficient. General standards for sanitation, cleanliness, and order were maintained at a high level.

In contrast, corruption was blatant and open in Constantinople. There were, in addition to the problems of order and security, enormous health hazards. The Ottoman lands were the scene of repeated epidemics of dangerous diseases and the plague. Long after it had passed as a threat in Europe, bubonic plague continued to menace the Ottoman lands. In 1770, 40,000 people died; between 1812 and 1814 the cities of Bucharest and Belgrade lost a third of their populations. In a year as many as 150,000 could die.[1] The situation was particularly bad for children; diseases such as scarlet fever could decimate a generation.

For the peasant – that is, for 90 percent of the Balkan people – questions of landholding were perhaps more important than political issues, although the two were certainly linked. It will be noted that in Chapter 2 trade and manufacturing were not discussed, even though these were, of course, important elements in the life of the monarchy. This omission reflects the fact that the Balkan people were almost entirely in agricultural or pastoral occupations. A very small minority of merchants and craftsmen, usually Greek or Serbian, lived in the cities, but for most Romanians, Serbs, Croats, and Slovenes the major economic questions were those connected with the land and agricultural production.

As we have seen, at the beginning of the eighteenth century, the majority of the peasants in the Habsburg Empire and in the Danubian Principalities were enserfed or dependent, with a subordinate legal status and only traditional rights to work a piece of land. They carried the major burden of state and church taxes, and they made payments for their land. In the course of the century the rulers Maria Theresa, Joseph II, and Constantine Mavrocordat introduced reforms, primarily for reasons of state interest, which changed the peasant's legal status but did little or nothing to assure him of security of tenure or ownership of the plots he cultivated. The massive discontent of the peasant population was thus a continual presence until it exploded in 1848. However, unlike the Ottoman Christian, the Habsburg peasant was not well

---

1 L. S. Stavrianos, *The Balkans since 1453* (New York: Rinehart, 1958), p. 134.

situated to express his desires either legally or by revolt. The nobility, not a village notable, ran the local administration; there were no peasant armed forces like those formed by the armatoles and haiduks. Among the Habsburg subjects only the Serbs of the Military Frontier had either the experience or the organization to act, and their influence was exerted chiefly in Ottoman lands. Agricultural conditions, not political, national, or religious issues, remained the prime peasant concern. The high cultural achievement of the monarchy, its architecture, art and music, of course held no advantages for this section of society, which had at the most only a primary level of education.

Despite the lower general conditions, some Ottoman Christian peasants did have advantages in landholding, if not in theory at least in practice. It is very difficult to make generalizations here because of the lack of comparative studies on agricultural conditions. However, if we use as the standard the goal of all peasant households to gain free control of a plot of land that could be farmed according to the desires of the family, this wish could more readily be fulfilled within the Ottoman domains, excluding Moldavia, Wallachia, Bosnia, and Hercegovina, which had a native nobility and a feudal organization. The landholding restrictions on the timars and chiftliks have been discussed. There were, however, wide areas where the equivalent of peasant farming was conducted or where the raising of livestock in the hills and pasturelands was the basis of existence. It must also be emphasized that the Ottoman Christians did have village administrations, local leaders, and sometimes armed forces at their disposal, which could back their claims in land disputes. There was, in addition, always a great deal of available unoccupied land, and movement was possible within the empire.

Although fundamental changes were not to occur in Balkan life until the nineteenth century, some indication had already been given of the direction that these would take. Leaders in both empires in the eighteenth century attempted to deal with what they regarded as the major problems. The Ottoman emphasis was on military reform to enable the state to control rebellious local pashas and to withstand foreign invasion. The Austrian monarchs, particularly Joseph II, attempted a fundamental reorganization of the government. As we have seen, these reforms, introduced from above, were largely unsuccessful. By the end of the Napoleonic Wars the conservative forces had reasserted their domination. The major issues were left unsolved. The Porte still faced the dangers of outside aggression and internal dissolution; the problems facing the Habsburg Monarchy in attempting to hold together an empire composed of widely different provinces remained. Moreover, new issues, arising from the economic changes of the era, were to add additional complications to the situation.

PART II

The revolutionary years, 1804–1887

4

The first national revolutions

THE HISTORY OF THE BALKAN PENINSULA from 1804 to 1887 is dominated by the theme of national revolt and the formation of the new governments. During these years an independent Greece, Serbia, and Romania and an autonomous Bulgaria were to be established. An Albanian national movement also arose. The first revolutions broke out in three separate areas – the pashalik of Belgrade, the Danubian Principalities, and the Peloponnesus and Rumeli – in the first three decades of the century. However, before discussing these events, it is necessary to consider certain general developments involving not only the Balkans but also the rest of Europe, which were to have an important effect on the revolutionary activities: first, the formulation and wide acceptance of national and liberal ideologies; second, the changing economic conditions; and third, the increasing intervention of the European great powers and the origin of the Eastern Question.

BALKAN NATIONALISM: THE BACKGROUND OF THE REVOLUTIONS

Balkan national leaders and intellectuals in the nineteenth century were to be deeply influenced by two political doctrines that had their origin in Western Europe: liberalism, with its roots in the ideas of the Enlightenment of the eighteenth century; and nationalism, whose basis was more in the romanticism and historicism of the nineteenth century. Many writers and philosophers in the eighteenth century, deeply impressed by the scientific discoveries of the previous period, came to believe that there existed certain laws or principles determining politics and society similar to the "natural laws" of the material world. They hoped that with the use of reason they could discover these and formulate them into statutes for the governing of the state. Most of these men were idealists; they had faith in the perfectibility of man and society. Since their goal was the assurance of human happiness and well-being, they wished state institutions to serve and benefit the governed. Their concepts were not necessarily democratic. As we have seen, one of their number, Joseph II, like other enlightened despots, fully intended to rule autocratically, but his aim was to act in the interest of all of the social levels of the Austrian population.

Although some of the doctrines of the Enlightenment did indeed serve the interests of the centralizing monarchies, other aspects strengthened their opposition. Attacking the concept of the absolute, mercantile state, some writers claimed that in accordance with the idea of natural law, all individuals were endowed with certain rights, which they held from birth and which should be regarded as "inalienable." In the American Declaration of Independence, a fine formulation of the basic ideas of this school of thought, these were declared to be "life, liberty and the pursuit of happiness." Private property was often added to this list of natural rights.

The argument was thus made that there were areas in the life of each individual in which the government should not interfere. In order to assure that intrusions should not take place, and to define what was private and what was public, it was believed that a constitution, a form of social contract, should be drawn up that would clearly set the limits of the state's power and guarantee the rights of the individual citizen. These concepts strongly stressed political equality; all men, no matter what their social or ethnic background, were to have the same rights in the state. The emphasis was on the freedom of the individual and his protection against the tyranny of government or society. These convictions were the basis of nineteenth-century liberalism. It will be noted that the liberal of this period, while usually espousing political equality, seldom if ever supported social or economic leveling, or the intervention of the state to aid one section of the population.

Nineteenth-century nationalism altered the direction of some of these ideas. For most of the writers of the Enlightenment, the state, or nation, was considered an association of individuals who were joined together by some sort of social contract, whether written or implied. The aim of the government should simply be to promote the general welfare in the widest terms and to protect the population against outside invasion. The subject of chief emphasis was the definition of the relationship of the individual and the state authorities, and the strict supervision of the power of the latter. The state was considered a rational organization of free-standing citizens; it had few if any mystical or emotional overtones.

In contrast, nationalist doctrines almost all took the emphasis off the individual and placed it completely on the collective entity, the nation. Much of the vocabulary of romantic nationalism was greatly influenced by the writing of Johann Gottfried Herder, a German philosopher, whose ideas were to have a great impact on Eastern Europe. He saw individuals in society only as part of the *Volk*, which can be roughly translated as the people or, better, the national group. Herder believed that art, music, literature, local customs, laws – in fact most forms of cultural and political life – were manifestations of the unique spirit, or *Volksgeist*, of each people.

In contrast to liberal ideology, which placed so much emphasis on assuring the citizen rights against both his government and his society, national ideologies often went to the opposite extreme. It was argued that God had divided mankind by nationality. Certain attributes, such as a common language, a single religion, similar customs, and long historical association, joined individuals in one nation. To some writers the citizen existed primarily as part of his collective group; he had no real rights against the nation and its institutions. Personal freedom was thus to be attained not through constitutions and similar legal documents, but through identification with and submission to the collective will of the nation, sometimes expressed by a charismatic leader.

The nationalist was extremely interested in the study and purification of his language, since he regarded this manifestation of national character as perhaps the most important. It was argued that one language alone was imprinted in each individual; it was the natural expression of the thought and innate character of the nation to which he belonged. Each writer should use only his own language, because in it alone could he express his true ideas and his national culture. Foreign words were to be rigorously expunged from the vocabularies of every language as detrimental to natural modes of expression. Nationalist philosophers were similarly concerned with the revival of the history of their nation and with folk and fairy tales. They delighted in delving into the murky past of their own people, and they professed a high regard for the peasant, whom they saw as the element of society least harmed by "foreign" cultural influences.

At first, it should be emphasized, these writers did not set up a hierarchy of superior and inferior nations. They merely argued that the individual could best realize himself through identification with the nation, the natural, God-ordained division of mankind. For instance, German writers, including Herder, showed great admiration for and interest in Balkan folk literature, in particular Serbian oral epic poetry, which was regarded as a superior example of the Volksgeist in action. It was only later, when these vague conceptions were translated into practice and into political programs, that national leaders came to emphasize the unique and marvelous qualities of their own people and to use this argument to justify their control over others. This trend, which can be seen in all the national movements, reached its culmination in National Socialist Germany in the twentieth century.

Extreme national doctrines in both Eastern and Western Europe were often followed with the greatest enthusiasm by those who had little practical administrative experience or actual political power. Revolutionary nationalism had a strong attraction for sections of the population, such as students, professors, writers, lawyers, and other members of professions, who were well educated but often excluded from high state positions. Their programs placed much emphasis on action and on the necessity of struggling for a noble goal; their efforts thrived in an atmosphere of conspiracy and violence. Most of them were convinced of the rectitude of their position, and they were sure that they held the key to the future.

The revolutionary movements throughout Europe in the nineteenth century combined liberalism and nationalism, although obvious contradictions existed between aspects of both doctrines. The leaders usually concentrated on the breakup of feudal or autocratic regimes and their replacement by constitutional governments. They accepted the national basis for the state, that is, that peoples with a common language and historical past should be joined together. As will be shown, they often compromised their liberal political principles once they had gained power, but their national enthusiasms seldom wavered.

The implications of liberal and national ideology for southeastern Europe were clear: both the Habsburg and the Ottoman empires should be dissolved and replaced by national states with constitutional governments. Theory aside, already in the eighteenth century certain events that served to impel the Balkan peoples along this course had taken place. Some aspects of this development, particularly the cultural revival and the increased interest in language, were exactly in line with nationalist doctrine.

Cultural revival: history and language

In a discussion of the age of nationalism in the Balkans it is important to emphasize first that neither Habsburg nor Ottoman rule had completely destroyed a feeling of unity among the individual nationalities or brought about a total loss of the memory of a more glorious past. There had, after all, been Byzantine, Serbian, Croatian, Bosnian, Bulgarian, Wallachian, and Moldavian states with distinct cultures and histories that recorded considerable achievements. The citizens of each state had shared a common language, religion, culture, and other attributes that defined the perimeters of a national unit in the nineteenth century. Certain institutions of the Ottoman system guaranteed that the remembrance of former triumphs would be carefully preserved, even among a largely illiterate peasant population.

Certainly the Orthodox church served as a major vehicle in the transmission and preservation of past traditions. Although the Patriarchate often collaborated closely with the Ottoman government, the church as a whole kept alive the idea that its members were distinct and superior and that the Muslims were transgressors on Christian territory. Providing the only available education, the Orthodox institutions could make certain that the Ottoman state authorities were never in a position to control Christian thought. The lack of a secular school system deprived the Muslim rulers of this convenient propaganda tool. In addition, a popular religious literature recounted tales of the lives of saints, martyrs, and heroes. Especially prominent were the stories of the neo-martyrs, who had suffered for their defense of Christianity against Islam. Religious art also carried the symbols and portraits of former rulers and reminded the viewer of the great Byzantine, Bulgarian, and Serbian empires of the past.

A second major method of cultural transmission was through the tight village community. Without a popular written literature, formal histories, or newspapers, succeeding generations of illiterate peasants learned about the past from their storytellers and their oral epic and popular poetry. In the nineteenth century European writers, including J. W. von Goethe, A. Mickiewicz, A. S. Pushkin, and Sir Walter Scott, were fascinated by the richness of the Balkan folk tradition and brought this literature to the attention of the West. All of the Balkan peoples had treasuries of myth, poetry, and song. Among the earliest were the Greek songs that told of the exploits of tenth-century Byzantine border warriors against Arab opponents. The best known of these was *Digenis Akritas*. Later Greek poems recounted the national tragedy of the fall of Constantinople. Epic poetry was particularly important among the Slavic people, whose tales were sung to the accompaniment of a one-stringed instrument, the *gusla*. The Serbian songs concentrated on the medieval state and its downfall, the Croatian on events after the fifteenth century. The Muslim Bosnians had folk poetry in which the Turks were the major figures. For the Christian Slavic people the common hero was Prince Mark, called Marko Kraljević in Serbian and Krali Marko in Bulgarian. His exploits and the battle of Kosovo became the central events of past history, though the concentration on this major defeat carried the assumption that at some time Christian liberation would be achieved.

In addition to the oral literature with religious or historical themes, all Balkan people had popular ballads, including the klepht or haiduk songs, which concerned the activities of these bandit groups. Although the outlaws were originally neither nationalistic nor even particularly patriotic, they did create a type of heroic figure that was to be much admired and was to have a place in the future national struggles. The songs, which emphasized the idea of freedom and the identity of man and nature, were concerned chiefly with the activities of individuals who alone or with a close band of faithful comrades fought fiercely and bravely against strong odds. Opposition to tyrannical rule and the glorification of the life of the hero had an obvious application to resistance to Ottoman rule.

Although these sources of knowledge about the past were to remain important in the village, other work would influence in particular the more educated and cosmopolitan elements of Balkan society. Beginning in the eighteenth century individual scholars became increasingly engrossed in the study of their language and history. Language involved some very difficult problems. As we have seen, the population of the peninsula consisted largely of a peasantry that spoke a multitude of dialects, all, nevertheless, falling into the major divisions of Greek, Albanian, Romanian, and South Slavic. As printing facilities became available and as more writers wished to use their national tongues, it was, of course, necessary to decide upon standard literary languages, which would also be taught in the schools. The language issue, which has caused major controversies until the present, will be discussed throughout this account.

The Greeks, with their superior educational facilities and their respect for learning, were the first to meet the question of the literary language. In some respects their choice was the most difficult. In addition to the many different Greek dialects spoken at the time, they had inherited the great tradition of the classical world and its literary masterpieces. The temptation was strong not to abandon the language that had been spoken and written in fifth-century Athens. There was, in addition, the heritage of Byzantine and Orthodox learning. This issue had to be faced at the time of the Greek cultural revival in the eighteenth century, which took place largely outside the Ottoman lands. The major center became Vienna when in 1783 Joseph II allowed books to be printed in Greek. Venice and the Ionian Islands also played a role in the movement. Two figures dominated the Greek literary scene: Rigas Feraios and Adamantios Korais.

For the language question the work of Korais was particularly significant. Influenced by European thought, particularly that of the Enlightenment, Korais was drawn to classical rather than Byzantine Greek civilization. Deeply concerned with the political education of his people, he wished the resurrected nation to express the spirit of the ancient culture. His main undertaking was the publication of seventeen volumes of classical texts, known as the Library of Greek Literature. As far as the contemporary written language was concerned, he believed that it should be as close to the classical grammar and vocabulary as possible. He was also in favor of expunging the Italian, Slavic, and Turkish words that had become a part of everyday speech over the past centuries. With these convictions in mind, he devised an artificial literary language, known as *katharevousa*, which was to be adopted as the official language for government and education in the future Greek state.

Rigas Feraios is best known as a revolutionary writer and agitator. Unlike Korais, he wrote in demotic Greek, the spoken language of his people. His highly emotional and nationalistic outlook is expressed in his "War Hymn," which well illustrates the passionate feeling of early Balkan nationalism.

> How long, my heroes, shall we live in bondage,
>   alone, like lions on ridges, on peaks?
> Living in caves, seeing our children turned
>   from the land to bitter enslavement?
> Losing our land, brothers, and parents,
>   our friends, our children, and all our relations?
> Better an hour of life that is free
>   than forty years in slavery.[1]

---

1 Quoted in L. S. Stavrianos, *The Balkans since 1453* (New York: Rinehart, 1958), p. 279.

The division on the question of the standard literary language was to become and remain a matter of major controversy and to have unfortunate repercussions in Greek political life.

The Serbian choice was to be different. The metropolitanate at Sremski Karlovci in the Habsburg Monarchy was the first modern cultural center, and the church played a major role in literary development. During the eighteenth century a close connection was maintained with Kiev and the Russian Orthodox institutions there. Russia, still the single Orthodox state not under foreign control, offered a greater attraction to the Habsburg Serbs than the Greek- and Ottoman-dominated Patriarchate. Because of this situation and the fact that many Serbian theological students were educated in Kiev, a considerable number of Russian words were incorporated into the literary language, which, it will be remembered, was Church Slavic. This so-called Serbian-Slavonic language, which was used by the church and the educated Serbs, did not conform either to the spoken idiom or to the standard form used elsewhere in the Balkan Slavic Orthodox world. It was nearly as artificial as katharevousa.

The major influence in diverting the language from this course was the work of two scholars, Dositej Obradović and Vuk Karadžić, both of whom wrote in the vernacular. The greatest influence on the development of the literary language was exerted by Karadžić, who chose the dialect of Hercegovina as the standard form and compiled a grammar and a dictionary. Deeply interested in the Serbian cultural heritage, he also collected popular songs and poems. As we shall see, the Croatian writers were to adopt the same dialect, a choice that would facilitate greatly the Yugoslav movement of the future.

The selection of the dialect that was to form the basis for the literary language was particularly significant for each Balkan Slavic people and was to have enormous political implications for the future. In all of the national movements language was the most important attribute of nationality. Although it was relatively easy to differentiate among Albanian-, Greek-, Romanian-, and Turkish-speaking people, the South Slav population presented certain major problems. From the Adriatic, across the peninsula to the Black Sea and the Aegean, the inhabitants spoke dialects that marked a gradual transition from Croatian and Serbian in the west to Bulgarian in the east. The efforts of scholars and politicians to divide these people by neat lines into Bulgarians, Croats, Serbs, and later Macedonians, with language as a chief consideration, was to lead to mutual recrimination and hatred in the future.

The study of history was also to have an important role in the national movements. Whereas a common language was regarded as the prime determinant of which people should form a state, their past history was seen as a major factor deciding the territory they should occupy. The writing of the Transylvanian School of historians and their emphasis on the prior and continuous residence of Romanians in certain lands since ancient times has already been discussed. Other writers representing their own national interests were to follow similar themes. Although descriptions of the fall of Constantinople and the battle of Kosovo might have the effect of bringing the Christian people together, other episodes did not. As historians delved into the pre-Ottoman era and revived the memories of past glories, the overlapping and conflicting jurisdictions of the medieval empires became obvious. When historic boundaries became a justification for national claims, sharp controversies were inevitable. Many issues in more recent times also brought the Balkan people into conflict. The entire question of Greek and Phanariot influence in the eighteenth century was a troublesome and divisive one. Both Romanian and South Slav writers protested Greek privilege and power. At this time Father Paisii, a monk at Mt. Athos, in an effort to protect his people against Greek pressure, wrote a highly nationalistic history of Bulgaria in which he asserted that "the Bulgarians were the most glorious of all the Slavic nations, they were the first to have tsars, they were the first to have a patriarch, they were the first to be Christianized, they ruled over the greatest area."[2]

In the previous pages religion has been given as one of the chief attributes of nationality. The role of the Orthodox establishment in preserving Christian identity has also been emphasized. In the future Orthodoxy would play an important role, especially in the struggle against the Ottoman and Habsburg empires and in defining and dividing the Serbian and Croatian nationalities. However, the organization of the national revolutions was to be predominantly in the hands of a secular leadership, particularly in the Ottoman lands. Some elements in the church were to fight against these movements and prefer the retention of the old order. Regrettably, the common Orthodox faith of the Balkan nations never hindered them from engaging in bloody conflicts with each other.

The three main determinants of Balkan nationality – language, historical association, and religion – continue to be major themes for the rest of this book. These attributes became both the basis for the building of the nation-states and the reasons for some of the conflicts between them. The fact that the nineteenth century was also an age of national development in Central Europe and Italy naturally fortified these currents within the Habsburg and Ottoman empires. Some political institutions were indeed to be imported from other parts of Europe. The national revolutions themselves, however, had their origins primarily in local conditions and past Balkan history. European ideology was later used to explain or justify the actions taken, but these ideas were not the cause of the events themselves.

In discussing the general ideological background to the revolutionary years, one other aspect is of interest. In the next pages, in the accounts of the revolts

---

2 Quoted in Charles A. Moser, *A History of Bulgarian Literature, 865–1944* (The Hague: Mouton, 1972), p. 42.

themselves, numerous examples are given of the activities of secret societies, some of which had their headquarters in Constantinople, and of propaganda activities carried on throughout the entire empire. The question arises why the Ottoman authorities were so inept in meeting this challenge and why they could not initiate an effort to combat the ideological warfare. Ottoman officials did indeed make a large number of arrests; executions of conspirators and traitors were common. Nevertheless, the government had few means either of "thought control" or of influencing the Balkan Christians in its favor. The organization of the empire precluded to a large degree any such efforts. As long as the Christian subject was primarily under the influence of the Orthodox church and the village community, the Porte had no means of reaching him directly or individually. It was thus weakly equipped to deal with internal subversion or to combat ideas detrimental to its control.

Economic considerations

One of the major elements contributing to the encouragement of the national movements was the improvement of general economic conditions, particularly the commercial revival of the eighteenth century. Despite the anarchy and lawlessness in some regions, trade between the Ottoman Empire and Europe increased rapidly both by the Balkan overland routes and by sea. The policies of the Habsburg Empire and Russia contributed to creating favorable conditions for Balkan merchants and seafarers. At the end of the seventeenth century, the Treaty of Karlowitz, on the Habsburg initiative, not only had set the boundaries between Austria and the Ottoman Empire, but also had provided for trade between the signatories. The Ottoman-Habsburg border thereafter witnessed a steady rise in the exchange of goods, especially in the import of raw materials and foodstuffs into the monarchy. A second important influence on commerce came with the Russian conquest and settlement of the lands north of the Black Sea. This region became thereafter a major grain-producing area. Its products were shipped by way of Black Sea ports, particularly Odessa, through the Straits to Western Europe. This situation gave the Russian government an economic as well as a strategic interest in the Straits. Although trade between Russia and the Porte did not attain significant proportions, the situation did develop to the benefit of the Greeks. The Russian carrying trade was almost completely in the hands of the Greek shipowners, who, by the terms of the Treaty of Kuchuk Kainarji, were allowed to fly the Russian flag.

As in the previous period, international commerce remained the province of the non-Muslim citizens of the empire, in particular the Greeks, Armenians, and Jews, but also other Orthodox Christians. Their advantageous position at the expense of the Muslims can be understood by reference to the relatively low standing of the merchant in Ottoman society, where prestige and power were traditionally associated with landholding, the military, and

179

public office. The Ottoman ruling classes, when they invested money, usually preferred to place it in land or in state-connected enterprises such as tax farming or the purchase of lucrative administrative positions. Christian notables also made their fortunes in real estate and tax collection. Although the merchant had a superior status in relation to the mass of the population, the peasantry, he ranked below those with the real power in the state.

Among the merchants, those engaged in international trade enjoyed certain advantages that did not pertain to those whose activities were limited to the Ottoman Empire. Local trade and the supplying of manufactured goods to the internal market were largely conducted by small merchants and craftsmen, concentrated in the cities, whose activities were tightly regulated by the guild system. The close control in effect here, however, was not applied to those who handled international or long-distance transport and trade. The vast possibilities in this field were exploited by an enterprising group who belonged neither to the top levels of Ottoman society nor to the guild-dominated merchant and artisan class of the towns. Orthodox Slavic and Greek merchants, as well as Jews and Armenians, were able to take full advantage of the situation.

The Ottoman Empire had, of course, been trading with Europe since the sixteenth century. The first commercial agreements, called capitulations, had been negotiated with France. They of necessity had to contain certain provisions that were to the advantage of the Europeans. Most significant for the future were the regulations concerning extraterritoriality, which gave foreign consuls legal jurisdiction over their citizens. This arrangement had originally been made to meet the problem that a Christian merchant could not expect to receive a fair trial in an Ottoman court, where his evidence would not be admitted. This privilege, later flagrantly abused, served to remove many foreign citizens from all Ottoman police control. Nevertheless, without extraterritoriality or some similar measure, it would have been difficult for a European to engage in trade in the empire.

The commercial agreements had other stipulations that were to be of great disadvantage to the empire. The first pacts usually set the tariffs at the low rates of 3 to 5 percent ad valorem. Agreements at this time and later hindered the Ottoman Empire from adopting protectionist policies; the condition depressed and discouraged native production. In the nineteenth century, as we shall see, all of the great powers cooperated to maintain what was in fact an unequal commercial relationship.

Despite the fact that European merchants were allowed to do business in the empire, they were faced with obstacles. Not only was there a great deal of hostility to foreigners, but the Western Europeans did not understand either the local languages or the methods used in conducting commercial affairs, including who should be bribed and how much. As a result, foreign entrepreneurs had to depend on Ottoman intermediaries, who were usually Orthodox Greeks. These agents were called dragomen, just as were those who served the Porte in similar functions. A great deal of corruption surrounded all commercial transactions, and the foreign consulates were deeply involved. The consuls were empowered to issue to Ottoman subjects papers, known as *berats*, that exempted them from local taxes and legal jurisdiction. These men could then enjoy the advantages of the capitulations. In addition, many consulates for a fee would grant citizenship of their states. An example of the extreme abuse of this system was to be found in the Danubian Principalities, where thousands of people, many of whom were Russian refugees, were able to claim Austrian citizenship.

The Greeks' monopoly of the position of commercial agent was paralleled by the strong hold of these people on all the enterprises connected with the sea. They dominated the positions from shipowner and shipbuilder to common sailor. Greeks manned the vessels of all of the trading nations; they were the major group from which the Ottoman navy recruited its sailors. After French shipping was driven from the Mediterranean during the Napoleonic Wars, and the activities of the other powers were severely reduced, Greek ships had almost complete control of the carrying trade.

The increased commercial activity in the Near East reflected certain changes in Western Europe that were to be of great advantage to Balkan agricultural interests. Europe was in a period of economic upsurge; this region, England in particular, was on the eve of the great transformation that was to take place with the industrial revolution. Both Western and Central Europe were soon to feel an increasing need for Balkan products, including raw materials for their factories and food to feed the growing city populations. The market was to be particularly good for such items as cotton and maize; livestock and animal products were always in demand.

Most of the produce for this market was to come from small peasant farms. The chiftlik estates, however, also shared in the benefits of the new commercial conditions. These estates, as we have seen, were concentrated in the river valleys, along the seacoasts, and near major trading centers. In theory, they should have been better able to exploit the situation, but in fact they never developed sufficiently to become the major source of goods for the international market. The units remained small, usually from fifteen to thirty acres in size, and new methods of scientific farming were not introduced. Sharecropping continued to be the regular basis of production.

In their international transactions the Balkan merchants imported manufactured goods and colonial products, such as spices, woolen cloth, glass, watches, guns, and gunpowder. In return they exported oil, raisins, wax, silk, wool, tobacco, timber, cotton, wheat, corn, and animal products such as salted meat, leather, and livestock. The distribution of such goods within the Balkans was also primarily in the hands of non-Muslim merchants, in particular the Greeks, Tsintsars, Serbs, and Bulgarians. The bulk of these wares were bought and sold in the city markets or at regular fairs held along the trading routes. Most of the major Balkan towns had a considerable population of merchants engaged in long-distance trade or acting as agents in commercial transactions. Since Greeks played such a prominent role in them, many cities came to have a high percentage of Greeks among the population, even though the countryside might be inhabited by another nationality.

Trade within the Balkans and over the frontiers was severely hampered by the poor communications and the lack of internal improvements. Roads were not adequately maintained, nor were waterways improved. Most goods had to be transported by water or by pack animal – horse, mule, donkey, or even camel. The advantage of this latter mode was that any track or trail could be used. Old Roman routes were regularly employed. Since the countryside was not safe, with both Christian and Muslim outlaws abounding, the merchant had to travel with armed guards and preferably in a caravan. A large number of the Balkan inhabitants, often Muslim, were regularly employed as muleteers, packers, and armed guards for merchant caravans.

The major trade routes of the peninsula remained much the same as they had been in ancient times; they extended both east to west and north to south. The great road remained, running from Constantinople to Plovdiv, Sofia, Niš, Belgrade, and then to the Habsburg lands, with a branch also going from Niš to the great port of Thessaloniki (see Map 16). Trade also passed from the Adriatic coast, from ports such as Split (Spalato), Durrës, and Dubrovnik, to inland cities such as Sarajevo, Novi Pazar, and Belgrade. A major trade route in the Danubian Principalities went from the Danube to Bucharest and then over the mountains to Braşov in Transylvania. The cities along these lines of communication were well prepared to receive the merchants and their animals; inns, called *hans*, were maintained at regular intervals along the roads.

Orthodox merchants similarly predominated in Balkan-related commerce within the Habsburg Empire. After the signing of the Treaty of Karlowitz most of this trade moved along the inland routes. Only toward the end of the eighteenth century and the beginning of the nineteenth could the monarchy exploit its newly acquired Dalmatian territory or begin to develop the port of Trieste. Although the Habsburg government attempted to adhere to mercantilistic policies, which called for a surplus of exports over imports, these principles could not be applied to the Balkan area. It has been estimated that in 1779 the ratio of overland imports to exports was 5:1. The main problem was that the impoverished Balkan region was a poor market for Austria's manufactured luxury goods, nor did it need the grain that the Habsburg Empire also exported. In contrast, there was a steady Habsburg demand for Balkan raw materials, such as cotton, wool, tobacco, timber, and livestock.

The merchants, usually Orthodox, who were engaged in these commercial ventures were subjects of the monarchy and principally Serb or Greek in nationality. Like their equivalents in the Ottoman territories, they were in a good position to study local conditions, and they had agents in the Balkans.

The transportation of goods

Map 16. The Ottoman Balkans, 1815

These Orthodox merchants formed an important part of the population of Vienna and other Habsburg cities. It has been estimated that by the middle of the eighteenth century there were eighteen thousand Serbian, Greek, and Tsintsar merchants in the monarchy, living in the highest concentration along the border between the two empires.[3]

3   John R. Lampe and Marvin R. Jackson, *Balkan Economic History, 1550–1950* (Bloomington: Indiana University Press, 1982), p. 60.

184

Thus, within both the Habsburg and the Ottoman states, the control of international trade was held by certain limited groups of the population; in the Ottoman Empire almost all foreign trade was in non-Muslim hands. Although there was some concern in Austria about the situation, there was no practical alternative. The Eastern trade was profitable and necessary. In the Habsburg Empire neither the enserfed peasantry nor the landed nobility had the talent or inclination to enter the business world. As in the Ottoman Empire, these groups preferred to invest in land. In the Balkans the Muslim population was indeed engaged in commerce, but usually only as small local traders, shopkeepers, and artisans, although there were some Muslim merchants engaged in long-distance trade within the empire, and some active in the Black Sea ports. The Ottoman attitude toward foreigners, however, and the limited knowledge of foreign languages were handicaps.

The existence of a large number of Balkan Orthodox people engaged in trade in the Ottoman Empire – and it must be remembered that the numbers include muleteers, porters, sailors, and others on the lower levels of these undertakings – was to have a definite effect on the political evolution of the Balkans. Although their numbers were small in comparison to the peasant population, merchants and their associates occupied crucial positions, and they traveled around. Some of these men were well satisfied with Ottoman conditions. The low tariffs encouraged trade; the Ottoman government did not impede or regulate international commerce. There were no major barriers to movement within the empire. Even the corruption of the system offered some advantages. With sufficient money it was possible to accomplish almost anything. Many operated efficiently in this atmosphere, and those who benefited from the situation naturally sought to maintain it.

In contrast, others in the merchant community were deeply dissatisfied. Some internal conditions were not conducive to trade. The merchant suffered from the poor roads and the unimproved waterways, and the disorder and anarchy in the countryside made his business dangerous. He could benefit from a government that would maintain adequate police forces and guarantee law and order. Most important, he was almost completely without protection abroad. Whereas European consuls were resident in almost all the major Ottoman trading centers, the Porte maintained no similar offices in other countries to assist its citizens. The empire thus did not offer protection and encouragement to its merchant class; it merely placed no particular hindrances or limitations on their activities.

Because of their travels and their residence in foreign cities, the merchants were in a good position to compare systems of government. The wide differences between conditions in the Ottoman Empire and those in Europe were most apparent to them. Moreover, many, particularly the Greeks, were well educated. Their travels brought them into contact with Europeans with similar interests, and they were thus enabled to become acquainted with current political doctrines. The ideas connected with the French Revolution were to prove particularly attractive to individuals who felt oppressed and restrained by the Ottoman system, or who felt that the government was backward and tyrannical. Those who had not made a success of their undertakings were most likely to be attracted by revolutionary ideology. Certain of the future leaders of the national liberation movements were directly affected by their commercial backgrounds, either as members of overseas merchant communities or simply as livestock dealers crossing between the two empires.

The Eastern Question

The solution of Balkan and Ottoman problems was infinitely complicated by the fact that in the nineteenth century this region became a major center of great-power conflict, and the fate of the area became intimately linked with the maintenance of the European balance of power (see Map 17). The entire cluster of issues surrounding the decline of the Ottoman Empire, the revolt of the subject people, and the European intervention became known as the Eastern Question. This problem was to become the single most important cause for diplomatic controversy among the powers and was to lead to the only two general wars in the century after the Congress of Vienna – the Crimean War and World War I.

The question that must be answered first is why this area was so important to the major European governments. Certainly Britain, Russia, Austria, and France, to be joined by Germany and Italy after their national unifications, all had competing and vital interests involved in the fate of the region. Many of the major issues had already arisen in the eighteenth century. At that time Russia and Austria, usually in alliance, extended their frontiers at the expense of the Ottoman Empire until the Russian boundary reached the Pruth and the Austrian the Danube-Sava line. During this period France usually stood for the integrity of the empire, since it wielded the greatest influence in Constantinople; Britain at first did not play a major role in the conflict.

The first power to shift its attitude radically was the Habsburg Empire. In the Treaty of Vienna, as we have seen, that government acquired the Dalmatian coast as well as a predominant position in the Italian peninsula and among the German states. Thereafter, the Habsburg statesmen ceased to work actively toward the incorporation of any more Balkan people into the empire; they had difficulty enough controlling the multinational population they already held. Although the Habsburg government remained in alliance with Russia, it sought to restrain any advance of its partner in the East because it could take no compensating benefits. Austrian leaders were well aware of the advantages that Russia enjoyed among the Orthodox people, and they feared that a further extension of Russian territory or influence would endanger Austrian security on the eastern and southeastern frontiers. Habsburg diplomacy in the first half of the nineteenth century was thus to become passive.

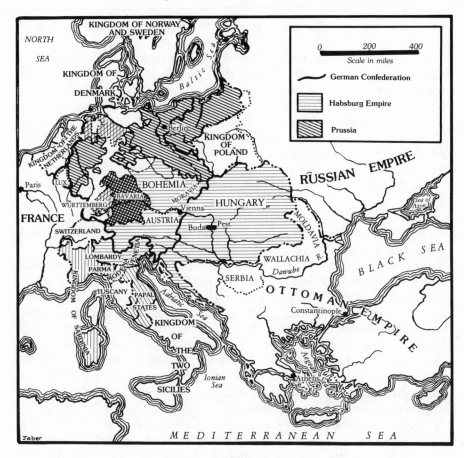

Map 17. Europe in 1815

Where possible, restraints were placed on the activities of other powers, but Austrian diplomats were no longer in the forefront of negotiations.

The former Habsburg position was now taken by Great Britain, which, as we have seen, had become actively concerned in Ottoman affairs only at the end of the eighteenth century. Previously the state had been engrossed in the duel for empire with France. After its victory over its rival and the acquisition of India, the British government gave its major attention to the protection of its vast colonial domains and the commercial routes to the East. These lines of communication ran directly through the Ottoman territories. The situation became even more serious with the development of steam transport and the opening of the Suez Canal in 1869. With the weakening of France, Britain regarded Russia as the chief threat to its world position. Britain's constant fear was that the Russian army would inflict a fatal defeat on the Ottoman Empire, which would be followed by the collapse of that state and the establishment of Russian domination in the Balkan peninsula and at the Straits.

The apparent Russian menace had an Asiatic perspective. During the nineteenth century Russia not only absorbed the Caucasus area, but extended control over the Central Asian steppelands and the three khanates of Khiva, Bokhara, and Kokand. The Russian border by 1885 thus reached that of British-protected Afghanistan. Russian advances in the Far East at the expense of China were also seen with apprehension in London. With points of conflict running from the Pacific to the Mediterranean, it can be understood why British diplomats watched the Russian moves with such care. Moreover, the key to the entire situation appeared to lie in Constantinople and the Turkish Straits.

Because of these concerns, the British government supported the maintenance of the Ottoman Empire and its continued domination over its wide territories. The alternative appeared to be an inevitable Russian control of the region, in particular of the Balkans and the Straits. This policy, together with its continued enthusiasm for colonial expansion, placed the British government in a contradictory position. At home, where liberal victories resulted in an ever-widening franchise, and on the Continent, where Britain usually joined with France in opposing the conservative powers, support was given to national and liberal movements. In contrast, in their own colonial possessions and in the Eastern Question, the British leaders followed quite different policies. Although they always encouraged efforts to reform the Ottoman administration, movements that had as their objective the dissolution of the empire were usually firmly discouraged.

Despite the defeat of Napoleon, France continued to pursue an active policy in the Mediterranean, but with the major attention directed toward North Africa and Syria, and not Constantinople and the Balkans. In the Mediterranean region, seen as a whole, the chief French opponent remained Britain, whose fleet controlled the waters of that sea. However, in the more restricted area of the Aegean and Black seas, the French government could cooperate with the British in opposing a Russian advance. French policy, in fact, preserved a great deal of freedom of action. When France's interests were served, its diplomats could support the maintenance of the Ottoman Empire. They had, however, the alternative of agreeing to a partition and of taking Egypt, Syria, and Algeria, areas to which claims had already been staked out.

As can be seen, although the policies of Britain, France, and Austria often conflicted in the Near East, all were extremely apprehensive about Russian actions. It had certainly been clear throughout the eighteenth century that the Russian government did have definite territorial goals, all of which could be achieved only at Ottoman expense. From the reign of Peter the Great onward, an active policy of expansion in the Black Sea region had been followed. By the end of the eighteenth century, not only had the lands north of that sea been taken, including the Crimea, but Russia was deeply involved in the affairs of the Orthodox Balkan people, in particular the Greeks, Serbs, Montenegrins, and, of course, the Romanians in the Danubian Principalities. Before 1812 the tsarist government had considered annexing the Romanian provinces, but had limited itself to the acquisition of Bessarabia.

In the nineteenth century the Russian government was to retain the advantages in Balkan affairs that it had enjoyed previously. Russian armies were in a position to menace Constantinople, and, as we have seen, the Balkan people did in fact offer a potential source of support. Some groups always called for Russian intervention. Should the Russian statesmen wish to exploit Ottoman weakness, they could usually count on Balkan allies.

Other considerations, however, tended to take precedence and to limit severely any temptation to pursue a forward policy in the area. In comparison with the West, Russia was a backward state. Throughout the nineteenth century, when Western and Central Europe were undergoing a period of rapid economic transformation with the industrial revolution, Russian development lagged behind. Although Russian armies were large in size, they were not particularly effective on the battlefield. The repeated victories won against the weak Ottoman empire were not easily achieved. The Russian borders were also long and difficult to defend. The great fear of the government throughout the century was that the adoption of an adventurous course in the Eastern Question would lead to the formation of a European coalition and a crushing military defeat. This possibility, which became a reality in the middle of the century, constantly hampered Russian actions.

Fortunately for Russian interests, the government had alternatives to war by which it could achieve diplomatic supremacy in the Near East. If the destruction of the Ottoman Empire were abandoned as a goal, Russia could instead adopt a policy of alliance, and through close cooperation control and supervise the actions of the weaker partner. Already Russian-Ottoman military actions had been undertaken during the Napoleonic Wars. The occupation and subsequent administration of the Ionian Islands had been a joint venture. Should this course of action be chosen, the Russian government of course could not actively support Balkan revolutionary movements. It too would have to counsel the Orthodox population to accept the situation, a policy that was often neither effective nor popular.

The Russian statesmen, however, had already discovered a partial solution to this dilemma. As we have seen, in the treaties dealing with the Danubian Principalities, provisions had been inserted enabling the Russian government to supervise the internal political conditions of the provinces. In Article VIII of the Treaty of Bucharest of 1812, similar stipulations gave St. Petersburg a right to interfere in Serbian affairs. There were, in addition, the numerous vague provisions in other treaties dealing with the protection of Orthodox Christianity. With these religious and political rights of protection, Russian officials could both wield great influence in Constantinople and also win favor among the Balkan peoples. They could exert their power to gain reforms

189

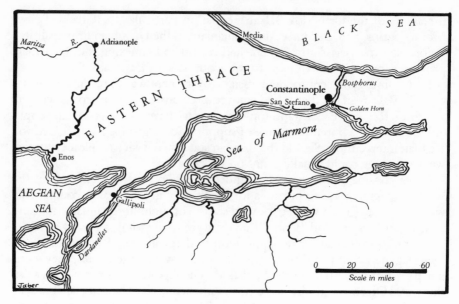

Map 18. The Straits

or more autonomous rights for their Orthodox coreligionists, if it suited their interests, or they could use their position to bolster the power and prestige of the Porte. This policy of manipulating the Ottoman domestic situation, rather than adopting military force to gain diplomatic objectives, was preferred by St. Petersburg through most of the century.

Because of the rivalry of the powers, in particular the conflict of Russia and Britain, the Turkish Straits assumed a major importance (see Map 18). It was generally recognized that the Ottoman Empire was extremely vulnerable to attack. Its capital, Constantinople, situated on the Golden Horn and the Sea of Marmora, could be taken from either land or sea. Modern weapons had destroyed the defensive capabilities of Byzantine times. A great power, once in possession of the city, would be able either to dominate the entire empire or, at the least, to force its division and decomposition. Russia, with Europe's largest land army, and Britain, the predominant sea power, both had the capability of taking Constantinople under favorable circumstances, but for either state to be successful, control of the Straits was essential.

The Straits played an equally significant role in the worldwide conflict of these two powers. Although in competition in both Europe and Asia, these states, with no contiguous boundaries, could fight only indirectly or on remote frontiers, such as Afghanistan. It was also difficult for a sea power to engage directly a nation whose strength was based on its army; it was the battle of the elephant and the whale. About the only region where the two competitors could meet in direct conflict was in the area of the Black Sea and the eastern Mediterranean. The British government was constantly apprehensive that Russia might gain control of the Straits and from there operate against British lines of communication through the Mediterranean. Russian fears concerned the ability of the British fleet to pass through the Straits and attack either the Caucasus or the relatively weakly defended shores of southern Russia and the Black Sea. Russia also had a strong interest in keeping the sea-lanes open once its grain trade through the Black Sea and the Mediterranean had attained significant proportions. It must be remembered that Russian Baltic ports were frozen for a large part of the year, so that these southern outlets were essential to trade, especially before the age of railroad transportation.

Because of these considerations, the control of the waterway was of international significance. Since both shores were Ottoman territory, the Straits were legally a part of the empire. Internationalization would not be easy to impose. The solution preferred by the powers, including the Porte, came to be the closure by international treaty of the Straits to the warships of all governments when the Ottoman Empire was at peace. This measure gave some protection to Constantinople, and it prevented the Russian and British navies from endangering each other's interests. It also assured the Porte of the right to regain full control in time of war. This entire question, however, remained an important subject of international diplomacy until after World War II, when atomic weapons made the immediate and complete closure of the Straits an easy option for any state armed with them.

The desire of all of the great powers to preserve peace and tranquility in the East after 1815 reflected the general fatigue and disillusionment felt everywhere after the previous quarter-century of warfare and revolution. Throughout Europe a wave of reaction arose against revolutionary movements and the climate of opinion associated with the French Revolution. Conservative principles and the maintenance of order were the prime concerns of the day. To protect their general interests the powers concluded two agreements: the Quadruple Alliance and the Holy Alliance. The first was little more than an association of the victors, Austria, Britain, Prussia, and Russia, guaranteeing the settlement; France adhered in 1818. The second, the Holy Alliance, was drawn up on the initiative of Tsar Alexander I, who was about to enter into a conservative, even mystical, period of his life. In this document, the signatories agreed to be governed by Christian principles in the administering of their states and in international relations. Only the tsar took the terms seriously, and the agreement certainly never functioned as a true alliance. The name was used after 1820 to designate the alignment of Austria, Russia, and Prussia, a combination that was, although with interruptions, to remain fairly stable until the 1890s. These three powers were joined by their common conservative political principles, their similar interests in international affairs, and their joint participation in the previous partition of Poland. Although this alliance was to function well in general European affairs, it was, as we shall see, to break down in crises involving the Balkans. In this area Prussia had no direct interests, and Austrian and Russian aims were often in open conflict.

Despite the conservative stance of all of the major powers, revolutionary movements continued to gain strength and to disrupt international affairs. Revolts took place in some German states, in Italy, and in Spain and her colonial possessions. The events in Central Europe and Italy were particularly damaging to Austrian interests. Habsburg foreign policy was under the direction of one of the most able diplomats of the time, Clemens von Metternich. Winning over the tsar to his views, he was able to implement a policy that called for military intervention wherever a legitimate monarch had been overthrown or was threatened by revolutionary activity. Under this program Austrian armies marched into Italy and put down revolts in the Kingdom of the Two Sicilies and Sardinia in 1821; French troops undertook the same mission in Spain in 1823.

Although Britain, and later France, withdrew from the Continental coalition, Russia, Austria, and Prussia remained joined in an alignment that not only stood for opposition to revolutions, but also favored positive measures for their suppression. For Alexander I "the revolution" had become a truly menacing presence. By the time of the opening of the Congress of Laibach (Ljubljana) in 1821, which had been called to deal with Italian affairs, the tsar was convinced of the existence of an international revolutionary committee, with headquarters in Paris, which organized revolutions throughout Europe and engaged in constant intrigue and agitation. Both the national and the liberal bases of most of the revolts did in fact constitute a direct threat to the three conservative regimes. It can thus be seen why Russia and the Habsburg Empire, the two states immediately adjacent to the Balkan Ottoman provinces, were strongly against change by revolutionary, violent means, and why they were committed to the defense of the status quo in international relations.

The revolutionary situation in the Balkans

In the previous pages the general background to the first Balkan revolutions has been examined. It would, however, be a mistake to assign too much importance to elements that were in some ways extraneous to the everyday experiences of the average Balkan inhabitant. Although European ideology, the revival of national consciousness among the intellectuals, the rise of an Orthodox merchant class, and the competing goals of the great powers in the Near East all play a role in our story, the immediate causes of the first revolts lay rather in the internal conditions in the peninsula, almost all of which had arisen in the eighteenth century. First in importance was the obvious failure of the Ottoman government to maintain law and order in the countryside and to control the unruly and brigand elements, both Christian and Muslim. This situation forced peaceful Christian as well as Muslim populations to organize in their own defense. Local centers of government thus arose, which in turn commanded the loyalty and obedience of the inhabitants.

The breakdown of central authority resulted not only in the formation of alternate political centers, but in the prevalence in many regions of armed bands, legal and illegal, with often competing interests and jurisdictions. The activities of the ayans, kirdzhalis, illegal janissaries, bandits, and Bosnian captains have been mentioned before. To these must be added the legal or quasi-legal formations of the armatoles, the police forces of the municipal authorities or the notables, the legal janissary units, the Serbs of the Military Frontier, and a Wallachian militia known as the *pandours*. A large proportion of the Balkan population was armed and had military experience, not so much as part of a regular army as in guerilla fighting. Local armies commanded by a native officer corps could thus be raised in times of crisis.

Local Balkan leaders also had a keen awareness of the use that could be made of the competing great powers. Although after 1812 no European government wished to be faced with an Eastern crisis, Balkan revolutionaries continued to expect outside intervention. As we shall see, Russian aid was often assumed. Although there was much rhetoric on the subject, both then and since, there were few signs of any deep affection linking the Balkan people to any European state. Despite the Orthodox connection, Balkan leaders regularly sought French, Austrian, and even British soldiers and money, as well as Russian. They were grateful for any assistance received, but they did not intend to recompense this aid with political privileges unless it proved absolutely necessary. Nevertheless, the fact that the revolutionaries were willing to gamble with great-power politics and to summon European assistance could create a dangerous situation.

THE SERBIAN REVOLUTION

The conditions just described were all present in the pashalik of Belgrade, which became the first center for a successful Balkan national revolution (see Map 19). This border province contained a population of around 368,000 prior to 1804,[4] and a high percentage of the people were experienced fighters. It will be remembered that during the war between the Habsburg and the Ottoman empires, which was concluded by the Treaty of Sistova in 1791, Serbian Freicorps under their own officers had fought on the Austrian side. Despite these services, the Serbs received no gains in the peace agreement. General disillusionment subsequently prevailed over the hope of winning advantages by cooperation with the monarchy. The goal of the Serbian leader-

4 Vladimir Dedijer et al., *History of Yugoslavia*, trans. Kordija Kveder (New York: McGraw-Hill, 1975), p. 263.

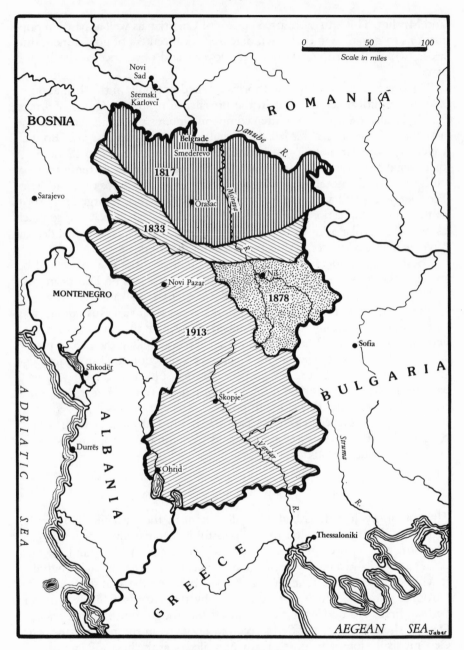

Map 19. The expansion of Serbia, 1804–1913

ship at this time was to reestablish peace and security in the countryside and achieve, if possible, the recognition by the Porte of certain local autonomous rights.

Sultan Selim III had a similar desire for tranquility in his lands. Not only had he been defeated by foreign armies, but in domestic affairs his rule was continually challenged by rebellious ayans and janissaries. It was certainly to his interest to conciliate his Christian subjects. Therefore, in 1791, 1792, and 1794 he issued firmans in which he acceded to many of the Serbian wishes; the relationship between the Porte and the Serbian population was better defined, and some autonomous rights were guaranteed. The Serbs were to collect their own taxes; they were to have the right to bear arms and organize a militia; assurances were given that measures would be taken to limit the abuses in the conditions of landholding on the chiftliks. In addition, the sultan appointed to local positions men who were given the task of conciliating the Serbs and suppressing the unruly elements. It will be remembered that at this time the Porte, under Russian pressure, had made similar promises of autonomous rights to the Principalities.

The grave weakness in this arrangement was that the Porte was in no position to fulfill its pledges. The unsettling element in Serbian affairs was, as elsewhere, the janissary corps. The Ottoman government had previously adopted a policy of sending these men out into the provinces to remove them as a source of trouble in Constantinople. In the Serbian lands, as in other areas, they proved impossible for the local Ottoman authorities to control. They were a menace in the countryside, where they seized lands and villages and established chiftlik estates on which conditions were much worse for the peasant than under the traditional landholders. The janissary actions were bitterly opposed not only by the Christians, but by the legal, established Muslim population of government officials, merchants, and sipahis.

In 1791, as part of the reforms to be made in the pashalik, the Ottoman government decided that the janissaries would be prevented from returning to Belgrade. The Habsburg army had occupied the city until the end of the war, so at the time there were naturally no janissaries in residence. They, however, were determined not to accept this decision, and they were in an excellent position to defy the sultan. Their ally was Pasvanoglu, the pasha of Vidin, who was successfully resisting Ottoman authority. The rebel ayan, of course, wanted his janissary supporters back in Belgrade, where they could aid him. With the support of Pasvanoglu and kirdjali forces, the janissaries launched an attack on Belgrade in the spring of 1797.

Meeting the danger of the rebellious janissaries and implementing the policy of conciliating the Christians were the responsibilities of Hadji Mustafa Pasha, the pasha of Belgrade. Probably of Greek descent, Mustafa had a favorable attitude toward the Serbs and approved of the concessions that had been made to them. At this time the Serbs were able to form a militia of fifteen thousand men, which gave them control of the strongest single armed unit in the pashalik, and they were able to defend Belgrade successfully. The Ottoman policies also led to an increase in cooperation between the Serbian local leaders. A front was thus formed between the Ottoman officials and the Christians against the lawless ayans and their associates.

At first, the measures taken by the Porte proved successful. The supporters of Pasvanoglu met defeat everywhere, and by 1798 he was under siege in his fortress at Vidin. However, this was also the year when Napoleon launched his invasion of Egypt. With only limited troops at his disposal, Selim was forced to withdraw his forces on the Danube to meet the new danger. The action proved to be a disaster for the Serbs. The Porte was compelled to make terms with the Muslim rebels; Pasvanoglu was recognized as governor of Vidin. Even worse, the janissaries were allowed to return to Belgrade, although they were required to respect the authority of Hadji Mustafa Pasha. The inevitable then happened. Once entrenched in the pashalik, the janissaries moved to take full power into their own hands, and Hadji Mustafa was killed. A period of chaos followed. Although the control of the province was in the hands of the rebellious elements, they quarreled among themselves. Nevertheless, Pasvanoglu and his janissary allies were clearly more powerful than the local Ottoman officials and the Serbs.

In 1802 four janissary leaders, called *dahi*s from their rank in the corps, rose to predominant power. The janissaries were able to take over control in the countryside. Again their actions were extremely damaging, not only to the Christians, but also to the loyal and peaceful Muslim population and the legal authorities. Nevertheless, despite the violent and destructive behavior of the janissaries, many Muslims opposed granting concessions to the Serbs or cooperating with Christians, since they had no faith in Christian loyalty to the empire. Faced with a reign of terror and unable to gain protection from the legal authorities, the Serbian population was forced to act in its own defense. Armed units were organized throughout the country. For the future the most important center of resistance was that established in the Šumadija under the leadership of the local notable and livestock trader Karadjordje Petrović. By the spring of 1804 he had thirty thousand men ready for combat.

The actual beginning of the revolt was occasioned by the dahis' plans to massacre the Serbian leaders. Convinced that they were faced by a rebellion, the janissaries decided to act first. In January and February they killed perhaps as many as 150 men. The Serbian population was thus forced to take measures of self-defense. At first there was no central leadership; the revolt took the form of a spontaneous response to janissary atrocities. However, in February about three hundred notables gathered in Orašac in Central Šumadija and chose Karadjordje as their leader. At this time there was no opposition to the nomination of a single commander. After May 1804 Karadjordje signed his proclamations with such titles as "Supreme Vojvoda" and

"Leader." Given the dangerous situation of the time, the Serbian notables accepted the necessity of establishing a strong authority.

Although the Serbs were in revolt, it is important to note that they were in rebellion not against the sultan, but against the janissaries who were themselves defying the Porte. Throughout this period the Serbian leaders continued to negotiate with the Ottoman government. The Serbian objectives remained consistent during this first period of rebellion. They sought simply the implementation of the firmans that Selim had already granted, and they thus merely desired that the Porte assure them of the fulfillment of promises already made. Their aim was to rid their land of the dahis, not to gain independence, although the firmans, if put into effect, would indeed have given them many autonomous rights. Limitations would have been placed on the Turkish presence in the pashalik. The Serbs wished to make certain that the janissaries would indeed be expelled and their ownership of rural property terminated. In addition, they themselves wanted to provide the military forces needed in the province; the Ottoman troops were to leave. They also insisted that the tribute and other taxes be levied and collected by Serbian officials.

Once again the Serbs won the approval and support of the central government. Not only were their forces successful in the field, but the sultan appointed Abu Bekir, the vezir of Bosnia, as pasha of Belgrade, with instructions to crush the janissaries. In August 1804 the dahi forces were defeated and the four leaders executed. With the elimination of this danger, conditions could be expected to improve in the province. In fact, little had been settled. The pashalik was still the scene of a three-cornered conflict among, first, the janissaries, who were still in residence; second, the pasha and the traditional Muslim elements; and, finally, the Serbs. The balance was soon upset. Once again the janissaries refused to accept the authority of the Ottoman officials. In the winter and spring of 1805 they laid waste to the countryside, and they secured the deposition of Abu Bekir.

Meanwhile, the Serbian leadership had gained in power and self-confidence. It had succeeded in organizing military forces that had won victories, and there was no intention of retreating. Moreover, it was decided that foreign assistance should be sought. Attempts were thus made to secure aid from both St. Petersburg and Vienna; a delegation was sent to Russia in 1804. What the Serbian leaders desired was some sort of a great-power guarantee for their autonomy. By this time, it will be remembered, Russia was acting as guarantor in the Danubian Principalities, and the Ionian Islands were under joint Russian and Ottoman protection. This issue was, however, very sensitive for the Porte. It naturally opposed granting any outside power a means by which it could interfere in internal Ottoman affairs.

In addition to attempting to secure outside aid, the Serbian leaders tried to gain the support of other Balkan Christians, in particular their brother Serbs living in Bosnia, Montenegro, and Hercegovina. The events in the pashalik were, of course, followed with intense interest by the Serbs living across the border in the Habsburg lands. As had happened regularly in the past, the disturbances in the pashalik caused thousands of refugees to flee into Austrian territories. Despite the efforts of the Habsburg authorities to prevent the crossing of the frontier, Serbian groups had little difficulty in moving freely across the boundary in both directions.

Selim thus once again faced a crisis. The janissaries were anything but obedient subjects, but the Serbs presented what might become an even greater danger to the interests of the empire as a whole. In the past many influential Muslims had always argued against concessions to the Christians; these conservative circles were also combating the sultan's attempts at military reform. Fearing Christian rebellion as well as Muslim opposition, Selim reversed his policy. Instead of conciliating the Serbs, he decided to suppress them. Hafiz Pasha, the governor of Niš, was ordered to march against them. In August 1805 the first major clash between Serbian troops and a regular Ottoman army took place. The Serbian victory marks the commencement of the Serbian revolution in the real sense of the word. In this battle the Serbs fought not against a Muslim rebel force, but against the sultan's troops. The Serbian military victories continued. In November 1805 the fortress of Smederevo fell; it became the first capital of the rebel government. Belgrade was captured in December 1806. The Serbian peasant soldiers had thus been able to take control of the entire pashalik.

Despite their military successes, the Serbian leadership remained willing to negotiate with the Porte on the previous terms. Efforts, meanwhile, continued to obtain Russian or Austrian intervention. The Serbian position was much improved in the summer of 1806 when war recommenced between Russia and the Ottoman Empire. Both sides had need of Serbian support. Even before the fighting was renewed, the Porte, fearing the probability of hostilities with Russia, was willing to make concessions. It now agreed to the entire Serbian program, including the removal of the janissaries and the use of local troops to garrison Serbian fortresses and the frontier. Although the Ottoman government was willing to offer what amounted to full autonomy, the question remained whether any agreement would be kept once the Russian danger passed.

Moreover, the Serbs had an alternate offer. Previously, their requests for aid had been regularly rejected in Vienna. The Serbian delegation sent to Russia in 1804 had received a similar negative reception. Although its members had held a meeting with the Russian foreign minister, Prince Adam Czartoryski, in November, he had advised them to negotiate with the Porte. At that time Russia was pursuing a policy of cooperation with the Ottoman government, but by 1806 the situation had entirely changed. Once at war with the Porte, the Russian government welcomed Balkan assistance, as it had in the past when it had regularly called upon the Christians for support during the invasions of Ottoman territory. At this time, a Russian army was in the Principalities; a fleet was cruising in the Adriatic, and, in cooperation with the Montenegrins, Russian troops were in occupation of the ports of Kotor and Budva. Serbia could form a link among the areas of operation.

In June 1807 a Russian emissary, Marquis F. O. Paulucci, arrived in Belgrade. His instructions were to assess the situation and to see what the Serbs needed. He was not authorized to negotiate a regular agreement. Nevertheless, in June he proceeded to conclude a formal convention. Its terms not only provided for Russian assistance to the Serbian rebels, but assured that Russian influence would remain strong in the future. The first article of the agreement read: "The Serbian people most humbly beg H.I.M. to appoint a capable governor who will bring order to the people, administer the Serbian land, and devise a constitution in consonance with the customs of the people. The promulgation of the constitution should be done in the name of H.I.M. Alexander the First."[5] Russian advisers and military garrisons were also to be sent.

In accepting the terms of this agreement, the Serbs had made a clear choice. Faced with the alternatives of agreeing to the Ottoman offer of an autonomous status or of joining Russia and fighting for full independence, they had decided on the second course of action. They had no means of knowing that the negotiations did not have the approval of St. Petersburg. Unfortunately for the Serbs, the wrong decision had been made. The acceptance of the Russian alliance in Belgrade coincided almost exactly with the meeting of Napoleon and Alexander I at Tilsit. Here the two emperors concluded a treaty settling most of the major controversies that divided them. In this agreement Napoleon undertook to attempt to negotiate an armistice between Russia and the Ottoman Empire. Certainly the pact precluded any major Russian effort to support the Serbian rebels. In August 1807 Russia and the Ottoman Empire concluded the armistice of Slobozia. Although Alexander did not approve its terms, two years of uneasy peace followed. The ultimate fate of the Serbian revolution now rested on the course of international events and also on the concurrent political struggle that was taking place in Constantinople.

After 1807 the fortunes of the revolution steadily declined. Not only was the fate of Serbia increasingly dependent on the relations between the great powers, but a split occurred in the Serbian leadership. As we have seen, Karadjordje had been chosen to head the rebel forces at the beginning of the revolt. He remained the outstanding figure during this period even though he had to face increasing opposition. The Serbian leader had been born in the Šumadija, probably in 1768. His family, which was poor, emigrated to the

5   Michael Boro Petrovich, *A History of Modern Serbia, 1804–1918*, 2 vols. (New York: Harcourt Brace Jovanovich, 1976), I, 54–55.

Vojvodina. During the Austro-Turkish war Karadjordje became a member of the Freicorps and fought in western Serbia. Once peace was restored, he returned to the Šumadija, where he became a livestock merchant. He engaged in trade over the border with the monarchy. He also joined the national militia that Selim III had authorized, and became an officer. He had thus acquired considerable practical military experience before the Serbian revolt. Although he held the title of supreme commander of the revolutionary troops, Karadjordje was only one of many such military men in Serbia. In their own districts similar local leaders held prestige and power. These men were anxious to protect their personal positions, and they were jealous of any single central authority.

These local loyalties naturally hindered Karadjordje. In addition to organizing the military effort against the Ottoman army, he was faced with the problem of administering the lands under Serbian control. He therefore had to arrange for the collection of taxes and the establishment of law courts. Although he had the necessary attributes of a military leader, being courageous, strong-willed, and skillful, he had more difficulty in governing the state. Moreover, his successes on the battlefield were bound to cause jealousy. What the Serbian lands needed in this time of danger was a strong central government that could organize the territory for victory. The local notables, however, were most reluctant to surrender any power to one of their number or to accept a secondary position in the government. They were also in a position to make their objections heard. The revolution was being fought not by a regular army, but by peasant soldiers led by their local leaders. Thus the notables had their own armed guards. Their attitude was to be that of opposition to any transfer of authority to a central regime that they and their adherents could not control. They sought means of binding Karadjordje's hands and assuring that he did not gain dictatorial powers. As we have seen, throughout Balkan history, the local aristocracy had consistently opposed a centralized state.

In order to meet the objections, Karadjordje agreed to the establishment of a Governing Council in 1805, which was supposed to be a check on his powers. At first, he was able to assure that the members were his supporters. In 1808 he had himself proclaimed hereditary supreme leader, although he agreed to act with the Governing Council. In fact, at this time he had no strong political rivals. He appointed his followers to the major political positions, and his candidates were sent to run the local administrations. Nevertheless, the opposition never ceased its efforts to weaken his authority. The situation became worse when Constantine Rodofinikin, the agent of the Russian army, arrived in Belgrade in August 1807. He cooperated with Karadjordje's critics and used them against the Serbian leader.

Meanwhile, the international situation was again worsening for Serbia. Although Russia was not actively at war with the Ottoman Empire, the policy of agreement with France had not been successful. The meeting between Napoleon and Alexander I at Erfurt in 1808 had resulted in an impasse over Eastern affairs. The internal situation in the Ottoman Empire had similarly deteriorated sharply. In Constantinople Selim III and his successor, Mustafa IV, were both deposed and killed; Mahmud II then ascended the throne. During this period of political crisis the Ottoman government again showed itself willing to offer the Serbs wide autonomy, but in the discussions between the representatives of the two parties, no agreement could be reached on the exact boundaries to be assigned to an autonomous Serbian state. The Serbs also still wanted a foreign guarantor. Because of these issues, no satisfactory arrangement could be made.

The lull in the fighting ended in 1809. Although the Serbs had expected military assistance from Russia, little was in fact delivered. The rebel forces were thus driven on the defensive; in August 1809 an Ottoman army marched on Belgrade. With this reversal of fortunes a mass exodus of Serbs across the Danube occurred, among them the Russian agent, Rodofinikin. Faced with disaster, Karadjordje appealed both to the Habsburg Empire and to Napoleon, again without success. Despite the fact that the Ottoman troops were not able to reconquer all of Serbia, a turning point had been reached in the first revolution. Rebel armies were now on the defensive; their aim became to hold what territories they had and not to make further gains. Some improvement in their position, however, took place in 1810, when a degree of Russo-Serbian military cooperation was established and when the brilliant Russian general M. I. Kutuzov was in command of the operations against the Ottoman Empire. Weapons, ammunition, medical supplies, and some financial aid also arrived at this time.

Unfortunately for Serbian interests, the Russian position soon underwent another radical change. Faced with the imminent danger of a French invasion, the Russian diplomats pressed toward a conclusion of the negotiations that were going on with the Ottoman representatives. In these discussions the chief Russian objective had been the acquisition of the Danubian Principalities, or at least Moldavia; Serbia was a secondary matter. Because it needed an agreement quickly, the Russian government was forced to accept the line of the Pruth River and thus the partition of the Moldavian territory. Serbia was not completely forgotten. Article VIII of the Treaty of Bucharest of 1812 provided for the full reoccupation of Serbia by the Ottoman authority, but with the promise of amnesty. Ottoman garrisons would return:

> But in order that those garrisons shall in no way annoy the Serbians contrary to the rights of the subjects, the Sublime Porte, moved by a feeling of clemency, will settle with the Serbian nation the necessary securities. It will grant to the Serbians, at their request, the same advantages which are enjoyed by its subjects of the islands of the

Archipelago and other countries, and will make it feel the effects of its high clemency in making over to them the administration of their internal affairs, in fixing the whole of their tributes, in receiving them from their own hands, and will, in short, settle all these matters with the Serbian nation.[6]

The Serbian government was not aware of the negotiations leading to the agreement, nor did the Russian government inform it of the contents. The terms were learned only when the Ottoman authorities sought their fulfillment. The Serbian leaders were naturally most concerned about the sections providing for Ottoman reoccupation of the fortifications and the cities of the pashalik, an action that would put the Porte again in full military control of the Serbian lands. Nor were the provisions for autonomy clear. The Russian advice was that the Serbs should negotiate directly on the subject with the Ottoman government; St. Petersburg would give diplomatic support. Even worse, the Russian government was now forced to withdraw all of its troops, not only from Serbia, where some units had been operating for almost two years, but also from Wallachia and Moldavia. Russia would thus not be in a position to exert pressure on Constantinople for the observance of treaty obligations.

The Serbian resources were by this time nearly exhausted. The constant fighting since 1804 had left the country without further means of resistance. Russia was fully occupied with the French invasion. The Ottoman government saw that it had the opportunity to settle the Serbian question, and in July three Ottoman armies converged on Serbia. In October 1813 Karadjordje, the metropolitan Leontije, and the other members of the government crossed the Danube into Austria. Four days later the Ottoman army reoccupied Belgrade, from which it had been expelled in 1806. The first Serbian revolution thus came to an end.

Once back in possession of the pashalik, the Porte at first tried a policy of conciliation. It had a great interest in securing peaceful conditions. A general amnesty was issued, and many emigrants returned from the Austrian lands. Other notables, who had not left the country, submitted to the authority of the new pasha of Belgrade, Suleiman Usküplü. Among these was the prominent notable, Miloš Obrenović, who in return was confirmed in his position as oborknez of Rudnik. The main force of the regular Ottoman army then left the country. Matters did not, however, settle down since the problems of internal administration remained. The Serbs were still armed, and they outnumbered the Ottoman troops left behind. The years of revolution and fighting had left a legacy of bitter feeling between the Christians and Muslims. Incidents and atrocities were bound to occur on both sides.

---

6 Edward Hertslet, *The Map of Europe by Treaty*, 4 vols. (London: Butterworths, 1875–1891), III, 2030–2032.

The future leader of the second Serbian revolution, Miloš Obrenović, first tried collaboration. When a local uprising broke out in 1814, he offered to suppress it on the condition that the participants be granted amnesty. The failure of Suleiman to abide by his assurances caused the outbreak of a new revolt. When the pasha executed some of the rebels, the Serbs feared that another massive outburst of Ottoman reprisals could be expected. Accordingly, they organized again for resistance, this time under the leadership of Miloš. The revolt commenced in April, but it was soon successfully concluded. The international situation was much more favorable this time. The wars with France were at an end, and the Porte did not want a new revolution in its lands that would draw European attention to its domestic problems.

From the beginning of the revolution Miloš declared that he was acting not against the sultan, but against Suleiman and his policies. He was thus always ready to negotiate a settlement. In Constantinople the Russian diplomats also prodded the Porte in regard to the implementation of Article VIII of the Bucharest treaty. Determined to follow a policy of appeasement, the Ottoman government removed the pasha of Belgrade from office. Negotiations then commenced between the Serbian representatives and Marashli Ali Pasha, the vezir of Rumelia. An oral agreement was reached in November 1815, which the sultan subsequently confirmed in a firman. Miloš requested and received terms similar to those which the Porte had been willing to grant to Karadjordje in 1807. The Serbian leader was recognized as supreme knez, or prince, of Serbia. A National Chancery of twelve Serbian notables was to be set up in Belgrade as the highest court of the land. Serbian officials were to collect the taxes and to administer local affairs. Janissaries were forbidden from owning land. Other provisions allowed the Serbs to keep their weapons, assured them of trading privileges, and granted a full amnesty to those who had participated in the rebellion. The terms of the agreement established Serbia as a semiautonomous state that was, nevertheless, still closely bound to the Ottoman Empire.

After the conclusion of the understanding both Miloš and Marashli, who remained vezir of Rumelia until 1821, attempted to maintain peaceful conditions. Miloš was faced with the problem of organizing a new administration and of combating the same type of opposition that had hindered Karadjordje. Questions of domestic politics were to be the chief concern of the prince throughout his relatively long reign.

Eleven years of revolutionary activity had thus gained for the Serbs many autonomous rights and a native prince. The achievement of this goal had not been easy. Serbian fortunes were closely tied to the ebb and flow of European politics, and repeated attempts to obtain Habsburg or Russian support had been necessary. Throughout this period the Serbian leaders suffered from the fact that the pashalik of Belgrade was of little general strategic value or interest to any European state. As we have seen, the Russian government, although offering some assistance, was quite willing to abandon its small ally when its European interests called for such a course of action. The Serbian revolution was a minor event of the time; it took place in a remote region, far from the European centers of power. In contrast, the second Balkan national revolution, that of the Greeks, caused the major European diplomatic conflict of the third decade of the century.

THE REVOLUTION IN THE DANUBIAN PRINCIPALITIES

Although the major events of the Greek revolution of the 1820s were to take place in the Peloponnesus and in Rumeli, the name by which southern mainland Greece was known at this time, the revolt was also to involve the Romanian Principalities. Here the Greek movement, which was based on Phanariot support, was first to parallel and finally to run counter to a native Romanian uprising led by Tudor Vladimirescu. For clarity and convenience the events in Greece proper are discussed here separately from those in Moldavia and Wallachia, although they were often concurrent and interdependent. The chief link between the actions in the two separate areas was to be the activities of the Greek revolutionary organization, the *Filiki Etairia*, or the Friendly Society.

The Serbian revolution, as we have seen, had been carried to success by peasant soldiers under their local leaders, with Karadjordje holding the central authority as supreme commander. The social basis of the Greek revolt was to be more complex. Greek society was divided into what were almost two separate worlds. The lower level was formed by the inhabitants of Greece proper. Its population of peasants, fisherman, notables, and military men was similar to that of the neighboring Balkan lands. At the top, other Greeks, in particular the Phanariots of Constantinople and the Principalities, the merchants engaged in international trade, and other members of the diaspora, enjoyed the privileges the Ottoman Empire could provide to those of its Christian subjects who cooperated. The aims of these two groups were also somewhat different, although both looked forward to the end of Ottoman rule. The desire of some Phanariots to dominate and eventually take over the empire has already been discussed. Their dream remained the reestablishment of the Byzantine Empire and the formation of a state whose boundaries would enclose a large non-Greek population. Some even equated the jurisdiction of the Patriarchate of Constantinople with their future nation.

Although individual Phanariots were to play a major role in the revolution, the Greek merchant community with its wide European connections was perhaps even more important. Especially influential were to be the Greeks who had settled in southern Russia, in Bessarabia, and in the port city of Odessa, the birthplace of the major central organization of the revolution.

The Filiki Etairia was founded in 1814 by three impoverished Greek merchants, Emmanuel Xanthos, Athanasios Tsakalov, and Nikolaos Skoufos. It was much like similar societies existing in Europe at the time; it had an elaborate ritual, levels of membership, and melodramatic practices. The "Great Oath" that new members were required to swear declared in part:

> Finally I swear upon your holy name, oh sacred and wretched fatherland. I swear upon your lengthy sufferings, upon the bitter tears of your imprisoned and persecuted people, shed for so many centuries until this moment by your wretched children. I devote my entire self to you. Henceforth, you will be the cause and the purpose of my thoughts. Your name will be the guide of all my actions and your happiness the reward of all my efforts. If ever I should, even for a moment, become oblivious to your sufferings and fail to fulfil my duty to you, may divine justice exhaust upon my head all the thunder of its righteousness; may my name, inherited by my heirs, be detested; may my person become the object of curses and anathema of my compatriots; and may my death be the inescapable punishment and reward for my sin, so that I may not infect the purity of the *Etairia* with my membership.[7]

The basic objective of the society was the organization of an uprising against the Ottoman Empire with the aim of establishing a Greek state with Constantinople as the capital. The goal was thus a revival of the Byzantine Empire, not the formation of a state on strictly national lines. The Etairia at first was not very successful. Between 1814 and 1816 only thirty members were enrolled; wealthy Greeks hesitated either to join or to contribute money.

The leaders soon realized that to advance further they would need Russian assistance, both military and financial, and a leader with power and influence. The ideal candidate for this position was, of course, Ioannis Capodistrias, who at this time shared the post of Russian foreign minister with Karl Nesselrode. Capodistrias had been born in Corfu. During the Napoleonic Wars he was associated with the Russian administration of the Ionian Islands. In 1809 he entered Russian service and thereafter rose rapidly through the ranks of the bureaucracy. He was approached in 1817 by Nikolaos Galatis, a member of the Etairia who had been sent to St. Petersburg to attempt to enlist his support. The Russian foreign minister, although an ardent Greek patriot, at this time believed that the liberation of Greece could best be achieved by a Russo-Turkish war. Since the time was not ripe for that event, he advised the

---

7 Quoted in George D. Frangos, "The *Philiki Etairia*: A Premature National Coalition," in Richard Clogg, ed., *The Struggle for Greek Independence: Essays to Mark the 150th. Anniversary of the Greek War of Independence* (Hamden, Conn.: Archon Books, 1973), pp. 99–100.

Greeks to organize only on an educational and cultural basis. At this stage it appears that both Capodistrias and the tsar learned of the plans for a revolt against the Ottoman Empire in some detail.

In 1818 the headquarters of the society were moved to Constantinople, and rapid progress was made thereafter. A new system of organization was adopted; twelve "apostles" were appointed and each was given the responsibility of organizing a definite district. The success of the Etairia was to be quite amazing. From the capital of the empire it set up a network of secret cells in Greek territory and the Danubian Principalities. Money was collected and instructions were sent out to all the centers of Greek life. Despite the failure to gain Russia's help, the leaders had no hesitation in implying that they were acting with the knowledge and support of that government. Since they had the open assistance of certain Orthodox church officials in Greece proper, and since Russian consulates had become recruiting centers, Russian sponsorship seemed obvious. Most of the Russian consuls in the Balkans at this time were Greeks; so they were naturally sympathetic to the cause. In view of the free use that the society made of the name of Russia, most of its members expected the tsar's active assistance in the future rebellion. At the head of the entire network of local cells was supposed to be an unnamed, secret leader, who was rumored to be Alexander I himself.

With this apparent high backing, the society was able to recruit very influential members. In Greece proper Theodoros Kolokotronis, the strongest military leader; Petrobey Mavromichalis, the ruler of Mani in the Peloponnesus; Germanos, the metropolitan of Patras; and other prominent men joined. In the Principalities the Phanariots were naturally drawn to this national movement. The merchant class, with about 54 percent, predominated in the rank-and-file membership. Of this number a high percentage were recruited in the Principalities or in southern Russia. Military men, the clergy, and the Greek notables also joined, but very few peasants became members. On a membership list of over a thousand, only six names were from the class that represented the overwhelming majority of the nation. In general, well-established merchants did not join, but the less successful, or those who had failed, were attracted.[8]

Despite its successes, the society recognized that it needed a real sign of Russia's approval and a leader who was directly connected with that power. In 1820 Capodistrias was again approached. Although he still refused to take the position, he may have suggested Alexander Ypsilantis, a general in the Russian army and an aide-de-camp of the tsar, as an alternative. The son of the former Wallachian hospodar Constantine Ypsilanti, Alexander had been educated in Russia. Despite his military rank, he had no experience in actual fighting. Although there is some controversy on the question, it appears that

8   Frangos, "The *Philiki Etairia*," pp. 87–94.

Capodistrias did not inform Alexander I of the new developments. In other words, the tsar's principal minister concealed from him the fact that preparations were being made on Russian soil for a revolt against a government with whom Russia was at the time on tolerable terms.

Once in charge of the organization, Ypsilantis gave every hint that Alexander I knew and approved of his activities. He took personally a title that meant "deputy" or "viceroy," implying that a "supreme authority" stood above him. Although the tsar was never named, the association seemed obvious. Certainly, it was this apparent connection with Russia that won so many converts to the Etairia, particularly in the Danubian Principalities. Moreover, Ypsilantis appears to have convinced the governors of Bessarabia and the Odessa region that he had some sort of official backing. That section of Russia became a staging area for the revolt. Although the Etairia did not obtain guns from Russian arsenals, other supplies and money were openly collected. Greek residents in Odessa could easily obtain passports for the Danubian Principalities.

Meanwhile, the plans for the revolution proceeded. The leaders of the society decided that the revolt should center in the Peloponnesus, but with a prior diversionary action in the Principalities. What seem rather wild plans were also made to burn Constantinople, kidnap the sultan, and sink the Ottoman fleet. Although the basic goal remained the establishment of an independent Greek nation, the advantages of the outbreak of a parallel general Balkan rebellion were obvious. Most important would be the attitude of Serbia.

A great effort was made to attract Serbian support. Karadjordje, who had emigrated to Bessarabia, was recruited into the Etairia, and he did take an active part in its work. In contrast, Miloš Obrenović was fully uncooperative. At this time the prince was following a policy of collaboration with the Ottoman government; his chief aim was to secure from the suzerain power the formal recognition of his title on a hereditary basis. The entire question also became entangled in domestic conflicts. When in July 1817 Karadjordje returned to Serbia, Miloš had him executed. His head was then sent to the sultan as a sign of fealty. Thereafter the prince continued to resist firmly any temptation to join the Greek efforts. Had Russia entered, his reaction might have been different. As it was, throughout the revolution he maintained his reserved attitude.

Although it had first been decided that the revolt should have its center in the Peloponnesus, preparations did not advance there as fast as expected. The first revolutionary action thus took place in Moldavia, and it was launched without adequate coordination with events in Greece. Nevertheless, the choice of the Principalities as the area from which to commence a Greek liberation movement was quite logical given the conditions of the time. The Phanariot regimes guaranteed that the authorities would be friendly. The Etairia had been able to recruit widely from among the Greek boyars, although not from those with a Romanian background. The prince of Moldavia, Mihai Suţu, was in the society, and the cooperation of a prominent Romanian, Tudor Vladimirescu, had been assured.

In addition, the geographic position of the Principalities was strategically excellent. If the Etairia wished to involve the other Balkan people – the Bulgarians, Serbs, and Romanians – the best plan was obviously to commence the rebellion in Moldavia; the victorious revolutionary forces could then march through the Balkan lands on the way to Greece. It was expected that the inhabitants along the route would flock to the Greek standards. Moreover, the provinces were adjacent to Russia, from whom help was still expected. The belief in Russian support remained widespread, even among those who knew of the previous refusals. Many apparently were convinced that if they started the revolt, they could force the tsar to act. They expected that a Greek uprising would be met by Turkish reprisals so appalling that the protecting Orthodox power would be compelled to intervene.

Internal conditions in the Principalities also made that region ready for revolt, but not in the direction desired by the Etairia. In fact, its leaders seem to have been singularly blind to the effects of the long period of Phanariot domination. The abuses of the regime had, in fact, increased after 1812. The two princes who were appointed at that time were Ioan Caragea, who ruled Wallachia from 1812 to 1818, and Scarlat Callimachi, who was in office in Moldavia from 1812 to 1819. During their reigns the Principalities were under extreme fiscal pressure both from the Porte and from the princes, each of whom had paid a high price for his throne and had to show a profit on his investment. Taxes were increased and peasant obligations became more oppressive. The situation was very bad indeed. The corruption and misgovernment under Caragea was so extreme that he was forced to flee the country. He was replaced in 1818 by Alexander Suţu, who arrived with eighty relatives and a suite of eight hundred, including an Albanian guard. Under these conditions it can be understood why hatred for the Phanariot rule was so widespread. The native boyars and the oppressed peasants were joined in a common cause.

Three potentially revolutionary forces were thus in existence in the Principalities. We have already discussed the Etairia and its links with the Phanariot regime. The native boyars constituted a second faction. Although many had indeed collaborated with the Greek princes, their main desire was to reestablish a native rule. Their attitude toward the Porte was ambivalent. They were willing to consider the retention of Ottoman suzerainty, but on the condition that the political authority in the Principalities be returned to their hands. If not, they preferred independence with foreign – that is, Russian or Austrian – protection. They were certainly not partisans of a great Hellenic revival. The third element in the situation was provided by the existence of mass discontent among the peasantry. Their grievances were over their taxes and the conditions of landholding; their goals were thus social rather than national in character. Their support, nevertheless, was absolutely essential to the success of any rebellion.

The importance of the availability of trained, armed men has been emphasized in connection with the Serbian revolt. Although the arming of the countryside was not as general in the Principalities as it was in some lands under direct Ottoman administration, certain local military fores did exist. There was, of course, no national army, but the princes had personal guards and the police at their disposal. In addition, during the wars of 1768–1774 and 1787–1792, other armed groups appeared. As in Serbia, local volunteers joined both the Habsburg and the Russian armies. Units also had to be organized to defend Wallachia against the kirdjali raids in the time of Pasvanoglu. Oltenia became the center of a legal militia, the pandours. They were recruited from the free peasants, and like the Habsburg soldiers of the Military Frontier, they combined agriculture with military duties. The pandours received a salary and tax-exemption privileges. They played a major role during the Napoleonic Wars; they fought against Pasvanoglu; and they cooperated with the Russian army against the Porte. By 1811 they were around six thousand strong.

An active member of this militia, Tudor Vladimirescu, who was to become the principal Romanian leader, had pursued a career which was in many ways similar to that of Karadjordje. Born in 1780 in a family of free peasants, Vladimirescu took part in the war against the Ottoman Empire as a commander of the pandours and received a Russian decoration for his actions. He later held the position of subprefect of Cloşani. He had by this time risen to the rank of a lower boyar. Terminating his military career in 1812, he subsequently became a very successful businessman and came to own houses, lands, and vineyards. Like his Serbian counterpart, he was active in livestock trading with the Habsburg Empire. In the course of his various pursuits, he was able to travel widely, visiting, for example, the Banat, Transylvania, and Buda. He lived in Vienna for about two hundred days in 1814 at the time of the Congress of Vienna. Although without a formal education, he was thus a man of wide experience.

In 1820 Ypsilantis was, as we have seen, in Bessarabia making plans for the rebellion. He had already chosen as the commander of the revolutionary troops operating in the Principalities a Greek, Georgakis Olympios, who had been in the pandours. Prince Mihai Suţu had been won over; the hospodar of Wallachia, Alecu Suţu, had not, but he was dying. A temporary Wallachian government was in office, and three of its members worked out an agreement with Vladimirescu, promising to support him if he would start a revolt in Oltenia. Vladimirescu also came to an understanding with the Etairia. It was expected that the society would commence its rebellion in the Principalities, but that, once it was successful, its forces would cross the Danube and proceed on to Greece.

In January 1821 Vladimirescu left Bucharest for Oltenia. At this time Alecu

Suțu died, leaving the temporary government fully in charge. In February, at the village of Padeș, Vladimirescu issued a violently revolutionary declaration, calling on the peasants to rise against the boyars. His words had nothing at all to do with Greek, or even Romanian, national liberation:

> Brothers living in Wallachia, whatever your nationality, no law prevents a man to meet evil with evil . . . How long shall we suffer the dragons that swallow us alive, those above us, both clergy and politicans, to suck our blood? How long shall we be enslaved? . . . Neither God nor the Sultan approves of such treatment of their faithful. Therefore, brothers, come all of you and deal out evil to bring evil to an end, that we might fare well.[9]

Although Vladimirescu himself tried to make a distinction between the "good" boyars who supported his movement and the others, the peasants, who joined him in thousands, were not so discriminating. They burned houses and barns, and they looted the boyar estates. A true social revolution was in progress. Vladimirescu formed an army, called the People's Assembly, whose basis was the group of six hundred pandours who had come to his support at once.

Vladimirescu's movement, it will be noted, was not directed against the Porte. He and his supporters called upon the suzerain power to restore "old conditions" – in other words, to return to the days before the Phanariot Greek rule. Vladimirescu also appealed to the Ottoman government to send a representative to investigate the conditions in the Principalities and to remedy the abuses and the sufferings of the people. Throughout this period he remained in touch with the Ottoman agents and with the pashas in command of the Danube forts.

The situation thus became extremely complicated. Vladimirescu had commenced a revolt after a prior agreement with the temporary administration in Wallachia and the Etairia. His call for peasant support had been enthusiastically received, but his followers had social rather than national or political goals. Extremely disturbed by the situation, the Bucharest regime sent a force to try to stop the Romanian leader; its members instead deserted to Vladimirescu. On March 12 the People's Assembly started to march toward Bucharest, where it arrived at the end of the month.

Meanwhile, Ypsilantis had gone into action. On March 6 he and a few associates crossed the border from Bessarabia. His victory in Moldavia was easy; he simply took over control of the government from Suțu. The local military forces supported him, and he appealed for volunteers. Appearing in the country wearing a Russian uniform, Ypsilantis gave his followers the

---

9 Quoted in Andrei Oțetea, ed., *The History of the Romanian People* (New York: Twayne, 1970), p. 317.

impression that a large Russian army was right behind him. On March 7, in a proclamation to the Moldavians, he informed them that his forces would march through the Principalities and then cross the Danube. There should be no fear of Ottoman reprisals: "Should the Turks dare to penetrate into Moldavia, an all powerful force was ready to punish them for their audacity."[10] At first, there was no reason to doubt the assurances of the Etairia. The Russian consul in Iaşi, Andrea Pisani, did nothing to disenchant those who were convinced that the Russian army would soon arrive. Under these circumstances, the Etairia received a great deal of support. Money, weapons, and recruits poured into its headquarters. Romanians as well as Greeks offered their assistance. In Iaşi, Ypsilantis and the Moldavian boyars composed a petition to Alexander I, entreating him to give aid.

Everything hinged on the Russian reaction. The fact that the reply was delayed for weeks added to the general confusion and allowed the Etairia to keep up the pretense of Russian involvement. Already on March 7, however, the Russian Foreign Ministry had sent instructions to the Russian consul in Bucharest denouncing Vladimirescu's revolt. The Romanian leader did not hear of the Russian attitude until toward the end of March. Until that time he too continued to assure his followers of Russian approval, probably basing his claims on declarations made by the Etairia. Finally, on March 17, the Bucharest consulate received the tsar's disavowal of Ypsilantis; an anathema from the patriarch of Constantinople also arrived. The Russian attitude was finally open and unequivocal.

Many aspects of Russian policy at this time are not clear. It does seem, however, that the tsar did not know about the existence of the conspiracy, although he was aware of some of the activities of the Etairia. The involvement of his foreign minister was obviously far greater. At the time of the revolt Alexander was meeting with his allies at Ljubljana to determine what measures should be taken in regard to the revolutions that had broken out in the Italian peninsula and Spain. The tsar's strong conservative views were strengthened by Metternich's increasing influence. It was extremely unlikely that Alexander would endorse the kind of revolutionary activity that was taking place in the Principalities. The authority of the legitimate ruler, the sultan, was being challenged; in the countryside revolutionary mobs were burning the houses of the Romanian nobility. The tsar's denunciation of the revolt was accompanied by a recall of the Russian consuls in Bucharest and Iaşi. Capodistrias was soon to lose his post as foreign minister.

Meanwhile, a crisis was developing in the Principalities. Valdimirescu arrived in Bucharest with about 65,000 men on April 2. At the same time Ypsilantis, with his troops, who numbered considerably fewer, set out for the Wallachian capital. Vladimirescu, with the strongest armed force, was working in cooperation with the Wallachian government and continued to remain

10   Oţetea, *History of the Romanian People*, p. 320.

in communication with the Ottoman authorities. He made attempts to tone down the social implications of his movement; the peasants were instructed to pay their taxes. Neither Vladimirescu nor Ypsilantis was in command of anything like a real army, nor did they have regular means of supply. Both forces lived off the country, and the Etairia had already caused much anger in Moldavia because of pillaging. Despite Vladimirescu's attempts to restrain his supporters, they too engaged in acts of violence and in looting. With disorder and anarchy increasing, a mass flight of boyars and merchants began. Some were frightened by the peasant uprising; others had been involved with the Etairia and feared Ottoman reprisals. Transylvania received most of the refugees; twelve thousand went to Braşov and seventeen thousand to Sibiu.[11]

On April 18 Ypsilantis finally arrived at the outskirts of Bucharest, accompanied by what was little more than a mob numbering about five thousand. His followers had no military training and few arms. The two leaders held a meeting on April 20, but it served principally to bring out their basic disagreements. Vladimirescu wanted the Greek forces to move out of the country and to cross the Danube as had been originally planned. He emphasized that he wished to remedy the abuses in the government, rather than to challenge Ottoman rule. Ypsilantis was in a dangerous military position. On April 6 a revolt had taken place in the Peloponnesus, and the Ottoman government was preparing to meet the insurrection there and in the Principalities. Without either Russian or strong Romanian support, Ypsilantis's motley force could not hope to defend itself against the regular Ottoman army.

Vladimirescu was similarly caught in a difficult situation. His army was strong, but it also could not defeat the Ottoman professional soldiers. In the negotiations with the Romanian leader, the Ottoman representatives insisted that his troops either lay down their arms or join in the fight against the Etairia. Not only did Vladimirescu not trust Ottoman assurances, but he also did not think that his men would march against Ypsilantis's army, whose ranks were likewise filled with Romanians. In this tense situation, Ypsilantis withdrew to Tirgovişte, while Vladimirescu remained in Bucharest.

Both armies feared an Ottoman intervention. One of the first acts of the Etairia in Moldavia had been the massacre of Turkish civilians in Iaşi and Galaţi (Galatz), and the Porte obviously had to act to restore its authority. On May 13 an Ottoman army entered the country and advanced on Bucharest. Vladimirescu and his forces abandoned the city, as did the Wallachian government, which left for Braşov. By this time both Ypsilantis and Vladimirescu had decided that their best course of action would be to retreat to the mountains. At this point the two movements came into direct conflict. Well aware of their relatively weak military power, the Etairia leaders deter-

11 Dan Berindei, *L'Année révolutionnaire 1821 dans les Pays roumains* (Bucharest: Éditions de l'Académie, 1973), p. 182.

mined that they should attempt to gain command of the pandour army. They also knew of Vladimirescu's negotiations with the Ottoman authorities, acts that they regarded as treason. Ypsilantis was aided by the fact that the Romanian leader had alienated some of his commanders when he executed pandour officers for looting. With the assistance of these dissidents, the Greek leadership was able to kidnap Vladimirescu. He was tortured and then executed on the night of June 8–9.

Thereafter Ypsilantis tried to take command of the pandours by announcing that Vladimirescu was alive and had been sent to Bessarabia. The move failed; this army was also in a process of dissolution. Once it became apparent that a social revolution would not take place, many of the peasants simply left. With the dissappearance of Vladimirescu, others joined the deserters. They were close to their Oltenian homes, and there was nothing for them to fight for. Ypsilantis was thus left with entirely inadequate forces to meet the advancing Ottoman army. He was also not an experienced or able field commander. On June 19 at Drăgăşani he suffered a disastrous defeat. Deserting the remnants of his army, he crossed over into Transylvania. There he was arrested, and he spent the last seven years of his life in an Austrian prison. A similar military collapse took place in Moldavia. Suţu abdicated and fled to Russia. The last stand of the Etairia in the Principalities was on June 29, at Sculeni on the Pruth River. With the defeat of the Greek forces, the Ottoman army was in complete control of the Principalities.

Although the Russian government had denounced the revolutionary movement, it remained deeply concerned with the events in these neighboring lands. At first the Russian ambassador in Constantinople, G. A. Stroganov, cooperated with the Porte, but disagreements soon arose. Russian advice had encouraged the Porte to suppress the revolts. However, when the Ottoman army entered the Principalities without a prior agreement with Russia, as was required by the treaties, the Russian government strongly protested. Even worse in Russian eyes were the actions taken in Constantinople as a result of the events in the Peloponnesus. There, as in the Principalities, the Greek revolutionaries had massacred Ottoman civilians. In reply, the Ottoman authorities commenced massive reprisals. As far as the Orthodox world was concerned, the worst atrocity occurred when a group of janissaries hanged the patriarch of Constantinople and some of his bishops on Easter eve.

Such a direct attack on the Orthodox population and its religious leader could not be ignored by Russia, any more than the Porte could allow the indiscriminate murder of Muslims. Moreover, the Russian government had certain obligations. In the past it had claimed repeatedly that it held a kind of religious protectorate over the Orthodox. As previously noted, the Treaty of Kuchuk Kainarji had a clause specifically referring to the Greek lands and stating that "the Christian religion shall not be exposed to the least oppression." Although Alexander I did not change his mind on the question of revolution, he did take a strong stand on the religious issue. The Russian government took the position that the Porte had the right to punish revolutionaries, but that it should not massacre innocent Christians. The distinction was, of course, often difficult to make.[12] These issues led to the breaking of diplomatic relations in August 1821.

The Ottoman army remained in occupation of the Principalities for sixteen months. Once again both provinces had to support a foreign army. The emigrés remained abroad, either in Transylvania or in Bukovina. It was, of course, to the interest of the Porte to try to restore a stable political situation. Russian pressure remained strong. In April 1822 two delegations with seven members each came to Constantinople. The Moldavians were led by Ion Sturdza, the Wallachians by Grigore Ghica. Both represented the interests of the Romanian boyars, and they presented similar programs. The major demand was the restoration of native rule and the end of Phanariot exploitation, with all high offices henceforth held by Romanians. The delegates similarly requested the removal of the Greek hegumens (abbots) of the Dedicated Monasteries and the appointment of native clerics. A Romanian militia to replace the former Albanian guard was also desired. The Porte agreed to these demands and named the heads of the delegations as princes of their provinces. These actions were not accepted by the Russian government, which insisted on its right under the treaties of passing judgment on the candidates for the thrones. Russo-Ottoman relations thus entered a period of crisis. The chief issues in dispute concerned the condition of the Principalities and Russian rights of intervention.

Many boyars returned to the Principalities at this time, although some remained abroad until 1826. Some local landowners took reprisals against those who had taken part in Vladimirescu's rebellion. Villages were disarmed, and the attempt was made to collect back taxes. In general, however, the matter was handled with moderation. The boyars were relatively content; they had gained much of their political program. A native administration was in power in both Principalities. The Porte had acceded to most, if not all, of the Romanian requests. It had taken no reprisals for the revolutionary actions of some Romanian boyars and peasants. Having achieved their goals, most boyars were in favor of maintaining the link with the Ottoman Empire.

THE GREEK REVOLUTION

Although the revolution collapsed in the Principalities, a similar movement was having greater success in the Greek lands, where conditions were much more favorable for a national uprising. As we have seen, local community government was strongly organized in the region; the Peloponnesus enjoyed

---

12 See the Russian circular despatch of June 22/July 4, 1821, in Barbara Jelavich, *Russia and Greece during the Regency of King Othon, 1832–1835* (Thessaloniki: Institute for Balkan Studies, 1962), pp. 124–128.

Map 20. The expansion of Greece, 1821–1919

an almost fully autonomous administration. The Greek islands too for all
practical purposes ran their own affairs. The very independence of these areas
was, however, to cause problems during the revolution. Once the revolt began, the Greek forces divided both on social and on geographical lines. In
general, the Greeks of the three main areas of Rumeli, the Peloponnesus, and
the islands formed separate groups with their own interests and objectives
(see Map 20). The Greeks of the diaspora and the Phanariots who were forced
to leave Ottoman service were a fourth category. On social lines the notables,

215

the wealthy shipowners of the islands, and the military men with their peasant followers constituted three distinct elements that could either ally with or fight against one another. It will be noted that there was no peasant movement similar to that in Wallachia. The individual peasant was closely tied to the social structure of his own tight community; he fought with the local captain for the interests of the area where he lived.

Fighting between Ottoman and Greek forces was already under way considerably before the outbreak of the revolution in April 1821. This conflict involved the old quarrel between the Porte and the disobedient provincial ayan Ali Pasha, whose headquarters were at Janina in Epirus. As we have seen, he was a continual thorn in the side of the Ottoman authorities. He had played between the rebels and the government in the western Balkans, and he had entered into relations with foreign governments. Although he was willing to accept the sovereignty of the Porte, his aim was the establishment of an autonomous state with all the power in his own hands. He formed ties with the Etairia, hoping to win Greek support for his own plans. In 1819 Mahmud II decided that he would have to be destroyed.

Well aware of the Ottoman danger, Ali prepared to resist. He began a great effort to win Greek and Albanian Christian aid. He improved conditions in the villages under his control, and he appealed to the local captains to join him. Some Greeks did indeed enter his service. Nevertheless, the Ottoman army was able to make advances against him, although with considerable difficulty. In 1820 considerable Ottoman forces were tied up in the conflict with Ali Pasha in the western Balkans. The involvement of so many Ottoman troops in this struggle offered the Greeks a fine opportunity for action. Recognizing the favorable aspects of the situation, the Etairia and Ypsilantis, as we have seen, decided to begin their rebellion, with an uprising scheduled for both the Peloponnesus and the Danubian Principalities. The revolt in Greece was delayed simply because the necessary preparations could not be made in time. The emphasis was then placed on the Principalities. They were to be a source of money and recruits and were to be used to draw Russia into the conflict. In fact, although Ypsilantis commenced his rebellion in Moldavia, preparations continued in Greece proper. There was little coordination, however, between the centers, and the revolt in the Peloponnesus arose primarily from local events.

Like the Principalities, the Peloponnesus offered extremely favorable conditions for the organization of a revolution. The Greek people had considerable autonomy under their own primates. The control of the countryside was more in Greek than in Ottoman hands. Moreover, there was a large concentration of military men in the area, particularly in Mani. It was also possible to maintain close contact with the islands, which had similar rights of self-government.

In the Greek lands the Ottoman authorities were concerned not so much about the activities of the Etairia as about the possibility that mass Christian support might be given to Ali Pasha. He had always been able to win some assistance from both Greek and Albanian Christians in the area. In March the Ottoman officials summoned the Orthodox leaders, including the primate of the Peloponnesus and the bishops, to Tripolitza for a conference. The Greeks were reluctant to obey the call because they feared what might happen to them. In fact, those who did appear were imprisoned. Some individuals then started taking direct action. Local leaders began attacking resident Turks, and such acts were widespread by the end of March. On April 2 a full revolt broke out in Mani. The symbolic act that was henceforth celebrated as marking the commencement of the revolution occurred on April 6. On that date, according to popular belief, Bishop Germanos of Patras raised the standard of rebellion at the monastery of Aghia Lavra. Uprisings then occurred throughout the Greek regions and in the islands, in particular on Hydra, Psara, and Spetsai, which would subsequently serve as major centers for Greek naval operations.

Some of the first Greek actions were taken against unarmed Ottoman settlements. It is estimated that fifteen thousand out of the forty thousand Muslim residents of the Peloponnesus were killed.[13] The survivors fled into the fortified towns, some of which held out until the end of the revolution. Other cities were captured; Tripolitza was taken in October 1821, and the inhabitants were massacred. Christian atrocities were fully matched by the Ottoman reaction. The hanging of the patriarch has been described. Similar events occurred in other parts of the empire that had a Greek population. In 1822 the massacre on Chios, where many thousands died, attracted general European attention. As a rule, Ottoman actions were fully reported in Europe, with all of the gruesome details; Christian atrocities tended to be ignored.

There was at first no massive Ottoman military operation against the Greek rebels; the empire continued to concentrate on defeating Ali Pasha. An army also had to be sent to the Principalities to deal with the revolt there. The involvement of the Ottoman forces in the western Balkans and the Romanian provinces allowed the rebels in the Peloponnesus time to consolidate their position. Finally, in January 1822, Ali was captured and executed, and his head was sent to Constantinople. The Porte was now free to deal with the Greeks. In addition to Epirus, the Ottoman forces were able to subdue Thessaly and Macedonia. The rebels, however, kept their stronghold in the Peloponnesus, and they controlled some territory north of the Isthmus of Corinth in Rumeli, including the cities of Misolonghi, Thebes, and Athens.

The chief Ottoman military effort was thus directed against this area. In 1822 and 1823 the Porte sent armies to relieve the fortress cities still held by Ottoman troops. The operation was not easy. The rebels had the services of

13 Douglas Dakin, *The Greek Struggle for Independence, 1821–1833* (London: Batsford, 1973), p. 59.

The tomb of Ali Pasha in Janina

a navy, which consisted primarily of individual shipowners acting on their own initiative, usually as pirates. They were very effective against the Ottoman naval forces, which were weak, and even more efficient in cutting sea communications. Because of this situation, the Ottoman invasion had to come by land. Armies were sent from both Epirus and Constantinople, but the supply lines were long and the campaigning season short. The troops were constantly harassed by Greek guerilla fighters, who, unlike their opponents, were masters in exploiting the advantages of the mountainous terrain. Wisely, the Greeks went into combat not as a regular, organized army, but in individual bands under the local captains.

With this even balance of strength, a stalemate had set in by 1825. Since victory seemed impossible without outside assistance, Mahmud II decided to appeal to the pasha of Egypt, Muhammad Ali. Like Ali Pasha, this Albanian chieftain had risen to high position in the Ottoman service. As the ruler of Egypt he had defied Ottoman authority, and it was only his own military weakness that induced the sultan to turn to this rebellious and independent vassal. Muhammad Ali was willing to intervene, but at a high price. For his services he demanded Crete for himself and the Peloponnesus for his son Ibrahim, who was a brilliant military commander. With the sultan's agreement to these terms, the Egyptian troops entered the conflict. Highly successful, they first took Crete and then, in February 1825, entered the Peloponnesus. In contrast to the Greek guerilla warriors, the Egyptian troops formed a disciplined army. They had been trained by French military advisers along modern European lines. They proved superior in fighting to the Greeks, who not only had inferior equipment, but lacked an organized plan of action. In April 1826 Misolonghi fell; soon thereafter Ottoman soldiers were in occupation of the Acropolis of Athens, the symbol of the ancient civilization. It seemed that the revolt would be crushed. Meanwhile, internal dissension had weakened and divided the revolutionary leadership.

In addition to fighting, the Greek rebels had to administer the regions under their control and organize some sort of national government. The problems that arose here were very different from those in Serbia, where one man had been able to take over both the civilian and the military leadership and hold that position, even against strong opposition, until he was defeated by the Ottoman army. In contrast, in Greece the forces of local autonomy were so strong that they were able to prevent one man or one center from predominating.

The Greek revolution suffered from certain basic weaknesses. There had been, as we have seen, no general Balkan rising, nor was there a mass peasant movement against Turkish rule. Instead, throughout the Greek lands, local military men led their followers in limited actions against the Ottoman forces. The entire revolution, in fact, was fought by armed bands under local captains. These men, with a klepht mentality, felt it a point of honor not to surrender control to a higher authority. As in the past, the captains individually were in strong competition with one another. During the revolution they continued to use whatever opportunities were offered to enlarge their jurisdictions. They seized booty, and they sought to extend their control over villages from which they could collect taxes for their own use. Some, to improve their own position, even collaborated with the Ottoman authorities. The lawlessness of this military element, which was the chief fighting arm of the revolt, was a continual problem for the civilian leaders. They had no means of compelling obedience from these armed men. Theodoros Kolokotronis was to cause the major problems, but there were many like him throughout the region.

Soon after the commencement of the revolt another political influence entered the Greek scene. The Porte at this point looked with extreme suspicion on all Greeks in its service, particularly on those who held important posts in Constantinople. Many were forced to leave; others, enthusiastic supporters of Greek freedom, wished to take part in the struggle on the mainland. After the defeat in the Principalities, Alexander Ypsilantis, as we have seen, spent the rest of his life in prison. His brother Dimitrios, who attempted to replace him, was not an able leader, and he did not play an important role in subsequent events. The Etairia as an organization faded into insignificance; other groups were to take over the direction of the revolution. Among the Constantinople Greeks who formed a part of this new leadership, perhaps the most important was Alexander Mavrokordatos, who was henceforth to play a major role in Greek political life.

Since the Phanariots and the diaspora Greeks usually did not hold extensive property in Greece or have a firm local political base, they tended to support the establishment of a single predominant central authority, which they could hope to control. They could win power in domestic politics by manipulating the competitive native political groups and exploiting local antipathies. Well acquainted with European political theory and practice, they were primarily responsible for the constitutional form of the first governments.

Greek political life was to involve, in addition to the members of the overseas Greek communities who arrived at this time, local leaders who based their influence either on regional loyalties or on class conflicts. The geographic division was among eastern and western Rumelia, the Peloponnesus, and the islands. The social conflict was primarily between the military men and their peasant followers, on the one hand, and the primates, who could ally with the shipowners and islanders, on the other. Much of the domestic history of the country during the revolutionary period revolves around the struggle between these groups to capture the central authority. The victor not only would dominate the administration, but would be the agent who dealt with foreign governments and received the loans that were being sought abroad. As in Serbia, prominent Greek leaders went by the principle that they would accept no central authority that they could not themselves control.

The story of the conflict and civil war within the revolutionary ranks is complex; only the outline can be presented here.

The first general meeting held to attempt to form a central government took place at Epidaurus in December 1821. Here the delegates, who came from the various parts of insurgent Greece, sought to draw up a constitution. Their chief effort was directed toward preventing any single individual from attaining a position of unfettered supreme power. Their ideal, like that of their counterparts in Serbia, was an oligarchy of primates. Their model document was the French Constitution of 1795. Following its example, they placed the executive power in the hands of a committee of five, headed by Mavrokordatos. Each member represented a region. This weak organization did not possess the power to control local authorities or defiant individuals.

In December 1822 another gathering of notables was held at Astros. Here some changes were made in the constitution. The major event, however, was the quarrel that arose between Kolokotronis, backed by his armed bands, and the government, which led to the outbreak of civil war. Kolokotronis held the city of Nauplion; his opponents at Kranidi formed an administration under the leadership of George Kountouriotis, who represented the interests of the islands. Although Kolokotronis was induced to surrender control of Nauplion, the bitter internal struggle continued. Neither faction succeeded in establishing a regime that could command general respect and obedience. Meanwhile, as we have seen, the Egyptian forces had landed in the Peloponnesus, and they were winning victories.

The national assembly held on Troezene in 1827 was to be more successful. By this date it was clear that the great powers would intervene in Greek affairs. A stable government with real authority had to be formed that could deal with the new situation. Another constitution was drawn up, but, most important, Capodistrias accepted an invitation to become president. At the same time, two British Philhellenes, Sir Richard Church and Alexander Cochrane, were given command of the land and naval military forces. The crisis of these years also served to give impetus to the formation of political parties. At the beginning of the civil war, political activity centered around the conflicts between strong individuals, each backed by a personal following. They might represent regions, factions, or social classes, but they were associated with no formal programs or organizations. Broader-based groups emerged at this time, taking the names of the great powers to which the members looked for support.

The involvement of the great powers in the Greek civil war is discussed in detail subsequently. For internal affairs the role that Russia, Britain, and France would henceforth play in Greek politics had equal significance. Local political leaders, recognizing the decisive importance of foreign intervention, sought to associate themselves with a power and to gain that government's support for their own ambitions. As could be expected, the Russian Party came into existence with the election of Capodistrias, although he did not follow a distinctly pro-Russian policy during his term in office. The French Party was led by Ioannis Kolettis, whose chief support came from Rumeli. This group favored a candidate from the French house of Orléans as the future ruler of Greece; it received some assistance from Paris. The British Party, with Alexander Mavrokordatos at its head, was in a particularly strong position. British naval power, which was predominant in the Mediterranean, could determine the fate of the Greek revolt; British Philhellenes were active in the Greek cause. All three parties put their faith in the intervention of their patron powers, and all sought subsidies from their consulates.

The first truly national government in Greece was formed by Capodistrias soon after his arrival in Greece in February 1828. After the tsar's denunciation of the Greek revolt, Capodistrias left Russian service and went to live in Switzerland. Despite his long years in Russian administration, he was primarily a Greek patriot. His experience in holding high office in the Russian government led him to seek to introduce into Greece the political institutions that were favored at that time, particularly by the conservative states. He thus wished to establish a centralized, bureaucratic, but "enlightened" regime that would give the executive a great deal of power. There was, however, no modern precedent for this type of government for the Greek lands, whose administration under Ottoman rule had been decentralized. Both the notables and the military men were strongly entrenched and determined to defend their tight local circles of authority. Moreover, as a new arrival in Greece, Capodistrias had not had time to build a large group of personal supporters, nor did he have a territorial base. At first he received the backing of Kolokotronis and his followers and of the Peloponnesian notables. The members of the French and British parties denounced him as a Russian partisan, which he was not, at least not in the detrimental sense they meant.

Nevertheless, during his short period in office Capodistrias did draw up plans for a centralized government and a national administrative system; this work is discussed in a later section in connection with its permanent influence on Greek political life. He also carried on negotiations with the great powers on the status of a future autonomous Greek state. It had been decided that Greece would be a constitutional monarchy. Since there appeared no possibility of the feuding Greek factions' agreeing on a single native candidate, the powers had decided that the country should have a foreign prince. The most popular candidate was Leopold of Saxe-Coburg, a German prince who was the British choice. He, however, refused because he was not satisfied either with the financial arrangements or with the boundaries of his kingdom. He later became the king of Belgium. Capodistrias, who may have discouraged the prince with the hope of gaining the high office for himself, was not to live to see the formation of the Greek kingdom. In October 1831 he was assassinated in an act of revenge by a family several of whose members he had imprisoned. Personal honor and the blood feud were living realities in revolutionary Greece.

With the death of Capodistrias, the government passed into the hands of a triumvirate consisting of Avgoustinos Capodistrias, the president's brother, Kolokotronis, and Kolettis. This group, too, was unable to maintain control over the country; once again anarchical conditions were prevalent everywhere. Meanwhile, the failure of the Greek revolutionary troops to win battles, together with the inability of the civil leaders to form a stable, lasting government, had led Russia, France, and Britain to take matters into their own hands. Great-power intervention took the form of military actions against the Ottoman and Egyptian forces and the determination of the form of the first Greek government. These states also named the king.

The Greek revolution provided dangers for the great powers that had not been present during the Serbian revolt or the events in the Principalities. Serbia was geographically remote from the sensitive areas of European diplomacy; the Principalities were a Russian and Habsburg sphere, and these two powers were in agreement. In contrast, the Greek strategic position and Greece's widely scattered islands made the control of its territory a matter of European concern. Of the great powers, the Habsburg Monarchy and Prussia were only peripherally involved in the fate of the area. Britain, France, and Russia, on the other hand, had major interests at stake. Of the three states, Britain, with naval domination in the Mediterranean, was in the best position to influence Greek affairs. France wished to maintain the balance of power in the Mediterranean and had influential partisans in Greece. The French government also had close relations with Muhammad Ali and a point of support in Egypt. In the past Russia had been the power that could exert the greatest influence, primarily because of the common Orthodox religion and the Russian involvement in Ottoman and Romanian affairs. We have already seen how the Etairia relied on eventual Russian aid; such support seemed entirely logical in view of the past relationships.

When the revolt broke out in 1821, no great power was ready for an international crisis in the East. Castlereagh, the British prime minister, and Robert Canning, his successor, were both for the maintenance of the Ottoman Empire. Metternich was extremely hostile to any revolutionary activity, and he wished to protect Ottoman territorial integrity. In his opinion the uprising was a clear case of a dangerous revolutionary challenge to a legitimate sovereign, and comparable to the movements in Italy, Germany, and Spain that the conservative monarchs were bent on suppressing. The Greek actions also opened the area to Russian penetration and could bring up issues that might endanger the Holy Alliance.

The Russian reaction, as we have seen, was of two sorts. Alexander I was in a period of intense conservatism; he also detested revolutionary outbreaks. Nevertheless, Russia did have treaties with the Porte concerning the government of the Principalities, and certain responsibilities toward the Orthodox Christians. The difference between the punishment of guilty rebels and the victimization of innocent Christians was impressed on the Ottoman government. In addition, the measures taken by the Porte were hindering Russian trade. It will be remembered that much of the Russian grain trade with Europe was carried in Greek ships flying the Russian flag. Not only had the revolt made the seas unsafe, but the Ottoman authorities were hindering the passage of these Russian cargoes through the Straits. Russia also had conflicts with the Ottoman government concerning the Caucasus.

Despite these points of dispute with the Porte, Alexander did not wish the crisis to lead to an outbreak of hostilities. He did not seek the dissolution of the Ottoman Empire, or even its severe weakening. Moreover, he was well aware that he could not take strong action without consulting other states, since unilateral intervention might lead to the formation of a European coalition against Russia. Thus, although diplomatic relations with the Porte were broken in 1821, no military action was taken. Instead, the Russian leaders preferred to follow the path of negotiation and act in cooperation with the other great powers. The basic Russian policy continued to be what it had been in the past: it favored the creation of autonomous Balkan governments under Ottoman sovereignty, similar to the regimes in the Danubian Principalities, which would, if that advantage could be obtained, be under Russian protection. In January 1824 Alexander circulated through the European capitals a plan calling for the establishment of three autonomous Greek states that were to be given the same status as Moldavia and Wallachia. The idea aroused little enthusiasm. To Britain in particular the proposal seemed little more than the attempt to extend Russian influence over yet another Balkan area. Despite British fears, the control of Greece was not a Russian goal. Russia was far more concerned about events in the Principalities, Serbia, and the Caucasus. On these questions, it will be noted, Russia negotiated with the Porte alone; on Greek affairs a policy of close cooperation with the powers was pursued.

Meanwhile, the British government was under increasing public pressure to act in support of the revolutionaries. In Britain, as in the rest of Europe, the romantic movement of Philhellenism was to influence the actions and attitudes of the government. In all the European states the political leaders and the influential members of the public had received a remarkably similar classical education in which the language and culture of ancient Greece had been prominent. When considering the Greek revolution of the 1820s, these men often transferred the impressions of Greece that they had gained in their youth to the contemporary Balkan scene. They thus saw the Greek captains and their peasant followers as the direct descendants of the mythological heroes of the ancient world. The Ottoman forces were regularly portrayed as brutal barbarians who were inflicting unprovoked terror on innocent and civilized victims. What was in fact Greek national propaganda was thus ably presented by painters, writers, poets, and politicians throughout the world.

For the formation of British opinion the most influential Philhellene was certainly Lord Byron, who died at Misolonghi in 1824. Quoted here to demonstrate the emotional appeal of Philhellene writing and the connection that it made between ancient and modern Greece are some verses of his that were written before the revolution:

> The isles of Greece, the isles of Greece!
>   Where burning Sappho loved and sung,
> Where grew the arts of war and peace,
>   Where Delos rose, and Phoebus sprung!
> Eternal summer gilds them yet,
> But all, except their sun, is set.
>
>   .   .   .
>
> The mountains look on Marathon –
>   And Marathon looks on the sea;
> And musing there an hour alone,
>   I'd dream'd that Greece might still be free;
> For standing on the Persians' grave,
> I could not deem myself a slave.
>
>   .   .   .
>
> Trust not for freedom to the Franks –
>   They have a king who buys and sells;
> In native swords, and native ranks,
>   The only hope of courage dwells;
> But Turkish force, and Latin fraud,
> Would break your shield, however broad.
>
>   .   .   .
>
> Place me on Sunium's marbled steep,
>   Where nothing, save the waves and I,
> May hear our mutual murmurs sweep;
>   There, swan-like, let me sing and die;
> A land of slaves shall ne'er be mine –
> Dash down yon cup of Samian wine![14]

In addition to the appeals from sections of its educated public, the British government had practical reasons for entering the conflict. Its trade in the Mediterranean had been injured by the events in Greece. Moreover, Britain feared that if it did not take action, Russia might decide the question alone. The wisest policy might thus be to join that power in order better to contain and control its moves. British intervention was slow. First, in 1823, the revo-

---

14 From "Song of the Greek Poet," in *Don Juan*, in Robert M. Gay, ed. *The College Book of Verse, 1250–1925* (Boston: Houghton Mifflin, 1927), pp. 358–361.

lutionaries were recognized as belligerents, an action that improved their position at sea. Then in 1824 a loan was floated in London. It was very badly if not fraudulently administered, but it did involve financial assistance to the revolutionary government. The great change in the British attitude came with the Egyptian army's invasion of Crete and the Peloponnesus. This move altered the balance of power in the Mediterranean and was detrimental to the British position there.

Alexander I died in 1825 and was succeeded by his brother, Nicholas I, who was to adopt a much firmer attitude toward the questions at issue with the Porte. Even more strongly conservative than his predecessor, he insisted upon Ottoman respect for Russian rights under the treaties, but he too favored cooperation with the other powers on the Greek question. In 1826 the British government sent the Duke of Wellington to St. Petersburg to attend Nicholas's coronation. There in April Russia and Britain concluded the Convention of St. Petersburg, an agreement obligating the two to seek to mediate a settlement of the Greek conflict. The aim was to achieve the establishment of an autonomous state; the borders were not designated. Although the Habsburg Empire stayed out of these negotiations, France joined in July 1827. The French monarch, Charles X, was a Philhellene; furthermore, France could not afford to stand aside on questions involving the Mediterranean.

The three allied powers then proceeded to take positive measures of intervention to stop the fighting in Greece. The revolutionaries accepted the mediation, but the Porte refused. As a consequence, the European powers took a step that was greatly in the Greek interest by setting up a naval blockade, enforced by a squadron composed of ships from the three states, to keep Egyptian supplies and men from crossing to the Peloponnesus. An incident was almost bound to occur under these circumstances. In October 1827 the allied force entered Navarino Bay, where a Turko-Egyptian fleet was anchored. Shots were exchanged, and a major battle began. The Ottoman fleet was demolished; fifty-seven vessels were sunk with a loss of eight thousand men. The majority of these Ottoman sailors were Greek nationals, since this sector of the population provided most of the manpower for the Ottoman navy. The incident at Navarino set in motion a series of events that were to be highly beneficial to the Greek cause, although this trend was not immediately apparent. The Duke of Wellington was by that time the British prime minister. Denouncing the entire episode, he withdrew his country from further participation in the mediation effort and thus reversed Canning's policy of associating with Russia in order to control and limit its actions.

During this period the Russian government continued to negotiate with the Porte on other matters in dispute. The Ottoman government had difficulty resisting demands from its powerful neighbor. The state was in a very weak position: it had not been able to handle the Greek rebellion; and it faced a coalition of powers who appeared determined to act in favor of the insurgents. Thus when Russia delivered a virtual ultimatum in March 1826, the Porte could do little more than accept and agree to negotiate the matters in dispute. In October 1826 the Convention of Akkerman was signed; the Ottoman government conceded almost all of the Russian demands. The agreement provided for the settlement of the Asiatic frontier and the commercial conflicts that had arisen. Most important for the Balkan states, two "Separate Acts" regulated the affairs of Wallachia, Moldavia, and Serbia. Russia received a clear protectorate over all three provinces. Despite this surrender, the negotiations gave Mahmud II time to proceed with internal reform. In June 1826 the sultan took the important step of abolishing the janissary corps. This act would allow him to embark upon a major reform of the army in the future, but it temporarily weakened the Ottoman military potential.

The news of the disaster at Navarino in October 1827 aroused a violent reaction in Constantinople. The Turkish fleet had been sunk by powers with whom the Porte was at peace. A strong wave of anti-Western religious feeling swept Constantinople. The empire broke relations with Britain, France, and Russia, but the chief animosity was directed against St. Petersburg. The Convention of Akkerman was denounced, and a Holy War was declared against Russia. The actual fighting did not commence until April 1828, when Russian troops entered the Principalities. During this new Russo-Turkish war, Greek issues for a short period ceased to occupy the center of the stage. However, with the Ottoman army fully engaged in meeting the Russian invasion, the Western powers could regulate Greek affairs. In August 1828 Muhammad Ali agreed to withdraw the Egyptian troops from the Peloponnesus. A French expeditionary force took their place, and British officers and men were sent to other areas of Greece.

Although at war with the Ottoman Empire, the Russian government was fully aware of the dangers in the situation. It did not want to impose a settlement in the East that would result in a massive reaction by the other governments. Its goals in the war thus became little more than the implementation of the provisions of the Convention of Akkerman, which the Porte had already accepted. The Russian leaders were aware that Constantinople could not be occupied even if the Russian armies were in a position to take the city. Despite the fact that they had cooperated with Britain and France in the Greek question, they fully recognized the limits that had to be placed on their ambitions.

These considerations played a major part in an important decision concerning future policy toward the Ottoman Empire that was made at this time. The Russian leaders decided that they would seek not to destroy or partition the Ottoman Empire, but rather to dominate it from within. Instead of directly conquering the state, they would assure that Russian representatives had the primary influence in the councils of the sultan. This policy naturally had an effect on Russian relations with the Balkan people. If the Russian government could achieve predominance over the entire empire, it would be less likely to support Balkan liberation movements that would weaken the Ottoman state. In fact, in the next years Russia was to become more interested in protecting the Porte than in aiding Balkan national movements. Firm support was given to the maintenance of the autonomous rights that had already been granted, but further changes were not encouraged.

The Treaty of Adrianople of September 1829, in conformity with this policy, was moderate in its terms. The achievement of victory had not been easy for the Russian army. Both Russia and the Ottoman Empire needed a conciliatory peace. In direct gains, Russia took control of the Danube Delta and some territory along the Caucasian boundary. A large indemnity was imposed, which the Ottoman Empire, in a bad financial condition, deeply resented. In addition, the terms of the Convention of Akkerman were reconfirmed. In Article X the Porte agreed to accept an autonomous status for Greece. The treaty also assured the opening of the Straits for the passage of Russian commercial vessels and guaranteed freedom of trade throughout the empire.

Although Russia had thus negotiated the questions dealing with Serbia and the Principalities with the Porte alone, it joined its allies to settle the Greek situation by mutual agreement. In these final stages, it will be noted, no Greek participants were included in the negotiations. The powers recognized that the chief difficulty in Greece was assuring a stable government. Capodistrias had attempted to set up a strong regime, but the British, regarding him as a Russian partisan, had not trusted him. After his assassination, the country again fell into political chaos. There was no recognized national leader with whom the allies could work, and a stable government was not in power.

The Treaty of London of February 1830 was the most important agreement for the formation of the modern Greek nation. Here the three powers set the boundaries and settled the form of government. Largely at British urging, it was decided that the state would be independent rather than autonomous. The British diplomats were highly concerned lest the country become a Russian satellite; they thought that this event would be less likely if all connections between Athens and Constantinople were severed. Although the Russian government would have preferred an autonomous status, it accepted the new arrangement. Britain's concerns over Russian influence also led it to wish to limit the size of the state as much as possible. To protect their interests in the future, the three powers appointed themselves the protectors, or guarantors, of the country – a provision of the treaty that was to provide unlimited excuses for intervention later.

Since the government was to be monarchical, a ruler had to be named. The search was difficult, since all of the new protectors had to approve the choice. Leopold of Saxe-Coburg, as we have seen, refused because of the difficult situation in Greece and his discontent with the conditions that were offered him. In 1832 the powers finally named Otto, the second son of Ludwig I, the Philhellene king of Bavaria. The new monarch, only seventeen at the time of his appointment, arrived in Greece in February 1833. He took the Greek form of his name, Othon. He was provided with a loan and what were in fact expanded boundaries for his kingdom. With the frontier finally drawn at the Arta-Volos line, the new Greek state was composed of only about 800,000 people, a quarter of the Greek inhabitants of the empire.

Although an independent Greece was finally in existence, it was a far cry from the dreams of the Greek nationalists. A small, impoverished Balkan state, it had little resemblance to the recreated Byzantine Empire that was the ideal not only of the Phanariots, but of most Greek political leaders. Moreover, its independence was severely limited. In the future the three founding great powers were to make full use of their right of protection. Furthermore, the Bavarian administration that was established had at first little Greek participation. A modern Greek state was on the map, nevertheless, and a national government was to come to power within the next decade.

CONCLUSION: THE ACHIEVEMENTS OF THE FIRST REVOLUTIONS

The first national liberation movements had thus won a measure of success, although not what their original organizers had wished. Serbia under Prince Miloš had gained many rights, but not a fully autonomous status. Further advances, however, were to be achieved with the application of the terms of the Treaty of Adrianople. In Wallachia and Moldavia both the Greek-led revolt and the peasant rebellion had failed. However, the Phanariot regime was brought to an end and a native government installed. As a result of the Russo-Turkish War, Ottoman sovereignty was to be further limited, but with a great increase of Russian influence in the country.

The consequences of the Greek revolution were not so clear. The Greeks as a nation had lost a great deal. They no longer provided the princes for the Danubian Principalities. Within the Ottoman Empire they were regarded as traitors, particularly by the Muslim population. Phanariots still held high offices, but they were no longer in a special, privileged category. The Greek position in business and commerce was also weaker. Armenians tended to replace Greeks in banking, and Bulgarian merchants became increasingly important in supplying state and military needs. Like the Greeks of Constantinople and of the diaspora, the population of mainland Greece had suffered severely. The land was devastated after ten years of civil war and foreign occupation. Moreover, the state established in 1830 was extremely limited in territorial extent. The powers had also felt it necessary to endow the technically independent nation with a Bavarian administration and, as we shall see, a mercenary army of foreigners.

Despite the fact that there was no general rising in the Balkans at this time, the movements in Greece, Serbia, and the Principalities shared certain common features. During this period the leaders in each area had to define more

Pass and waterfall in the Balkan Mountains

closely their goals for the future. Only the Filiki Etairia started out with a full-fledged political program, calling for the establishment of a free Greece with wide boundaries. The Serbian revolution began as a spontaneous defensive action against unruly janissaries; the revolt in the Peloponnesus, despite the previous preparations of the Etairia, took place because of the primates' fear that the Ottoman authorities might take reprisals against them. Vladimirescu's rebellion was never ostensibly directed against Ottoman control. Nevertheless, by the end of this revolutionary period, in every region the clear desire of the leadership was the formation of a national state with either an independent or an autonomous status. Each area also had a government that could both negotiate with the powers and present a common front in relations with the Porte. Central administrations existed in both Serbia and Greece, where previously there had been scattered communal authorities. In the Principalities native princes governed the country, not Greek agents of the Porte.

The movements shared certain other similarities. All used terrorist methods, and these succeeded. We have seen how the massacre of Muslims was among the first actions of the Christian insurgents. These atrocities were often directed not against individuals or officials who had been guilty of cruel or unjust acts, but rather against civilians who had no means of defending themselves. The Ottoman authorities replied with even harsher means of reprisal, although the Porte found it very difficult to deal with Christian rebellion without the use of the regular army. The government did not have adequate police control on the local level anywhere in the empire. In the Principalities, of course, it had no armed forces.

The Christian revolutionaries also used cruel measures against uncooperative members of their own faith and nationality. One account, discussing methods of recruitment for the Serbian revolt, informs us: "It was the custom to persuade the hesitant to join the rebellion by having more resolute neighbors set fire to their houses or for Karadjordje to hang a Turk on their threshold."[15] In the latter case the rebels would denounce the householder to the authorities, and he would then be forced to flee to the hills and join the insurgents. In the course of the revolt, its participants often did more damage to their own countrymen than to the Ottoman opponent. Vladimirescu's peasants burned and looted. The breakdown of order and the lack of adequate police control gave free reign to criminals and violent individuals. Ioannis Makrigiannis, one of the leading military men of the Greek revolution, found that he could not keep his followers from destructive actions. He described an event of 1824 as follows:

> After my men had seen how the troops under Gouras and others were pillaging the country people while they themselves were for-

15 Dedijer et al., *History of Yugoslavia*, p. 266.

bidden to do so by me, they too would no longer listen to me on the march. In a village near Tripotamon some of them plundered the village without taking thought for me as their senior commander. I feared they would rob me too and young Sisinis and others, and I should be taken for a liar and a man of no honour . . . As my own men had looted the village, when the wretched inhabitants came before me in tears and I could not help them, I felt a deathly shame.[16]

Balkan history to the present has regularly been filled with accounts of great physical cruelty not only to equal adversaries, but to the defenseless, the defeated enemy, and prisoners. Although some of the stories are an extreme exaggeration, they do reflect the atmosphere of bitter and merciless warfare that went on not only between the Christian population and the Muslim rulers, but also among the nationalities themselves. Many of the customs of the time were deeply repulsive to Western observers. We have seen previously in this account the practice of sending a severed head to the sultan. The staking out of heads and impalement were regular methods of public control. In some primitive areas head collecting was part of the local culture. To the Montenegrins, for example, the practice had great symbolic significance. A prominent modern Yugoslav writer explains:

> The severed head was the greatest pride and joy of the Montenegrin. He regarded the taking of heads as the most exalted act and spiritual solace – having been nurtured in mythical history and in the naked struggle for life. He had not felt hatred for the cut-off head, the hatred he was bound to feel for it in its live state, but only esteem and solicitude. He washed it, salted it, combed it. After all, it was a human head and the badge of his own highest merit. The Montenegrins did not exhibit heads to terrify their enemies, as the Turks were wont to do, but as signs of public acclaim and recognition. The number of heads one took was remembered, handed down, and marked on gravestones . . . That which seemed like savagery to the foreigner was for the Montenegrin the poetry of warfare.[17]

Although Serbia, Greece, Wallachia, and Moldavia undoubtedly gained a great deal of freedom from Ottoman control in this period, the authority of the Porte was replaced by a domination that could, if fully exercised, become even more difficult to withstand. By 1830 the Principalities and Serbia were under a recognized Russian protectorate; Greece was under the three-power guarantee of Britain, France, and Russia. This great-power control exerted a

---

16 Ioannes Makriyannis, *The Memoirs of General Makriyannis, 1797–1864*, trans. and ed. H. A. Lidderdale (London: Oxford University Press, 1966), p. 57.
17 Milovan Djilas, *Njegoš* (New York: Harcourt, Brace & World, 1966), pp. 245–246.

Pass in the Balkan Mountains

233

determining influence on the political development of the Balkan states over a long period. The terms *protection* and *protectorate*, as used here, describe the establishment by a single state or a group of states of a right of interference in or control over the internal or foreign policy of another country, one that is recognized in some form by an international treaty or a tacit understanding. The working of this institution for the rest of the century is described in detail later in this account. However, in summary, the Principalities were to be under Russian protection to 1856 and then under great-power supervision to 1878; Serbia was under Russian protection to 1856 and under great-power authority until 1878, and then it became a client of the Habsburg Empire until 1903; Bulgaria was in the Russian sphere from 1878 to 1886; Greece had the misfortune to have three protectors, who kept this position until 1923.

The degree of influence exerted by a protecting power depended on the circumstances of the time and the issues involved. However, the generally recognized principle of the right of European supervision meant that the first governments of the Balkan states were organized more by the great powers than by the national leaders. An exception is to be found, however, in the case of Serbia, whose first administration was the work of Prince Miloš. The European states, together or singly, determined the form of the Greek kingdom in the 1830s, the organization of the Danubian Principalities in 1856, the government of autonomous Bulgaria in 1878, and that of Albania in 1913. Thereafter, the powers repeatedly intervened in the internal affairs of each state. In the coming years the Balkan leaders thus had to deal not only with the Porte, but also with the European states, who had enormous military, political, and economic strength behind them.

5

The formation of the national
governments

IN THE PREVIOUS CHAPTERS the stages by which four Balkan people won a wide degree of control over their own administration have been examined. By 1816, under the rule of Prince Miloš, Serbia had gained rights of internal self-government, although not a fully autonomous regime. Montenegro had succeeded in maintaining a defiant attitude that made the attempt to collect regular taxes or interfere in its local affairs too costly a policy for the Ottoman Empire to undertake under normal circumstances. The Danubian Principalities by 1822 had been able to get rid of their Phanariot governors; the exact relationship with both the Porte and Russia had still to be determined. Greece by 1830 was at least in theory a fully independent state, despite the Bavarian administration and the great-power protection.

Although Montenegro was to continue to engage in almost constant border warfare, and the Danubian Principalities were to undergo another Russian and Ottoman occupation in 1848, with these exceptions the Balkan states enjoyed a period of relative tranquility that was to last until the 1870s. One major European conflict, the Crimean War, did involve Balkan issues directly, but, though the Principalities did once more experience a Russian, followed by a Habsburg and Ottoman, occupation, there was no fighting on the peninsula and local armies were not engaged. These years could thus be devoted to the consolidation of the internal regimes and to attempts to modernize and improve the lives of the inhabitants. Problems of domestic administration accordingly dominate the history of these four areas in this period. Although they were to develop both socially and politically along differing paths, all shared certain common problems.

The first task that had to be undertaken was the formation of national administrations; in each state a strongly centralized regime was established. As we have seen, under the Ottoman system the Christian population had enjoyed wide rights of self-administration through local communities and the millet system. The Christians did not, however, have national secular organizations within the Ottoman Empire. The church took the place of a Serbian, Bulgarian, Albanian, and Bulgarian civil administration. An exception, of course, could be found in the Principalities, with their princely courts in Bucharest and Iaşi, but these provinces had never been directly administered by the Porte. In practice, the building of national governments involved taking power from local authorities, who had functioned effectively in the past in their own spheres. This move inevitably met with much opposition in both Christian and Muslim areas where the local notables were jealous of their power and prestige. However, it was obvious that the small states could not survive without central, strong leaderships that could in each case mobilize and use the resources of the entire nation.

Closely tied with the formation of the administration was the extremely sensitive issue of who or what group would control the state apparatus. As we have seen, throughout Balkan history there had been conflicts between the ruler, or whoever held the executive power, and the notables and military men with their ties to definite localities. The latter regularly followed the principle that we have seen in the Greek and Serbian revolutions of refusing to recognize the authority of an executive they could not control. As we shall see, this group was often to adopt Western political ideology to the extent of calling for constitutions or charters, which would limit the power of the ruler, and for the establishment of some sort of council or assembly to share in the control of the state. These were not democratic movements. Powerful families and strong individuals fought for predominance in the government; they wished to control it for themselves and their followers. Although many gained their strength from their authority in the countryside, few called for a decentralized administration or a widening of the franchise to include the peasant majority.

In addition to building domestic institutions, the Balkan leaders had to determine their relations with their neighbors and with the great powers. The autonomous states in theory should not have conducted foreign relations – that was the privilege and the duty of the Porte. In fact, all did in one form or another. Usually special agents were sent to the European courts to present the individual national point of view in times of crisis. Even more effective, however, were the direct relations established between the European consulates in the Balkan capitals and the national governments. European consular agents were very active throughout this period. They competed with one another for predominant influence, and they interfered constantly in domestic affairs. They championed rival political factions, and they sought special privileges for their clients. Their position was often very strong. Owing to the capitulations they had a special legal standing, even in the autonomous states, that put them outside the jurisdiction of the local courts. They could also offer protection and favors to natives; some could even sell their own country's citizenship.

As part of their foreign relations the governments had to formulate a national policy. Of course, none of these states included all of the Balkan inhabitants of the nationality concerned. Obviously, diplomatic and military plans had to be made for the eventual acquisition of further territories. At the same time the national idea had to be propagated. It is impossible to judge the extent to which the people in any Balkan area held deeply nationalistic convictions – that is, in the sense of believing that the nation-state was the natural moral and political division for mankind and that it should command the first allegiance of the citizen. The majority of peasants were probably emotionally most closely attached to their families and regions and perhaps their local churches. Certainly the new governments did take seriously the task of teaching patriotism to the population. National propaganda, for both internal and foreign consumption, became a major state industry and was perhaps the strongest component of the education given in the new school systems.

With the achievement of autonomy or independence, the new regimes had to regulate their relationships with the Orthodox church, which, as we have seen, fulfilled many important functions under the Ottoman rule. One of the first moves that each government made was to attempt to separate its ecclesiastical organization from the Constantinople Patriarchate. Although it was obvious that the churches could not remain under the jurisdiction of a hierarchy closely associated with the Ottoman Empire, the move also was to the benefit of the state. What occurred at this point was not a separation of church and state, as happened in liberal Western Europe, but the subordination of the religious to the secular authorities. The government took over those aspects of life that had formerly been under millet jurisdiction, including not only matters such as education and social welfare, but also to an extent the moral guidance of the population. Under Ottoman rule the Orthodox church had major political responsibilities; it held the Christian people together and ordered their lives. The new national churches were to be run by synods whose members were often political appointees; their main concerns were often not to center on purely ecclesiastical problems.

Although a small minority of the population in each state was to decide the major political questions, their actions, of course, involved the fate of the peasant majority. Excluded from direct participation in the political activities, the peasants were primarily interested in the land question, particularly in the issues involving ownership, or payments where plots were held on the sharecropping or leasing system. State taxes and labor dues were also a grievance. The major objective of most peasant families was the securing of direct control over a definite piece of land, and then, if possible, the extension of this property. We have seen the great confusion of the land system in the eighteenth century, with the multiple methods of landholding and the weight of taxation and labor dues carried by the individual. A regulation of this question was an absolute necessity for the national regimes, and the solutions they adopted were to have a determining effect on the future evolution of each state.

All of the Balkan governments were acutely aware that their economic development lagged behind that of Western Europe. By the end of the century, despite the emergence of the independent states, the gap between Balkan and Western European levels of development had widened considerably. The efforts made to modernize Balkan societies and to introduce advanced Western technological achievements, such as railroads and the telegraph, are an important part of the history of the region. The principal emphases of this chapter, however, are the problems of political organization, the relations among the Balkan states and with the great powers, and the land and peasant question. General economic issues are covered in a subsequent section.

SERBIA FROM MILOŠ TO MILAN

The status of the Serbian principality had been settled, it will be remembered, on the basis of the agreement between Miloš and Marashli Ali Pasha, the vezir of Rumelia. Miloš was recognized as supreme knez; his government was to administer the country and collect the taxes. His rule, however, was not hereditary. Moreover, in contrast to the situation in the Danubian Principalities, in Serbia the Ottoman presence was still strong and obvious. An Ottoman governor was appointed for Belgrade; other officials and judges remained in residence. The sipahis, the merchants, and the garrisons of the fortress cities were further reminders of Ottoman control. The main objective of the first period of Miloš's rule was to change these conditions. He wished to strengthen his personal position and win further autonomous rights for the state.

Serbia at this time was an extremely primitive land. It was, one authority writes,

> a poor and primitive pashalik with the physical appearance of an American frontier region and with cultural characteristics reflecting the past centuries of Ottoman rule.
>
> The few roads that were cut through the forests could be traversed only on foot, on horseback, or by oxcart. Two roads alone were fit for carriage traveling, but this did not cause hardship because only two people boasted carriages, the pasha in Belgrade and Prince Miloš himself. The Serbian peasants regarded the surrounding forests as a nuisance to be rid of as soon as possible and, like the American frontiersmen, they set fire to vast stands in order to scatter corn seed between the charred stumps. Also, the manner of everyday life in the Morava Valley closely resembled that in the Ohio Valley – the same log cabins, home-made furniture and clothes, plain food but plenty of it, plum brandy in place of rum, books and schools conspicuous by their scarcity, and an abundance of malaria and other diseases which were treated by a combination of home remedies, barbers, and quacks.[1]

1 L. S. Stavrianos, *The Balkans since 1453* (New York: Rinehart, 1958), p. 251.

Only the outward appearance, however, linked Serbia with the American West. Miloš's reign was to demonstrate how deeply the Ottoman rule had affected the political outlook of the Balkan people.

Miloš's first task was to organize a central administration. He had inherited only one state institution, the National Chancery, which was a higher court; otherwise he had no basis on which to build. Miloš was not an educated man; he could not read or write. Nor had he experienced life outside the Ottoman Empire. With this background he naturally adopted Ottoman examples in running his state; essentially he acted like a Turkish pasha. He was opposed by the local notables, who resented his attitude as well as the elevation of one of their number to the supreme position. They were used to running their own districts with little interference from a central authority. The struggle between the prince and the dissident notables was to be the central theme of Serbian political history over the next decades.

Miloš had the advantage of being an extremely clever and wily politician. He succeeded not only in dominating the political situation, but in making himself very wealthy. Rising from his origins as a poor peasant, he became one of the richest men in Europe. Since the public money and his private funds were not clearly separated, he did not hesitate to use his advantage in his speculations. He took possession of state lands and property that had been confiscated from Ottoman owners. Using the state labor taxes, he had the peasants work off their obligations on his private undertakings. He held a monopoly on livestock exports and on the sale of salt. He also owned large estates and seventeen villages in Wallachia.

Despite his autocratic attitude and his obvious corruption, Miloš was a popular and respected leader among the population at large. He was a figure that the peasant could understand. Illiterate and rude in manner, he was not far separated from the average man. Throughout his reign the prince had difficulties in dealing with the Porte and the notables, but the majority of the people gave him their full support.

Miloš's controversies with the Porte concerned both his personal authority and the exact rights of the Serbian government. His position was not hereditary, and the borders of the principality had not been finally determined. Although Miloš remained in touch with the Russian government, which assured him of backing in the attempt to secure the implementation of Article VIII of the Treaty of Bucharest, the prince preferred to deal directly with the Porte. His method was still to make gains through collaboration with the Ottoman authorities; he made frequent professions of loyalty and devotion to the sultan, and he distributed rich bribes widely. His first objective was to secure the right of hereditary succession for his family.

Because the prince did not want to jeopardize his relations with the Porte, he refused to cooperate with the Etairia in its endeavor to organize a great Balkan rising. There were certainly no close ties between the Serbs and the Greeks, and the Serbian interests had been adversely affected by the Phanariot influence in Constantinople. The Greek leaders for their part were primarily interested in using the Serbian lands as a base of operation for their national revolt. Moreover, the entire question became entwined in Serbian internal politics and the opposition of some notables, who saw in Karadjordje a preferable alternative to Miloš. The return of the leader of the first revolution was thus a challenge to the power of the prince. The assassination of Karadjordje in July 1817 marked the commencement of a feud between the Obrenović and Karadjordjević families.

When Miloš failed to win Ottoman approval of hereditary succession, he summoned an assembly in 1817 and had it declare him hereditary prince. Without the assent of the Porte or the great powers, the act had, however, little real value. Thereafter, Miloš turned to consolidating his rule in the country. The National Chancery was filled with his adherents. He similarly made certain that he would not be opposed by the communal authorities. He personally appointed the oborknez in each locality and paid him a salary; the local assemblies were deprived of their former authority. With the assistance of his relatives and friends, the prince was able to maintain his control of the state. Although there were frequent conspiracies against him, he suppressed them by direct and brutal methods.

He was, however, unable to expand Serbian autonomous rights through the policy of collaboration. As was true in the Principalities, changes in the political relationship with the Porte were to come only as the result of international crises and the actions of Russia. This great power did continue to support the Serbian position. In Article V of the Convention of Akkerman of October 1826, the Porte gave assurances of the fulfillment of its obligations under previous agreements. These were further defined in an Additional Act as the granting to Serbia of

> freedom of religious worship, the choice of its chiefs, the independence of its internal administration, the re-annexation of the districts detached from Serbia, the consolidation of the various taxes into a single sum, the making over to the Serbians [of] the administration of the properties belonging to Muslims, subject to the payment of the proceeds thereof at the same time with the tribute, liberty of commerce, permission for the Serbian merchants to travel in the Ottoman dominions with their own passports, the establishment of hospitals, schools, and printinghouses; and, finally, the prohibition to Muslims, other than those belonging to the garrisons, to establish themselves in Serbia.[2]

The accomplishment of these aims, of course, was to depend on the Russian victory in the Russo-Turkish War of 1828–1829, a conflict in which Ser-

---

2 Edward Hertslet, *The Map of Europe by Treaty*, 4 vols. (London: Butterworths, 1875–1891), I, 758–759.

bian participation was not requested. Article VI of the Treaty of Adrianople confirmed the previous conditions and made additional mention of a cession of territory. This stipulation concerned the status of six districts that Serbia claimed, but that were not administered by Miloš.

In a firman of October 1830 the Ottoman government granted the Serbian principality a fully autonomous status. Miloš was recognized as hereditary prince; he was to rule with an assembly. The tribute was to be fixed, and no Muslims were to live in the state except for the soldiers attached to the six fortresses that remained under direct Ottoman control. Other Muslims would have to sell their property and leave. The question of the six districts was not finally settled until 1833. At that time the Porte, hard pressed by a conflict with Egypt, ceded the territory in question, and the tribute was set at 2.3 million piastres a year. With the establishment of firm boundaries and the definition of the relationship with the Porte, Serbia's main attention could be devoted to the question who, or what faction, would run the autonomous government.

According to the firman of 1830, Miloš was to rule with a council and an assembly, bodies that in theory would serve as a check on his authority. In Serbia there was also a traditional institution, the *skupština*, a popular assembly of the male population of a district that was called together in times of crisis to hear and ratify the declarations of its leaders. By 1830 the arbitrary rule of the prince had created a united opposition composed principally of notables, merchants, government officials, and others who had been harmed by Miloš's actions or who hated him personally. In the ensuing decade they attempted to force the prince to establish a council or an assembly that would share his powers, an action that indeed was called for by the agreement with the Ottoman Empire. Miloš, as could be expected, would not voluntarily limit his authority. In 1835 an assembly of about four thousand met and drew up the so-called Presentation Constitution, which called for these institutions. The prince did appoint a council, but he then ignored it and the rest of the provisions of the document.

The constitutional question also involved the great powers, who followed Serbian domestic events through their consulates in Belgrade, most of which were established in this period. Russia already had representatives in the principality; they were joined in 1835 by an Austrian consulate, in 1837 by a British, and in 1838 by a French. As in Constantinople and in every other Balkan capital, these consulates vied for influence over the government and participated actively in domestic quarrels.

In this political crisis the opposition to Miloš was known as the Constitutionalist Party; its chief was Toma Vučić-Perišić. The goal was the acceptance of a constitution that would limit the powers of the prince and force him to govern in association with the leading men of the country. The issue was not that of popular participation or democratic reform. The alternatives offered were rule by a corrupt prince or by an oligarchy. With these choices, the

British and French governments gave their support to Miloš and his absolutist system; Russia, in contrast, backed the Constitutionalists. Under strong
pressure from the domestic opposition, Miloš was forced to agree to an alteration in the government. A Serbian delegation was sent to Constantinople, where the discussions were influenced primarily by Russia. The Ottoman
Empire was in the midst of a new Egyptian crisis, and Russia's support of
the empire assured this power a predominant diplomatic position in Constantinople. In December 1838 a document known as the Turkish Constitution was issued. More an administrative statute than a true constitution, this
charter was, nevertheless, to form the basis of the government of Serbia until
1869. Its most important aspect was the limitation that its provisions placed
on the previously arbitrary power of the prince. Henceforth, he was to govern in association with a council of seventeen. He was to nominate the members, but they could not thereafter be removed. The prince and the council
were to be jointly responsible for legislation; Miloš had the right of veto. The
document also regulated other aspects of state life, such as the bureaucracy
and the judicial system. Unable to accept this new arrangement, Miloš abdicated and left the country.

Despite his departure under these adverse circumstances, the prince had
accomplished much during his reign. He had regulated the status of Serbia
within the Ottoman Empire, and he had gained a very favorable boundary
settlement. Although Russia was by treaty the protecting power, neither that
state nor any other great power was able to exercise the type of political
domination that we shall see in operation in neighboring states. Moreover,
the prince had established the framework for the internal administration. The
foundations were thus laid for the state bureaucracy. By the end of Miloš's
reign the state officials numbered 672, of which 201 were police. These men
were to form an influential group in the future and to develop their own
organization and interests. Under the first prince, however, posts in the state
service were filled primarily with Miloš's supporters.

Despite the fact that the ruler, like many other revolutionary leaders, was
himself illiterate, he was concerned with the development of education. In
the 1830s both elementary schools and a high school were opened. A printing
press was in operation in 1831. At first the situation was very difficult. There
was a shortage of adequately trained teachers, as well as of books and school
supplies. During the first decades of the autonomous state the chief intellectual influence was to come from the Serbs of the Habsburg Monarchy, who
had had better opportunities than the Serbs under Ottoman rule to obtain
an education. These Serbs from across the border, known as *prečani*, were
also to form an important element in the new bureaucracy, since they had the
skills needed by the state. The Vojvodina was to remain the cultural center of
the Serbs until the young state had the chance to catch up.

The status of the Serbian church was also regulated during Miloš's reign.
In 1830 the sultan agreed to restore its former autonomy; the national orga-

nization was headed by the metropolitan of Belgrade, who was from 1833 to 1859 the very able Peter Jovanović. Although Orthodoxy was indeed to play an important role in Serbian national development, the leadership of the state was henceforth clearly in the hands of the secular authority, that is, the prince and his government.

As we can see, the peasant was given no role in the new constitutional order. The Turkish Constitution placed the political power in the hands of a narrow group of influential men. There was no provision for the summoning of a skupština. Political authority had been fully transferred from the village and the nahije to the capital, Belgrade. Formerly, under Ottoman administration, the peasant had often played at least a limited political role as part of his community or as a revolutionary fighter; he was now to be governed by agents of the central government sent to his locality. Nevertheless, much had been gained as a result of the revolution. Most important, the peasant did receive the type of land settlement that he preferred.

Serbia, as has been shown, was traditionally the land of the small peasant farm. As a result of the revolt and the subsequent agreements, those peasant families which had formerly been attached to estates owned by Muslims did gain full possession of the land they worked. During and immediately after the revolution every effort was made to force the Turkish landowners out of the countryside. Life was made difficult and dangerous for those who attempted to remain. Where possible, Miloš seized Ottoman state property. The later treaties, which forbade the settlement of Muslims in Serbia, compelled these people to sell their property and emigrate. The sipahis were forced to leave in 1830, but they did receive indemnification for their losses. Their land then passed to the small owner. Of course, the land question was not as pressing in Serbia as in certain other regions. There were still huge stretches of forests and unused land. Nevertheless, the settlement made at this time assured that Serbia would become a land of small peasant proprietors, not of great landed estates. In 1836 an act was passed to protect the peasant from losing his land to creditors; it set a minimum, including a house, a small plot of land, and some livestock, that could not be taken away from the peasant household.

After Miloš abdicated in June 1839, the sucession passed to his son Milan. This prince, who was very ill with tuberculosis, died after twenty-six days without ever having taken charge of the government. A regency held power until his brother Michael returned from abroad in March 1840. This sixteen-year-old prince was in a most difficult position. He faced the opposition both of the Constitutionalist Party and of those who wished his father to return. In 1842 he too was forced to leave the country. An assembly, which was dominated by the Constitutionalists, was then summoned. They chose as ruler Alexander Karadjordjević, the son of the great revolutionary leader.

The reign of Alexander was marked by the domination of the Constitutionalist Party, led by Toma Vučić-Perišić, Avram Petronijević, and Ilija Garašanin. They were backed by the notables, bureaucrats, and merchants who had formed the opposition to Miloš's regime. The power in the government now lay in the council, not in the office of the prince. The aim of the new administration was a well-run state. It was interested in assuring the rule of law, economic freedom, and a good educational system. The leaders were not democratic; they expected their party to dominate the state. During their period in power, they did achieve some of their goals. The centralized, bureaucratic regime was strengthened. A law code, based on Austrian models, was issued in 1844. Like Miloš, the Constitutionalists filled the government posts with their supporters. These men, often born in the Habsburg Monarchy, were at least better educated than their predecessors in office, but they too had little in common with the peasantry. They formed a bureaucratic elite and, as such, caused much discontent among those whom they were sent to administer.

Alexander, as can be readily understood, did not have control of the situation. He was personally not a strong man. His position was affected by the fact that the Karadjordjević family did not enjoy the right of hereditary rule, which had been conceded only to the Obrenović dynasty. The prince had no popular base of support in the country; he could not summon the peasantry in his defense against the bureaucratic regime. His rule was also disliked by both Russia and the Habsburg Empire, who were cooperating in international affairs. Of course, always in the background there was the threat of an Obrenović restoration, although its proponents were divided between the candidatures of Miloš and of Michael.

Alexander's reign covered the years of two major events in European history – the revolutions of 1848 and the Crimean War, both of which will be discussed in greater detail elsewhere. The revolutionary situation in the Habsburg Empire naturally aroused much interest in the principality, particularly the events involving the Serbian population of the monarchy. Some Serbs did cross the border to participate in the revolts or to fight against the Hungarian insurgents. The Crimean War caused an even greater problem. When the Ottoman Empire became involved in war with Russia in 1853, there was naturally a temptation to take advantage of the Ottoman distraction to make territorial gains. In 1854 France and Britain joined the Ottoman side. These powers, together with the Habsburg Empire, wished to keep the conflict out of the Balkans and to protect their ally's interests. Strong pressure was thus put on Belgrade not to act.

During this period the Serbian government was closer to France than to any other power. Both Russia and Austria continued to look with disfavor and suspicion on the Karadjordjević administration. Since Serbia could not hope for support for an aggressive policy, no concrete advances were made in foreign relations. Nevertheless, the question of future territorial objectives was a matter of constant discussion. In 1844 Garašanin drew up a plan, called the Načertanije, which probably best illustrates the direction of Serbian nationalist thought. The document called for the unification of the lands that were considered predominantly Serbian and Orthodox, including Bosnia, Hercegovina, "Old Serbia" – that is, the Kosovo region – Montenegro, the Vojvodina, and northern Albania.

Although the prince was in a weak position, he still made constant efforts to protect or strengthen his authority. A major point of conflict was the composition of the cabinet, whose members were chosen by Alexander from the council. This body was divided between the adherents and the opponents of the prince. The Constitutionalists at this point proposed that an assembly be convened to define the powers of the executive branch of the government. Such meetings had been held in the past to consider other problems. In December 1858, 439 representatives attended the St. Andrew Assembly. Despite their belief that they could control the participants, the Constitutionalists found themselves outmaneuvered. There was indeed a great deal of opposition not only to Alexander, but also to the Karadjordjević dynasty. As a result, the assembly deposed Alexander and voted to call back Prince Miloš and the Obrenović dynasty.

Returning after a long period in exile, Miloš reigned for only a year and a half before he died at the age of eighty. His political ideas had not changed; he fully intended to rule as an absolute monarch. In 1859, however, it was agreed that the assembly would meet on a regular basis every three years, but as an advisory rather than a legislative body. The Serbian government was thus composed of three potentially conflicting elements: the prince, the council, and the assembly. These competing centers were to form the basis for new political alignments and for two parties. In the future the Liberal Party was to serve to rally the supporters of the assembly, whereas the Conservative Party backed the authority of the council and the prince.

In 1860 Michael Obrenović commenced his second reign. Now thirty-seven and far more experienced, he was well educated and he had traveled widely. He was acquainted with the general international situation, and this aspect of his reign is of principal significance. His internal policy was, in general, also successful. Like his father he was determined to rule, but he was willing to give his authority a constitutional form. As required, he held the assemblies every three years, but he assured that his supporters dominated the proceedings. He used the police to supervise the elections, and he made certain that the bureaucracy was composed of his partisans. He cooperated principally with the Conservative Party; the Liberals were forced into opposition. His chief minister was Ilija Garašanin, who had also been prominent in the previous reign.

Although Michael's early death precluded the accomplishment of his wider goals, he did achieve certain definite advances in foreign policy. His first objective was the strengthening of the army. Here he met with great success. His military forces became the strongest among the Balkan states. In 1861 he introduced regulations that made all males from twenty to fifty years old liable to military service. He could thus count on having approximately ninety thousand soldiers available in case of war. Although their training and equipment left much to be desired, the numbers were impressive. The next obvious move was to rid Serbia of the Ottoman military garrisons in the six fortress cities. Of these, Belgrade held a particular significance. The city had a Muslim population of about three thousand, composed principally of soldiers and merchants. Incidents between the Christian and Muslim inhabitants were difficult to avoid, and such an event in 1862 resulted in the shelling of the city by Ottoman troops from the fortress of Kalemegdan. The Serbian government, appealing to the great powers for backing, began a long period of negotiation with the Porte aimed at removing all of the garrisons, a goal that was accomplished only in 1867.

Michael's reign is known particularly for the sponsorship that the prince gave to the formation of a Balkan alliance system aimed at the overthrow of Ottoman rule. This period of national and revolutionary agitation in the peninsula, as well as in Central Europe, is discussed further in a later section. However, it should be noted here that Michael was able to conclude agreements with Montenegro in 1866, with Greece in 1867, and with Romania in 1868. The prince made Serbia the center for revolutionary and national activity in the Balkans. His sympathetic attitude toward Bulgarian groups in Serbia was to be of great assistance in furthering their aim of organizing a revolutionary movement within the Bulgarian lands. As far as Serbian objectives were concerned, the goals for the future were enlarged to include Catholic Croatian as well as Serbian Orthodox lands under Habsburg rule. The leadership of any South Slav movement, no matter what territory or people it embraced, was, of course, to remain in the hands of Belgrade. Michael's ambitious program was cut short when he was assassinated in June 1868.

Since Michael had no direct heirs, his nephew Milan succeeded him. The new prince was only thirteen at the time, so a regency had to be appointed. Milan had an unfortunate background for his high position. He had been born in Wallachia in 1854. His mother, Marie Catargiu, became the mistress of the Romanian prince Alexander Cuza after her husband died. Milan, who at the age of nine had been sent to Paris for his education, did not have a happy childhood. His entire reign was characterized by his personal weakness and instability; it also covered a period of war and national disaster.

The young ruler was to receive a new constitution, replacing the document of 1838. Under the sponsorship of the regency a constitutional assembly was summoned in 1869. It will be noted that although Serbia was still under Ottoman sovereignty, there was no interference in the activities of this body either by the Porte or by the powers. The constitution that was issued left the prince with a strong position in the state. The assembly too had important powers. Three-quarters of its members were to be elected; one-quarter were to be appointed by the prince, who also had the power to dismiss it. The council was reduced to little more than an administrative committee.

The document contained declarations on civil rights, including freedom of speech, assembly, and the press.

From 1815 to 1869 Serbia had thus advanced from the position of a semi-autonomous province to that of a state with almost complete self-government. In theory, the Ottoman Empire was still the suzerain power; a tribute was paid. In practice, however, the Porte made little effort to influence internal affairs. There was more interference in foreign policy, but this consideration did not hinder Michael from pursuing active and aggressive programs. As far as the internal administration was concerned, the government had advanced from the primitive level at the time of Miloš, where the ruler held complete power and made use of the state treasury, to the constitutional regime of 1869. During this period, as we have seen, local government was placed under the control of the centralized bureaucracy.

Although it can be argued that most of these changes were beneficial to the development of the nation, certain other attributes of the autonomous regime were not. The use of the police in elections and the prevalence of corruption in politics have been mentioned. It should, nevertheless, be pointed out that in Serbia, as in other Balkan states, certain practices were accepted as either normal or inevitable that would have been strongly criticized elsewhere. The Ottoman rule, in a period of decline, had been deeply corrupt, at least by Western European standards. It could not be expected that the new Balkan regimes would change traditional practices overnight.

MONTENEGRO

Similar moves toward political consolidation were made during the same period in the second Serbian state, Montenegro. At the beginning of the century this country was without recognized boundaries, and its status in relation to the Ottoman Empire had yet to be defined. Montenegrin leaders often maintained that they were independent; the Ottoman Empire, in contrast, firmly insisted that these lands were an integral part of its territory. It was an extremely backward region, both politically and economically. Despite the existence of the bishopric in Cetinje and the office of governor, the real authority remained with the tribes. Loyalty was to the local leadership and to family-based groups. The extreme poverty of the land was due to its mountainous and rugged character. Since few areas were suitable for cultivation, the principal occupation was animal husbandry, with the concentration on the raising of small animals like goats and sheep. Raiding and cattle rustling were, as we have seen, a part of the economy. Throughout the century the basic problem of hunger remained. The land was too poor to support its population. Emigration or territorial expansion were among the few solutions to the dilemma that appeared possible, and throughout this period Montenegrins left for Serbia, Russia, or the Habsburg lands.

The alternative, an active policy of expansion, was not easy to implement.

Access to the sea at Kotor had not been gained despite the Montenegrin exploits during the Napoleonic Wars. In fact, there was a threat that the neighboring military leaders might endanger the state itself. The western Balkans were at this time in a condition of almost continual turmoil and warfare owing to the fact that the Porte could not subdue the local notables. In addition to Ali Pasha of Janina, Bosnian and other Albanian beys continued to resist control from Constantinople, and they quarreled ceaselessly with each other. Rival centers were established at Shkodër, Mostar, Sarajevo, and Travnik. Although the Montenegrins could play between these groups to some extent, the danger always existed that they might combine against their Christian neighbor. The threat was to become even greater later in the century, when Ottoman reform measures succeeded to the extent of forcing all of the rebellious pashas to recognize the authority of the Porte. Montenegro then faced the possibility of an Ottoman occupation.

The constant threats from without had the positive effect of virtually compelling the Montenegrin clans to accept a single authority. Obviously, without unity, the land could fall under the domination of one or several of the contending Muslim forces, or under the direct administration of the Ottoman Empire. Montenegro had, as we have seen, two recognized leaders, the bishop and the governor, of which the first had generally been the more powerful. Aside from these offices, the Cetinje government consisted of very little else. It did not carry on the normal functions of a state; there was no regular collection of taxes, no army, no administration for the various regions, and no system of justice. It has been estimated in the first part of the nineteenth century there were about 120,000 people, divided into thirty-six tribes and living in 240 villages. There were no roads; communication was by horse or pack animal. The capital, Cetinje, contained the monastery and only a few stone houses. The leaders thus had to start from the beginning in building a political structure, and they had very poor material with which to work.

Some important steps toward forming some sort of central administration had already been taken in the eighteenth century under the leadership of Bishop Peter I. In 1798 an assembly of tribal chiefs met in Cetinje to consider common problems and to coordinate the defense of the territory. Decisions were taken for both Montenegro and Brda. This assembly accepted a code of laws and established a central court, known as the *kuluk*, which had both administrative and judicial functions. Despite these accomplishments, Peter I, during his long reign, had little success in establishing anything like a central government with real authority in the countryside. It was impossible to set up an administrative system or organize an army unless taxes could be levied, and the tribes were no more willing to pay taxes to Cetinje than to the Porte. Efforts to stop their raiding and looting were equally futile, as were attempts to prevent the tribes from fighting each other.

Justice also remained primarily a tribal matter. The elders of each tribe judged their members. Relations among the tribes were based on customary law. One serious problem that the central administration was to attempt to end was the blood feud, a tradition that existed throughout certain of the backward areas of the Balkans. According to this custom, if one member of a clan, or a similar association, killed a member of another, the life of one of the murderer's fellow clansmen had to be taken. Since this act in turn called for revenge, the chain of deaths could be very long. Even when the central government ordered executions after a regular legal process, the sentence was carried out by a firing squad, all shooting simultaneously, so that the responsibility for the death could not be assigned to one individual or family.

The problems raised by the existence of the dual offices of bishop and governor were to be solved by Peter's successor. The governorship had been held regularly by the Radonjić family, just as a Petrović always became bishop. The position of bishop had traditionally passed from uncle to nephew, since bishops were required to be celibate. The choice now fell upon Rade, who in 1830, the year of his selection, was just seventeen. He was not a monk, and he had received no formal education. An open struggle for power broke out between the Petrović and Radonjić families. Although the jurisdiction of the governor had never been clearly defined, the Radonjić supporters had usually claimed that his powers were equal to those of the bishop. At this time, however, Vuk Radonjić attempted to establish the superiority of his office and to claim full jurisdiction over secular affairs. He was unable to win the support of the clan chiefs, who instead backed the Petrović family, probably seeing in an ecclesiastical leader less of a threat to their own local power. As a result, the office of governor was abolished and the members of the Randonjić family were either killed or banished. This move left the bishop the undisputed secular and religious leader.

Following tradition, Rade became a monk and adopted the name Peter II, although his subsequent life did not give any evidence of a deep religious calling. He also used the name Njegoš. Like his uncle he faced severe limitations on his power. He had no army, militia, or police under his command; he could use only the military forces provided by his family and clan. His greatest problem was the management of the tribes on the outer fringes of the state, who often refused to obey him or joined his opponents. There was constant resistance to his authority among all the clans. It was impossible for him to control their raiding into Ottoman territory, which had become an element in the economic life of the region. Nevertheless, he was able to take some steps toward establishing a regular administrative apparatus.

In the creation of state offices, the tutorial hand of the Russian court was again apparent. As we have seen, Russia had shown at times a great interest in Montenegro, especially when the strategic position of these lands could be of value to its policy. The Russian subsidy, which had been paid intermittently, had constituted one of the metropolitan's few financial resources. In 1831 the Russian government sent two envoys, Ivan Vukotić and Matija Vučićević, who were both Montenegrins; they were accompanied by D. Milaković, who subsequently became Peter's secretary. Their principal task was to assist in the establishment of stronger institutions of central government.

Another assembly of chiefs was held, and in 1831 the Administrative Senate of Montenegro and Brda was formed to replace the court created in 1798. The senate was composed of sixteen men who were to receive salaries from, and represent the interests of, the central administration. Possible opposition was blunted by the appointment of chiefs and prominent men to the positions. At the same time, an organization known as the Guard was formed; its members were sent to the districts and the clans, where they served both police and judicial functions. The commanders were called captains and were chosen from the prominent men of the clans. All the members received salaries. Their duties were to serve the central government, to assure that the decisions of the senate were fulfilled, and to guard the frontiers.

The essential role of Russia in these reforms is clear. The salaries and the state expenses came chiefly from the Russian subsidies. Attempts were made again in 1833 to introduce regular taxation, but even though the rates were low, the taxes were strongly resisted. The amount of the Russian subsidy remained higher than the revenues that could be collected in the country. In that same year Peter II went to Russia on his first visit and was there confirmed as bishop. He was received by Nicholas I, and he returned home with rich gifts, including a sum of money, the promise of an increased subsidy, books and ikons for the church, and a printing press. Now in a stronger position, Peter dismissed Vukotić and took full control of the government.

Despite these moves, Peter was well aware that the principal power was still in the hands of the clans, whose chiefs were chosen on a hereditary basis and who had a vested interest in maintaining political conditions as they were. The best policy for the bishop to adopt was simply to try to manipulate his rivals and play them against each other. He had his uncle, Peter I, canonized to increase the prestige of his family. He enjoyed constant Russian support, at least in the first part of his reign. His closest contact with official Russia was through the consul in Dubrovnik, Jeremija Gagić, a Serb who had joined the opposition to Karadjordje in the revolutionary period. Forced to emigrate, he had entered Russian service. In 1815 he was appointed consul in Dubrovnik, where he remained for forty years.

In addition to these attempts at internal consolidation, Peter carried on an active foreign policy. The major goal remained, as in the eighteenth century, that of securing an outlet to the Adriatic. As before, the Habsburg Monarchy was firmly opposed. Vienna, like the other powers, was convinced that Montenegrin acquisition of a seaport would signify principally that Russia had acquired a base on the Adriatic. In this respect, the Russian connection was a hindrance to Montenegrin interests. On the other borders, attention was paid chiefly to three strategic points: Spuž and Podgorica (Titograd) in the east, and Grahovo in the northwest. In 1831 and 1832 attempts to take Pod-gorica failed, even though the Porte was in a weak military position because of the concurrent conflict with Egypt. In 1842, after similar local skirmishes, both sides agreed that Grahovo would be neutral territory. During this period, Peter faced continual revolts from the clans. In 1837 he went to Russia to explain his difficulties, and there received an increase in the subsidy and wheat to relieve a famine that was going on at the time. He was accompanied on his return by another Russian agent, Iakov Ozeretskovskii.

Although Peter was an able ruler, he is better known for his writing. He is considered the greatest Serbian poet. His chief works are *The Mountain Wreath* (1847), *Light of the Microcosm* (1845), and *The False Tsar Stephen the Small* (1851), the last of which, of course, dealt with the career of the eighteenth-century adventurer. Although primarily concerned with problems of human existence, Peter wrote passionately about the Serbian (identified directly with the Montenegrin), past. This quotation comes from the beginning of his most famous work, *The Mountain Wreath*:

> Our God hath poured His wrath upon the Serbs,
> For deadly sins withdrawn His favour from us:
> Our Rulers trampled underfoot all law,
> With bloody hatred fought each other down,
> Tore from fraternal brows the living eyes;
> Authority and Law they cast aside,
> Instead chose folly as their rule and guide!
> And those who served our kings became untrue,
> Crimson they bathed themselves in kingly blood!
> Our noblemen – God's Curse be on their souls –
> Did tear and rend the Kingdom into pieces,
> And wasted wantonly our people's power.
> The Serbian magnates – may their names rot out!
> They scattered broadcast Discord's evil seed,
> And poisoned thus the life-springs of our race.[3]

Certainly internal dissension was the major problem with which Peter had to deal. Once again, in 1846–1847, he was faced with revolt. The rebels co-operated with the pasha of Shkodër and had to be suppressed by force. Although the bishop was able to hold his country together, the central government remained weak, with the Russian subsidies continuing to be the main source of income. There was no treasury; Peter had a safe in which he kept the state money. There was no judicial system or laws to command general respect. The captains judged some small cases, and the senate handled larger

---

3   Quoted in Milovan Djilas, *Njegoš* (New York: Harcourt, Brace & World, 1966), p. 294.

crimes; but the organization remained primitive. Although the first primary school was opened in 1833, education was not readily available even on the lowest level.

In 1851 Peter II died of tuberculosis, after having previously named his nephew Danilo as his successor. Danilo had been educated in Russia and, like his uncle, had not received a religious training. Moreover, he had no desire to be a bishop and he wished to marry. With the approval of both Russia and the Habsburg Empire he secularized his office and in 1852 proclaimed himself prince. Like his predecessors he had a great deal of difficulty exerting his authority over the tribes. In fact, the situation deteriorated at this time because of changes that had taken place in Constantinople.

In an era of reform, the Ottoman Empire had succeeded in reestablishing its authority in Bosnia over the dissident beys. Here an active and strong policy was being carried on by Ömer Pasha Latas, the governor, whose goal was the reestablishment of Ottoman control in the entire region. His first move was to try to detach the Piperi tribe from allegiance to Cetinje. An open conflict broke out when Montenegrin forces attempted to seize Žabljak on Lake Shkodër in 1853. Ömer Pasha was able to advance into Montenegrin territory, and Danilo was forced to call on the powers for assistance. He was able to obtain the strong backing of the Habsburg Empire, which at this time preferred to have the prince rather than the Ottoman authorities in control of this region bordering on Dalmatia. An ultimatum was delivered to Constantinople, and as a result Ömer Pasha was recalled and the captured Montenegrin territory was returned.

After this conflict, Danilo attempted to build a stronger military organization. He registered his fighting men, but he had to leave the tribe as the basic military unit. In his internal administration, he met some opposition from the senate, which had gained more power at the end of Peter's reign. Danilo was, however, a strong leader, and he was able to maintain his authority. In 1855 a law code was issued that was based on the principles of equality before the law and the protection of the rights of private property. The Montenegrin rulers, unlike the Serbian, did not have to deal with the land question; in fact they probably did not have sufficient power to do so. The basic means of livelihood was animal husbandry. Problems of land usage were handled by the tribes and the villages.

During the Crimean War there was naturally much enthusiasm about using the opportunity to capture some neighboring Ottoman territory. Under strong pressure from Austria, Danilo remained quiet. His passive attitude caused some tribes to attempt again to withdraw from his authority, but he was able to subdue them. With Russia in a weak position, the prince attempted to establish closer relations with France. Once the war ended, however, Russian influence was reestablished. In 1858 another crisis with the Ottoman Empire occurred. At this time there was much unrest among the Christian population of Hercegovina. Uprisings there often involved the participation of

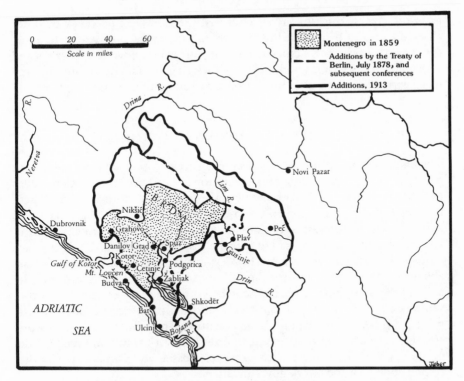

Map 21. The expansion of Montenegro, 1859–1913

Montenegrin tribes, who raided the area even in relatively peaceful times. In May 1858 a Montenegrin and Hercegovinian force took Grahovo. At this time both France and Russia intervened with the Porte in favor of Montenegro, and the boundary between the principality and the neighboring Ottoman lands was finally fixed. An extension of territory that included the city in dispute was secured (see Map 21).

In 1860 Danilo was assassinated. He was succeeded by Nicholas I, who was to rule until the end of World War I. This last Montenegrin ruler was born in 1841 and educated in France. He inherited a principality that had won a remarkable position in international relations, one that was entirely incommensurate with its small size and extreme poverty. We have seen how Russia was willing to send large subsidies, which were the main support of the central administration. Austria also paid careful attention to events in this region. It was to be a common witticism in Europe that Cetinje consisted of thirteen foreign consulates and a hotel.

The exact status of Montenegro in relation to the Ottoman Empire remained murky. The Porte continued to claim that the region was an integral part of the Ottoman Empire, but it was unable to collect taxes or a tribute. The Ottoman government was certainly not able to influence internal administration, and by this time it was clear that the European powers would not allow the area to be subdued by military means. In the next years Montenegro was to continue to contribute to the unrest in the western Balkans and to remain in close touch with Serbia, which shared the same desire for territorial expansion and a clear break from any vestige of Ottoman control.

GREECE UNDER KING OTHON

The first attempts at the organization of a Greek central administration were made, as we have seen, during the revolution. At that time the Greek notables established governments patterned on Western constitutional forms. These regimes broke down owing to the rivalry between factions of primates and military men. In contrast to the situations in Serbia and the Principalities, in Greece no single man emerged to take the leadership of the revolt. The greatest degree of success was achieved by Ioannis Capodistrias, who was at least able to lay the foundations for the future. An experienced administrator, he attempted to establish a government based on the rule of law. Like other statesmen of his era, he had as his ideal a strongly centralized state with the principal power in the hands of the executive. The failure of his successors, after his assassination, to maintain an orderly government reinforced the determination of the three powers, France, Russia, and Britain, to take full responsibility for the Greek government.

The new king, Othon, arrived in his first capital, Nauplion, in February 1833; the government did not move to Athens until 1835. Since he was still a minor, the king was accompanied by three regents. King Ludwig I, who wished to provide his son with the best support possible, appointed able men to the regency. At its head he placed Count Joseph von Armansperg, an experienced administrator. The other two members were Ludwig von Maurer, a jurist and professor of law, and Major General Karl von Heideck, a Philhellene who had served in Greece during the revolution and was thus well acquainted with local conditions. Karl von Abel became the secretary. A ministerial council, composed of Greeks, was also formed. Nevertheless, the real power in the government was in the hands of the regents, particularly in the period before Othon came of age.

Well prepared for their duties, the Bavarian officials attempted to introduce an enlightened administrative system on the pattern of the best of monarchical governments. They divided the tasks. Maurer concerned himself primarily with the codification of laws, church affairs, and education. Heideck organized the armed forces. Abel was responsible for internal affairs and foreign relations. Another adviser, Johann Greiner, handled economic problems. Although several constitutions had been drawn up during the revolutionary period, the Bavarians were not in favor of the introduction of representative institutions at this time. King Ludwig I had indeed given some vague assurances about a constitution when his son was chosen as king, but the regents proceeded to establish a centralized absolute monarchy.

The situation facing the regents was a difficult one. Greece had a far more complex social and political heritage than Serbia or Montenegro. Some parts of the new kingdom were as primitive as Montenegro; in contrast, many of the former Phanariots who arrived during the revolution had an education and experience equal to the regents'. In addition, the notables of the Peloponnesus had long been accustomed to handling their own local affairs. Many problems were to be caused by the fact that the Bavarians, like Capodistrias, and with the best of intentions, attempted to impose on the Greek kingdom patterns of life and government that had been developed elsewhere. The Greeks were accustomed to the Ottoman system, both in basic spirit and in appearance. An example of the differences that could occur, on a not especially serious level, is given by Maurer. When Othon arrived in Greece, some of his Greek officials did not wish to remove their hats.

> They maintained that they also were not accustomed to taking off their hats before the sultan. The question of taking-off-hats or not-taking-off-hats was officially considered, and in the end the present Greek officials were given the alternative of either presenting themselves in the eastern fashion, that is, throwing themselves on the floor in order to kiss the royal feet, and in this case they could keep their hats on their heads, or presenting themselves according to the European manner, and in this case appearing with bare heads.[4]

The chief tasks before the regents were the organization of the administration, the establishment of a judicial system, the codification of the law, a settlement of the church question, the organization of an army, and the formulation of a land policy. The first problem was that of local administration. Here the foundation laid by Capodistrias was developed. Greece was divided into ten provinces (nomarchies), which were subdivided into counties (eparchies), and then into municipalities (demes). The chief officials of the provinces and counties were appointed by the central government. Despite the fact that more allowance was made for participation at the lowest level, the system as a whole ended the former traditions of local self-government. As in other states that underwent similar political reorganizations, Serbia in particular, community offices tended to be headed by men appointed from the capital who had no previous experience in the locality to which they were assigned and no personal connections with the inhabitants. Although in theory this condition should have assured an impartial attitude among the officials, and should have provided at least a partial check on corruption, the final

---

4 Georg Ludwig von Maurer, *Das Griechische Volk*, 3 vols. (Heidelberg: Mohr, 1835), II, 69–70.

effect was not in the interest of the local population. As the century progressed, the public officials not only received better educations than the rest
of their countrymen, but became increasingly a class separated by manners
and economic status from the peasant majority. As elsewhere, the strengthening of the central regime was to limit popular participation in government
severely.

Both the establishment of a judicial system and the religious settlement
were the work of Maurer, perhaps the best of the Bavarian advisers. A code
of laws was drawn up under his supervision, based on Greek customary law
as well as on Byzantine and Western models. The question of the relationship
of the Orthodox church of independent Greece with the Patriarchate was, of
course, a matter of grave importance. During the revolution the patriarch
had excommunicated the Greek religious leaders, who, of course, had been a
major support of the movement. It was also clear that the independent state
needed a church hierarchy that was not even indirectly under the control of
the Porte. Maurer himself was a liberal Protestant who had received his legal
training in Napoleonic France. The final arrangement was worked out in
consultation with an ecclesiastical commission, but Maurer's influence was
strong. His attitude has been described as follows: "Maurer looked upon the
church as a department of the state and subordinate to it. The situation in
his homeland was a model for him, for in Bavaria both Catholic and Protestant churches were dominated by the secular power. Catholic bishops were
allowed to correspond with Rome only through the intermediary of the king."[5]

A strong dependence on the secular authority was, of course, in conformity with Orthodox tradition. In the settlement made at this time, which was
not accepted by the Constantinople Patriarchate until 1850, the Greek church
was separated from the Patriarchate. Othon was its head; he administered
church affairs through a Holy Synod whose members were royal appointees.
An attempt was also made to reform the monasteries, many of which were
in an extremely bad condition. Those with less than six members were closed,
with their property taken by the government.

One of the most difficult questions facing the regency was the organization
of a national army that could both defend the state and assure civil tranquility.
The country certainly could not rely on the captains and their military bands,
the forces that had fought the revolutionary war. Their disruptive activities
and feuds had been chiefly responsible for the anarchy and violence of the
period. Recognizing the necessity of assuring the new regime a firm support,
the protecting powers had arranged that Othon would have the services of a
mercenary force of about 3,500 soldiers. These men, most of whom were
German or Swiss, had to be paid relatively high salaries, and they were a
severe strain on the Greek budget.

5   Charles A. Frazee, *The Orthodox Church and Independent Greece, 1821–1852* (Cambridge: Cam-
    bridge University Press, 1969), p. 106.

With the regular army composed mostly of foreign soldiers, the problem of what to do with the Greek veterans became serious. Thousands of these fighters remained from the revolutionary period, many without alternative means of employment. Even if the government had wished, they could not easily have been integrated into a modern army. They did not like uniforms, drill, or discipline. Some simply went home and were absorbed into their village life. They might be given honorary military titles and land. Others became policemen or joined the bandits. They remained, nevertheless, a disturbing element for quite a while. The foreign troops also caused difficulties. They were naturally resented by the population. Although some stayed permanently in Greece and eventually became citizens, the majority had left by the end of the 1830s. Thereafter the army was completely Greek in composition, but as had been feared, it did not form a loyal and reliable backing for the monarchy. In fact, political activities by the military were then and were to continue to be a major source of disruption in Greece. It should also be noted that, although the soldiers were at first in the majority German in nationality, the navy remained completely in Greek hands.

In Greece as in Serbia, one of the major questions to be settled by the national administration concerned the ownership and distribution of the land. Again the decisions taken would largely determine the future social and political life of the country. The status of a considerable amount of land had to be decided. It must be remembered that only a small percentage of Greek acreage is arable; farmland was thus scarce and valuable both from the economic aspect and because ownership conferred prestige and power. Before the revolution it has been estimated that in the territory of independent Greece about 65,000 Muslim landholders controlled over half of the land.[6] Much of the rest was held by Christian notables who had assembled large estates. The Greek population thus consisted largely of a peasantry who worked on a sharecropping arrangement on both Muslim and Christian estates.

During the revolution, as we have seen, the Muslim population was driven out or massacred and its property plundered. Christian landowners did not receive a similar treatment. In Serbia during and after the revolution, the peasant on a Muslim estate in general simply took possession of the land that he worked. There was thus an automatic transfer to small peasant ownership of much Muslim property. This process did not take place in Greece. The revolutionary governments were in the control of notables who often held large estates. These regimes also needed money. In 1821 it was decided that Christian peasants on former Ottoman-held lands would continue to make payments, but at a reduced rate and to the state. The peasants thus continued

---

6 On the land question see William W. McGrew, "The Land Issue in the Greek War of Independence," in Nikiforos P. Diamandouros et al., eds., *Hellenism and the First Greek War of Liberation (1821–1830): Continuity and Change* (Thessaloniki: Institute for Balkan Studies, 1976), pp. 111–129.

to be sharecroppers. This action was to form a precedent for the future. In the Epidaurus constitution the former Ottoman properties were declared to be national estates. This decision was logical and intelligent given the conditions of the times. The state lands could be used as collateral for essential foreign loans, and they also provided about the only regular source of income during the revolutionary period. As in the past, the taxes were farmed by the notables, who thus kept intact their former privileges.

During the war, however, the government used the promise of land for recruitment purposes. These assurances proved impossible to fulfill. The notables with large estates did not want to be faced with demands from their peasant sharecroppers for a radical reform; and if former Ottoman estates were divided among their cultivators, the application of the same principle might be demanded of the Christian owners. Despite the fact that there was no general land distribution, some state land did in fact move into private hands. During the revolution notables and captains were in the position simply to appropriate property that fell under their immediate jurisdiction. Since land was the principal investment and source of wealth, the temptation to seize it where possible was great.

The Bavarian regime in Greece in theory favored the small landowner. Bavaria, after all, was a land of prosperous peasant farming. In 1833 it was estimated that only a sixth of the Greek peasants owned land; the rest cultivated private estate land or state property. For the use of the national land, the cultivator paid a tax of 25 percent of the produce, as compared to the 10 percent that was levied on freeholders. In 1835 a law was passed that allowed all the veterans of the revolution to purchase land. However, payment had to be made, and most of the eligible buyers did not have the necessary funds. Thus the peasant was neither assigned a plot nor allowed to keep the land he worked. He could simply bid for plots at a state auction. There was little response. The Greek peasants were not organized as a class, and they had no general feeling of grievance or solidarity. Moreover, at this time there was little pressure of population on the land. Alternate means of livelihood existed; Greeks found employment in large numbers as fishermen, sailors, small merchants, shepherds, and artisans.

The Bavarian regency accomplished a great deal during these first years, organizing the country on the pattern of a modern state. The process was not easy. Jealousies and rivalries divided the regents, and Armansperg was able to secure the recall of both Maurer and Heideck. In 1835 Othon reached his majority, but he kept Armansperg as his chief counselor even after the dissolution of the regency. By 1837 the opposition to this official had become so intense that he was replaced by the weaker Ignaz von Rudhart. By this time Othon had gained confidence and was determined to rule the country himself. In 1836 he married the Protestant princess Amalia of Oldenburg, who as queen was to play a prominent role in national life. Although Othon was an absolute monarch, he was not authoritarian in either attitude or manner. He had, however, some serious personal problems.

A major division between the king and the Greek people was always the Catholic faith of the monarch. Orthodoxy was a serious matter; it was an integral part of Greek life and certainly of the national movement. Othon was not only a Catholic, but a devout and faithful member of his church. At the time of his nomination, it had been agreed that he would bring up his heir in the Orthodox faith. If indeed he had been fortunate enough to have had children, his problems might have been less serious, but it soon became apparent that Othon would probably remain childless. The state needed a royal heir, both to assure the stability of the throne and the dynasty and to end the religious controversy surrounding the ruler.

In addition to the criticism of the monarch arising from this issue, Othon and his advisers met the type of opposition that had faced the central government during the revolution and that we have seen in Serbia and Montenegro, which had native rulers. Greek notables and military men who had previously run the government found themselves displaced by the Bavarian officials and the Greeks who worked with the regime. As elsewhere, these groups formed political alignments and parties to win back influence or to displace their adversaries. As has been noted, throughout the Balkans families and family-based relationships were basic to the social and political system. In Montenegro the bishops had to meet the opposition of the clans and rival families. A similar situation existed in Serbia, where both Karadjordje and Miloš had to fight against local leaders with personal and family backing. In Greece too political life revolved around the activities of strong leaders whose supporters looked to them for guidance, protection, and favors. This patron–client relationship could form a network of considerable influence, since a patron could himself become a client of a yet more powerful man, who could in turn seek a protector at a higher level. There were other institutions that also served to connect families. Most important was the *kumparia*; a strong and ambitious man could become godfather to literally hundreds of children, thus forming blood ties with their families. He did them favors, but could also command their allegiance.

In politics this situation could have important consequences. The institutions of government that were adopted in Greece depended on at least some standards of honesty and efficiency among the officials. Neither a centralized bureaucracy under an absolute monarch nor a representative system could function without public responsibility and some awareness of the needs of the entire nation. Yet Greek political life was not to center on specific issues. There were no equivalents to the Serbian Constitutionalist, Liberal, or Conservative parties. Instead, political conflicts were likely to involve the struggle between factions led by powerful individuals to control the government. Once in office, the successful politician was expected to reward his supporters. Administrative appointments and patronage went to the victors and their adherents; those who lost were simply dismissed from their positions. Elections thus usually involved the simple issue of which group would control the spoils. In this situation the temptation to adopt illegal and violent means was strong. The officials in power could use the police and their local agents; the opposition could organize riots and employ brigands.

During the first part of Othon's reign the three political parties of the revolutionary period – the French, the Russian, and the British – dominated the political scene. Despite their attachment to the foreign consultates, they too were each essentially based on the leadership of a strong individual. Of the three, the most popular was probably the French Party, headed by Ioannis Kolettis. At this time France could give more encouragement than Britain or Russia to Greek expansion and was less concerned than they about protecting the territorial integrity of the Ottoman Empire. Kolettis was also an able political leader. Next in influence was the Nappist, or Russian, Party. Its political orientation was conservative and Orthodox. The most influential members were, first, Capodistrias, and then Kolokotronis and Andreas Metaxas. The party with the greatest potential influence, however, was the British, under the direction of Mavrokordatos. With naval supremacy in the Mediterranean, Britain was always in the best position to impress its views on the Greek government. The major impediment to the popularity of this group was the British desire to uphold the Ottoman Empire, a policy that precluded aid to Greek expansion. The Russian Party enjoyed the strongest position during the Capodistrias regime; the British were supreme with Armansperg; the French were to have the chief influence after 1844. Despite the fact that these parties carried the names of foreign powers, they were not blind tools of the patron consulates. In fact, the parties sometimes manipulated the great powers more than the powers were able to exploit the parties. Nevertheless, their existence allowed a degree of foreign interference that had no parallel in Serbia or Montenegro.

The king, it will be noted, did not have the support of a Bavarian or royal party. He could not even be sure of his army. By 1838 most all the foreign soldiers had returned home, although some officers remained. Without a firm military or political backing, the king had to play between the factions. He also had to deal with a bad financial situation. State expenditures now far exceeded income. A major problem was the high payments that had to be made in connection with the foreign debt contracted during and after the revolution. Dissatisfaction with Othon's rule and with conditions in the state increased in the early 1840s. The protecting powers pressed for financial reform. Chiefly concerned with the repayment of the debt, they asked for a reduction of military expenses and the size of the army. There was also criticism of the autocratic government. As in other states, the opposition to Othon sought to limit the royal powers through other institutions. To many the introduction of constitutional government seemed the best means of meeting the situation.

In 1843 the British and Russian parties, who were temporarily out of power, joined to back a military coup d'état. In September the Athens garrison marched on the palace and took the king prisoner. Since the alternative was abdication, Othon agreed to dismiss his remaining Bavarian advisers and accept a constitution. In November an assembly was convened, composed of delegates not only from the Greek kingdom, but also from Macedonia, Epirus, and Thessaly. The leading roles in the deliberations were taken by Mavrokordatos and Kolettis. The Russian Party was forced to stand aside because Nicholas I would not condone participation in the making of a constitution whose acceptance by the king had been forced by an armed revolt. The Greek government, however, received constant advice from the British and French consulates, representing protectors that were favorable to the introduction of a constitutional regime, but wanted it to be conservative in nature. They wished to avoid any situation that might make Greece a center of revolutionary disturbance or might lead to the reopening of the Eastern Question.

The constitution of 1844 was fully satisfactory to conservative opinion. It provided for a limited constitutional monarchy, but the king had wide powers. Othon could veto legislation, and he appointed and dismissed the ministers. A two-house legislature was established, with the lower chamber elected on the basis of universal manhood suffrage and the upper, the senate, nominated by the ruler. The leaders of the revolt of 1843 had thus attained their objective: the king was to share his authority with an elective assembly. It will be noted that the movement had been carried through by a small group of opposition politicians who obtained military support. The action had not involved the population at large. It was, however, to serve as a precedent and to show the power that could be exerted in the government by the military.

The introduction of a constitutional regime in fact led to no real change in Greek politics. The first elections gave the victory to the French Party and Kolettis, who until his death in 1847 held the principal position in the government. Working closely with Othon, his regime was to follow the classical pattern of a royal dictatorship in the Balkans. Kolettis appointed his supporters to the principal positions, and he used government patronage to assure loyalty. Exercising his official powers, he made certain that he maintained control of the assembly. He had no hesitation about using violence and terror against his opponents. Nevertheless, he was an extremely popular leader. Much of the opposition to Othon had come from notables who had no wide popular support themselves. Moreover, Kolettis and the king both came to stand for the kind of national expansion that won enthusiastic support. The Philhellene Bavarian regents had seen modern Greece as a reborn Athens; the classical, pagan civilization had been their ideal. Kolettis and most Greek nationalists were in contrast to base their programs on the Byzantine tradition and the Orthodox faith. The Great Idea, whose influence in the eighteenth century has already been discussed, became their objective too. They tended to believe that the correct boundaries for a resurrected Greek state should encompass all the lands that had been under Byzantine rule or under the jurisdiction of the Patriarchate of Constantinople at any period. These goals were made clear by Kolettis in a speech before the constitutional assembly in January 1844:

> The kingdom of Greece is not Greece; it is only a part, the smallest and poorest, of Greece. The Greek is not only he who inhabits the kingdom, but also he who lives in Janina, or Thessaloniki, or Seres, or Adrianople, or Constantinople, or Trebizonde, or Crete, or Samos, or any other country of the Greek history or race . . . There are two great centers of Hellenism, Athens and Constantinople. Athens is only the capitol of the kingdom; Constantinople is the great capital, the City, *i Polis*, the attraction and the hope of all the Hellenes.[7]

The great hindrance to the promotion of a national irredentist policy at this time, however, was the fact that most of the great powers were firmly against any Greek action. In the 1830s two Ottoman–Egyptian crises occurred, the first from 1831 to 1833 and the second from 1839 to 1841. At this time Britain and Russia, usually at odds in Eastern affairs, joined the Habsburg Monarchy to support the maintenance of the territorial integrity of the Ottoman Empire. In 1841 Greek public opinion was aroused when a revolt broke out in Crete. An even tenser situation developed during the Crimean War, when Russia, the great Orthodox power, was fighting the Ottoman Empire, France, Britain, and Sardinia. Despite the imbalance of this coalition, there was enthusiasm about using the opportunity to acquire more territory. Irregular bands did operate in the Greek lands under Ottoman control, but these were easily suppressed by the local authorities. To make certain that the Greek government remained passive, the Western allies sent a squadron to Piraeus, where it remained from 1854 to 1857. The two protectors also imposed a Mavrokordatos ministry on the king.

The failure to exploit the situation or to make any other concrete gains in foreign affairs was an important element in the king's increasing unpopularity. After the Crimean War the parties connected with the foreign consulates dissolved. The new political combinations represented little more than the interests of strong leaders and their supporters. In the elections the candidates won who could control local patronage and the police. The individual voter, when he had a free choice, preferred the man who promised him the greatest benefits; issues were infrequently a matter of political debate. Con-

---

7 Quoted in Edouard Driault and Michael Lhéritier, *Histoire diplomatique de la Grèce de 1821 à nos jours*, 5 vols. (Paris: Les Presses universitaires de France, 1925–1926), II, 252–253.

stitutional government and a wide franchise had thus caused little alteration in traditional political methods.

Although Othon was anything but a tyrannical ruler, he had by the 1860s gained many opponents. His most vulnerable point was the fact that he had no children. Even worse, there was no obvious candidate for the throne. The constitution made it obligatory that the next ruler be Orthodox. Othon's brothers were not enthusiastic about changing their faith or endangering by such an act their possible succession to the Bavarian throne. This situation would be dangerous for even a highly popular monarch.

In addition, Othon had to face criticism from a new generation of Greek youth, which was not only better educated than its predecessors, but also more aware of current European political ideology. The young men were strongly influenced by the liberal and national ideas of the mid-century and by the revolutions of 1848. They had studied at European universities or at the University of Athens, which opened in 1837. Extremely critical of the constitution of 1844 and the entire Greek political system, they wanted to introduce a parliamentary democracy and reduce the king to a figurehead.

Despite widespread dissatisfaction, the revolt that broke out in October 1862 resembled closely the events of 1843. There was no revolutionary movement involving the general population. Instead, once again the revolution was essentially a military coup. At the time Othon and Amalia were on a cruise on their yacht; when they heard that several garrisons had revolted, they did not return to Athens. There were some minor disorders, but the transition of power was relatively smooth. A provisional government under the leadership of Dimitrios Voulgaris was formed, which then turned to the task of choosing another prince and framing a new constitution.

After the departure of Othon, the three protecting powers immediately asserted their authority. They named the new ruler, although they did not interfere in the drafting of the constitution. The Greek leaders themselves would have preferred Prince Albert, the second son of Queen Victoria, as their king. They had hoped by this choice to acquire the Ionian Islands, which were still under British rule, and support for further expansion. The protecting powers, however, had agreed among themselves not to nominate a candidate from a reigning dynasty, so this choice was impossible. They finally chose the seventeen-year-old Prince William George of the Danish Glücksburg dynasty. A constitutional assembly in Athens accepted the nomination of this prince, who on his accession took the name George. In 1866 King George I married Grand Duchess Olga and thereby gave his dynasty a valuable link with the Russian imperial family. Since George was the British favorite, Britain agreed to surrender the Ionian Islands; they became a part of the Greek kingdom, although they were neutralized.

The new king was given a constitution, based on the liberal Belgian Constitution of 1831, that was designed to limit sharply the royal power. Article XXI stated: "All power has its source in the nation and is exercised in the manner appointed by the constitution."[8] There was to be no question of an absolute or a divine-right monarch in the future. Nevertheless, the king still held the authority to appoint and dismiss the ministers; he could also dissolve the chamber. Like other rulers of the day, he could declare war and make treaties. The legislative branch of the government was composed of a single chamber; the senate was thus abolished. The representatives were to be elected by direct, secret, manhood suffrage and were to serve for four years. The ministry was responsible to the assembly.

These changes too had remarkably little effect on Greek politics. Conditions remained much as they had been before. George I arrived with a Danish adviser, Count Sponneck, who became a controversial figure. As had been the case with previous foreigners, he soon faced so much opposition that he was forced to leave. The political parties were still little more than factions organized around leaders, among whom the most prominent were Dimitrios Voulgaris, Alexander Koumoundouros, Thrasyvoulos Zaimis, and Epaminondas Deligeorgis. The political scene gave an appearance of extreme instability; from 1864 to 1881 there were nine elections and thirty-one governments. The liberal constitution also had no effect on the corrupt system. Whenever the government changed, all of the civil service positions were filled by the winning faction; the losers simply lost their jobs. It was still important for a political party to be in office when elections were held, so that it could use the police to control the voting in its own interest. Although there were indeed disagreements on national issues, the real struggle involved the spoils of office and personal honor and prestige.

THE DANUBIAN PRINCIPALITIES UNDER RUSSIAN PROTECTION

The pattern of political development in the Principalities from 1821 to 1854 contrasted in many respects with that in Serbia, Montenegro, and Greece. One particular difference was in the degree of control exerted by an outside state. Although the protecting powers had interfered a great deal in Greek domestic politics and Russia had strongly influenced events in Serbia and Montenegro, the Russian domination in Wallachia and Moldavia was far more pervasive. Despite the fact that the aim of Russian policy was the improvement of conditions in the provinces, the pressure exerted aroused a great deal of resentment. The national movement of the mid-century was thus to be directed more against the Russian protector than against the Ottoman suzerain.

Russian intervention in Romanian affairs had its legal base in the Treaty of

8   The constitution is printed in George Finlay, *History of the Greek Revolution and of the Reign of King Otho*, 2 vols. in 1 (London: Zeno, 1971), pp. 345–357.

Kuchuk Kainarji; these rights were strengthened in the agreement of 1802. In 1821 the Russian government broke relations with the Porte because it had failed to come to an agreement with St. Petersburg concerning the military intervention in the Principalities. The Russian government was serious about enforcing its treaty rights, and these were strengthened considerably in the Convention of Akkerman of October 1826. In a separate agreement attached to the treaty, Russia was recognized as the protecting power. In addition, changes were made in the political organization of the provinces. The hospodars were henceforth to be elected by the divans – that is, the councils of boyars – from among this class, and they would hold office for seven years. The elections would have to be confirmed by both St. Petersburg and Constantinople. Both Principalities were to be given new administrative regulations. Although the Ottoman government denounced this treaty after the disaster at Navarino, its terms were repeated in the Treaty of Adrianople of 1829. Here the rights of the Porte in its vassal states were limited to the collection of a fixed tribute and a voice in the choice of the princes. Article V stated that Moldavia and Wallachia were under the suzerainty of the Porte and that Russia "guaranteed their prosperity." They were to "enjoy the free exercise of their worship, perfect security, an independent national government, and full liberty of commerce."[9]

An Additional Act to the treaty defined the new conditions in greater detail. Most significant for the future was an end to the Ottoman right of preemption on the products of the Principalities. The provinces thus no longer had to provide articles such as grain, sheep, and timber almost exclusively to Constantinople; instead, they could trade freely with the rest of the world. In addition, the payments to be made to the Porte were henceforth to be limited to the annual tribute, whose amount was to be set, and a sum to be paid on the investiture of each prince. As in Serbia, Muslims were not to live in or hold property in the Principalities, except under special circumstances. The Ottoman government was to withdraw its garrisons from the fortress cities of Turnu Severin, Giurgiu, and Brăila. The Muslim inhabitants were to sell their property within eighteen months. Also very important was the provision that a quarantine was to be established along the Danube. This stipulation gave force to the idea that a definite break existed between the Principalities and the rest of the Ottoman lands. Finally, the treaty allowed both provinces to organize militias, and the provision requiring new administrative regulations was repeated.

In the treaty Russia compelled the Ottoman Empire to pay a very high indemnity. Until this obligation was fulfilled, Russian troops were to remain in occupation of the Principalities. They did not leave until 1834, and during this period Moldavia and Wallachia were both under Russian military rule.

9 Hertslet, *Map of Europe*, II, 817.

The reorganization of the administration of the provinces was thus carried through under Russian supervision. This action was taken under the direction of Count Pavel D. Kiselev, an extremely able and enlightened administrator. As president of both divans from November 1829 to April 1834, he was principally responsible for the reforms that were introduced. After assuming his post he immediately took action to establish the quarantine because of the threat of plague and cholera. He imported wheat from Russia to meet the famine conditions, and he organized a national militia. His chief contribution, however, was his supervision of the formulation of new administrative statutes for both provinces.

The Principalities remained an important strategic area for Russia. Even though the government did not wish to annex the region, it wanted to make certain that the provinces would remain a buffer and under Russian domination. The land was also a convenient base from which to move southward toward Constantinople should another war occur. This policy, as we have seen, had been followed consistently since the eighteenth century. As before, it was to the Russian interest to assure that the provinces were both prosperous and contented. A great effort was thus made to try to introduce a practical and progressive political system.

After the signing of the Akkerman convention, committees had been formed to draft new administrative regulations, but little had been accomplished. Now two other committees, each composed of four members (two chosen by the divans and two by the Russian officials), were appointed. They met under the chairmanship of the Russian consul-general, Matei Leovich Minciaky (Minchiaki). When their work was completed, Kiselev made some changes in the texts and forwarded them to St. Petersburg. There they were approved and returned to the divans, who were allowed to discuss but not change the final version. The statutes were issued in Wallachia in July 1831 and in Moldavia in January 1832.

These documents were not constitutions, but rather detailed administrative regulations. They created parallel, but not identical, institutions in both provinces. Accordingly, they marked a definite step toward an eventual unification of the two Romanian states. Like the measures taken by the Bavarian regency in Athens, the Organic Statutes (Règlements organiques) established a system of government based on the best examples of current administrative practice as seen by a conservative, monarchical, but enlightened leadership.

Each province was to be ruled by a prince, who would be elected for life by an extraordinary assembly of 150. He would be chosen from among the great boyars. The legislative power was to be exercised by boyars' assemblies that were to be held in each province, with thirty-five members in the Moldavian and forty-two in the Wallachian body. These assemblies passed the laws, but the prince had a right of veto. With the approval of both the Porte and Russia, he could prorogue, but not dissolve, the assembly. Similar means of interference by St. Petersburg were inserted in other parts of the documents. The Organic Statutes were a clear advance over the system previously in existence, but they gave the control of the country to the great boyars and Russia. The strong position of the privileged noble class was similarly reflected in the sections of the reform dealing with the land and peasant questions.

In the eighteenth century, as we have seen, Romanian serfdom had ended, but the question who owned the land had not been settled. The issue was not critical at that time because the main source of peasant support was cattle raising. The peasant, who had a plot of land that he cultivated, could graze his livestock on the common pasture land and could gather wood in the forests. There was no shortage of land. If conditions on the estate became too bad, he could simply flee.

The Organic Statutes brought about certain fundamental changes. Most important, the boyar was designated as the owner of the land; the peasant families were allowed a share based on the number of cattle that each owned. Families were divided into three categories: first, those who had four oxen and a cow or ten sheep; second, those who had two oxen; and third, those who had no animals at all. The first group was allotted nine acres, with the others receiving proportionally less. If a peasant wanted more land, he had to make a special arrangement with the boyar. The labor obligation was set at twelve days, but again the work period was defined by tasks accomplished, and in practice it came to amount to about twenty-four to thirty-six days in Wallachia and over fifty in Moldavia. In Wallachia, where the landowners tended not to operate their estates personally, they often preferred to take cash payments rather than labor dues. They then rented out all of their land on terms agreed upon with the peasantry; the estates were managed by stewards while the owners lived in Bucharest or traveled in Europe. In Moldavia the owners were more likely to supervise their estates personally.

The unequal relationship between the peasant and the boyar can best be understood when it is remembered that the latter had complete control of the administrative and judicial system. The peasant could not rely either on the police or on the courts to defend him against unjust exactions. In addition, although he was not technically bound to the soil, he did not have unlimited freedom of movement. He had to give six months' notice if he wished to leave his land, and he had to pay his share of the village taxes. Kiselev was deeply critical of the situation. He commented concerning the boyars' assembly that,

> having constituted itself judge in its own cause, it is only natural that
> it seeks to extend its own privileges at the expense of others, who
> are neither represented nor defended by anyone. That goes so far,
> that by an insidious clause regarding labor dues they have bound the

villagers to the soil, though they are free by right, and every day they tend to make of them slaves, to oppress them the more.[10]

The Romanian boyar made another great gain in this period. The end of Ottoman preemption rights opened the Principalities to trade with the West at a time when demand for grain to feed the growing Western industrial population was increasing. The market for Romanian agricultural products thus rose during the century. It was to the interest of the Romanian land-owner to secure control of as much land as possible and to assure an adequate labor supply. The Organic Statutes thus gave the boyar the type of agrarian regime that was to his best advantage.

In January 1834 Russia and the Ottoman Empire signed the Convention of St. Petersburg. The Porte accepted the Organic Statutes, and the tribute was set at 3 million piastres. In an action that was an exception to the provisions of the new regulations, the two powers named the first princes, who were to reign for only seven years. The Russian choices, Alexander Ghica in Wallachia and Mihail Sturdza in Moldavia, assumed office; the Russian army then evacuated the provinces. The Russian government had achieved most of the objectives formulated at the time of the Russo-Turkish War. It held a position of preeminence at Constantinople and in the Balkan peninsula in general. Although some Russian officials, including Kiselev, had advised the annexa-tion of the Principalities, an alternate solution had been found in the intro-duction of a regime that gave Russia domination without the complications and expenses of direct rule.

The political system established at this time, based on the Organic Statutes, lasted until 1854. It gave the direct control of the country to the boyars, with Russia as overseer. The dominating class represented only a small fraction of the population, and as we have seen, there was little cohesion among the boyars. Like other Balkan notables, they would not accept the authority of one of their number unless they could control him or unless he represented their interests. The constant intrigues among the boyar factions and against the prince were to weaken the governments and to make them more open to Russian intervention.

After the departure of the Russian troops both Principalities faced the same major economic and political problems. Neither was in a prosperous condi-tion, and heavy expenses had to be met. The tribute had not been paid during the Russian occupation, so the back installments were due. A payment also had to be made when the princes were invested by the sultan. The cost of the Russian occupation and administration in the past years was charged to the provinces. Moreover, the political situation was not stable. Three centers of authority existed: the princes, the assemblies, and the Russian consulates.

10 Quoted in Barbara Jelavich, *Russia and the Rumanian National Cause, 1858–1859* (reprint ed., Hamden, Conn.: Archon Books, 1974), p. 3; see also p. 4

The opposition to the princes centered, as could be expected, in the assemblies. In each province the boyars did all they could to embarrass and hinder the work of the prince. For their part, the Russian representatives kept a close watch on the situation and interfered constantly in the government. They also became involved in the domestic intrigues. According to the Organic Statutes, appeals could be addressed to both the Porte and Russia. Dissident groups not only followed this path, but also turned to other foreign consulates, which in turn were not averse to embarrassing the Russian government. An atmosphere of conspiracy and discontent thus existed in both Bucharest and Iași.

The situation was worse in Wallachia. There Alexander Ghica, the brother of the former hospodar, found himself faced with formidable opposition. The Russian government had supported his appointment because it considered him reliable. He, however, had many enemies, whose numbers increased once he became prince. He appointed two of his brothers as ministers; and their actions made his rule still more unpopular. Even more serious, Ghica came into conflict with the protecting power. Minciaky was replaced as consul-general in Bucharest by P. I. Rückmann (Rikman). This agent had a difficult task to perform. The Russian government was pressing for the acceptance of a so-called Additional Article to the Wallachian Organic Statute, which it claimed had been "inadvertently" left out of the original version. This provision stated that the Principality could not change the statutes without the consent of the Russian and Ottoman governments. If accepted, this stipulation would have been a real blow to the autonomy of the province, and it was deeply resented as such. Great influence was exerted. When the Wallachian assembly would not accept the article, it was dissolved. Russia was finally forced to act through the Porte to compel a second assembly to accept the measure.

The Wallachian assembly was a center of opposition to Ghica as well as to the Russian consulate. In 1840 another consul-general, I. A. Dashkov, was appointed, who proved sympathetic with the prince's adversaries. What happened next is described by Nicholas Karlovich Giers, who was attached to the Russian consulate in Iași and who was impressed by the corruption of Romanian politics. Commenting on the past activities of the boyars, he wrote:

Each had his own party, and all of them joined together to overthrow Ghica. A complaint was drawn up at the General Assembly of Deputies . . . enumerating the abuses of Prince Ghica's administration, and it was resolved by an overwhelming majority of votes that the complaint be submitted to both courts. As a consequence of these *doléances*, as they were called in diplomatic language, the Russian and the Turkish governments appointed . . . commissioners to investigate the case . . . The Turkish commissioner, as is customary, took full advantage of the situation, and made a fortune by taking bribes from the hospodar as well as from each of the candidates for the office of prince by promising each individual the support of the Porte. While our representative, listening to anybody and everybody, tried to form a fair opinion on the state of affairs, he was deceived, being unfamiliar with both the region and the people.[11]

As a result of this investigation, Ghica was deposed in 1842. An election was then held according to the stipulations of the Organic Statute, and George Bibescu became prince.

A rich boyar who enjoyed Russian favor, Bibescu had studied in Paris. Although he had been at the head of the opposition to Ghica in the assembly, he found that this body would not accept his direction either; again the boyars conspired to bring down one of their number. Once more, too, the question of the special privileges to be allowed to Russia came into question. A Russian engineer, Alexander Trandifilov, had been given a concession to survey the province for minerals and then to exploit the resources he found. The assembly attempted to block the agreement. With the approval of both Russia and the Porte, Bibescu prorogued the assembly and governed by decree for two years. The Trandifilov grant was nevertheless not upheld. In 1846 an assembly that was more favorable to the prince was elected. His enemies, who remained numerous, sought support in the British and French consulates, where they received encouragement and assistance. Russia continued to back the prince. Even with this difficult internal situation, Bibescu was able to secure the passage of some important legislation. Extremely significant for the future were to be the customs union with Moldavia, put through in 1847, and the law on naturalization of the same year, which made it easier for a Moldavian to become a Wallachian citizen. Bibescu was also responsible for improvements in the city of Bucharest and for measures to improve education.

Events went more smoothly in Moldavia, where the prince, Mihail Sturdza, was both clever and strong. He too was faced with the problem of constant opposition from the boyars, but he was able to control them. When they denounced him to the Porte and Russia, he successfully defended himself. He had no difficulty in securing the passage of the Additional Article, so that question did not form a matter of dispute with Russia. He took care to remain on good terms with the Russian consulate in Iaşi; he was also in touch with the rival French and British agents. Although his regime, too, was corrupt, he did attempt some internal improvements. Roads, bridges, and hospitals were constructed, and the postal system was developed. Measures were passed to improve education, which nevertheless remained poor.

The regime of the Organic Statutes was in most Romanian opinion closely

11   Charles Jelavich and Barbara Jelavich, eds., *The Education of a Russian Statesman: The Memoirs of Nicholas Karlovich Giers* (Berkeley: University of California Press, 1962), pp. 192–193.

associated with Russian domination. Therefore the discontented elements tended to blame the problems of the time on the protecting power. Most of the Russian representatives were responsible diplomats who were concerned about the welfare of the Principalities. They did, nevertheless, allow themselves to be drawn into the domestic intrigues between the boyar factions and into the controversies between the assemblies and the princes. This participation in Romanian political life was bound to win Russia enemies among those who were not given support. Moreover, the Russian activities, no matter what their intentions, were representative of Russia's special position and its domination of Romanian political life. In addition, the regime of the Organic Statutes was extremely conservative in nature. Russia's support of this system gained it the hatred of those who wished further political reform. In the future, the nationalists, who wanted a truly independent government, and the liberals, who sought a genuine constitutional regime, were to see Russia as the principal obstacle to the introduction of their programs.

At this time the Principalities were undergoing a period of rapid social and cultural change. By the 1840s the influence of Western Europe was becoming increasingly apparent. This trend was shown in the manners and dress of the boyar class. The older generation still retained the national costume with long robes, whereas their children prided themselves on wearing the latest Paris fashions. The differences were to be more than superficial. Not only Western styles were introduced, but also the political ideologies currently in favor among the more radical groups. These were absorbed by the new generation that was educated outside the Principalities.

There were no institutions of higher education in the Principalities. This lack affected in particular the considerable number of wealthy young men, sons of boyars, who could afford to travel and who had no pressing need to follow an occupation. They could live off the proceeds of the family estates. The point of attraction for them was Paris, which had the advantage of combining elegance and culture with revolutionary excitement. Before 1848 this city was the center of liberal and national political agitation. Particularly important was the influence of the Polish emigrés who had been forced to leave their country after the failure of the revolution of 1830 against Russian rule. The most prominent, Adam Czartoryski, the former minister of Alexander I, established what was in fact a government-in-exile, which was in touch with nationalist movements all over Europe. Italian, German, and Hungarian young men were also deeply involved in the revolutionary activities. Like their contemporaries, the Romanian youth entered into the conspiracies and elaborated plans for a national revolt in the Romanian lands.

Although they agreed upon no single program, most of the future Romanian revolutionary leaders stood for the unification of Wallachia and Moldavia under a constitutional regime that would provide full guarantees of civil liberties and some sort of a representative system. They were united in their opposition to the Organic Statutes and to Russian protection. For the Romanians, as for the Poles, Russia was the main obstacle to national liberation. The revolutionaries organized both within and without the country. Literary societies and secret associations were formed in the Principalities, but Paris remained the center of organization and agitation.

In February 1848 a revolt broke out in Paris that was to touch off a wave of revolution throughout Europe. The German states, the Italian peninsula, and the Habsburg Empire were chiefly affected; conservative, monarchical regimes were toppled. The aim of the victors was the introduction of constitutional and national governments. There were no uprisings in Russia; in the Ottoman domains only the Danubian Principalities were to be involved. The first action occurred in Iaşi, and it was mild indeed. On April 8 about a thousand people, primarily townsmen, liberal boyars, and opponents of the prince, assembled in the St. Petersburg Hotel. Speeches were made attacking Sturdza, and a petition was drawn up for submission to the prince. His reaction was swift. He arrested about three hundred people, some of whom were later exiled. There were no prisons in which boyars could be kept; they were usually confined in monasteries for the length of their sentences.

The revolution in Wallachia was a far more serious matter. The participants were to provide much of the national leadership for the next decades, and the movement was to set the pattern for future Romanian development. The principal figures were Ion and Dumitru Brătianu, Nicolae and Radu Golescu, C. A. Rosetti, and Nicolae Bălcescu. In May a revolutionary committee headed by Bălcescu, Rosetti, and A. G. Golescu was formed. This group immediately dispatched Ion Ghica to Constantinople to reassure the Porte on the intentions of the revolutionaries. It is interesting to note that once again, as in 1821, Constantinople was informed that the objective was not an end to Ottoman rule, but the regaining of "old rights." The formal beginning of the Wallachian revolution was the issuance of the Islaz Proclamation on June 21. This document contained a standard liberal program of twenty-one points. Its aim was the replacement of the regime of the Organic Statutes and an end to Russian protection. The leaders at this time appointed a provisional government and moved from Islaz to Bucharest, where the revolutionary forces had also achieved a victory. Bibescu at first agreed to the Islaz program, but on June 26, after an assassination attempt, he abdicated and left for Transylvania. A new government was set up, with Metropolitan Neofit at its head; it included also Bălcescu, A. G. Golescu, I. C. Brătianu, and Colonel Ion Odobescu, who was in command of the limited armed forces of the Principality.

Bucharest was thus once again the center of a revolutionary movement, although the conditions were in many ways quite different from those of 1821. Of great significance was the fact that the revolutionaries did not have an army at their command. There was no force that was the equivalent of the pandours and volunteers who joined Tudor Vladimirescu. The commander of what troops were available, Odobescu, used them in July in an unsuccessful coup against the government. This situation saved the provinces from the ravages of a violent civil war, but it meant that the revolutionary leadership would have to achieve its goals by negotiation and diplomacy.

In addition, in contrast to the 1821 uprising, this action was in no sense a peasant movement. In fact, the land question caused a split in the leadership when it came up for debate. The revolutionaries, with few exceptions, were boyars themselves. They were not eager to undermine their economic base with a radical peasant reform. Of course, the new regime had little time in which to implement any kind of a program. Its three months in power had to be devoted to immediate tasks of organization and defense. Some attempt was made to put into effect parts of the Islaz Proclamation, but the main effort was directed elsewhere.

The chief fear of the revolutionary government was a Russian armed intervention. In July a Russian army entered Moldavia, although its purpose was to keep watch on the revolutionary situation in Transylvania and the Habsburg Empire, rather than to suppress the movement in Moldavia, which Sturdza had well under control. The presence of the Russian force in the neighboring province, however, caused so much concern in Bucharest that the revolutionary leadership left the city. A new regime based on the Organic Statutes and headed by Metropolitan Neofit was then set up. When a popular reaction overthrew this administration, the insurgent government was restored. Plans for a constitutional assembly were prepared. Meanwhile, attempts were made to placate the Porte and to gain French and British diplomatic support.

The Ottoman government found itself under contradictory pressures. The French and British representatives, happy about the Russian embarrassment, wished to restrain any intervention. Russia, in contrast, strongly urged the Porte to take action against the revolutionary movement. The Ottoman government limited its moves to the dispatch, first, of an army to stand watch at the Danube and, second, of a commissioner, Suleiman Pasha, to Bucharest. There Suleiman negotiated with the Romanian leaders a settlement that called for the replacement of the revolutionary regime by a regency that would, nevertheless, include some members of the insurgent administration. Under Russian pressure, the Porte rejected this solution and sent another representative, Fuad Pasha, to secure the establishment of a government based on the Organic Statutes, with all revolutionary influences removed.

At the same time, the Russian and Ottoman armies prepared to occupy the provinces. Ottoman troops entered on September 25, with the Russian army following on September 27. Since the revolution did not have an armed force, it could not resist. Some volunteers had been assembled in Oltenia, but they disbanded when it became obvious that the opposition was overwhelming. A new government under Constantine Cantacuzino was then organized, and the revolutionary leaders fled the country. Russia next moved to reestablish a firm control of the situation. In May 1849 the Convention of Balta Liman was signed with the Porte. Under its provisions the princes were to be chosen by Russia and the Porte for seven-year terms; the assemblies were to be replaced by divans whose members would be nominated by the prince and the Ottoman government. This agreement marked the height of Russian power in the Principalities. Russian troops remained in occupation until 1851 and returned again in 1853 at the commencement of the Crimean War.

The revolution of 1848 in Wallachia had thus been a failure. Despite the popular enthusiasm for reform, there had been no great peasant uprising to accompany the actions of the boyar leadership; no people's army made its appearance. Of course, such a force would have had little chance against the Russian and Ottoman armies. It would also have brought up embarrassing questions for the revolutionary leadership, since mobilization of the peasantry could easily have led to actions against the social and economic interests of the boyar group. The revolt, nevertheless, did have important results. The major national leaders for the next decades were to come from the ranks of the revolutionaries, who were known as the "forty-eighters." Although Bălcescu died of tuberculosis, the Brătianu and Golescu brothers and Rosetti, among others, were to play major roles in subsequent events, as were two prominent Moldavians, Mihail Kogălniceanu and Alexander Cuza. Once in exile these men, concentrating on the achievement of the national rather than the liberal aspects of the revolutionary program, continued their activities in the national interest. Their goal was the unification of the Principalities and, because they recognized that rule by native hospodars had resulted in continual intrigues and domestic instability, the nomination of a foreign prince. As before, they saw Russia, not the Ottoman Empire, as their chief obstacle. Until that power was eliminated from its position of protector, they had little hope for national or liberal advancement.

OTTOMAN REFORM: THE CRIMEAN WAR

We have seen in the preceding pages how Serbia became an autonomous state, Greece won its independence, the Principalities loosened their connections with Constantinople, and Montenegro remained out of the control of the Ottoman government. At the same time, within the empire, powerful Muslim leaders, such as Muhammad Ali, Ali Pasha, and others, were able to set themselves up as the real rulers of their provinces and to defy the commands of the Porte. The question naturally arises what the sultan and his ministers were doing to counter this disintegration of their domains.

Throughout this period the Ottoman statesmen were well aware of their dangerously declining power; they recognized that the existence of the empire was at stake. They, however, faced problems not shared by the Christian leaders. Of first importance was the fact that the conservative, religious forces were much stronger in the Muslim community. For five centuries the Ottoman system had apparently worked. Emphasis on Muslim predominance and religious division had built a mighty empire. Moreover, those with vested interests in the maintenance of the old conditions held powerful positions; Christian notables as well as Muslim beys could block change. As could be expected, the Muslim religious establishment was a hindrance to reform. It could not be expected that the ulema would give support to reforms whose ultimate aim was the secularization and modernization of Muslim society.

A matter closely connected with the reform question was the trouble the Porte had in meeting pressures from the great powers. Although these states regularly referred to the empire as the "sick man," they were among the chief contributors to this condition. They intervened in Ottoman affairs for many reasons – for instance, to advance their own spheres of control, in response to appeals by Balkan people, or to preserve the balance of power. In the eighteenth century the Russian and Austrian objectives had been to acquire Ottoman territory. In the nineteenth century the powers often concerned themselves with Eastern crises primarily in order to assure that one of their number, usually Russia, did not use the opportunity to acquire disproportionate territory or influence and thus upset the balance of power in the area. After 1815 the powers principally involved in this struggle were France, Britain, and Russia. Mutually antagonistic, any two could ally should the third threaten to gain a predominant position. At this time, it will be noted, the Habsburg Empire, absorbed in serious problems in Central Europe, maintained a passive, negative attitude. Of the three major powers concerned, France, with its ambitions in Africa and Asia Minor, posed the greatest immediate threat to Ottoman territorial possessions. In 1830 France annexed Algiers; its claims were to extend further to Egypt and Syria. The French government, however, without a large army in the area and with a navy second to the British, could not endanger the Ottoman Balkan interests or directly threaten Constantinople.

Great-power intervention in Ottoman affairs was selective and capricious. Each government sponsored that party or nationality which would support its general diplomatic interests. In the autonomous states and in Greece the local consulates took part in the domestic factional struggles and in the conflicts between the ruler and his powerful opponents. Great-power sponsorship also upset the balance within the empire. The interference was always solely in behalf of the Christians. No outside state spoke for the Muslims, although they suffered from similar conditions of bad government under Ottoman administration and from outright repression under Christian rule. There was little the Porte could do about the situation. It did not have the military power to prevent foreign interference, and it could not keep order in its own house.

The desperate need for change had been recognized even in the eighteenth century. Selim III had concentrated on military reform. In the nineteenth century the condition of the army remained the first concern, but the Ottoman leaders went much further in attempting to reorganize the empire to

Constantinople

meet the challenge of the great powers and their own restless subject people. Like their Christian contemporaries, they took as their ultimate objective the establishment of a centralized bureaucratic monarchy, with a single law for all of the citizens, based on equal rights and, in theory, on equal responsibilities. Whether such a goal was obtainable, given the national and religious composition of the population and the history of the area, was to be decided at this point.

Mahmud II, who came to power as a result of the revolutionary actions of 1808, fully realized the necessity of reform. Unlike his predecessor, he moved very slowly. In fact, eighteen years of preparation preceded his first step. His main task was to deal with the military vulnerability of the empire. The janissaries had become little more than a mob of unruly men who were more capable of pulling down the central government and creating anarchy in the countryside than of defending the state against a foreign invader. The sipahis had settled down to be provincial country gentlemen. With the traditional forces thus in disarray, it was clear that the country needed an army organized on modern, Western European lines. The sultan did have certain troops at his command, but these were not sufficient to protect a great empire. Before a real reform could be instituted, the problem of the janissaries had to be met. They were difficult to oppose because of their close connections with the ulema. Proceeding with care, Mahmud II worked carefully to reassure the religious authorities, and he also introduced his own men into positions of command in the janissaries.

At the same time, Mahmud II was faced by the opposition of the rebellious pashas, in particular Ali Pasha of Janina. Although the Ottoman authorities knew of the activities of the Etairia in Greece, they had chosen to concentrate on subduing the Muslim rebel. Their success here, however, eliminated the one strong Muslim military force in the area that could have been used against the Greek revolution. Without an adequate army and with no readily available Balkan Muslim ally, Mahmud II was forced to appeal to another refractory vassal, Muhammad Ali, and offer him Crete and the Peloponnesus for his services. As we have seen, the Egyptian army was very effective; under the command of Muhammad Ali's son, Ibrahim, it took Crete and landed in the Peloponnesus. In the north the Ottoman army captured Misolonghi in April 1826.

Also at this time, the sultan prepared to destroy the janissaries. Not only had they demonstrated their incapacity in the Greek events, but in June 1826 they staged another revolt, this time in protest against the formation of a special corps in the army, which they saw as a challenge to their influence. Having prepared his ground, Mahmud was able to abolish the corps and also to move against the Bektashi dervish order that had been closely associated with it. The janissaries had been more than a military organization; they had been the chief support of the traditional conservative forces, who thus lost their military auxiliary. Although the sultan's action succeeded, the empire was left temporarily in an unusually exposed situation. Because of this weakness, the Porte was forced to bow to Russian demands and accept the terms of the Akkerman convention. The Russian ultimatum caused great anger in Ottoman official circles, where opinion was divided on the question whether the empire should fight or not. In this atmosphere the news of the battle of Navarino came as a great shock. Mahmud II had introduced reforms in the navy; it had now been effectively destroyed, and by powers who were not at war with the Porte. Their squadrons continued to patrol the Greek coasts. The outburst of anger and frustration was directed chiefly at Russia, who had been responsible for most of the past humiliations. The war that broke out in 1828 was fought under the worst of circumstances. The military forces were not ready for combat, and no help could be expected from the European powers. Although the Treaty of Adrianople was a blow to the empire, it was far from deadly. For the Porte the worst aspect was the heavy indemnity, which it was not able to pay. Some territory in Asia was surrendered, but with the exception of Greece and the Danube Delta, the Balkan lands remained intact. The independent Greece created by the Treaty of London of 1830 meant the loss of only a fraction of the Greek-inhabited lands. Of course, Russian influence over both Serbia and the Danubian Principalities had been greatly strengthened. Nevertheless, when the internal condition of the empire is considered, the final outcome of the revolutionary events of the 1820s had not been especially destructive. The state itself had never been in danger.

The next decade was to present exactly this threat. After the settlement of the Greek question and the peace with Russia, the Porte faced a major challenge from Egypt. Muhammad Ali was certainly the strongest and the most able of the rebel ayans. He was born in Macedonia in 1769 of an Albanian family. In 1798 he had been sent to Egypt with an Albanian force to fight Napoleon, and there he subsequently rose in the administrative and military service. In 1805 he was named governor. Once in power he introduced an extremely effective reform program. He was assisted by French advisers, whose presence gave France a stake in his success. His goal, too, was the establishment of an efficient centralized bureaucratic administration under his absolute control. He was able to introduce many of the reforms that were subsequently to be attempted by the Porte. For instance, he replaced the tax farmers with salaried officials; he issued standard law codes; he set up an educational system; and he employed foreign teachers and technicians. His greatest achievement, however, was his organization of a modern disciplined army. His son, Ibrahim Pasha, was to prove a brilliant military commander.

The settlement of the Greek crisis was a great disappointment to Muhammad Ali. Although he was given the administration of Crete, he naturally lost control of the Peloponnesus, which was a part of independent Greece. He thus demanded Syria as a replacement. When the Porte refused, he sent his army to capture the prize. He succeeded in winning a great victory over the Ottoman army at Konya in December 1832. The road was then open for the conquest of Anatolia, and Constantinople was itself in danger. Faced by this crisis, Mahmud II was forced to turn to his former adversary, Russia. No other government would come to his assistance. In July 1833 the two powers signed the Treaty of Unkiar Iskelessi (Hünkâr Iskelesi). Although this was a mutual defense treaty, the pact in fact marked the achievement by Russia of a position of predominance in Constantinople, which was a major goal of Russian policy at the time. The Egyptian advance was stopped, but Muhammad Ali gained much of what he wanted, in particular the control of Syria. He was in a position to develop a great Arab empire centered on the Red Sea; Egypt, which enjoyed the diplomatic backing of France, had the potential of becoming a major power.

These military disasters brought into sharp focus the urgent necessity for reform in the empire. Measures had to be taken to strengthen the central government at the expense of the religious, military, and provincial influences that had been so strong in the past. Changes were implemented that were designed to make the administrative organization more efficient and honest and to bring it more in line with contemporary European practice. Departments headed by ministers were established. A Council of Ministers was formed, which functioned like a cabinet and coordinated the activities of its members. Officials were to receive regular salaries, and a hierarchy was set up for the bureaucracy. Reforms were also introduced in the local governments, with the objective of securing more central control over their activities.

Because of the nature of the Ottoman government, nothing equivalent to the struggle between the prince and the notables that we have seen elsewhere could occur. However, two centers of influence did develop. The first, the Porte, represented the bureaucracy; the second, the Palace, included the sultan's immediate family, his servants, and the officials of the royal household. The same intrigues and personal rivalries took place here as in other governments.

One of the great accomplishments of Mahmud's reign was his attempt to open Muslim society more to the outer world. Concerned about form and style as well as content, the sultan dressed like a European ruler and compelled his officials to follow his example. The robe and turban were replaced by the frock coat of the European bureaucrat, and the fez became the official Ottoman head covering. The sultan himself attended concerts and receptions at the embassies, and his manner of living became more open than before. The other branches of the government naturally reflected this change of attitude toward the outside world. In 1836 a Ministry of Foreign Affairs was established, and at the same time permanent embassies were opened in the major European capitals. The need to know foreign languages was recognized, so schools were set up for that purpose.

The central government was thus reorganized and the basis laid for a closer understanding of the European states. These changes were very difficult to accomplish. The strength of the conservative opposition, which probably

Entrance to the government buildings, Constantinople

represented the opinion of the majority of the Muslim population, was shown particularly in the question of education. The state desperately needed technical and professional schools. In the Balkan states secular school systems had been set up without a major confrontation with the Orthodox church, even though education had traditionally been under its jurisdiction. The situation was quite different in Constantiople, where the ulema remained a major obstacle. Nevertheless, certain special institutions, such as a medical school, were opened. The same problems were met here as in the Balkan states; there was a shortage of books, equipment, and competent teachers.

Military reform remained the chief focus of interest. The defeat at Konya had taught a costly lesson. Foreign advisers were once again employed; this time they came chiefly from Prussia. The Porte naturally preferred to rely on assistance from a state with a high reputation in military achievement, but one that until then had shown little interest in the Eastern Question. The great Prussian general Helmut von Moltke came to Constantinople and played a major role in military reorganization; British advisers were used for the same purpose in the navy. Ottoman students were also sent to European military institutions. The progress made in the military field was evidently grossly overestimated by Mahmud II, who appears to have made a complete misjudgment of the capabilities of his army. He had never accepted the defeat by Egypt; revenge was always uppermost on his mind. In 1839 he declared war on Egypt with the aim of destroying Muhammad Ali and regaining the lost territories. This campaign was a disaster from the beginning. Mahmud died of tuberculosis in June 1839 without learning the full extent of the defeat.

His son, Abdul Mejid, came to the throne at the age of sixteen in the midst of a dangerous crisis. Fortunately for the empire, the international rivalries were to aid in the maintenance of Ottoman integrity. The close association of France with Muhammad Ali's Egypt awoke the fears of both Britain and Russia about the balance of power in the Mediterranean. Russia was also under the obligation to defend the empire after the conclusion of the Treaty of Unkiar Iskelessi. A coalition was therefore formed among Russia, Britain, Austria, and Prussia in support of the Ottoman Empire. A protracted crisis followed, but neither France nor Egypt could withstand this combination. Muhammad Ali was forced to withdraw from Syria and Crete, but he retained the hereditary rule of Egypt. The powers came to a further understanding. In 1841 the Convention of the Straits, which for the first time placed the Turkish waterway under international supervision, was signed. According to the terms of the treaty, the Straits would be closed to ships of war of all outside nations in time of peace. This stipulation protected the interests of Russia, Britain, and the Ottoman Empire equally. British warships would not be able to menace Russian southern shores; similarly, Russian squadrons could not endanger British shipping in the Mediterranean; and the Porte was assured that a hostile fleet could not appear to threaten Constantinople. In time of war, of course, the Ottoman Empire was free to summon allied navies into its territorial waters. Russia allowed the Treaty of Unkiar Iskelessi to lapse. These agreements reflected a close Russian–British understanding and Nicholas's desire to work with Great Britain. He considered France the main danger to Europe, chiefly because of its influence on the revolutionary movements.

With the settlement of the Egyptian question, the Ottoman Empire was free to concentrate on domestic affairs. The great period of reform, known as the *Tanzimat*, or "Reordering," was about to begin. Measures undertaken at this time were a continuation of those of Mahmud II, and the goal remained that of saving the empire. Certain changes were made in the basic principles of administration. Previously, the Ottoman government had worked through other institutions and agents. For the Christians the millet and the village communities had been most important; these authorities, not the central offices in Constantinople, were in touch with the individual. Now the government was to attempt to control its citizens directly. In order to do this, new institutions had to be adopted, most of them patterned after European examples. The aim remained the establishment of an efficient administration conducted by honest bureaucrats dedicated to the service of the state.

The general goals were stated in the first great document of the reform period, the imperial rescript of the Gülhane (Rose Garden) of November 1839. Basically a declaration of intention, it promised a government based on security of life, honor, and property; equal justice; and a regular system of taxation. A very able group of statesmen attempted to achieve some of these objectives. It will be noted that the reform movement centered in the Porte, that is, in the government, rather than in the Palace. Abdul Mejid and, at first, his successor Abdul Aziz played a less important role than the ministers, a situation that naturally caused friction between the two centers of influence. The first reformer of prominence was Mustafa Reshid Pasha, who was grand vezir six times and foreign minister three times. Associated with him were Âli Pasha and Fuad Pasha, both of whom had wide experience in Europe. Ahmed Cevdet Pasha was known for his work in supervising the drawing up of a new law code, known as *Mecelle* (Law Collection), which was issued between 1866 and 1888. Midhat Pasha was experienced in provincial affairs. After the Crimean War the influence of France and Britain was paramount in Constantinople. The Ottoman reformers, like their Balkan contemporaries, preferred to use French examples for their administrative reforms. Britain was, of course, a strong supporter of both the maintenance of the empire and internal reorganization. In 1838 the British and Ottoman governments signed the Treaty of Balta Liman, which was exceedingly favorable to Britain's commercial interests. Both trade considerations and the strategic importance of the Ottoman lands gave this naval power an interest in the maintenance of Ottoman integrity.

At this time the chief governing institution was the Council of Ministers, which included representatives of groups such as the ulema, the military, and officials from the palace. In addition to those affecting the central government, reforms were also undertaken in the provinces. At first the attempt was made to lessen the powers of the governors; councils were associated with them in which Christians as well as Muslims sat. The process of reform was interrupted in the 1850s by the crisis that led to the Crimean War. This conflict, the only general European war between 1815 and 1914, arose directly from the familiar issues associated with the Eastern Question: the necessity felt by most European powers of maintaining the Ottoman Empire and thus the balance of power in the Near East.

The question of the religious protectorates has been discussed previously. Austria in the Treaty of Karlowitz, France in various agreements, and Russia in particular in the Treaty of Kuchuk Kainarji had acquired certain vaguely defined rights to speak in favor of their coreligionists. In 1851 a conflict arose between France and Russia concerning religious jurisdiction over the Holy Places in Jerusalem, which involved the Catholic and Orthodox churches. In February 1853 the Russian government sent to Constantinople a special emissary, Prince Alexander Menshikov. An arrogant and overbearing diplomat, Menshikov not only insisted on satisfaction in regard to the original issue, but demanded a clear recognition of the Russian right to protect the Orthodox Christians of the Ottoman Empire and thus to speak in behalf of 12 million Ottoman subjects. The Russian officials may have genuinely believed that their previous treaties gave them this privilege. Nicholas I also seems to have felt that he had some sort of an understanding with Britain over eastern affairs. Nevertheless, the demand, particularly in the form in which it was presented, could be accepted neither by the Porte nor by the powers, since it would have signified the domination of the empire by Russia and a complete upset of the diplomatic equilibrium in the eastern Mediterranean.

By slow stages the Western powers and Russia were drawn into war. When the Porte refused to accept a Russian ultimatum, whose demands included the question of protection, a Russian army was sent in July 1853 to occupy the Principalities. In October the Ottoman Empire declared war. At the same time the British and French fleets entered the Straits in support of the Ottoman position. In November the Russian Black Sea fleet sank the Turkish navy at Sinope (Samsun); all of the ships and four thousand men were lost. Finally, in March 1854, France and Britain entered the conflict. It was very difficult for the belligerents to find a battlefield. In June 1854 the Habsburg government presented the Russians with an ultimatum demanding that they evacuate the Principalities. Habsburg troops, in cooperation with Ottoman forces, then entered the region. At the same time, the monarchy and the German states came to an agreement to keep Central Europe neutral. Under these circumstances the allies, which included Piedmont as well as France, Britain, and the Ottoman Empire, were reduced to attacking in an unlikely spot, the Crimea. Although a year of fighting did result in the capture of the main fortress of Sebastopol, this victory was in no way decisive for the Western powers. However, Russia too was in difficulties. The defeat on its own territory was a humiliation for the army and the tsarist regime. Both sides were willing to make peace.

The Treaty of Paris of 1856 gave certain advantages to the Ottoman Empire, although most of its provisions were overturned within the next quarter-century. Most important, the military defeat and the terms of the peace were a sharp check for the principal Ottoman antagonist. Russia was to concentrate henceforth on internal reform and not renew its Balkan adventures for twenty years. For the Porte the most important stipulation of the treaty was that concerning the neutralization of the Black Sea. To assure Ottoman safety and to protect British interests, it was agreed that neither Russia nor the Ottoman Empire was to maintain warships in the Black Sea or fortifications on its shores. The Ottoman Empire could, however, station a fleet in the Straits. Other sections of the treaty were similarly beneficial to the Porte. Three districts of southern Bessarabia were given to Moldavia, an action that removed Russia from the ranks of the riparian states of the Danube; this measure was of primary importance to Austria. The treaty also returned the Danube Delta to Ottoman control.

Other provisions of the peace, in contrast, were to prove extremely damaging to Ottoman authority in the Balkans, although their implications were not at first obvious. Russia was required to surrender any claim to a protectorship of the Balkan Christians. The question, however, was not dropped. Instead, the signatory powers assumed the position of joint guarantors. It will be noted that the Habsburg Empire and Prussia, as well as the belligerent states, took part in the peace conference and signed the treaty. Contradictory clauses in the agreement complicated matters. In Article VII the signators promised "to respect the independence and the territorial integrity of the Ottoman Empire." As regards the Christian nationalities, the sultan communicated to the powers the text of a firman, the Hatti Humayun, which he intended to release on the question. The Christian states in return agreed that they did not have the right "to interfere, either collectively or separately, in the relations of His Majesty the sultan with his subjects, nor in the internal administration of his empire."[12] In practice, these provisions were to lead to great confusion and to serve to facilitate a massive interference by the great powers in any crisis between the sultan and his Christian subjects.

With the conclusion of the Crimean War another period of reform commenced. Âli and Fuad were the chief Ottoman statesmen concerned. The Hatti Humayun was issued in 1856; as we have seen, it became a part of the Treaty of Paris. Drawn up under foreign pressure, the document was a declaration of intentions and an assurance that Christian and Muslim would be treated on an equal basis. As far as the practical measures undertaken are

12 Hertslet, *Map of Europe*, II, pp. 1254, 1255.

concerned, the most important for the Balkan people were those dealing with provincial administration and taxation. Provincial reform, of course, had begun before the Crimean War. The Ottoman experience with the rebellious Muslim pashas had shown that it was essential that the provinces be controlled. A major effort was made to reassert the authority of the Porte in areas such as Bosnia, where local authorities had often acted quite independently. In this reorganization the empire was divided into vilayets, then into livas or sanjaks, then into kazas, which were subdivided into nahiyes, and further into villages. At the head of the vilayet was a governor. Associated with him was an Administrative Assembly including the heads of the administrative divisions as well as three Muslim and three Christian representatives, who were chosen by their communities. A similar system was applied to the lesser subdivisions. Although at first the power of the governor was reduced, he was later given more authority and control over the administrative apparatus.

One of the strongest complaints expressed by the Christians against Ottoman rule had always been the system of taxation. Reform in this area was fundamental to the continued existence of the state. The wars and reforms had absorbed huge sums of money. If anything, the amounts collected had to be increased, but reform was needed in both assessment and collection. The question of assessment had already been taken up in the reign of Mahmud II. A census and a land survey were conducted from 1831 to 1838 in the interests of a better allocation of taxes. In the new reforms, attempts were made to simplify and reduce the number of the taxes that the government collected. The effort was also made to abolish tax farming and to have the collections made by salaried officials. When such measures proved impossible to implement, new regulations were issued to control the abuses of the old system. In the 1840s the Christian community leaders were made responsible for the collection of the head tax and later for the tithe. In actual practice, very little was done to reduce the extreme corruption in this area of administration. There were too many vested interests involved. Both Ottoman officials and Christian notables regarded this source of income as part of the rewards of their offices.

The continued corruption at the bottom was paralleled by a condition of growing chaos at the top of the Ottoman financial institutions. To meet the cost of reform, as well as its regular military and administrative expenses, the Ottoman government resorted to unwise borrowing. The first loan was received in 1854; by 1860 the state was paying 20 percent of its income on the service of the debt, and by 1875 the figure had risen to 50 percent. In 1877 payments on the debt had to be suspended, since the funds could not be raised. Some attempts were made to control the situation. In accordance with measures introduced after 1858, annual budgets were prepared. Their value was reduced by the fact that the government was never able to collect the revenues that were expected, and so the budgeted expenses were not covered.

Basic to the Ottoman financial problems was the relative poverty of the empire. Agricultural methods were primitive; subsistence farming was the rule in most areas. Industrial growth was stifled by the difficulties within the empire, such as the scarcity of capital for investment, the insufficient legal framework, and the lack of safe and easy transport facilities. The commercial agreements made previously, which allowed foreign powers to import their products virtually duty free, were also extremely detrimental to Ottoman development. Austrian and British manufactured goods flooded the Ottoman market to the detriment of the native producer, who could not meet the competition. The treaties prevented the Porte from taking effective measures to protect its own industries in their period of growth. A similar shortsighted policy governed the handling of state lands. In the Land Law of 1858 the attempt was made to regain control over property that had passed into private hands, but the effect was quite the opposite. Tenants and tax farmers continued to regard their holdings as private property.

In addition to the financial burdens mentioned, the Ottoman government had to undertake the expenses resulting from the tragic fate of the Muslim inhabitants of former Ottoman territories. The Russian occupation of these lands created conditions that led to the emigration of hundreds of thousands of Muslims. Between 1854 and 1876 it has been estimated that 1.4 million Tatars left the Crimea. Russian forced resettlement policies carried through between 1863 and 1866 resulted in the immigration into the Ottoman Empire of around 600,000 Circassians. The Porte was not prepared to handle this mass movement, and there was an enormous loss of life. Although the male Muslim element in the Ottoman population was increased despite the losses, the problem of the resettlement of these people within the empire was overwhelming. The Christian great powers, who were to prove so sensitive about the fate of the Balkan people, felt no necessity to assist here.

In 1861 a new sultan, Abdul Aziz, came to the throne. Despite the growing criticism of the Tanzimat reforms, he continued his predecessor's policies. Âli and Fuad remained in power. Throughout the Tanzimat period the Porte was the center of government. The bureaucrats, as could be expected, gained a large number of enemies, both on the right, from those who resented the secularizing and westernizing influences, and on the left, from a new group, the Young Ottomans, who felt that the changes had not gone far enough. The men who formed the latter group had grown up in the reform atmosphere. Usually civil servants, writers, army officers, or businessmen, they were educated and well aware of events in the rest of the world. They combined progressive ideas with a deep respect for Islam and the Ottoman past. Although they were willing to take from Europe anything that would strengthen their state, they wished to preserve what they considered the essential nature of their society. Their specific aim was the introduction of representative institutions into the government.

After the death of Âli Pasha in 1871, a basic change in direction occurred. Abdul Aziz was determined to rule himself. Russian influence increased, particularly during the vezirates of Mahmud Nedim. The sultan followed a policy of balance among his ministers. By this time it was apparent that the reforms were not achieving the major goal of pacifying the Christian population. In 1866 a revolt broke out in Crete; in 1875 and 1876 rebellions swept through Bosnia, Hercegovina, and Bulgaria. Although these movements had economic as well as political aspects, it was quite apparent that the Christian population wanted independence under their own leaders, not equal citizenship in a reformed Ottoman state. The Tanzimat reforms had satisfied few in the empire. Those who lost their former positions were deeply aggrieved; the progressive elements of Muslim opinion wanted more radical measures. In May 1876 the conservative and liberal forces joined hands in a revolt that overthrew Abdul Aziz and introduced another period of extended crisis for the empire.

As far as the Christian population was concerned, the reforms had simply come too late. They could only have worked if they could have been based on a unifying principle stronger than that of nationalism or religion. None such existed. Ottomanism, symbolizing the unity of the empire's citizens, was not a term to attract wide support. The Ottoman Empire was no longer a great conquering power. It had suffered from repeated foreign intervention, humiliating defeat in war, and financial bankruptcy. Moreover, the new measures themselves had not been very popular. The centralizing institutions were difficult to apply to a population that had for centuries been governed on another basis and that was divided by religion, national background, and provincial loyalties. The Tanzimat officials were no substitute for the former religious and communal leaders. The parting of the ways between Christian and Muslim was clear at the beginning of the century, and the reform era made the divisions even more apparent. If communal and church authority was reduced, the Balkan people wanted their own national governments, not continued control from a centralized administration in Constantinople.

THE FORMATION OF THE ROMANIAN STATE

The stipulations of the Treaty of Paris of 1856 had a greater effect on the Danubian Principalities than on any other area. Russia's protectorate was brought to an end; that power could no longer exercise control over Romanian political life. The significance of the substitute European guarantee had yet to be shown. Moldavia was given back three districts of southern Bessarabia, part of the larger region lost in 1812 (see Map 22). The neutralization of the Black Sea affected Romanian interests also, in that it limited the Russian military and naval capabilities in the region. With the end of the Russian protectorate and the internal regimes based on the Organic Statutes, it was clear that a new political organization would have to be introduced in the Principalities. Since the powers were divided on its nature, it was decided that the question would be settled by diplomatic negotiations after the ad-

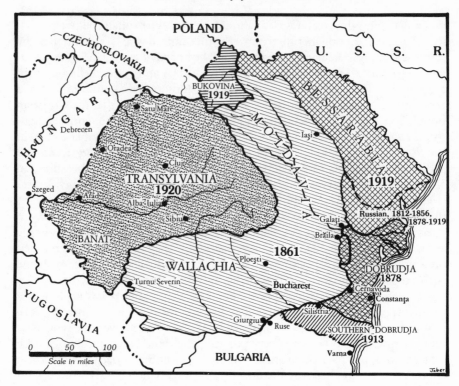

Map 22. The expansion of Romania, 1861–1920

journment of the conference at Paris, and that the wishes of the inhabitants would be consulted.

Important as these stipulations were for future Romanian national development, the diplomatic revolution that occurred following the Crimean War was of potentially even greater significance. In the first part of the century Continental politics had been dominated by the Holy Alliance, the combination of Russia, Prussia, and the Habsburg Empire, whose common goal was to maintain the status quo on the Continent and keep the conservative governments in power. They had cooperated to suppress revolutionary activity throughout Central Europe and in the Italian peninsula. In 1849 a Russian army had been sent to Transylvania to put down the Hungarian revolution and maintain the Habsburg domination. The failure of Vienna to repay this debt in 1854 aroused enormous bitterness in Russia. Habsburg actions during the Crimean War were, in fact, extremely damaging to the Russian cause. Once the war was concluded, the Russian statesmen were determined to take revenge. Not only was the Holy Alliance shattered, but the field was open for liberal and national movements that could only be to the detriment of the monarchy.

The Sulina Channel, the mouth of the Danube

Russian foreign relations were to be almost completely reversed. Nicholas I had regarded France as the foremost Russian adversary because of its sponsorship of revolutionary movements. Certainly the French ruler, Napoleon III, made no secret of his sympathy for national and liberal ideas. His policy became if anything more pronounced after the Crimean War. Yet Alexander II, who came to the throne in 1855, and his ministers were to work closely with Paris in the postwar years. Russia was about to enter a period of internal reform. The state could not afford to remain isolated. An informal alliance was thus established with the French government that was to have great significance for the Principalities. Whereas previously the Russian representatives had acted to suppress liberal and national agitation, they now stood with France in support of a nationalist program.

After 1848 the leadership of the Romanian national movement lay principally in the hands of those who had participated in the revolution. With the radical change in international alignments, they could hope to obtain their objectives through diplomacy. The national program remained the unification of the Principalities and the nomination of a foreign prince. A more radical plan, which would include full independence and the inclusion in the union of all the Romanian lands – that is, Transylvania, Bukovina, and Bessarabia – was regarded as impossible to fulfill. There were even strong hindrances to the accomplishment of the more limited objectives.

At the end of the war an Austrian army was in occupation of the Principalities. The Habsburg aims were not clear. In the negotiations that took place on the Romanian question, France became the champion of the national cause, and its stand was supported by Russia, Prussia, and Sardinia. The Russian position signified the change in attitude that had taken place. The Russian statesmen also hoped that they could divide France from Britain and thus break the Crimean alliance. Prussia and Sardinia, with their own programs for German and Italian unification, naturally associated themselves with France. These four powers were willing to accept the organization of the Principalities in the form desired by the liberal Romanian leaders.

Most strongly opposed to a program of unification and a foreign prince were the Ottoman Empire and Austria. The Porte saw any alteration in the status of the provinces as a further erosion of its rights as suzerain. The Crimean War had been fought in theory to defend the empire, rather than to contribute to its dissolution. The Habsburg Monarchy at this time and later feared that a strong Romanian national unit would exert too great an influence on the Romanian population of Transylvania. The British government wavered between the two positions. Finally, it decided that the formation of a united Romanian state would be detrimental to its policy of building up the Ottoman Empire as a bulwark against Russia.

Not only could the powers not come to an agreement between themselves, but their attempt to learn the opinion of the Romanian people led to even further controversies. Two sets of elections were held in the Principalities;

both showed majorities for union and a foreign prince. After a period of tension, the powers met in Paris in the summer of 1858 to decide the question. Despite the results of the elections, the convention agreed upon in August 1858 changed the stipulations of the Organic Statutes but did not provide for union. Wallachia and Moldavia were given parallel, but separate, institutions. They were each to have a prince and an assembly. In order to appease the unionists, a central commission was established at Focşani, but its functions were limited. The princes were to be elected by special assemblies and approved by the sultan. The representatives to the assemblies, with the franchise limited to the boyar class, were to hold office for seven years. Their duties were to oversee the budget, taxation, and the ministries. Elections were held on the basis of this statute in the winter of 1858–1859. In both provinces the special assemblies chosen to name the prince selected the same man, Alexander Cuza, a liberal and a forty-eighter. Although the convention had not precisely forbidden such an action, it was certainly against the spirit of the entire document, which aimed at maintaining the separation of the Principalities. The double election was a triumph of liberal–national policy, but it was a question whether the powers would accept it.

Once again the protectors took the responsibility of deciding an internal question. They split, as could be expected, into two camps. The Porte and the Habsburg Monarchy were firmly opposed to the personal union; France, Russia, Prussia, and Sardinia supported it. Britain, the ostentatious proponent of constitutional government elsewhere, did not like the action, but did not see how it could be changed. From this time on the Romanian liberals benefited from the fact that the powers recognized that they could not easily enforce their wishes on the provinces. The obvious measure would be an entrance of the Ottoman army, an alternative that the majority of the states would not consider. The agreement of all the protectors was needed for an Ottoman intervention. Neither the Russian nor the Habsburg army could be used as a policeman because of the antagonism between the two governments and the general distrust of their motives. The crisis that arose at this time was eased in June when Austria became involved in a war with France and Sardinia. The defeat of the monarchy removed one opponent of union and made a settlement possible. In September 1859 the guaranteeing states recognized the double election, but only for the lifetime of Cuza. Despite the limitation there was a general recognition that once the provinces had been joined, they would be difficult to separate.

Although Cuza was prince of both Moldavia and Wallachia, his position was very difficult. He faced the same opposition from the boyars as his predecessors. His problems were compounded by the fact that he had to govern in both Principalities. He thus had to deal with two separate assemblies and administrative systems. He had personally little experience in national administration, and he was well aware that liberal opinion preferred a foreign prince. He had no reliable political support. The franchise assured that the conservatives would be predominant in the assemblies. The prince thus had to secure a change in the electoral laws before he could be certain of adequate backing in the legislatures.

Two political parties competed for political power. The Liberals, henceforth stood for the national program, and, with some reservations, they called for franchise and land reform. The Conservatives, with no set objectives, preferred the maintenance of the status quo and the preservation of the special political and economic privileges of the boyars. A convinced Liberal himself, Cuza recognized that his major goals would have to be, first, an amalgamation of the legislative and administrative institutions of the two provinces and, second, an electoral reform that would break the Conservative control and allow the country to take further measures that would benefit wide sections of the population.

The administrative and legislative union was accomplished with surprisingly little difficulty. Relying on diplomatic means, Cuza turned first to France and the Porte to convince them of the necessity of the move. He then presented the question to the other guarantors. By the end of 1861 he was able to win their consent, although again the union was to apply only to the reign of the prince. With the establishment of a single assembly and administrative system, a true Romanian national state had been established, although it was officially known only as the United Principalities of Wallachia and Moldavia. The first goal of the liberal revolutionaries of 1848 had thus been accomplished.

Even with this advance, Cuza had great difficulties in controlling his government. As in Greece and Serbia, the prominent men were reluctant to concede authority to one of their number. The assembly thus once again became a center of opposition to the prince. Cuza had a definite program that he wished to implement, but he was blocked by this situation. In 1863, however, he took an action that was bound to gain public approval by secularizing monastic property, including the lands of the Dedicated Monasteries. These institutions had played an important role in the life of the Principalities in the past. They were under the authority of the patriarch of Constantinople and were administered by Greek ecclesiastical officials. Over the centuries they had amassed great wealth through pious donations, until by the nineteenth century they controlled 11 percent of the arable lands of the provinces. The profits on their holdings were "dedicated" to certain Holy Places, such as Mt. Athos. They had become extremely unpopular. Conditions for the peasants working the estates were worse than for those on private lands. Although they were supposed to maintain certain charitable institutions, such as hospitals, for the benefit of the population, they had failed to do so. In previous years the princes had made efforts to regulate their activities, but with little success. The institutions had the backing not only of the Patriarchate, but also of the Russian government, which made use of the monasteries during the frequent occupations. In December 1863 the assembly passed the expropriation measure; compensation was offered, which the Patriarchate refused. Negotiations on this matter dragged on for years. In the end the Patriarchate received nothing.

All parties could unite on this issue. In contrast, the great domestic question, that involving the peasantry, was to cause a bitter conflict. Obviously, some move had to be taken to regulate the status of the majority of the population. The position of the peasant had been a major issue in the revolutions of 1848 in the Habsburg Monarchy; neighboring Russia in the 1860s was undergoing a period of radical peasant reform. Here the serfs were liberated and they received land. The Romanian peasant was not a serf – that is, he was not legally tied to the estate – but he did owe labor dues and payments for the use of his land. Some changes clearly had to be made in the relationship of peasant and the landowner. Such measures, however, were not likely to be carried through with the cooperation of the Romanian assembly, dominated as it was by boyars whose interests were closely involved. Cuza solved the problem by a coup d'état in May 1864. When the assembly passed a vote of censure of his ministry, he used soldiers to dissolve the body. He then announced a new statute that would both give him more power and widen the franchise. The measure was approved by a plebiscite with the vote of 682,621 to 1,307. Quite obviously, the methods of coercion available to the prince had been used freely.

This alteration of the political institutions that had been established by the great powers was a clear challenge to their authority over the country. Their reaction was very weak. As usual, France supported the Romanian decision. The chief opposition came from the Habsburg Empire, backed by Russia, who disliked the methods used. Once again the disunity of the protectors and the recognition that they had really no means of enforcing a negative decision led them to accept an accomplished fact.

With the government securely under his control and with the assistance of his most important minister, Mihail Kogălniceanu, Cuza proceeded with the regulation of the land question. The Agrarian Law of 1864 was perhaps the major piece of legislation introduced in the century because of its effects on social and economic conditions in the Principalities. The intention of the law was to guarantee each peasant direct ownership of a plot of land and to create a prosperous and independent class of small proprietors. Previously, it will be remembered, the peasant had only the right to a collective share in a portion of the estate. In the new law, once again, ownership of draft animals was made the basis of the distribution of land. A family owning four oxen and a cow received 13.6 acres (5.5 hectares); those with two oxen and a cow were given 9.6 (3.9), and those with one cow got only 5.7 (2.3). A peasant with no animals could keep his house and garden plot, or about 0.5 acre (0.2 hectares). In return for the tithe and labor dues that he lost, the boyar was to receive compensation. The peasant paid the state over a period of fifteen years, and the government in turn indemnified the landholder. The peasant land was declared inalienable for thirty years, a measure designed to prevent the landlord from regaining full control of his former estate.

The reform did not work as intended; a strong and prosperous class of peasant farmers did not appear. The major problem was that the peasants, except perhaps those in the first category in the division, did not receive adequate amounts of land to support their families. Moreover, the boyar kept control of the forests and pastures that previously had been regarded as common land and had been used for the raising of cattle. The change had an immediate effect on the diet of the inhabitants. Less meat and dairy products were available; corn became the staple in the peasant diet. The more valuable wheat was sold as a cash crop, eventually destined for export. Under these circumstances the peasant, to supplement his meager income, was forced to work on the land still retained by the boyar, who had been required to surrender not more than two-thirds of his estate. Since this class dominated the local administration, the individual landholders had often used their position to assure that they kept the best land or to cheat on the amounts surrendered. Thus in most areas the boyar land continued to be cultivated by the peasants, usually on a sharecrop basis; they provided their own tools and animals.

Despite the original intention of the Agrarian Law, its ultimate effect was to improve the position of the boyar. With the continuing rise in demand abroad for the agricultural products of the Principalities, the large landowner remained in a good position to benefit from the economic conditions of the time. Although Moldavian boyars often ran their estates, the Wallachian landowner still generally preferred to live in Bucharest or abroad and to appoint a steward to run his affairs. He was not interested in improving the use of his land or introducing modern agricultural methods. With so much cheap labor available, there was no incentive for change. The entire situation was to the great disadvantage of the peasantry, whose position worsened considerably during the second half of the century, particularly as the population continued to rise. The Principalities were to remain a land of large estates and a depressed peasantry, in contrast to neighboring Serbia and Bulgaria, where small peasant farms predominated.

In addition to these reforms, the Cuza administration was responsible for other important measures. A civil code based on the French Code Napoléon was issued, and local government was organized on the centralizing principles that we have seen elsewhere. The control that could be exerted over the local officials and police by Bucharest gave the men in office the advantage in the elections that prevailed in Greece and Serbia. A system of primary and secondary education was established, and universities were opened in Bucharest and Iaşi. The measures could not, of course, be put through without opposition. It was to be expected that the Conservatives would seek Cuza's overthrow, but he had also won the dislike of the Liberals. They made no secret of their preference for a foreign prince.

By 1866 Cuza was thus faced with enemies on all sides, and he had received very little credit for his achievements. He was himself not an intensely ambitious man. He had repeatedly declared that he regarded himself as a temporary substitute for the foreign prince whom the Liberals desired. Moreover, like King Othon, he did not have an obvious successor. He had no legitimate sons. His mistress, Marie Obrenović, did have children, but their sucession was improbable. Cuza was also unpopular with the protecting powers because of his acts of defiance in the past; they supported his maintenance in power chiefly because they could envisage no better alternative.

The overthrow of Cuza in February 1866 thus came as no great surprise. The action was a military coup; a group of army officers entered the prince's room and forced him to sign an abdication. He made no resistance and assured the local consuls that he too preferred the foreign prince desired by the leaders of the revolt. The conspiracy had been the result of an understanding between the Conservatives and the Liberals. Ion Brătianu and C. A. Rosetti were to play a particularly active role in the next weeks. A provisional government was appointed and a regency set up. The goal of the leaders was the maintenance of national unity, a foreign prince, and constitutional government. They did not seek to break the link with the Ottoman Empire. The assembly next proceeded to choose a prince. The first preference was Philip of Flanders, a brother of the king of Belgium. When he refused, Ion Brătianu undertook the task of finding an alternative candidate who would accept the position.

The Principalities were in a potentially dangerous situation. According to the treaties, Moldavia and Wallachia should have separated with the end of the reign of Cuza. Although France still supported a united Romania, Russia, the Habsburg Empire, the Ottoman Empire, and Britain preferred a return to the former situation. Europe, however, was on the eve of the war between Prussia and Austria that was to decide the issue of supremacy in Germany; the principal attention was on this area. In the Principalities the regency argued that the choice of a prince was a purely internal matter not subject to great-power interference. Meanwhile, Brătianu had found a possible candidate in Charles of Hohenzollern-Sigmaringen. This prince, the son of the head of the Catholic branch of the Prussian royal family, was also a cousin of Napoleon III. With close French and Prussian connections, he was a good candidate for the Romanian throne. With the tacit consent of both France and Prussia, the prince accepted the offer. The provisional government in April held what proved to be a classic example of a controlled plebiscite; the choice was approved 685,969 to 224.

Since Charles was an officer in the Prussian army and war with Austria was about to break out, the prince had to travel through Habsburg territory to Romania in disguise. He arrived in his new country in May 1866. The subsequent Prussian victory in the war with Austria and the obvious impossibility of securing his removal without a military intervention led the powers to recognize his election by the end of the year. With a foreign prince securely on the throne, the Romanian Liberals had thus achieved the second part of their national program. The Ottoman suzerainty was nominal; the Porte had no influence on internal affairs. The next step in the national movement was to be the attainment of full independence.

This goal fully corresponded with the ideas of the new prince, who did not want to be an Ottoman vassal. After his accession to the throne he strongly supported any measure that would weaken the few remaining ties with the Porte. His initial years in power, however, were primarily devoted to dealing with the internal opposition. His first government was under the leadership of the Conservative Lascăr Catargiu, but it contained both Rosetti and Ion Brătianu. A constitution was approved to replace the convention of August 1858, which had previously been the basis of government. Based on the Belgian Constitution of 1831, the document contained guarantees of free speech, press, and assembly. The prince was given a strong position; he named and dismissed the ministers; he could dissolve the assembly and veto legislation. The two-house legislature consisted of a senate and a chamber of deputies. An indirect system of election assured the continued predominance of educated, wealthy, and property-holding sections of the population.

With the political organization determined, Charles embarked upon a program designed to strengthen and modernize the country. Proud of his military background, he devoted particular care to building an efficient Romanian army. He asserted as great a degree of independence from Constantinople as possible; his principal attention was directed to securing the right to carry on more of the normal functions of an independent ruler, including the minting of coins, the awarding of military decorations, and, most important, the negotiation of treaties with other governments without the intervention of the Porte. Postal, telegraph, and consular conventions were concluded at this time. The prince also wished to secure international recognition of *Romania* as the official name of the state. In 1869 he made a popular marriage with Elizabeth of Wied, a Protestant, who was later to become known in Europe for her writing about Romania under the name of Carmen Sylva. Like King Othon and Alexander Cuza, Charles did not produce an heir. His one child, a daughter, died at a young age.

This foreign prince found the task of governing no easier than had the native rulers. Charles, in fact, was himself in much the position that Cuza had been in. He had no personal party, and he had to play between the opposing factions and individuals. In 1870–1871 a major internal crisis almost led to his abdication. In July 1870 the Franco-Prussian War commenced. The prince naturally supported Prussia, whereas most of the politically influential men in the state preferred the Romanian patron, France. Russia used the occasion to denounce the Black Sea clauses of the Treaty of Paris, and there was anxiety in Bucharest that a claim would be made for the three districts of southern Bessarabia acquired in 1856. Some groups were also opposed to the conservative monarchical form of government that had been established. In this atmosphere of domestic unrest, agitation directed against the prince rose. A small uprising that took place in Ploeşti in August was suppressed, but a jury subsequently freed the participants. These events, together with his great difficulties in governing the country, deeply depressed the prince, who came to the conclusion that he could not rule under the constitutional regime in effect. Like Cuza, he felt that the executive powers had to be expanded. He thus wrote a letter to the governments of the guarantor states stating his problems and expressing his willingness to abdicate.

This message was received most unsympathetically in all the capitals, where it was felt that the prince was simply laying the groundwork for a declaration of independence. The Franco-Prussian War and the Russian denunciation of the Treaty of Paris had caused dangers enough; the powers dreaded another Eastern crisis. They were certainly not going to go to the aid of the prince in his domestic quarrels. The agitation against Charles reached its height on the night of March 22–23, 1871. Demonstrations held by French sympathizers when the German colony in Bucharest was holding a dinner to celebrate the Prussian victories resulted in a major crisis in the government. Already unhappy with the conditions of his rule, Charles was now ready to leave. Realizing the dangers to the nation if such an action occurred, the responsible Romanian leaders acted to calm the situation. Catargiu formed a Conservative ministry, which was to last for five years. Retaining control of the legislature, this regime assured a period of domestic tranquility.

The defeat of France and the unification of Germany, following closely on similar events in Italy, created a new diplomatic balance on the Continent. In the early 1870s Russia, Germany, and the Habsburg Empire joined together in an informal association known as the Three Emperors' Alliance, a combination that was to dominate European diplomacy for the next years. None of these powers wished a new Eastern crisis. Despite the fact that the international situation was not favorable to attempts to expand its autonomous position, the Romanian government continued in these endeavors. Its greatest success was the conclusion of commercial conventions with Austria-Hungary and Russia without the intervention of the Porte.

Despite the temporary check to further major accomplishments, it can be seen that between 1856 and 1875 real advances had been made in the Romanian national program as enunciated in particular by the Liberal Party. Moldavia and Wallachia had been united, and a foreign prince was on the throne. Neither the suzerain power nor the protectors had been able to prevent Romanian moves toward greater autonomy. In internal affairs a constitutional government had been established, and attempts, at least, had been made to meet the peasant problems. In these years the principal supporter of the Principalities in foreign affairs had been France. Its defeat in 1871 was to have important consequences for the future. In fact, no other power was subsequently to assume a similar attitude of assistance and patronage.

CONCLUSION: THE BALKAN NATIONAL
REGIMES

By the 1860s national governments had thus been established in four areas. The single fully independent state was Greece. Serbia and the Danubian Principalities were still under Ottoman sovereignty, although this status involved little more than the payment of a tribute and some other minor obligations in regard to internal affairs. The position of Montenegro was unique. Despite the fact that the state was generally recognized as part of the Ottoman Empire, the Porte had no control over Montenegrin internal affairs and could not collect a tribute. In foreign policy the Balkan governments acted in an equally independent manner. The Ottoman foreign ministry was still in theory supposed to handle the international relations of the entire empire, but in practice the Balkan states had regular and direct contact with other governments.

In their internal development the new national regimes tended to follow the same general pattern and to face similar difficulties. In each state the centralized bureaucratic monarchy was considered the best form of government. Political control was thus shifted from the village communities and the regional divisions to the capital city. Here the struggle to control the central authority, and with it the administrative network, dominated the scene. The major conflict was that between the executive and the legislative branches of government, that is, between the prince and his supporters, on the one hand, and the groups who were excluded from power, on the other. The opposition first demanded the establishment of councils or assemblies of notables to check the power of the executive. Later the idea of a representative assembly and constitutional government was introduced. The vocabulary of the liberal and democratic movements of Europe was used, but in fact the issue was whether a strong ruler or an oligarchy should run the country. The average peasant did not have a direct political role in the state except as a revolutionary fighter.

Domestic controversies involved not only this conflict between the ruler and the notables, but also the struggle for political power among the prominent men who joined competing factions or parties. Some organizations were formed around a strong leader, whereas others were based on issues, such as support or opposition to the prince, or questions of domestic reform. Victory in an election meant more than the triumph of a man or an idea. It gave the winning party the control of the bureaucracy and thus of the appointments to major posts, which in turn allowed access to sources of real profit. Much has been said about the corruption of the Ottoman political system. The Christian states were to follow in the same path. It should first be emphasized that all governments are to a degree corrupt; the problem in the Balkans was that this aspect of political life limited and weakened the entire society to a notable extent.

When discussing corruption in office, it must be remembered that many practices that were not acceptable in Western Europe were regarded in the Balkans not only as correct, but in some instances as admirable. For example, nepotism was a standard practice. It was thought normal for a man to appoint members of his family to high offices when he gained power; it was a sign of his attachment and loyalty to those closest to him. Similarly, he was expected to reward friends and supporters. The assignment of public posts on the basis of political patronage rather than merit caused little violent outrage. Once in office, such officials regularly followed the Ottoman practices and took advantage of their positions. Again, many of their activities were accepted. Payments for services rendered were not regarded as unusual. The term *bakshish* covered both outright bribes and what the Western European would regard as tips. Officials in the lower branches of the bureaucracy were often so miserably paid that they had to augment their incomes through these practices. The total effect was unfortunate. Balkan states were not only impoverished, but also badly administered.

The Ottoman government, as we have seen, attempted to halt the disintegration of its empire by a policy of reform. By the 1870s, if not long before, it was clear that the major aim of these changes, the reconciliation of the Balkan people still under direct Ottoman rule, could not be accomplished. The attraction offered by the national idea was too strong. Moreover, the leaders in Greece and the autonomous principalities had regularly used real and invented Ottoman horrors to back their own position. The concept of a "Turkish yoke" became an integral part of national mythology and official propaganda. The constant emphasis on this theme served to influence the population under Ottoman administration and to obscure or draw attention away from the defects of the Balkan governments.

The high degree of interference by the great powers has been emphasized in the preceding pages. These practices were legal and based on international treaties. Russia had the right to intervene in the Principalities and Serbia until 1856; the three-power protectorate over Greece remained theoretically in effect until 1923. In addition, Austria and France could speak for the Catholics and Russia for the Orthodox of the peninsula, although what this protection entailed was never clearly outlined. After 1856 all of the signatories of the Treaty of Paris were guarantors of the Balkan states, but again no definition of what this involved was attempted. In any event, the major powers, Russia, Austria, France, and Britain, did take a decisive role in determining the fate of the Balkan nations. They not only exerted control over foreign relations, but entered with enthusiasm into local politics. Each consulate had its clients. This intervention on every level was not evenhanded. It seriously interfered with the Ottoman ability to run the empire, and it became a major factor in the relations of the ruler in each country with opposition politicians and with the Porte.

6

The national issue in the
Habsburg Empire

THE HABSBURG EMPIRE AFTER 1815:
THE HUNGARIAN PROBLEM

A FTER THE CONGRESS OF VIENNA the Habsburg government was again in a favorable position in international affairs, but most of the domestic problems remained unsolved. In the eighteenth century, as we have seen, the principal opposition both to the establishment of a strong autocratic monarchy and to reforms of any kind had come from the nobility, with their base of power in the provinces. They defended their privileged position on the grounds of historic rights and traditions. The French Revolution had deeply frightened this group. During the long period of warfare it had shown itself more willing to cooperate with the court and accept a central direction, but with the return of peace the former attitude of criticism and resistance was again adopted.

The major challenge to Habsburg authority was to come, however, from another direction. The doctrines of the French Revolution continued to have an appeal to certain sections of the population, for instance, members of the professional classes, the lower gentry, the non-Catholic church leaders, and some merchants, artisans, and students. These people were educated and aware of general European conditions, but they had no political power. They were to support programs calling for the introduction of representative institutions and a guarantee of civil rights. They were also to espouse national programs strongly. In other words, their goals and activities resembled closely those of their contemporaries in the Balkan states.

Throughout the century the Habsburg government was to remain continually on the defensive in domestic and international affairs. To understand the repeated retreats made in this period it is important to recall the basic nature of the state. As in the eighteenth century, the monarchy remained a collection of lands united by a dynasty that had control of the army and the bureaucracy and that could ally with various other political elements. The Habsburg government was still largely dependent on the provinces and their diets for financial support and recruits for the imperial army. To maintain control the Habsburg leaders had to accomplish a juggling act among the various interests, both national and social, within the empire. They had to ally with those groups whose support was essential and to maintain a balance among the political opponents – in other words, to follow a divide-and-rule policy.

We have seen how both the Ottoman Empire and the Balkan states became in the nineteenth century centralized monarchies with strong bureaucracies. At the time of Maria Theresa and Joseph II, reforms had been made in this direction, but the provincial, class, and national opposition had always been too strong for any great success. Some advances could be made, but the provincial authorities could never be completely subordinated to the central administration. In this struggle with the dissident elements the Habsburg government suffered from the fact that it could not use the popular slogans and catchwords of the day for education and propaganda. Loyalty to the monarch and the church was serving less and less as a principle commanding widespread support. Liberalism and nationalism, the ideals of a large part of the politically active segment of the population, could endanger the monarchy. The government itself could appeal to no individual national group as such. Although German was the preferred language for state affairs, the court did not represent specifically German interests. In fact, in the period under discussion, the principal danger to the empire was to come from the growing power of Prussia in the German states and the attraction of German liberalism within the empire. German liberal and national movements, if brought to their logical conclusion, would mean the end of Habsburg rule and possibly the dissolution of the state. There could, of course, be no "Habsburg," any more than there could be an "Ottoman," nationalism in the true sense of the word.

The solution that the government adopted to deal with these problems was simply to attempt to maintain the status quo as long as possible. When this endeavor failed completely in 1848, an opposite approach was adopted and experiments were made with different systems of political organization. The weakness here was that political adjustment and reform require a period of peace and stability in international affairs. From 1848 to 1866, the crucial years for the settlement of its internal problems, the monarchy was faced with continual challenges abroad. Many of these, involving national movements in neighboring states, had repercussions within the monarchy.

After the Congress of Vienna, as before, Clemens von Metternich was the chief architect of Habsburg foreign policy. In internal affairs he was not a centralist. He regarded the empire as a federation of historic provinces, each with its own customs and traditions that should be preserved. Essentially a man of the eighteenth century, he respected historic rights, but he denounced the revolutionary principles of the equality of individuals and nations. Although his influence on Habsburg internal policy was never as great as on international relations, he recognized the close links between the domestic and the foreign policy of any state. He thus felt strongly about preventing the accession to power of revolutionary governments in regions of importance to Habsburg interests. He supported the close cooperation of the European powers, in particular Austria, Russia, and Prussia within the bounds of the Holy Alliance, and their intervention in the internal affairs of other states when the legitimate authorities were threatened by revolutionary activity. Like Alexander I and Nicholas I, he was willing to send the Habsburg army to restore or protect a ruler whose position was endangered by revolutionaries using methods of force and violence.

Until 1870 the principal Habsburg concern centered on events in the German and Italian lands. The protection of Habsburg interests in these regions was the main aim of foreign policy, and Balkan and Eastern affairs usually were distinctly secondary in importance. The generally negative Habsburg attitude in the Eastern Question and the desire not to become involved in the Balkan controversies reflected this attitude; Habsburg neutrality in the Crimean War, for instance, was made necessary at least in part by conditions in Italy. The Habsburg diplomats took a more active role in the negotiations over the Danubian Principalities, because of the effects that any changes in this region might have on the Romanian population of the empire.

In 1835 Francis I died, to be succeeded after much controversy by his eldest son, Ferdinand, but this monarch did not have the mental ability to govern. The state, whose main unifying element was the dynasty, thus had at its head an incompetent emperor, with the actual authority transferred to the ministers and other members of the Habsburg family. The chief problems that had to be met at this point were the rising demands for a settlement of the peasant land problem and the increased dangers from Hungarian nationalism.

The major social problem of the monarchy was the discontent of the peasantry. Although conditions differed widely, in many areas even the reforms of the enlightened despots had not been put into effect. The situation was becoming increasingly unsatisfactory from the point of view of both the peasant and the progressive elements among the large landholders. Peasant attitudes in particular were changing. There was less inclination to believe that God had assigned each individual a role in life and that people should fulfill their functions without complaint. As in the Balkan lands, the peasant in the monarchy wanted to end all feudal dues and services and to obtain full ownership of a definite plot of land. He had ways of expressing his feelings: peasant revolts had been common in the past, and more passive tactics were also employed. Often sick chickens and rotten produce were sent to fulfill feudal obligations; the peasant assigned to robot tasks might loaf on the job.

The nobility too was discontented with the agricultural situation. Some disliked or were bored by their feudal duties, such as holding manorial courts and providing local administration. Others lived in dread of massive peasant uprisings like that of Horia in the previous century. The more enlightened among them wished to extract greater profits from their estates. Following the example of their class in Britain and Prussia, they sought to gain full control of their lands and farm them with wage labor. They were perfectly willing to end the robot, but they wanted to be indemnified for any losses, with the state taking the responsibility. For the noble the ideal solution to the agrarian problem would have been the full emancipation of the peasant, with the ownership of the land remaining in the noble's hands.

The agricultural situation reached a state of crisis in the late 1840s, with bad harvests in 1845, 1846, and 1847. Even before 1848 some peasants were refusing to fulfill their obligations. As a class they remained extremely weak. There were no organized groups and no recognized leaders. The future revolutions were to be led by members of the middle class or the gentry, whose programs called for liberal and national reforms whose implementation would put them in power. They claimed to talk for the "nation" and the "people," but the reforms desired by the majority of the peasants were either of low priority or tacked onto the revolutionary programs, if they were included at all.

The strongest opposition on a national basis faced by the Habsburg government in this period came from Hungary. It was recognized in Vienna that the Austrian position in the German and the Italian lands could not be maintained with a militant, discontented Hungary at the rear. Moreover, the empire needed financial support and soldiers from Hungary. The Hungarian leadership was always fully aware of the strength of its position. From the end of the seventeenth century, when the Hungarian territories were finally freed from Ottoman control, emphasis had regularly been placed on the provincial and historical rights of the lands of the crown of St. Stephen. The nobility, as the political nation, had led the resistance to the central authority. It showed a strong determination to maintain control over all the regions that had been a part of historic Hungary, although the special position of Croatia was recognized.

Whereas previously the Hungarian leadership had been feudal and aristocratic, in the nineteenth century another group, primarily from the small landowners, or gentry, and the middle class, was to play an increasingly important role in national life. Strongly influenced by the ideology of the French Revolution, the new leaders used the vocabulary of this movement in their attacks on the autocratic Habsburg government. In their relations with the non-Hungarian nationalities, their attitude was quite different. It is important to emphasize that the Hungarians themselves were divided between moderates, like Stephen Széchenyi, who favored cooperation with Vienna and a limited reform program, and radicals, best exemplified by Lajos Kossuth. Born of a Slovak father and a German mother, Kossuth supported a radical political program that called, on the one hand, for individual liberties, the abolition of special noble privileges, and peasant emancipation and, on the other, for Hungarian national predominance. This position, which was to be the basis of the revolutionary demands in 1848, had extremely negative implications for the other nationalities in the Hungarian crownlands. The Hungarian liberals offered them a regime based on liberty and equality, but on an individual basis and on the condition that they accept Magyar national supremacy. Like the Ottoman attitude of complete acceptance of the Christian convert to Islam, that of the Hungarian radical was one of willingness to receive as an equal citizen any member of another national group who would learn his language and adopt the culture and customs associated with it. Some revolutionaries were to regard it as treason if an individual supported his unique national interests in a controversy with the Hungarian authorities.

A very complicated game was thus being played in the Habsburg lands. Hungarian radicals stood for their unique national rights in the struggles against the centralizing endeavors of Vienna, but they worked for Hungarian domination in their own lands. The Habsburg statesmen, with a much weaker national basis than their opponents, feared Hungarian liberal agitation because of its effect on the other people in the monarchy. They knew, nevertheless, that they could not continue to have a major role in European affairs or hope to hold their empire together without a cooperative Hungary. This struggle had, of course, direct effects on the South Slav lands and Transylvania. In theory it should have given the national leaders in these regions the opportunity to play between the two rivals and extract the maximum benefits. Although such a policy was attempted at times, it was often not wisely conducted. As will be shown, in most controversies it was the Hungarian leadership that was able to control the situation, and with a realistic and clever attitude, to gain its major objectives.

CROATIA AND SLAVONIA: THE ILLYRIAN MOVEMENT

After 1815, in the Habsburg lands with which we are principally concerned, Vienna had under its jurisdiction the Slovenian lands, Dalmatia, Transylvania, and the Military Frontier zones. Croatia and Slavonia, with certain autonomous provincial institutions, were part of the Hungarian crownlands. The Romanian and Serbian populations of the Banat and southern Hungary were under direct Hungarian administration. The position of Croatia had been weakened, it will be remembered, when in 1790 the local assembly, the sabor, had voluntarily surrendered a great deal of authority to the Hungarian diets, which met either in Buda or in Bratislava and which included only a few Croatian representatives. Financial control lay in their hands. As in the eighteenth century, the Croatian administration was headed by a ban, appointed by the Hungarian Chancellery in Vienna, which was the major administrative office for the Hungarian lands.

The predominant class in Croatia was still the landed nobility. It, however, provided no strong national leadership. The upper nobility had a majority of Italian, German, and Hungarian families, and it was cosmopolitan in its views.

This attitude was shared by the lower nobility, which was primarily Croatian, but was more concerned with its position as a privileged class than with defending Croatian national rights. As elsewhere in the empire, this latter group dominated the local government and provided the membership of the sabor.

In all the lands of the Hungarian crown, the language of administration and education was Latin. Latin had the enormous advantage of being international in the true sense: it was known to educated men throughout Europe, and it was also the language of the Catholic church. Prior to the nineteenth century this linguistic unity made the administration of the Hungarian lands easier. There was a common language of politics and culture. However, Hungarian nationalists now began to press for a change. They wished to replace Latin with Hungarian in government and education. This attitude was a reaction against the use of German by Vienna, but it was not a sentiment that could be shared by the other nationalities. Hungarian was not a world language; it could not compare in any respect with Latin in the literary and cultural horizons that it opened for those who mastered it, nor was it spoken outside Hungary. Moreover, as an Altaic tongue, it was difficult for Slavic, Romance, or Germanic speakers to learn.

At first the Croatian nobility showed little opposition to Hungarian pressure. Because of the large-scale intervention in Italy in the 1820s to suppress the revolutionary movements, Francis I needed to recruit in the Hungarian kingdom. The counties refused to levy troops without directions from the Hungarian diet, which was called into session in 1825 for the first time since 1811. The sabor also met to choose its delegates to this body. The diet used the opportunity to demand the replacement of Latin with Hungarian as the official language. Since they were interested in checking the authority of Vienna, the Zagreb delegation supported this action, as well as the introduction of the study of Hungarian into the educational system. In 1827 and 1830 the sabor approved the learning of Hungarian as a compulsory subject in Croatian schools.

This language decision was to become the major subject of attack by the Croatian national opposition. The membership of this movement was relatively limited. The nobility, as we have seen, was in the majority not nationally minded. There was no specifically Croatian commercial or industrial class. The cities in Croatia and Hungary proper had a strong German element, as well as a mixed population of other nationalities. Croatian national interests were enunciated and defended largely by a group drawn from the educated sections of the population, including men from the lower nobility, the clergy, the professions, and the army. Moreover, as in the Principalities, an important role was taken by the educated youth, who shared many ideas of their generation throughout Europe. Unlike the wealthy Wallachians, the Croatian students could not afford to study in large numbers in Paris. They could, however, attend institutions in Graz and Vienna. Here they came in touch with revolutionary ideologies and, even more important, with romantic nationalism as propounded by German writers such as Herder and by Slovak scholars, in particular P. J. Šafařik and Jan Kollár.

The most important figure among the Croatian intellectuals in this period was Ljudevit Gaj, who was to inaugurate the Illyrian movement. Born in 1809 of a family of German background in a small town north of Zagreb, Gaj as a student in Buda and Graz was immensely influenced by the work of Šafařik and Kollár. He was also brought in touch with the work of Vuk Karadžić, and he came to admire the Serbian songs and poems that were enjoying a vogue among the intellectuals. The objective of many of the scholars of the time was to uncover the Slavic past and establish a unified Slavic culture that could be used to counter claims of preeminence by Hungarians and Germans. As we have seen, all the national movements placed a great emphasis on language and history. Gaj moved in the same direction. Like the Romanians in Transylvania, he sought to link the Croatians with a people who had lived in the area before the Germans and Hungarians. Just as the Romanians used the Dacians and Romans, Gaj claimed that the South Slavs were the descendants of the ancient Illyrians and thus were the original inhabitants of the land. All of those associated with him did not hold this view, and even Gaj later modified his arguments, but the entire program that they supported is known as the Illyrian movement.

Once the term *Illyrian* came into use the question naturally arose what regions this Illyria had included and which people were its contemporary representatives. Gaj himself spoke in vague and romantic terms of lands stretching "from Villach to Varna," which would include Slovenia, Croatia, Serbia, Montenegro, northern Albania, Bulgaria, and southern Hungary. Gaj's major supporter from the nobility, Janko Drašković, wrote that "Illyrians are the descendants of the ancient Illyrians of Greco-Roman times," who were later "broken up into Croatians, Serbs, Slovenes, and Bulgarians."[1] Whatever the boundaries and people included, the chief significance of this program was its claim that all South Slavs were basically one people and that, by implication, they should form a political unit.

Gaj's major direct influence was to be on language. Since he believed in a unified South Slav culture, he wished the differences in language to be minimized as much as possible. First in importance was the question of orthography. Croatian was written with different spellings in the various districts. Gaj favored a Czech system using diacritical marks. Even more important was his adoption of the *štokavian* dialect for the Croatian literary language.[2]

---

1 Quoted in Wayne S. Vucinich, "Croatian Illyrism: Its Background and Genesis," in Stanley B. Winters and Joseph Held, eds., *Intellectual and Social Developments in the Habsburg Empire from Maria Theresa to World War I* (Boulder, Colo.: East European Quarterly, 1975), p. 88.

2 In Vladimir Dedijer et al., *History of Yugoslavia*, trans. Kordija Kveder (New York: McGraw-Hill, 1975), p. 103, n. 1, the following clear explanation of the dialects is given: "The Serbo-Croatian language is divided into three basic dialects according to the form of the interrog-

This form was spoken by all of the Serbs and the great majority of the Croatians, and a common literary language would constitute a bond among them. The choice was entirely logical since this dialect was in general use, and it had a literature. The alternative, the *kajkavian*, was used only in Zagreb and districts to the north of the city, and was a less-developed language. The Croatian language reformers did not face the type of opposition that confronted Karadžić. There was no equivalent of the "Slavo-Serb" literary language, since the Catholic church used Latin.

The Illyrian movement was by far the strongest intellectual current among the Croatians before 1848. Since it was to the interest of Vienna to counter Hungarian activities, the Habsburg authorities at first made no move to hinder the activities of proponents of these ideas. In 1835 Gaj received permission to publish two journals, *Novine Horwatzke* (Croatian News), which appeared twice a week, and *Danica* (Morning Star), a weekly literary supplement. Reading rooms were established and societies formed to propagate the ideas of the movement. From a cultural and intellectual point of view, Illyrianism was a great success. Štokavian was used in the schools, and it did become the Croatian literary language. "Illyrian" could thus be placed in competition with Hungarian.

The activities of Janko Drašković were also important to the movement and to Croatian politics. Educated in France and active in political life, Drašković used the Illyrian conception to assert the independence of Croatia within the framework of the monarchy. He was in favor of the reorganization of the empire into a federation of nations. That he was sent as a representative to the Hungarian diet in 1832 is a reflection of a change of attitude that was taking place toward Hungary.

Instead of cooperating against Vienna, the Croatian members of the diets of 1832–1836, 1839, and 1840 resisted the Hungarians' efforts to impose their language, and they stood strongly for the maintenance of Croatian autonomous rights. They were not able to check the Hungarian actions themselves, but the Habsburg government vetoed the offending legislation. The Croatian agitation naturally disturbed the Hungarian politicians. To appease them, Vienna in 1843 forbade the use of the word *Illyria*. The adherents of the movement simply switched to the word *national* and continued their activities.

The Illyrian movement was to involve much wider issues than the question of Croatian relations with the Habsburg and Hungarian authorities. It was a Croatian-sponsored program, but its basis was Yugoslav; that is, it embraced all of the South Slav people and not merely the Croats. As a tactic to oppose

ative pronoun *what*: kajkavian (what = kaj), čakavian (what = ča), and štokavian (what = što). Kajkavian is spoken today in northwestern parts of Croatia, čakavian in the northern coast area and on the Adriatic islands, štokavian in all other regions. Štokavian is the basis of modern standard Serbo-Croatian. Štokavian has three subdialects according to the pronunciation of the original Slavic vowel represented by the letter *jat*."

Hungarian and German influences, this direction had its advantages, but to be effective it needed the cooperation of the Serbs and Slovenes. Their reaction was to be prophetic for the future and to bring out the fundamental weaknesses of a Yugoslav orientation. Most Slovenian intellectual leaders from the first rejected the idea. With a developing cultural life of their own, they did not want to associate with a movement with its center in the Hungarian lands. Few Serbs saw any advantages in it in comparison with their own strictly Serbian orientation. Certainly the Illyrian conception had little to offer them. They were proud to be Serbs and Orthodox; why should they be Illyrians? There was no reason to abandon the emphasis on Kosovo and the medieval Serbian kingdom for this mythical ancient basis. Most Serbian nationalists followed the ideas of Karadžić, who believed that all who spoke the štokavian dialect were Serbs. They thus regarded the Croats as schismatic Serbs who had broken away and joined the Catholic church. The question of leadership was also involved; an Illyrian orientation would make Zagreb the center. To nationalistic Serbs the whole movement had the taint of Habsburg expansion and Catholic or Uniate proselytism.

The Illyrian movement, it will be noted, did not use the word *Croat*. In fact, this term tended to be identified with the opposition and with those who supported cooperation with the Hungarians against the Habsburg government on the old basis. The first true political party in Croatia was formed in February 1841 with this program. The Croato-Hungarian Party, whose members were also known as Unionists or Magyrones, stood for a close association with Buda, and they rejected the wider Yugoslav orientation. Other opposition to the Illyrian principles came from those who disliked the new literary language and preferred the kajkavian dialect, or were even willing to accept Hungarian. Some Catholics disliked any close links with the Orthodox Serbs. Members of the old nobility did not approve of the revolutionary principles associated with the movement.

Nevertheless, by 1848 the Illyrian influence was predominant in Croatian cultural activities. In politics its victory was not so complete. Its standpoint was represented by the Illyrian, or National, Party, which was organized in September 1841. Although it was to become the most influential Croatian political organization, an important element in the population still supported a strong union with Hungary. Another party was soon to arise that would challenge the emphasis on Illyrianism or Yugoslavism at the expense of Croatian nationalism.

THE HABSBURG MONARCHY, 1848–1867

From 1848 to 1867 the Habsburg Monarchy was in a period of internal and external crisis. The challenge came from liberal elements within the empire who attacked the absolute monarchy and from the national movements at home and abroad. Within the monarchy the main problem remained Hungary. In Europe German and Italian revolutionaries fought against Habsburg influence and sought to establish unified national states. The attempts of the Habsburg government to deal with this situation affected the political conditions in both Croatia and Transylvania.

The major danger to the continued existence of the Habsburg Empire came in 1848 and was the result of internal rather than external pressures. In January 1848 a revolt broke out in Sicily; in February a major revolution in France forced King Louis Philippe and his government out of power. In March the revolutionary wave engulfed Central Europe and Italy. On March 13 a revolution in Vienna resulted in the formation of a new government and the dismissal of Metternich. The court attempted to meet the situation by issuing a constitution similar to the Belgian, but the revolutionary leaders preferred to draft one of their own. It was thus agreed that a constitutional assembly would be called. The court, feeling endangered, moved to Innsbruck.

The spring and summer of 1848 was a period of intense political activity not only throughout the monarchy, but also in the German and Italian states. The kingdom of Piedmont took the leadership in the Italian peninsula; an all-German parliament, also attended by delegates from the Habsburg Empire, was convened at Frankfurt. Parallel to this German gathering, a Slavic congress was organized in Prague and opened at the beginning of June. Under Czech influence the representatives supported a program of Austroslavism, which called for the reorganization of the monarchy into separate autonomous national units, an action that would strengthen the influence of its Slavic people. The empire was thus not to be dissolved, but transformed into a federation of nations. The meetings were disbanded only a few weeks later by the Habsburg army. Although the Prague congress met but a short time, the Austroslav idea was to remain an alternative solution for the reorganization of the monarchy that was to enjoy support among some Slavic groups.

Despite the fact that a revolutionary regime held power in Vienna, the court retained control over the army. In July the Habsburg forces commanded by General Radetzky defeated the Sardinians at the battle of Custozza. Bohemia was brought under control soon thereafter. Meanwhile, delegates arrived in Vienna for the opening of the constitutional assembly. Under the presidency of Archduke John, this parliament abolished the remaining feudal obligations of the peasantry. With their major demands satisfied, the peasants' interest in further revolutionary activities declined rapidly. In October another revolutionary outbreak forced the court to move to Olmütz; the parliament transferred its meetings to Kremsier. The Habsburg army then marched on Vienna, and by the end of October the imperial forces were in full control of the city. Although Habsburg authority had been reestablished over most of the imperial lands, it was quite apparent that Ferdinand I could not fulfill the duties of emperor in times of crisis. He thus abdicated in December in favor of his nephew Franz Joseph, who was eighteen years old. Actual authority in the government was wielded by Prince Felix Schwarzenberg, under whose intelligent leadership the imperial authority was to be reimposed throughout the Habsburg domains.

Back in control in Vienna, the government had to face the immediate question of the future organization of the empire. The revolutionary events had made clear that a constitution would have to be issued and changes made. The issues to be decided were the familiar ones of choosing between a centralist or a federal form of administration and establishing a balance between the executive and legislative branches of the government. In March 1849 the court produced its own constitution and simply prorogued the Kremsier assembly. The new document provided for a highly centralist regime with a single parliament, common citizenship, and one legal and administrative system for the entire empire. A strong program of civil liberties was also included.

The constitution was particularly damaging to the Hungarian position. The ruler was to be crowned only as emperor of Austria, not also as king of Hungary. The lands of the crown of St. Stephen were divided among the Kingdom of Hungary, the Grand Principality of Transylvania, the Military Frontier, and the Kingdom of Dalmatia, Croatia and Slavonia, as the new territorial divisions were named. Croatia received the port of Rijeka (Fiume) and the possibility of eventually acquiring Dalmatia. The advantages that could be won by the non-Hungarian population of these lands were clear. The constitution took little account of the dangerous situation in the Hungarian regions. In fact, it was a question whether the document could be applied there at all. The Habsburg government had reestablished its authority over the Habsburg lands, it had defeated the revolution in Italy, and it would ultimately regain its former position in the German areas; but the major challenge was to still come from the Hungarian revolutionary regime, which was at the height of its power in the spring of 1849. Its main army, led by General Arthur Görgey, controlled Hungary proper; a second army, under the command of the Polish general Jozef Bem, had defeated the imperial forces and held Transylvania. The Habsburg leaders could not allow the secession of the Hungarian lands. With their loss, the empire would no longer be a great power.

The most successful of the revolutionary movements in the empire was undoubtedly the Hungarian. Although it was finally defeated, it did bring about the formation of a functioning government under a strong leader, Lajos Kossuth, and the organization of a very effective army. Once in control, the revolutionary regime introduced a highly centralized system of administration, but one accompanied by liberal reforms. At first, facing attacks on all sides, the court accepted the new conditions. After October 1848, however, with control again reasserted in its other lands, the Habsburg government turned its attention toward the Hungarian situation. A strong factor in Habsburg favor was the extreme dissatisfaction that the new measures had aroused among the non-Hungarian nationalities. As we shall see in the next section, Vienna was able to rally support from the Croatian, Serbian, and Romanian population. Even with this assistance, the Habsburg army was still unable to defeat the Hungarian forces.

Faced with this situation the court came to a fateful decision. A Russian army, it will be remembered, was stationed in Wallachia and Moldavia, where it had been sent to suppress the revolutionary activities in the Principalities. In January some Russian troops had already undertaken an unsuccessful action in Transylvania against the forces of General Bem. In May 1849 Franz Joseph wrote to Nicholas I and requested a far more extensive intervention. As a result of the tsar's favorable reply, a Russian army of 150,000 men crossed the frontier. By August the Hungarian forces had been defeated and Habsburg rule had been reestablished over all the land of the Hungarian kingdom.

With the end of the Hungarian revolution, the Habsburg government could proceed with the reorganization of the empire. The new system, which was to be in effect from 1849 to 1860, was primarily associated with the name of Alexander Bach, the minister of interior. A German of liberal inclinations, he, like many of his peers, wished to establish an enlightened regime modeled on the ideas of Joseph II. The constitution of 1849 was never put into effect. Instead the state went back to the absolutist pattern, by which the emperor held complete power unchecked by a representative assembly. With the defeat of Hungary, there was no effective opposition left to the adoption of a strongly centralized administrative organization. The empire was divided into districts that were governed by officials appointed from Vienna. The objective was a unitary state whose administration would stand above the nationalities and the historic divisions and would guarantee the same rights to all Habsburg citizens. The same laws and regulations were to be applied throughout the empire. As in the time of Joseph II, the language of government was to be German.

The new arrangement was a particular shock for the Hungarian leadership. Those who had participated in the revolution, of course, had fled the country or had been imprisoned. Many had emigrated to the Ottoman Empire. Over the next years members of this emigration slowly returned to take active roles in the resistance to the Bach regime. Under the new system Hungary was fully incorporated into the empire, with its lands divided into five districts. Hungary, Croatia, Transylvania, the Vojvodina, and the Military Frontier were separate jurisdictions. The county organizations and the diet in Buda, the central organs of Hungarian autonomy, were dissolved. The country was governed by a German-speaking bureaucracy, a great number of whose members were Czech in nationality.

The disasters suffered by the Habsburg Empire during the Bach period were the result more of foreign than of domestic complications. The Austrian position in international relations after the Congress of Vienna had rested on the Holy Alliance, the partnership of Prussia, Austria, and Russia. Although this combination had not always worked well in the Eastern Question, it had fulfilled its main function of stabilizing political conditions on the Continent and protecting its members' interest in partitioned Poland. As we have seen, a Russian army came to the rescue of Vienna in 1849. To the extreme dissatisfaction of Russia, the Habsburg government did not adopt a similarly benevolent attitude toward Russia during the Crimean War. At that time the Habsburg Empire remained neutral, but its actions rather favored Russia's enemies. During the war the primacy of Austrian concerns in the West was again demonstrated. The Habsburg statesmen feared that if they assumed a pro-Russian attitude, the French would raise a revolutionary movement in Italy. The adoption of a neutral policy, however, broke the Holy Alliance, and thus the main dam to national revolutionary activity in Central Europe and Italy was eliminated. In the next years Russia worked in cooperation with France. The first product of this entente, as we have seen, was the union of the Danubian Principalities against strong Austrian opposition. The second, even more serious, was the unification of Italy between 1859 and 1861. Although the empire still held Venetia-Lombardy, it no longer influenced the rest of the peninsula.

The defeat in Italy brought the Bach regime to an end. A centralized system had not created a government strong enough to defend the empire's interests, and other alternatives thus had to be tried. At this point decisions were being made by Franz Joseph and a group of close advisers. The changes were introduced by decree and without much prior warning. In the October Diploma of 1860 a return was made to the former basis of provincial control, and an attempt was made to meet Hungarian grievances. The conditions existing before 1848 were thus reestablished, except that some reforms, in particular peasant emancipation, were retained. A central body, the *Reichsrat* (Imperial Council), was created; its members were nominated by the provincial diets, which, of course, were again functioning. No sooner had this organization been announced than the government again reversed itself. Strong internal opposition to the diploma, particularly from the German Liberals, resulted in the issuance of the February Patent of 1861, which reinstated centralism and made the Reichsrat a real parliament with an upper and lower house. The provincial diets, losing some of their previous rights, now had as their chief function the election of delegates to the central assembly.

From 1861 to 1865 Anton von Schmerling was the principal minister. Although he received the support of some of the national leaderships, he was strongly opposed by the Hungarians. When they refused to send delegates to the Vienna parliament, their diet was dissolved. At the same time, in an effort at appeasement, the government returned the Vojvodina and a section of disputed Croatian territory to Hungarian jurisdiction. Meanwhile, with the Hungarian problem still acute, the probability of a showdown with Prussia over predominance in the German lands was becoming constantly greater. The Habsburg leaders were well aware that they could not risk a war if there was the possibility that complications might arise in Hungary. A settlement here was thus essential for Vienna.

Despite the defeat in 1849, the Hungarian position had remained firm. Moreover, unlike the other nationalities, the Hungarians had demonstrated their ability to organize a strong revolutionary government and to bring an army into the field. Under pressure from the international situation, the Austrian government therefore commenced discussions with the Hungarian moderates, led by Ferenc Deák. In 1865 a ministry under Count Richard Belcredi was appointed and given the task of reaching an agreement. Deák was willing to accept a settlement based on a personal union of the Hungarian lands with the rest of the empire, with a common policy for foreign affairs and defense, but with the complete control of the administration of the kingdom left in the hands of a national government responsible to a Hungarian parliament. In 1866 the Habsburg army was defeated by Prussia, which then proceeded with the organization of the North German Confederation. The Habsburg Empire was excluded from influence in German affairs. This second major defeat in less than a decade made inevitable the empire's acceptance of the Hungarian demands.

The Ausgleich (Compromise) of 1867 represented a major reorganization of the empire that was to last until the end of the monarchy in 1918. An expression of the moderate Hungarian program, the document divided the empire into two distinct political units (see Map 23). The lands of the Hungarian crown were henceforth to be administered as a centralized state under the provisions of the March Laws of 1848, which had been passed in Pest during the revolution. Franz Joseph was recognized as king, but his position in Hungary was that of a limited, constitutional monarch. The two sections of the empire were to have only three common ministries: Foreign Affairs, Defense, and Finance, the last of which would have jurisdiction only over the expenses connected with the other two. Delegations from the reorganized Reichsrat and the Hungarian parliament were to meet regularly to consider common problems. A customs union, which was to be renewed every ten years, was also agreed upon. To reflect this fundamental change, the state was to be known as Austria-Hungary. The name *Hungary* was used to refer to all of the lands under its authority; the choice for the other half was not as obvious. At the time, the term *the Kingdoms and Lands represented in the Reichsrat* was used officially. The names *Cisleithania* for the areas under Vienna and *Transleithania* for Hungary, based on the line of the river Leitha, have also been adopted by some authors. For the rest of this narrative, the name *Austria* will refer exclusively to the non-Hungarian half of the empire. Franz Joseph's title was king in Hungary and emperor in Austria. Vienna was the capital of Austria and the home of the joint ministries. In 1872 Buda was united with Pest, and Budapest was henceforth the Hungarian capital.

The Ausgleich was an enormous Hungarian victory, although it did not

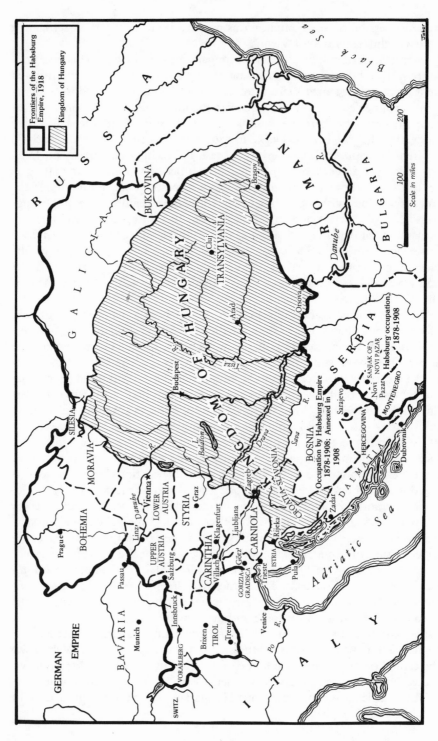

Map 23. Austria-Hungary, 1867–1918

fulfill the expectations of those who had sought complete independence. In practice, however, there was not to be an equal division of power. In the next years the Hungarian government was able to present a united front on all major issues. In contrast, the Austrian section underwent a series of internal crises that weakened its ability to deal with Budapest. The predominant influence of Hungarian interests in foreign affairs was to be amply illustrated in the next years. Thus the Hungarian section, with a smaller population, of which only about a half were actually Magyar in nationality, was able to exert a disproportionate influence over the life of the entire state. The Ausgleich, of course, was to have a devastating effect on the political life of the South Slavs and Romanians, particularly those living in the lands of the Hungarian crown.

CROATIA, SLAVONIA, AND THE VOJVODINA, 1848–1868

The years 1847 and 1848 marked the culmination of the Croatian and Hungarian conflict over language. There was also a dispute over the extent of the territory that should fall under Croatian jurisdiction. The sabor was dominated by the National Party, which held Yugoslav or Illyrian views. Its immediate program called for the unification of Dalmatia, the Military Frontier, and the port of Rijeka with Croatia and Slavonia under an autonomous administration. In addition, the party wanted a bishopric established in Zagreb and a university. In 1847 the sabor declared Croatian the official language. Meanwhile, the diet in Budapest was proceeding along the same nationalistic path. Whereas the sabor was seeking to widen the territorial limits of its control, the diet wished to restrict Croatian authority even in the lands that had previously been recognized as Croatian. In 1847 another law sought to impose Hungarian as the language of government. Its provisions stated that Latin could be used within Croatia, but all dealings with Budapest had to be in Hungarian, which was also made a compulsory subject in the schools. The Croatian language was to have no place in official correspondence between Zagreb and Budapest. The sabor and the diet were thus proceeding in diametrically opposite directions.

Before the revolution broke out, the court had attempted to maintain a balance between the disputing parties. In March 1848, when Vienna was under revolutionary control and the court was forced to leave the city, the Habsburg officials were compelled to assent to Hungarian demands. As long as the army was tied down in Italy, they had no means of assuring obedience in any of the imperial territories. Although the central government was thus paralyzed, the non-Hungarian population of the Hungarian kingdom organized both in favor of revolutionary ideals and against the Hungarian actions. The Habsburg government accordingly had alternate centers of power with which it could cooperate.

Simultaneously, with the rebellions in Buda and Vienna, the revolutionary fever took control in Zagreb. The basic national program remained the same, but the demand was expressed for further liberal reforms, in particular an end to feudal obligations. The movement in Croatia was aided by the services of an able leader. In March Baron Josip Jelačić, a colonel in the Military Frontier, was named by the court as ban of Croatia; he was at the same time raised in rank to general and put in charge of the Military Frontier. His appointment as ban was accepted by the sabor. Jelačić first directed the Croatian officials not to follow any instructions except those issued in Zagreb, and in April relations with the Hungarian government were severed. A proponent of the Illyrian idea, Jelačić cooperated with the National Party. He also organized a national guard and called for new elections for the sabor, which was to meet in June.

Meanwhile, similar events were occurring in the regions inhabited by Serbs. Meetings were held in centers such as Sremski Karlovci and Novi Sad, which had a large Serbian population. The demands remained what they had been in the previous century: the recognition of Serbian as an official language, a position of equality with the Catholics for the Orthodox church, and annual meetings of the church assemblies. The latter, it will be remembered, contained strong lay elements and concerned themselves with matters of general interest to the Serbian population. As before, the Serbian program called for the assignment of a definite geographical jurisdiction and the appointment of a military commander, or vojvoda. In May a national assembly attended by several thousand people met in Sremski Karlovci. The delegates chose Josip Rajačić as patriarch and Stephen Šupljikac as vojvoda. They further sought the recognition of a national territorial unit, consisting of the Banat, Bačka, Baranja, and a part of Srem, known collectively as the Vojvodina. The general area, according to the military census of 1851, had a population of 407,000 Serbs, 395,000 Romanians, 325,000 Germans, 241,000 Hungarians, and 32,000 others. The total number of Serbs in the empire was given as 1,438,000.[3] The Serbian program called for the close association of the Vojvodina with the Croatian state and an autonomous position in relation to Hungary. Naturally these claims were completely unacceptable to the Hungarian revolutionary leaders, who tended to see the Serbs as intruders on their historic territory. More encouragement, however, came from Vienna. In December the new emperor, Franz Joseph, approved the appointments of both Rajačić and Šupljikac and gave assurances concerning the establishment of a national organization for the Serbs. Clashes had already begun in June between Serbian and Hungarian bands. During the revolutionary period there was little fighting in Croatian territories, but the Vojvodina was to be devastated.

---

3 C. A. Macartney, *The Habsburg Empire, 1790–1918* (London: Weidenfeld & Nicolson, 1968), p. 447.

In June the newly elected sabor met in Zagreb and proceeded to enact a program of liberal reform, including the abolition of all feudal obligations. Representatives were sent to the Slav Congress at Prague; the Austroslav views expressed there received Croatian support. The sabor fully approved of the reorganization of the empire on a national and federal basis. Its major goal was the revival of the Triune Kingdom, with territories that would include Croatia, Slavonia, Dalmatia, Rijeka, and Medjumurje, a piece of territory that had formerly been a part of Hungary. Strong support was given to the principle of cooperation with the Vojvodina Serbs, and the leaders of the two movements worked closely together. The question of relations with Vienna and Buda remained; negotiations were carried on with both. The Croatian leaders were willing to come to an agreement with Hungary, but only on the basis of political equality. They demanded from Buda essentially what the Hungarians were seeking from Vienna. In both cases, the objective was the establishment of a close relationship but with guarantees of complete autonomy in internal affairs. Croatian representatives carried on discussions with the Habsburg government on the same basis.

By September negotiations had broken down between Zagreb and Buda on the one hand, and Vienna and Buda, on the other. Imperial troops, led by Jelačić, crossed the Drava River into Hungarian territory. In October the Habsburg government declared the Hungarian diet dissolved and appointed Jelačić commander of the army operating in the area. These events brought about the complete victory of the radical element in Hungary; Kossuth took full control. When the October revolt broke out in Vienna, Jelačić was forced to suspend his operations in Hungary so that his troops could take part in the recapture of the city. The subsequent failure of the Habsburg army to subdue the Hungarian rebellion and the entrance of the Russian army have been described previously. In this campaign Croatian, Serbian, and Romanian soldiers joined with Russians and Austrians against the Hungarian revolutionaries, who were supported by a large Polish contingent.

By the end of the revolutionary period the Croatian leaders thus saw defeated the Hungarian attempts to impose unity. The sabor had enacted reform measures of which by far the most important concerned peasant emancipation. In April 1848 in Buda and in August in Vienna, laws were approved concerning the peasants. Similar measures were enacted by the sabor in June. All of the obligations of the peasant to the lord, including the tithes, labor dues, and other payments, were abolished. The peasants were to obtain allotments of land. An indemnity was paid, set at the amount that it was estimated the lord would have received over a period of twenty years; this standard had been used regularly in other regions. The government was to compensate the landlords and then to collect payments from the peasants in installments over twenty years. Pasture and forest lands were also divided. The lord held his assigned sections of the estate in full ownership; the peasant's share was given to the communal associations. The nobility and the church were henceforth to be liable to taxation on the same basis as the peasantry. This settlement was not implemented, of course, without much controversy. The major difficulty lay in determining the amount of compensation to be given the individual noble.

After the defeat of the Hungarian revolution with their assistance, both the Croats and the Serbs expected to be rewarded with the granting of extended autonomous rights and the recognition of the territorial divisions to which they laid claim, that is, the lands of the Triune Kingdom and the Vojvodina. Instead, they, like the defeated Hungarians, were forced to accept the Bach system. Croatia was divided into six districts whose officials were appointed by Vienna; the sabor did not meet. All vestige of Croatian autonomy disappeared. Jelačić remained as ban until his death in 1859, but his title was largely honorary. The administration was in the hands of German-speaking officials who were sometimes Croatian but often German, Czech, or Slovene. The Austrian legal system and civil code were enforced. Nevertheless, some advances were made in this period. The measures concerning the peasantry were carried out; Zagreb once again became a bishopric. Rijeka was assigned to Croatia, but Dalmatia and the Military Frontier retained their former status. In 1849 the Vojvodina became a crownland, with Franz Joseph taking the position of grand vojvoda. It too was governed directly from Vienna.

The establishment of the centralized system naturally displeased almost all the Croatian political leaders. They had received nothing for their support of the monarchy in 1848 and 1849. A succinct remark, made by a Hungarian to a Croat, summed up the situation: "What we received as a punishment was bestowed upon you as a reward."[4] At this time political alignments were formed that were to last until 1914. The former parties, the National Party and the Unionists, or Magyrones, remained active. The first was to split on the issue of cooperation with Vienna, but the Unionists remained firm in their support of Hungary on about any terms. In 1861 another group, the Party of Rights (meaning Croatian state rights), which stood for Croatian nationalism in the true sense of the word, was formed under the leadership of Ante Starčević and Eugen Kvaternik. As we have seen, the National Party believed in South Slav cooperation and placed Croats, Serbs, and Slovenes on an equal plane. The Party of Rights, in contrast, emphasized the historic rights of Croatia and opposed the Yugoslav orientation of the Nationalists. Starčević, a former adherent of the Illyrian idea, argued that all South Slavs were really Croatians; the Serbs and Slovenes had broken away from the main body of the nation. His views thus paralleled some Serbian contentions that Croatians were simply apostate Serbs. Apart from these extreme opinions, which were not held by all the members, the Party of Rights wished a

---

4 Quoted in Robert A. Kann, *The Multinational Empire: Nationalism and National Reform in the Habsburg Monarchy, 1848–1918*, 2 vols. (New York: Columbia University Press, 1950), I, 126.

permanent partnership neither with Vienna nor with Buda. At best, it would accept union only through a common monarch.

The most influential figure supporting the Illyrian position at the time was Bishop Josip Strossmayer, who worked closely with Franjo Rački. Appointed bishop of Djakovo in 1849, Strossmayer took a prominent part in Catholic activities. A strong believer in South Slav cooperation, he preferred the term *Yugoslav* to *Illyrian*. As a leader of the National Party, he played a major role in formulating the decisions that were made at this point. In 1861, it will be remembered, the February Patent established a central assembly, the Reichs-rat, to which delegates from the provinces were to be sent. The Hungarian diet refused to participate in this parliament. The ban of Croatia, Josip Šokčević, tried to win Croatian support for the new organization of the empire. As might be expected, the Unionists, who followed the Hungarian lead, and the Party of Rights, which wanted a fully autonomous or independent state, opposed cooperation. The National Party divided on the question. One group, under Ivan Mažuranić, favored the sending of representatives to the Reichs-rat if an agreement could be made that would add Dalmatia and the Military Frontier to Croatia. The majority of the party, however, under Strossmayer's leadership, preferred to refuse participation. In 1863 Mažuranić formed the Independent National Party, which supported a policy of agreement with Vienna. In 1865, however, the original National Party won the elections to the sabor. On instructions from Vienna, this assembly nominated a delega-tion that attempted unsuccessfully to negotiate a new political relationship with its Hungarian counterparts.

Meanwhile, the discussions that were to result in the Ausgleich com-menced between the Habsburg government and the Hungarian representa-tives. In the final agreement, as has been seen, Hungary demanded and suc-ceeded in acquiring the inclusion of Croatia in its part of the Dual Monarchy. Croatian representatives were not seriously consulted on this decision, which decidedly shaped the political future of the country. Henceforth, the Hun-garian authorities would have the commanding position in any further ne-gotiations.

The significance for Croatia of the altered relationship between Vienna and Buda was soon made obvious. In 1867 the newly appointed ban, Levin Rauch, who was also the leader of the Unionist Party, took measures to suppress the activities of both branches of the National Party and of all of those who would not accept the situation. Elections were then held for the sabor. Using the means in his control to influence the vote, Rauch was able to assure that the Unionists won fifty-two out of sixty-six seats. When the opposition del-egates refused to recognize the results of this fraudulent election, the ban simply appointed other men to take their places. The sabor next appointed a twelve-member delegation that was sent to Buda to negotiate with a similar committee chosen by the Hungarian diet.

Despite its strong position, the Hungarian government was willing to recognize some Croatian rights to political autonomy. The Nagodba (Agreement or Compromise), negotiated in 1868, established Croatia as a separate political unit within the Kingdom of Hungary with autonomous jurisdiction over its internal affairs, police, justice, religion, and education. The Croatian language could be used in domestic administration and in the Hungarian parliament when joint problems were being discussed. Forty Croatian deputies were to be members of that body. Other provisions, however, were not so favorable. The powers and position of the ban were to prove particularly critical. This official was to be appointed by the king on the nomination of the minister-president of Hungary, a procedure which guaranteed that he would represent Hungarian interests. Moreover, he had the right to prorogue the sabor and to govern until the next election. The Hungarian government also retained a strong control over Croatian economic and commercial affairs, including banking, railroads, weights, measures, coinage, and the conclusion of commercial treaties. The territorial arrangements similarly did not coincide with Croatian desires. Croatia did acquire the lands of the Military Frontier in 1881, but Hungary took Rijeka, and Dalmatia remained under Austrian rule. In September 1868 both the sabor, with its Unionist majority, and the Hungarian parliament accepted the settlement.

As can be imagined, the Nagodba was greeted with violent opposition within Croatia. Only the Unionists supported it. In October 1871 Kvaternik organized an uprising in Rakovica and was killed during its suppression. There was little, in fact, that the Croatian leaders could do. Both the Austrian and the Hungarian governments approved of the agreement. The intensity of the reaction, however, influenced the Hungarian authorities to agree to make some revisions. Another delegation, consisting of six Unionists and six members of the National Party, which included Strossmayer, asked for alterations that included the nomination of the ban by the king without the intervention of the Hungarian government, the recognition of the right of the sabor to send five representatives to the joint Austro-Hungarian delegations, and the assurance that Croatia would administer its own finances. None of the major demands were met, although some concessions were made on lesser matters. Disillusioned, Strossmayer retired from active political life. He nevertheless remained bishop of Djakovo, and he was to wield great personal influence until his death in 1905.

The political evolution of Croatia, Slavonia, and the Vojvodina after 1848 was thus to the detriment of the South Slav population. The conditions in Dalmatia and Slovenia, which remained under Austrian administration, will be discussed in a later section, but here too there had been few advances for the national movements. In the lands of the Hungarian crown one national idea, and one only, achieved an astounding success. From crushing defeat in 1849 the Hungarian leaders were able to guide their nation to a position of partnership in a reorganized empire by 1867. The new situation was unfavorable not only for the Slavic population, but also for the majority of the inhabitants of Transylvania.

TRANSYLVANIA

Before 1848 Transylvania was administered through the special chancellery in Vienna. The Habsburg government appointed the governor and the chief officials. The diet, which was not convened between 1810 and 1834, was made up of representatives from the privileged section of the population and members appointed by the imperial authorities. The former system of the three recognized nations, the Saxon, the Hungarian, and the Szekler, and the four accepted religions, Catholic, Lutheran, Calvinist, and Unitarian, continued. In the diet the consent of all three nations had to be obtained for a law to pass.

Despite the fact that they formed the majority of the inhabitants of Transylvania, the Romanians continued to have no official representation in the government. A population composed largely of peasants, they were excluded by their social class as well as by their nationality. As was the case with the Orthodox Serbs in the Banat, the national leadership was in the hands of the clergy, which was divided between the Orthodox and the Uniate hierarchies. Although the two churches had certain points of friction, they were able to cooperate a great deal on the political and cultural level. In the eighteenth century, as we have seen, the cultural leadership was in the hands of the Uniates. It was to pass to the Orthodox largely because of the efforts of Bishop Andreiu Şaguna, who was to play a major role in the Romanian national movements.

The hold of religious institutions on Romanian cultural life was the natural result of the fact that the churches provided most of the education available to the Romanians. The church trained the teachers for the elementary schools; higher education was available at the Uniate school in Blaj and the Orthodox seminary in Sibiu. The only Romanian-language publishing house was run by the Uniate church at Blaj. The emphasis in religious training was, of course, not nationalism but religion and the duties of a good citizen. The central position of the churches and their national leadership was recognized by the Habsburg government, who dealt with them as the agents of the Romanian people.

In the 1830s and 1840s this monopoly was challenged by a rising group, consisting mainly of middle-class intellectuals, such as teachers, lawyers, civil servants, doctors, artisans, and merchants. They were critical of the church leadership, and most were liberal and national in political conviction. Like their contemporaries among other Balkan people, they were convinced of the importance of language as the true expression of a national culture. Placing an emphasis on the Latin base of Romanian, they favored removing Slavic and other foreign words and using the Latin rather than the Cyrillic alphabet. Although they accepted the concept of the Roman origins of their people and the continuity of residence in Transylvania, they did not rely wholly on historical arguments. Following contemporary liberal doctrine, they argued that since the Romanians were the majority of the population of Transylvania and provided the most taxes and recruits for the army, they should have adequate representation in the political institutions. Their concrete demands went beyond recognition as a fourth privileged nation. They wanted, in addition, a position in the government proportionate to the size of their population. Their demands were thus revolutionary and struck at the aristocratic and feudal basis of Transylvanian society. These views soon appeared in print. In 1838 George Barițiu and his collaborators began publication in Brașov of the *Gazeta de Transilvania* (Transylvanian Journal) and its literary supplement, *Foaia pentru minte, inima și literatura* (Paper for Mind, Heart and Literature). These became the chief vehicles for the expression of the opinions of the intellectuals.

It is difficult to judge the size of this group, which was to be very influential in the future. There were about two million Romanians in Hungary proper and Transylvania at this time. In 1838 there were only about five hundred subscribers to *Gazeta de Transilvania*; there was little change by 1860.[5] Yet these men were to form the political and cultural leadership for the rest of century. At first they shared this position with the Orthodox clergy. The cooperation between the intellectual and religious leaders was not always easy. The intellectuals were not anticlerical, but they did want some changes in church management. They believed that the lay members should have a stronger influence in the administration, and they wanted to introduce more nationally oriented topics, such as Romanian literature and history, into the educational system. They also wished the Uniate and Orthodox churches to work more closely together. The outstanding figure among the intellectuals was Simion Bărnuțiu, a teacher of philosophy in the high school in Blaj. Among the clergy, the bishop of the Orthodox church, Andreiu Șaguna, was by far the most important; his contemporary, Ioan Lemeni, at the head of the Uniate hierarchy, was eventually to abandon the Romanian national movement.

In Transylvania, as in Croatia, the Hungarian leaders made the language question the central point in their national program, and they argued in the diet for the replacement of Latin with Hungarian. They were supported by the Szeklers, but opposed by the Saxon deputies. The German interests were threatened as much as the Romanian by these demands. The Saxons, however, were hampered by the fact that they wished to preserve the political structure in Transylvania intact. As long as they sought to maintain complete control over the Saxon districts, they could not cooperate with the Romanian

5 Keith Hitchins, "The Sacred Cult of Nationality: Rumanian Intellectuals and the Church in Transylvania, 1834–1869," in Winters and Held, *Intellectual and Social Developments*, p. 135.

majority whose leaders demanded representation in proportion to their numbers.

After the outbreak of the revolution, in March and April 1848, the Hungarian diet proclaimed the full union of Transylvania with the rest of the Hungarian lands. Transylvania was to lose its diet, but to receive sixty-nine seats in the Buda assembly. Hungarian interests were clearly served by this move. The Hungarian population was a minority in Transylvania. If, however, the province were added to Hungary proper, the Hungarians would have a bare majority in the united territories. As elsewhere, the Hungarian revolutionaries offered liberal reforms in other spheres. Any Romanian or Saxon who accepted the Hungarian language and cultural domination would enjoy a position of full equality in the state. Naturally this attitude won little favor among the non-Hungarian people.

In 1848 local meetings were held throughout the Romanian-inhabited territories in Transylvania, the Banat, and Hungary itself. There was also considerable peasant agitation. The laws on emancipation passed in Hungary were delayed in their application in Transylvania, and when the nobility attempted to continue to collect their feudal dues and labor services, the peasants reacted with violence. The situation in Transylvania was further complicated by the fact that a Hungarian nobility held control over a Romanian peasantry. The peasant representatives joined with the intellectuals and clergy in formulating and presenting a national program. Their center of organization was to be Blaj.

The first Romanian national meeting of significance in this revolutionary year was held at the end of April. On May 8 another conference was held, attended by Şaguna, Bărnuţiu, Avram Iancu, who was to lead the peasant movement, and other intellectuals and clergy. The Romanian leaders faced exactly the same problem as their contemporaries in Croatia: Should they cooperate with Vienna or Buda? A solid front was presented against full union with Hungary, but there was disagreement on the question of negotiation with these rival centers. However, even those who wished to work with the Hungarian revolutionaries desired a recognition of Romanian national rights, an impossible condition. The strongest group, including Şaguna and Bărnuţiu, favored cooperation with Vienna. The aim was to achieve recognition as a nation with authority over a definite territory – in other words, a program very similar to that desired by the Serbian leadership. In the future, Şaguna was to be the chief link with the Habsburg government, which in turn recognized the bishop as the representative of Romanian interests.

The main task of the previous meeting was the preparation of a national assembly, which was called to meet in the middle of May. Here, on May 15–17, the major decisions were again made by the intellectuals and the clergy. Şaguna and Lemeni were chosen as presidents of the assembly, with Bărnuţiu and George Bariţiu as vice-presidents. Their program was announced to a gathering of thirty thousand in a field outside Blaj. The Romanian demands were presented in a sixteen-point petition to the emperor. Its content clearly demonstrated the enormous advance that had been made from the previous Romanian goal, which had been simply recognition as the fourth political nation. The Romanian objective was now stated as the complete reorganization of the administration of the province, with the Romanian population assigned a position commensurate with its numbers, including a proportionate share in the representation to the diet and in the public offices. Romanian was to be an official language. The changes were to be accomplished by a constitutional assembly, and, until it met, the question of union with Hungary should be postponed. The petition also included the standard list of liberal reforms that we have seen elsewhere, such as guarantees of freedom of speech and the press, the abolition of special privileges, peasant emancipation, and an end to restrictions on trade and industry.

Two delegations, headed by the bishops, were then chosen; one was sent to Vienna to present the petition to the emperor and the other to Cluj to the meetings of the Transylvanian diet. At the same time a permanent Romanian National Committee was established with its headquarters in Sibiu. Şaguna became president and Bărnuţiu vice-president. Of the twenty-three members, there were six priests, five professors, and twelve lawyers and officials. The assembly at Blaj was dominated by moderates. No violent revolutionary activities were contemplated. Instead, the leaders proposed legal means of action. They composed petitions to the government, and they formed delegations with bishops appointed to head them. At the end of the meeting, the bishops cautioned the assembled crowd to be patient and to wait for the reaction of the government.

The Romanian initiative was to be unsuccessful. Şaguna arrived in Vienna in June at a time when the court was in a very weak position. In action taken just before Şaguna was received, the emperor, fearful of Hungarian opposition, had approved the revolutionary March and April laws, which included the union of Hungary and Transylvania. The bishop then went to Buda, where he held discussions with the Hungarian officials from June until September. Lemeni was similarly disappointed. The Transylvanian diet met in May, with the bishop and a few others who were of noble rank as the only Romanian delegates. In June peasant reforms were approved; the Hungarian laws served as the model. Since the Hungarians and Szeklers had a majority, they were able to secure the acceptance of the union with Hungary. It could not be expected that the Romanian leaders would either approve the decision or recognize the authority of the diet to carry through such a measure.

Meanwhile, the Wallachian revolution had gone down to defeat. In September Russian and Ottoman armies were in occupation of both Principalities. Refugees streamed into Transylvania; Braşov and Sibiu were central places of refuge. Most of these people passed through the province and continued on to Western Europe. Some, like Nicolae Bălcescu, became involved in the events in Transylvania. The leaders of the Wallachian revolt had much sympathy for the Hungarian revolutionary regime, which had many principles in common with their own short-lived movement. Before 1848, and in the years afterward, Romanians from the Principalities and Hungarian liberals cooperated. At this time Bălcescu attempted to bring the Hungarian and Romanian leaders together to form a common front against Russia and the Habsburg Empire, the two conservative powers who had stood as the main block to revolutionary change in Europe. The problem remained the Hungarian government's refusal to give sufficient concessions. Although it was willing to recognize that Croatia had certain historic rights, it would not extend a similar recognition to Romanian or Serbian claims. Not until July 1849, on the eve of defeat, was the Hungarian position in regard to these nationalities modified.

Meanwhile, violence increased in the countryside. Atrocities were committed both by Hungarian soldiers and by Romanian peasants seeking to obtain the implementation of the emancipation laws. In areas where the regular government broke down, Romanian popular leaders were able to take control. An important center of Romanian authority was established in the Western Mountains. Here Avram Iancu headed a group of armed peasants who were able to defend their position until the end of the revolution. Fighting had, of course, already commenced in other sections of the empire. The Serbs in the Banat and the imperial troops were both at war with the Hungarian revolutionary forces. In Transylvania the Romanians supported the Habsburg army; the Szeklers joined the Hungarians. The military situation was radically altered when General Bem took charge of the Hungarian forces. By the end of the year he was able to bring under control almost all of Transylvania except the Western Mountains. Transylvania was thus under Hungarian military rule.

In December the Romanian leaders held another meeting, over which Şaguna again presided. The program remained the establishment of a Romanian autonomous region. It was to be governed by a Romanian official named by the emperor who would have a position similar to that of the ban in Croatia. The Romanian National Committee still favored cooperation with Vienna, even though the Habsburg government had not recognized it as an official body. An immediate problem had also arisen. The Romanian representatives had to decide what to do about the danger presented by General Bem's campaign. At this time, the Romanian, Serbian, and Saxon leaders all agreed that the intervention of the Russian army stationed in Wallachia should be requested. The power that had crushed the revolution in the Principalities was to be asked to protect the Transylvanian Romanians against the Hungarian threat. Şaguna thus went to Bucharest to attempt to gain this assistance. As a result of a Habsburg request, a Russian force did enter Transylvania. It was, however, defeated. The major Russian intervention did not come until summer.

Şaguna went next to Olmütz with a delegation to present to Franz Joseph, who had just become emperor, a petition requesting the formation of an autonomous Romanian principality. In March 1849 the constitution issued at Olmütz recognized a separate Transylvania and Vojvodina, but it went no further in meeting Romanian demands. All subsequent negotiations had to wait until the Hungarian problem was settled. In June the Russian army, answering a Habsburg appeal, entered Transylvania, and by the middle of August the Hungarian forces had been defeated.

In the revolutionary period, as we have seen, the Romanian and Saxon as well as the Croatian and Serbian support had gone to the Habsburg side. Each of these national leaderships had expected a reward for their loyalty in the form of political concessions favorable to their cause. All were to be equally disappointed. The Bach system, of course, was no more acceptable to the Romanians than to the Croatians, the Serbs, the Saxons, or the defeated Hungarians. Transylvania was divided into districts, which were governed by officials appointed from Vienna. The governor now lived in Sibiu. Although the official language of administration was German, the new regime did not favor the Saxons, who lost all of their autonomous privileges. Among the Romanians the influence of the clergy remained strong; Şaguna was still the dominant figure in their political life. The Uniate bishop, Alexander Şuluţiu, who had been appointed in 1848 when Lemeni was suspended for his pro-Hungarian activities, was less active. The Romanian leadership maintained its policy of cooperation with Vienna despite the limited success obtained in 1849.

An opportunity for national advancement came in 1860 and 1861 at the time of the constitutional experiments. Şaguna was a member of the Reichsrat that met from May to September 1860, and there he again presented the Romanian demands. The policy of collaboration was continued after the issuance of the February Patent of 1861. At this time, it will be remembered, the Hungarians refused to send delegates to a central parliament, but the Habsburg government was determined to proceed with its establishment. In order to choose its delegates, the Transylvanian diet was summoned to meet in Sibiu in July 1863. A new electoral law issued at this time extended the franchise to more Romanians. As a result, forty-six Romanian, forty-two Hungarian, and thirty-two Saxon representatives were chosen. After the government had nominated its members, the diet was composed of fifty-seven Romanians, fifty-four Hungarians, and forty-three Saxons. Almost all the Hungarian delegates refused to attend the sessions, arguing that the legal basis of the Transylvanian government was that established by the March 1848 laws: Transylvania was a part of Hungary, and only the Buda diet had jurisdiction. After a second election was held, with the same results, the diet was opened without Hungarian or Szekler representation. Dominated by the Romanians and Saxons, the body proceeded to grant the Romanian request to be accepted as the fourth recognized nation; the Uniate and Orthodox churches were placed on the same basis as the older religions, and Romanian became a recognized official language. The basic demands of the eighteenth century had thus been met. However, the entire internal and international position of the Habsburg Empire had meanwhile changed, and the Hungarian viewpoint was about to prevail.

The decision of Franz Joseph to accept the Hungarian position on Transylvania was communicated in a personal audience of the emperor with Şaguna in 1865. The policy of cooperation with Vienna in order to gain recognition of the Romanian rights had thus ended in dismal failure. Only one real advance had been made. In December, 1864 the Romanian Orthodox church had been separated from the authority of Sremski Karlovci; it now had its own center at Sibiu with Şaguna as metropolitan. Nevertheless, in the vital question of political autonomy, the worst possible solution from the Romanian viewpoint had been adopted. Since they were not recognized as a "historic" nation, the Romanians, like the Serbs, received no special political rights, such as those included in the Croatian Nagodba. Instead, they were granted some privileges in the Nationalities Law passed by the Hungarian parliament. Its provisions, however, though they were liberal in appearance, were never fully implemented.

In the next years the intellectuals were to take control of the national movement. Strongly critical of the previous policies, which had involved cooperation with the government, they adopted a policy of "passivism" and withdrew from active participation in political life. They were not to alter their attitude until the 1880s.

CONCLUSION: THE HABSBURG EMPIRE IN 1867

The year 1867 was to be a decisive break in Habsburg history. The Ausgleich marked the victory of the most active and aggressive nationality in the empire. The Hungarians were henceforth to enjoy the principal benefits of the association with Vienna and to make few sacrifices for it. During the previous years the political history of the Croats, Serbs, and Romanians had been strongly influenced by this struggle between the Habsburg government and the Hungarian leadership. There was much sympathy with the Hungarian position. The nationalities were opposed to Austrian absolutism, and they usually supported arguments of historic privilege. The liberal and national doctrines of the Hungarian revolution were favored by many groups throughout the empire. The major problems arose when it became apparent that the Hungarian program, which called for a unitary state embracing all of the lands of the crown of St. Stephen, clashed directly with the demands for territorial autonomy and national recognition that were being made by Croatian, Serbian, and Romanian leaders. Just at the time when the Hungarian government sought to obtain the maximum historical boundaries and to weaken as much as possible the central imperial authority, similar desires were being expressed by the other nationalities. After 1848 it was clear that Hungarian national goals were just as incompatible with Croatian, Serbian, and Romanian desires as were the policies of the previous Habsburg absolutist regime.

Before 1867 the nationalities had at least some possibility of playing between Vienna and Budapest. They chose different paths. Şaguna sought to cooperate with the Habsburg government; Strossmayer preferred to seek an agreement with Hungary. In the end neither alternative was satisfactory. The Hungarian leaders were able to maintain a firm and unyielding position. In contrast, the Habsburg government, weakened by the defeats in Germany and Italy and the multitude of domestic problems that arose in all its lands, could not withstand Hungarian pressure. No other nationality was strong enough to provide an alternate partnership.

We have seen an evolution in some of the national programs in the years before 1867. In the eighteenth century the emphasis was placed on historic rights guaranteed by treaties or charters. By 1848 the idea of individual and national rights had become important. Thus petitions from Romanians emphasized that their nationality formed the majority of the population of Transylvania and paid the most taxes. Historical arguments, however, were never abandoned. There was also some change in the leadership, although the paramount position of the church is amply demonstrated in the careers of Strossmayer, Rajačić, and Şaguna. At this time members of the educated middle class assumed active political roles. They were primarily professionals, for example, teachers, doctors, lawyers, officials, and army officers. Politics, however, remained the concern of a small proportion of the population throughout the empire. The peasants as a class were almost totally excluded from political activity, except when they were called upon to fight either in the Habsburg army or as members of revolutionary bands.

7

War and Revolution,
1856–1887

THE TWO DECADES AFTER THE CRIMEAN WAR were to offer an open field for revolutionary activity, largely owing to the disarray of the previous alliance system. After 1815, it will be remembered, the cooperation of Austria, Russia, and Prussia in the Holy Alliance had provided an effective dam against the overthrow of conservative, monarchical regimes by national liberal movements. The Russian assistance to the Habsburg Monarchy in 1849 marked a climax in this activity. The Habsburg actions during the Crimean War and the intense reaction of the Russian government against this policy split the former alliance, and for a brief period Russia cooperated with France. Napoleon III, who had himself come to power through revolutionary action, was willing to sponsor and assist other such movements. His chief interest was Italy, but he was also concerned with events in the Danubian Principalities and Poland. The entente with Russia held through the unifications in Italy and the Principalities, but fell apart on the Polish question. In 1863 a revolution broke out in the Russian-ruled Polish lands, which won a great deal of open support and sympathy in France, Britain, and the Habsburg Empire. Thereafter, Russian relations with Paris cooled. Instead, the Russian government turned to Prussia as the only possible partner in international affairs. Russia's subsequent backing of the Prussian unification of Germany was to have a profound significance for the Habsburg Empire and, indeed, for the Balkan peninsula.

Although the diplomatic aspects of the revolutionary period are important, the movements themselves, of course, were organized by the national leaderships. They were often in touch with other groups with similar aims, in particular with Italian, Hungarian, and Polish organizations. Most influential for Eastern Europe were to be the activities of such men as Czartoryski and Kossuth, who had held high political positions in their states and who continued to play leading roles even in exile. After the failure of the Polish revolts of 1830 and 1863 and the Hungarian revolution of 1848–1849, Polish and Hungarian emigrés were actively involved in further conspiracies. Their leaders regarded themselves as heads of governments-in-exile, and they dealt with other European statesmen often on an equal basis. They had agents throughout Europe, and they continued to play important roles in international diplomacy. Their goals were the reconstruction of their states rather than social or political reform. Although they might be liberal and might support a widening of the franchise to include the educated, property-holding classes, they were seldom democratic. Balkan events were to be strongly affected not only by Hungarian and Polish influences, but also by the Italian unification movement. There were connections both with the left wing of Mazzini and Garibaldi and with the right, under the leadership of Cavour and the kingdom of Sardinia.

The revolutionary situation in the Balkans was also affected by the activities of revolutionary groups on the left who espoused programs ranging from moderate liberalism to socialism, anarchism, and communism. Often emphasizing the social instead of the national aspects of revolution, they aimed at the introduction of democratic regimes. They also, of course, supported the idea of the national state. Unlike the more conservative groups, the leaders on the left did not have access to heads of government and officials. They tended to work through secret committees and to base their hopes for success on revolution rather than on diplomatic negotiations or regular political procedures. It is important to note that underground revolutionary activity was widespread. Innumerable secret societies with elaborate programs for action existed, although only a few were to be successful or to influence the course of events. Because of their large number, it was often difficult for officials and governments to distinguish among them or to decide who and what each truly represented. It was the secretive, conspiratorial tone of many of these movements that disturbed conservative regimes, in particular tsarist Russia. National movements with a conservative leadership might receive support, but democratic or socialist agitation, which would endanger the social or political structure of the great powers, became the target of intense police investigation.

The two great national movements after 1856 were, of course, the German and the Italian. Both were carried through on traditional lines by basically conservative leaderships. They succeeded through war and diplomacy, namely, the war of Sardinia and France against the Habsburg Empire in 1859 and the subsequent conflicts of Prussia with Austria in 1866 and with France in 1870–1871. All of these events had immediate repercussions in the Balkans. The defeat of the Habsburg Empire and the unification of Italy had a negative effect on the reign of King Othon, but greatly aided in the unification of the Principalities. The Prussian victory in 1866 contributed much to the final negotiation of the Ausgleich; it thus had a detrimental influence on the Habsburg Balkan nationalities. This crisis, however, allowed Prince Charles to consolidate his position in Bucharest. The defeat of France in 1871 and the subsequent weakness of that state in international relations was a disadvantage in particular to the non-Slavic states of Greece and Romania, who thereby lost their most effective patron.

In an age of national upsurge, when the map of Europe was rapidly changing, it was natural that the Balkan governments should seek to follow a similar path. National unification and advancement were the watchwords of the day. A united Italy and Germany had been created; Hungary shared in the control of the Habsburg Empire. Independent or autonomous governments held power in the Principalities, Greece, Montenegro, and Serbia, but the Ottoman Empire still controlled the greater part of the peninsula – Bosnia, Hercegovina, Epirus, Thessaly, Macedonia, Thrace, and the Bulgarian and Albanian regions. As we have seen, Balkan statesmen and writers had already drawn up many schemes for the partition of these lands. For instance, the Megali Idea, aiming at the recreation of the Byzantine Empire, in its furthest extension foresaw the Greek acquisition of lands south of a line running through the Balkan Mountains to the Albanian coast. Garašanin's Načertanije aimed primarily at the annexation of Bosnia, Hercegovina, and the Kosovo region; union with Montenegro; and the securing of an outlet on the Adriatic. The Romanian nationalists sought the unification of Transylvania, Bukovina, and Bessarabia with the two autonomous provinces. Within the Habsburg Empire proponents of the Illyrian idea supported the joining of all South Slavs from "Villach to Varna."

Not only were these programs mutually contradictory, but they obviously involved the interests of the great powers. The most difficult problem was faced by the Romanian nationalists. There seemed little probability that the Habsburg Empire would surrender Transylvania and Bukovina or that Russia would give up Bessarabia. The extension of the Serbian and Greek boundaries at the expense of the Ottoman Empire also met obstacles. Great Britain after the Crimean War, as before, supported the territorial integrity of the Muslim state. The Habsburg Monarchy had a similar interest. It certainly had no desire to have a strong Serbia as its southern neighbor. The Russian government, with its attention devoted primarily to internal reform, wished to maintain good relations with the Porte and conditions of tranquility in the Balkans. After the defeat by Prussia, France was in no position to exert influence in Eastern affairs. Under these circumstances, the Balkan leaders could expect to meet not just a lack of support, but outright opposition from the great powers, should they attempt a policy of territorial expansion.

With this negative attitude among the European states, the Balkan statesmen had to look to other alternatives. After 1856 an isolated national military action was not a practical policy. The reformed Ottoman army could defeat any regular Balkan force. Diplomatic negotiations, such as those which resulted in the unification of the Principalities and the acceptance of a foreign prince, could succeed only if they involved the internal affairs of the states and not the extension of their boundaries. The only other possibility, unless hopes of expansion were abandoned, was the organization of a cooperative undertaking by the Balkan governments and their adoption of measures of mutual support. Attempts were indeed to be made to bring the Balkan governments together and to enlist the aid of the Italian, Polish, and Hungarian national and revolutionary leaders. Questions of conflicting objectives and the partition of Balkan territories still under Ottoman rule had to be met at this time.

BALKAN COOPERATION

Although this narrative has been primarily concerned with the relations of the Balkan people with the Porte and the great powers, some signs of mutual cooperation have already been noted. In the eighteenth century both the Russian and the Habsburg governments had called for a general Balkan rising to aid them in their military endeavors. The Etairia had envisaged a similar united action in support of its goals. Thereafter, student and revolutionary groups with similar aims were in touch, particularly in centers such as Paris, Geneva, and London. It is very important, however, to emphasize that these movements, with their many interconnections, were not necessarily anti-Ottoman. In fact, after 1849 they were more likely to be primarily directed against Russia and the Habsburg Empire. Italian, Romanian, Polish, and Hungarian revolutionaries certainly considered these two governments to be their principal adversaries. In contrast, all three were more friendly toward the Ottoman Empire. Exiled from their own countries, many Hungarians and Poles entered Ottoman state service. The aim of these emigrés was not the partition of the Ottoman lands, but the establishment of Hungarian and Polish states at the expense of Austria and Russia.

The conspiracies organized by these groups could be quite complicated. In 1859 the French and Piedmontese governments were in contact with Hungarian revolutionaries, who in turn carried on negotiations with Cuza. The aim was to arrange for the delivery to the Principalities of French weapons, which would be given to Hungarians resident in Moldavia, who would then make raids into Transylvania and thus divert Habsburg forces from Italy. The action required negotiations between Hungarian and Romanian agents who had clashed quite sharply during the revolution of 1848 over the political conditions in Transylvania. In these discussions the Hungarian representatives agreed that a plebiscite would determine the ultimate fate of Transylvania, should a victory be achieved. The aim was the establishment of a Danubian Confederation whose members would be Hungary, Serbia, and Romania, all independent states. These plans had to be abandoned when Napoleon III concluded the Truce of Villafranca with the Habsburg Empire in 1859 and thereby withdrew French military backing from further revolutionary conspiracies. Under strong pressure from the powers, Cuza had to suppress Polish and Hungarian intrigues organized on Romanian territory. Nevertheless, in the future the Principalities were to remain a center of revolutionary activities and a safe haven for radical groups; the Romanian government looked on these organizations with a very tolerant eye.

Other movements were directed solely against the Ottoman Empire. The

most serious attempt to form a Balkan alliance was made by Michael Obrenović. By the middle of the century the dangers of great-power interference
in Balkan affairs had become apparent. No Balkan state wished to substitute
European, that is, Austrian or Russian, rule for that of the Porte, which was
in fact becoming increasingly less burdensome. Could the Balkan governments agree among themselves, they might be able to obtain their objectives
without calling in outside assistance. The major flaw in this policy was the
obvious fact that the Balkan armies were not strong enough to defeat a reformed
Ottoman army. It has been estimated that the Serbian army, the best force
available, numbered only about ninety thousand men; Greece had a
scant eight thousand under arms.[1] The Romanian army was to be developed
later, during the reign of Prince Charles. All of the governments put their
faith in the organization of their military forces along Western models instead
of concentrating on the development of the techniques of guerilla warfare,
in which they were in fact most effective. Despite this drawback, almost all
the Balkan leaders were eager to undertake aggressive national programs.

The center of the negotiations was Serbia. Working with his foreign minister, Ilija Garašanin, Prince Michael maintained contact throughout his reign
with the other Balkan rulers, although alliances were not signed until 1866,
1867, and 1868. The Serbian territorial goals remained much the same as those
outlined in the Načertanije. There was much discussion about a wider South
Slav conception that would involve the Habsburg Croats and Serbs; Michael
had dealings with Strossmayer. However, the major emphasis remained on
the acquisition of what were considered historic Serbian lands.

The most important negotiations were carried on with Greece, beginning
in 1861 when Othon was still on the throne. Eager to gain prestige in foreign
policy to buttress his declining influence, the king willingly entered into the
discussions. The major obstacle to an agreement was the difficulty of dividing
the Ottoman territory. Neither government was hindered by any ideas of
"self-determination." They felt little concern about possible Bulgarian claims
and none at all about the Albanians. The Greek government wished to acquire all of Macedonia and suggested a partition of the Bulgarian-inhabited
territories, with Serbia taking the land north of the Balkan Mountains and
Greece that to the south. Serbia sought Macedonian regions, the Kosovo
area, Bosnia, and Herecegovina, without much real interest in or knowledge
of the exact ethnic composition of the areas. The negotiations were in abey-
ance from 1862 to 1866, and in this period Othon was replaced by George I.

A great opportunity for the Balkan states appeared to come in 1866, a year
of crisis in Europe. In February a revolution resulted in the overthrow of
Alexander Cuza. In the summer Prussia defeated Austria, a prime foe of Serbian expansion. At the same time a revolt broke out in Crete. The first Balkan

---

1   Michael Boro Petrovich, *A History of Modern Serbia, 1804–1918*, 2 vols. (New York: Harcourt
    Brace Jovanovich, 1976), I, 329.

agreement, that between Serbia and Montenegro, was signed at this time. In his attempts to bring the Balkan states together, Michael had cooperated well with Montenegro, whose inhabitants considered themselves Serbs. Prince Nicholas was willing to relinquish his throne should a union of the two states be possible. Since Michael was childless, the Montenegrin ruler evidently had hopes that, if the Serbian throne became vacant, he might succeed. The treaty signed at this point provided for cooperation to prepare for an uprising against the Ottoman Empire. The goal was the formation of a single Serbian nation with Michael as prince.

Discussions with Greece were again taken up, but serious problems soon arose. The Greek government, deeply involved in Crete, wished the Serbs to undertake obligations to go to war with the Porte to divert Ottoman forces from the island. Instead, the Serbian leaders used the difficulties in which the Porte found itself to gain from it the final evacuation of the fortresses on Serbian territory. Nevertheless, in August 1867, Serbian and Greek representatives signed an agreement at Vöslau, a town near Vienna, in which the two states agreed to aid each other should either be attacked by the Ottoman Empire. The problem of the division of Macedonia was avoided; a declaration was made that, as a minimum, Serbia would receive Bosnia and Hercegovina and Greece would annex Epirus and Thessaly in any situation that made these territorial changes possible.

Negotiations were also proceeding with Bucharest. The major obstacle to Romanian participation in a Balkan union directed against the Ottoman Empire was the simple fact that no major Romanian territorial objectives were involved. The next great goal was Transylvania. Although the Serbian government did indeed regard Austria as a principal block to expansion into Ottoman territory, neither the Serbian nor the Romanian leaders could contemplate a campaign against Vienna. Thus, although Serbia and Romania had as yet no direct interests in conflict, they also had no common goals. In February 1868 a treaty was signed, but it was simply a declaration of friendship.

In addition to carrying on discussions with the neighboring powers, the Serbian government gave support to conspiratorial groups who were planning insurrections in Ottoman lands. Assistance to Serbian secret committees in Bosnia was to become a standard policy throughout the century. Even more important was the aid offered to Bulgarian leaders, in particular to George Rakovski. Cooperation with Bulgarian revolutionaries naturally complicated further the question of the division of Ottoman territory. Like the Greeks and the Serbs, the Bulgarian committees had developed their plans for a future state, which in most of their programs included Macedonia and Thrace.

Michael's assassination in 1868 brought an end to these schemes of Balkan cooperation. Even before his death, the prince appears to have changed his views, in particular in regard to Austria. He had close relations with Hungarian nationalists, and their attitude toward Vienna shifted sharply after the conclusion of the Ausgleich. Another serious attempt to bring the Balkan states together to achieve a common goal was not to occur until 1912. This early effort had shown the grave weaknesses in any pan-Balkan movement, and the contradiction between the territorial objectives of the states was to become even more evident after the Albanian claims were introduced.

In the next crises each Balkan government was to follow an independent policy. Only in some instances was there cooperation to achieve a common goal. Once again the leaderships showed a preference for seeking the assistance of a great-power patron, a practice that caused European attention to focus on the Balkans in the 1870s. Although in the future there were always to be some groups and individuals, generally left-oriented and underground, who supported programs of Balkan cooperation and appeasement, in general, on the official level, the Balkan governments, who were competing for the same territory and whose prestige and power were in question, retained a suspicious and competitive attitude toward one another. In other words, the relations among the Balkan states resembled closely those among the European great powers.

THE BULGARIAN NATIONAL MOVEMENT

By the 1860s both the Greek and the Serbian governments were faced with a Bulgarian national movement whose territorial goals conflicted seriously with their own. The comparatively late development of Bulgarian national agitation can be easily understood. Situated geographically nearer to Constantinople than the other Balkan regions, the Bulgarian lands were always subject to closer surveillance from the central government and were more open to military control. Greek cultural dominance, which was a natural result of previous historical developments and which was approved by the Porte and to an extent by Russia, was also difficult to throw off. Moreover, in contrast to the Serbs, Montenegrins, Romanians, and Greeks, the Bulgarians had no central institutions that could organize and unite the people; the church was under Phanariot control. They also had at first no links with a foreign power who could act as a patron in foreign relations. A further hindrance to the national movement was the fact that after 1830 the economic conditions in the country improved rapidly. With the Ottoman reforms and the restoration of order in the country there no longer existed the type of provincial anarchy and blatant economic exploitation that had pushed other areas into revolt. As shall be shown, there were local peasant rebellions against the landholding and taxation system, but no great internal uprising similar to the Greek and the Serbian revolutions.

The rise of national consciousness in Bulgaria, as elsewhere, was preceded by a cultural revival. Like the Serbs and Greeks, the Bulgarians preserved remembrances of their past history through the church and through folk-

Village near Adrianople

songs and folklore. However, the higher offices in the church were in Greek hands. In the late eighteenth and early nineteenth centuries Church Slavonic, a language close to Bulgarian, had been replaced by Greek in most services. The establishment of Bulgarian as the literary language was thus essential. The first history of Bulgaria was completed in 1762 by Paisii, a monk at the monastery of Hilandar at Mt. Athos. His aim was to demonstrate that the Bulgarians too had a glorious past history. In 1806 another cleric, Sofronii, bishop of Vratsa, published a collection of sermons entitled *Kyriakodromiom* (Sunday Book) which was printed in Rimnik in Wallachia. Other books in Bulgarian appeared in Constantinople, the Danubian Principalities, and other places, with their numbers increasing in the 1840s and 1850s. After the Crimean War the printing of books was permitted in Bulgaria. A great interest was shown in history, grammar, arithmetic, and translations of foreign works. In addition, educated Bulgarians had access to Russian publications because of the similarity of the languages.

As elsewhere in the Balkans, education was at first available only in the churches and monasteries. On the lower level what schools there were concentrated on reading and writing and on Church Slavonic. They did not provide the training necessary for commerce, nor did they introduce their pupils to the affairs of the wider world. The best secular institutions were the so-called Helleno-Bulgarian schools. There the students learned Greek, which had the advantage of being the commercial language of the Black Sea region. The Greek schools also introduced their pupils to the progressive political ideas of Europe, in particular liberalism and nationalism. The first purely Bulgarian school of higher education was established in Gabrovo in 1835. It became a model for similar institutions in other cities, such as Kazanlŭk, Triavna, and Sofia, which were trade and manufacturing centers. There was no Bulgarian establishment on the university level. For an advanced education the Bulgarian student could attend the Protestant missionary schools, which were opened around the middle of the century, or go abroad. Some studied in universities in France, Austria, and Germany, but the group that was to be the most significant in the future received a Russian education.

Although the Russian government was to play a major role in the establishment of an autonomous Bulgarian state, the first relationship was quite one-sided. At the beginning of the century Russian interest was naturally focused on the Principalities, Serbia, and Greece, whose national movements directly involved Russian interests. Until the 1870s Russia also stood behind the authority of the Patriarchate of Constantinople, because it was believed important to maintain as far as possible the strength and unity of the Orthodox world. Russian armies were, of course, in occupation of the country during the Russo-Turkish War of 1828–1829. Thereafter, it will be remembered, Russia supported the maintenance of the territorial integrity of the Ottoman Empire. The subsequent defeat in the Crimean War prevented the Russian government from adopting a forward policy on any Balkan issue for almost twenty years. Official Russia thus offered the Bulgarian nationalist little hope for assistance. Yet this great power was the best source of foreign support.

Encouragement, however, came from another direction. In 1858 the Slavic Benevolent Society was founded. Representing the views of the Panslavs, it offered scholarships to young Bulgarians to study in Russia. A basically conservative organization, it sought to bring the Slavs together under Russian leadership. However, the Bulgarian students who received these grants came in contact with the radical Russian youth, who were under the influence of writers such as D. I. Pisarev, N. G. Chernishevsky, and Alexander Herzen. Thus, instead of being instilled with love and respect for Orthodox, autocratic Russia, many absorbed the more radical European ideologies. Others were deeply affected by the Panslav orientation. Panslav interest in Bulgarian affairs was to remain constant and to have an enormous influence on later Bulgarian history.

The development of the Bulgarian national movement was naturally deeply affected by the events that have been previously described, in particular the Greek revolution and Ottoman reform. At the beginning of the nineteenth century the situation in the Bulgarian lands had been very bad indeed. The effects of the breakdown of Ottoman central authority had been disastrous. The bandit state of Pasvanoglu had been based in Vidin, and the kirdjali raids had devastated the region north of the Balkan Mountains. Thereafter conditions improved markedly. Bulgarian merchants and businessmen benefited especially from the decline of Greek influence in Constantinople after the Greek revolt; they were able to replace their former Greek competitors in many fields. Although strong Bulgarian merchant colonies already existed in Constantinople, Bucharest, and other localities, these expanded in size and became more prosperous. The end of Ottoman preemption rights in the Principalities was also in the Bulgarian interest. With the loss of control over Wallachia and Moldavia, the Porte came to prefer to rely on Egypt and Bulgaria for its supplies, particularly for the city of Constantinople. When a regular Ottoman army was created in 1826, its clothing and food was provided principally by Bulgarian sources.

From 1830 until 1876 Bulgarian merchants and manufacturers enjoyed the market of the entire empire. During these years an active cloth industry, based on home handicraft production, developed in the Balkan Mountains. In this period of prosperity, the Bulgarian cities were centers for the manufacture of carpets, metalwork, shoes, and clothing, the production and sale of which were regulated by merchant and artisan guilds. Bulgarian merchants handled these items and also natural products, such as grains, cattle, honey, wax, animal products, wine, pig iron, and salt. They had offices in Constantinople as well as in major trading cities. After 1856, they like their Ottoman colleagues, were affected by the increasing penetration of British and Austrian products. Local handicrafts could not compete with the low prices of machine-manufactured goods. Although the main effects were not to be felt until later, the free-trade policy adopted by the Porte under British influence was eventually to have an extremely detrimental effect on the economies of all the Balkan nationalities.

In addition to enjoying relatively prosperous economic conditions, the Bulgarian lands had a great deal of local self-government at the lowest administrative level. Although no single central Bulgarian authority existed, the communities controlled virtually all their internal affairs. Most Bulgarians were thus governed directly not by Ottoman officials, but by their own notables. In general, each locality elected one or two mayors, who were assisted by a council of five to twelve men. The communal organization had many functions. For instance, it dealt with legal questions, such as the drawing up of contracts, and disputes between Christians; it controlled the educational system, including the appointment of teachers and the building of schools; and it acted as an Ottoman agent in tax collecting. It also handled most of the relations of the citizens with the Ottoman authorities, including matters such as the quartering of soldiers, bribes, and gifts. During the Tanzimat period this community system was made part of the Ottoman administrative organization; standard regulations were set in the Provincial Reform Law of 1864. As in other Balkan lands with similar institutions, problems arose within the communities themselves. They tended to be controlled by a minority of notables who benefited from certain privileges, such as tax collecting. These men were usually conservative, and they wanted to maintain the system that was favorable for their personal interests. Nevertheless, the communities did play a major role in the struggle to establish a national church and to develop an adequate educational system. They also gave the individual Bulgarian some support against unjust actions by officials representing the central Ottoman administration.

The Bulgarian peasantry, which constituted the overwhelming majority of the population, shared in the general improving conditions in the Ottoman lands. The peasant's position was certainly superior to that of his contemporary across the Danube in the Principalities. The free peasants and shepherds lived predominantly in the hill and mountain areas; the chiftlik estates were in the lowlands. All the peasants paid taxes and labor dues to the government; the dependent class gave a share of its products and labor service in return for its land. Here too the major objective of every peasant was to secure full control over his plot or to enlarge his holding. He also had an interest in a reform of the tax system and in securing recognition of the equality of Muslims and Christians in the empire. The peasant revolts prior to this period were directed primarily toward correcting the abuses in the landholding and taxation systems, rather than toward securing national liberation.

The abolition of the janissaries in 1826 and the sipahis shortly thereafter brought up the question of the disposal of their lands, which should have reverted to the state. The sipahi control had already commenced to disintegrate; some individuals had converted their holdings to chiftlik estates. At first the sipahis continued to hold their lands in return for tax payments, but the Porte later replaced this system with regular pensions. With the removal of the landholders, the peasant who actually worked the lands considered his plot his private property. He did not want to pay redemption costs, and he resisted attempts of Muslim landholders to retain their estates. A complicated pattern of land ownership emerged from this situation, but in general the agricultural land was passing into the possession of the small peasant proprietors. The process, however, was slow, and it caused much discontent.

With these generally favorable conditions, Bulgaria should have been a good place to test the success of the Tanzimat reforms. If they worked anywhere, they should have improved conditions there. In fact, the problems met in Bulgaria were typical of those encountered throughout the Ottoman provinces, and thus they merit examination in greater detail. The aim of the Tanzimat was, as we have seen, to promote the tranquility and prosperity of the empire; a condition of equality was to be established between Muslims and Christians, and the major abuses of the administration were to be corrected. The two areas of government that were in urgent need of change were the provincial administration and the means used to collect taxes. The securing of an efficient and honest administrative system was particularly difficult. Officials had to be found who would be loyal to the Porte and not open to corruption. The local notables and military men, both Christian and Muslim, who had strongly entrenched interests, had to be brought under control. At first the swift rotation of officials was used as a means of preventing any individual from developing a center of personal power or sources of private profit. This measure meant that often the men appointed came from other parts of the empire and had little knowledge of or sympathy with local conditions.

The major effort at administrative reform took place after the Crimean War, when the Porte decided to establish a model province out of the regions south of the Danube. In 1864 the Danube vilayet, composed of the districts of Silistria, Vidin, and Niš, was organized. The able Ottoman reformer Midhat Pasha was placed in charge. The attempt was made to place Muslims and Christians on an equal level; Christians sat on the administrative councils. The Porte also appointed Christian officials to serve in the area, but most of these were Poles, Croatians, or Albanians, not Bulgarians. Midhat made a great effort to improve the conditions in the country through a program of public works. He built roads, bridges, schools, and model farms. He was particularly interested in providing a better education so that the Bulgarian youth would not be compelled to study abroad. Despite his good intentions and successes, Midhat was replaced after only three years. His endeavors were not sufficient to counter the prevailing trends both in the Ottoman government and in the Christian society.

Similar failures met the Ottoman efforts to reform the methods of tax collection and assessment. During the reign of Mahmud II a census and a land survey were taken for purposes of distributing the taxes on a fairer basis. At this time and in later years the entire question of tax collection was reviewed repeatedly. The possibility of levying a single tax to replace the multitude of minor payments was similarly discussed. Since it proved impractical for the Porte to collect taxes directly, the necessity of regulating the tax-farming system arose. The major issue here was whether it was better to assign the contracts for a single year, opening the danger that an agent might simply clean out his district, or for a longer period, in which case he might develop his own special interests. During this period Christian notables took over an increasing share of tax collecting. This method did not end the abuses, but it did bring this group into the Ottoman system. In the end the tax reforms simply did not work. Even when in theory just one tax was to be collected, the tax farmers and local officials would levy it several times a year, or collect it and other payments as well. The basic problem remained the difficulty of finding honest government officials. The Porte attempted to control the situation by sending out special investigators or commissions, but these too could be corrupted.

Despite an improvement in conditions during this period, there was in fact an increase in the number and intensity of peasant revolts after 1835.[2] They were caused at least in part by rising expectations. The peasants were well aware of the assurances of the Tanzimat reformers, and they expected the promised benefits. When these did not occur, there was great discontent. From the point of view of the peasant majority, one of the great problems was that they had no way of making their complaints known directly to Constantinople. They sent multiple petitions to officials, but they lacked institutions through which they could express their views. The reforms did not help here. Although in the 1840s Christians were added to local administrative councils, this measure did not improve the situation. Higher officials often just ignored the recommendations of these councils, or they appointed docile representatives or notables who were deeply involved in local corruption. In general, the Bulgarian population blamed the local authorities, not the central government, for administrative abuses, but there were no means of circumventing incompetent and dishonest officials.

When the reforms failed to stifle domestic discontent, the Ottoman officials often blamed either Russian or Serbian agitation. Although it was true that the Serbian government was giving support to Bulgarian revolutionaries in exile, these men were not particularly effective in organizing internal subversion. The Russian government was certainly not in the business of promoting rebellions. Russian pressure for reform was exerted directly through

2 See Mark Pinson, "Ottoman Bulgaria in the First Tanzimat Period – the Revolts in Nish (1841) and Vidin (1850)," *Middle Eastern Studies* 11, no. 2 (May 1975): 103–146.

diplomatic channels or the Orthodox church. The chief cause of unrest within the Bulgarian lands came from local conditions. The peasant program was clear. The chief emphasis remained on the land question, with the objective of assuring that each family held full property rights over a given plot, for which it would be assessed only a light tax burden. Freedom from labor dues either to the state or in connection with landholding was also desired.

Even if the reforms had achieved a greater success, the development of a Bulgarian national movement was to be expected. National doctrines were becoming generally accepted throughout Europe. Moreover, some measures had to be taken to defend Bulgarian interests, in view of the attitude of both the Greek and the Serbian government toward the territories still under the jurisdiction of the Porte. If the Bulgarians' claims were not asserted, the regions they inhabited might be partitioned among other states. The question that first had to be decided, however, was the path to be followed. As elsewhere, the national leaders had two basic choices. They could seek to achieve their goals through diplomacy and negotiations with the Porte and the great powers. This method had been adopted by the Principalities after 1856 and by Miloš in Serbia. The alternative was the organization of revolutions on the line of the revolts in Greece and of Karadjordje in Serbia. The first course of action was favored by the group known as the "Elders," which consisted primarily of merchants and notables. They desired an extension of Bulgarian autonomous rights within the empire, not a destructive revolution. They had a stake in the system, and they were used to dealing with Ottoman officials. They expected to be able to reach their objectives by an agreement with the Porte. Their center was Constantinople, where a large colony of merchants lived.

This stand was challenged by those who preferred direct and violent means. As was the case with the forty-eighters in the Principalities, the main support for this position came from the educated youth, usually from prosperous families, who had traveled and who were influenced by the radical ideologies of the day. More democratic and socialistic than their elders, they nevertheless retained the romantic fervor of earlier revolutionary endeavors that we have seen in other areas. They wished to obtain national liberation through their own efforts, and thus they did not seek great-power support. These men organized a number of separate committees. Conspiratorial centers were established in Bucharest, Belgrade, and Odessa. The leaders were in touch with similar groups in other parts of Europe.

Despite the sincerity of many of these men and their firm belief in the romantic conception of a great national rising to defeat the forces of tyranny and oppression, such a policy was simply impractical at the time. The importance of the availability of an armed force for a successful revolution has been emphasized previously. Except for a relatively small number of armed men engaged in legal and illegal activities, the Bulgarians did not have the military organization necessary to start a revolt. Moreover, the relatively long period of tranquility in the Bulgarian lands, the generally good economic conditions, and the Ottoman reform attempts had affected the population. Many were indeed extremely discontented, but there was certainly no large body of desperate men willing to risk their lives for national liberation. The situation was not comparable to that in Serbia in 1804 or in Greece in 1821, when armed peasants were often faced with the alternative of fighting or being killed. Moreover, the Bulgarian lands were too close to the center of Ottoman power. The reformed Turkish army, although it might have difficulty with a great-power adversary, was fully capable of dealing with any force that could be raised in Bulgaria.

Under these circumstances the patronage of a great power was urgently needed. Quite obviously, assistance could come only from Russia. The Habsburg Monarchy consistently opposed Balkan national movements; Britain supported the maintenance of the empire. There were no direct links to France. Although the Russian government in the post-Crimean period had neither the ability nor the desire to embark on Balkan adventures, it remained the best hope for the Bulgarian nationalist. In 1864 one of the most influential Russian diplomats, Nicholas Pavlovich Ignatiev, was appointed as the Russian representative in Constantinople. He thereafter attempted to keep in close touch with all Balkan revolutionary and national movements. An enthusiastic Panslav, he was a strong proponent of measures leading to Slavic unity and increased autonomous rights for the Balkan people. However, he was first and foremost a Russian nationalist. He expected the national movements to contribute to Russian prestige and power and to accept direction from St. Petersburg, and he opposed actions that were not under Russian control. The first victory for the Bulgarian national cause involved his mediation, but he did not achieve the result he desired.

As we have seen, the Greeks, Serbs, and Romanians had insisted upon a separate national church organization as soon as they won autonomy or independence. Under the leadership of the moderate elements in Constantinople, an attempt was made to separate the Bulgarian hierarchy from the Patriarchate even before advances had been made in the political sphere. The Gülhane decree of 1839, with its assurances of religious equality, was used as an argument against the continued authority of the Greek-dominated Patriarchate in the Bulgarian lands. This first step toward religious autonomy failed. Russia at the time was backing the Patriarchate. The problem of the Dedicated Monasteries in the Principalities and the separation of the church of independent Greece had already caused the Russian government much concern. The Bulgarian cause, however, did make one advance. In 1849 the sultan agreed that the "Bulgarian millet" could have its own church in Constantinople. This was the first official recognition that a Bulgarian nation existed.

The situation became more favorable after the Crimean War. Not only did the new reform measures give more hope, but the Patriarchate appeared willing to make some concessions. These, however, were never sufficient to meet the Bulgarian demands. Most important was the change in the Russian attitude. Filaret, the metropolitan of Moscow and the most influential Russian religious leader, was worried about the activities of the American Protestant missionaries and the Uniates, who represented French and Polish influences, in Bulgaria. He was thus willing to support the Bulgarians' desire to have their own hierarchy, a share in the church revenues, and services in Church Slavonic.

With the arrival of Ignatiev in Constantinople, active Russian intervention commenced. The church councils discussed the question, but they accomplished very little. The Patriarchate naturally opposed a further limitation of its direct jurisdiction and a loss of income. It will be remembered that in 1863 Cuza secularized the lands of the Dedicated Monasteries, an act that dealt a serious blow to the Patriarchate's finances. Throughout the negotiations over the Bulgarian question, Ignatiev attempted to mediate and to find a compromise between the two positions. Neither he nor the Russian government wanted a further weakening of the Patriarchate or quarrels among the Balkan Orthodox.

When no results were obtained through negotiation, the Bulgarian church leaders acted and in 1866 expelled the Greek bishops. The Porte became seriously concerned. Unwilling to face a Bulgarian revolt on the matter, the Porte agreed to the formation of a separate Bulgarian church. The debate then shifted from the question of the establishment of such an institution to that of its territorial jurisdiction. The Greek government also entered the controversy. Although it had insisted on a national ecclesiastical organization after independence, it could not readily accept a similar Bulgarian demand because of the implications for the future. Obviously, the territory that would be assigned to the jurisdiction of the new church might eventually be included in a future Bulgarian state and thus lost to Greece. The issues were too explosive to be easily decided by negotiation. In 1870 the Porte took the major step toward the solution of the question, when it issued a firman that established the Bulgarian Exarchate, as the new institution was called. The territory under its jurisdiction included the lands north of the Balkan Mountains and the Varna and Plovdiv regions. Most important, in Article X it was decreed that if two-thirds of the inhabitants of a district wished to join the Exarchate, they would be allowed to do so. This act opened a bitter conflict among the Christian church organizations. In the next years the Exarchate was able to make considerable progress at the expense of the Greek Patriarchate.

Naturally, this solution was unacceptable to either the Patriarchate or the Greek government. In March 1872 Antim I became exarch. He then announced the separation of his church from Constantinople. In reply, the patriarch declared him schismatic. Nevertheless, with or without the Patriarchate's approval, a Bulgarian church was in existence. Its creation was largely the result of the efforts of moderate Bulgarian leaders and of the Ottoman government. Ignatiev and his government had been willing to accept a separate Bulgarian organization, but they disliked the manner in which it was accomplished. The advance had been achieved essentially through cooperation with the Porte. It did not win prestige for the Russian diplomat, and it weakened Orthodox unity.

Meanwhile, at the time when the moderates were concentrating on the religious question, those who favored revolutionary action were organizing. Their activities naturally had to take place primarily outside the Ottoman lands. Serbia and the Principalities were to offer the most favorable conditions for these conspiracies. The Bulgarian revolutionary movement had no single organization or leader. There was also disagreement among the committees on many important issues, including those of soliciting the aid of a great power and of cooperating with other Balkan revolutionary organizations. From the beginning the Bulgarian actions included the use of armed bands, or *chetas*, which were organized in Wallachia and then sent across the Danube. Their objective, which was to attempt to instigate a great peasant rebellion, was never attained. The first action of this type was organized in 1841 by Vasil Hadzhivulkov and Vladislav Tatich. It should be emphasized that the chetas, like the Bulgarian movement in general, enlisted the support of very few people. There was never to be the mass peasant support for a revolt that we have seen in Serbia or even in Wallachia at the time of Tudor Vladimirescu.

During the reign of Michael Obrenović, Serbia offered a place of refuge for the revolutionaries. The principal figure at this time was George Rakovski, who in 1861 commenced the publication of a journal, *Dunavski Lebed* (Danubian Swan). He favored the organization of an uprising in Bulgaria and the winning of great-power assistance. Should his projected rebellion succeed, he was willing to enter into a federation with Serbia and the Principalities, but not with Greece, The revolutionary groups had the same difficulties as the governments in deciding questions concerning the future boundaries of the national states. After conflicts with the Serbs over this and other issues, Rakovski moved in 1862 to the Principalities, and Wallachia henceforth became the major center of Bulgarian revolutionary activity. Conditions were extremely favorable there. Many Bulgarians lived in Bucharest and the Danube port cities, with ready access to their countrymen across the river. The Romanian government was also extremely lenient in its treatment of the conspirators and lax in enforcing measures to control them. Although the great powers repeatedly warned the Romanians about tolerating these organizations, little was ever done. Many Romanian Liberals were sympathetic to the Bulgarian cause. Moreover, even if the government had wanted to be strict, it was difficult to suppress small-scale clandestine activities of this kind.

The Russian government was particularly strong in its protests to Bucharest over the actions of the radical revolutionary groups. In the past it had objected to the use of Romanian territory by Hungarian and Polish revolutionaries; it was no more sympathetic to the Bulgarians. In 1868 a cheta was organized by Hadzhi Dimitŭr and Stephen Karadzha. They led 120 men across the river, where they were quickly defeated by the Ottoman troops. The Russian consul in Bucharest had warned the Romanian government before the raid was begun that Russia wished the action stopped. The Russian representatives were sympathetic to the Bulgarian desire for greater autonomy, and they were close to conservative Bulgarian circles in Bucharest, in particular to the Bulgarian Benevolent Society, which had close links with the Russian consulate; the Russian diplomats, however, stood strongly against revolutionary acts under radical leadership and any undertaking that they could not control.

Despite the opposition of the powers and the failure to find any serious response among the Bulgarian people, the left revolutionary forces continued to organize and to prepare for future action. In 1870 the Bulgarian Revolutionary Committee was formed for the purpose of uniting all of the radical groups within and without Bulgaria. Its goal was declared to be the formation of an autonomous or independent state and a possible federation with Serbia, Greece, Montenegro, and Romania. After Rakovski died of tuberculosis in 1867, the leadership passed to the moderate Liuben Karavelov. Prominent in the movement were two other men, Vasil Levski and Khristo Botev, who were directly in the Balkan romantic revolutionary tradition. Levski believed that Bulgarian liberation should come through a mass peasant revolt and that foreign assistance should not be sought. In 1869 he went to Bulgaria to organize support for an uprising. Botev, Bulgaria's greatest modern poet, was a socialist and a supporter of the idea of a general revolution. A disaster for the movement occurred in 1872. At that time Levski and a fellow conspirator, Dimitŭr Obshti, were once again in the midst of preparations for a rebellion in Bulgaria. In order to obtain money, Obshti robbed a train. When he was caught, he confessed the plan of the revolt, in order to demonstrate that he was not a common criminal. With this information the Ottoman authorities had no trouble capturing those involved in the conspiracy. Levski and Obshti were hanged. The failure of this attempt caused Karavelov and some others to leave the committee. They felt that some sort of outside assistance, even if only from the Balkan states, was indispensable for success.

Other members of the committee, nevertheless, continued the preparations for rebellion despite the discouragements of the past. Another attempt, the Stara Zagora revolt of 1875, had equally dismal results. Badly planned and led, it received little support inside Bulgaria. Still undiscouraged, the revolutionary leaders continued their preparations. The Ottoman government had its hands full with a revolt that had broken out in 1875 in Bosnia and Hercegovina, and had concentrated its main military forces in the western Balkans. The plans for the new uprising were under the direction of George Benkovski. Preparations were made inside Bulgaria, and Plovdiv was to be the central point of the revolution.

Although the Bulgarian leaders had not wished to commence the rebellion until the middle of May, they were forced to advance the date when their plans became known to the Ottoman authorities. On May 2 (or April 20 by Old Style dating) a revolt broke out in the Balkan Mountain towns of Koprivshtitsa, Panagiurishte, and Klisura. The fighting thereafter was largely concentrated in this area; there was no mass uprising in other regions. The original rebellion was quickly crushed. Its last episode led to the death of Botev, who at the end of May seized a Danube steamer with a group of two hundred supporters and crossed the river. The Ottoman officials learned at once of this landing and had no difficulty in quickly annihilating the force.

The April Uprising, which became the major event in later Bulgarian nationalist mythology, was a complete failure as a revolution. Quite apart from the disasters that it brought upon the Bulgarian people, its leaders were unable to enlist the support of even a small percentage of the population. Only a few localities were involved. It certainly did not gain the support of the peasantry; its leaders did not have an agrarian program. Most of the participants – artisans, merchants, teachers, and students – were from the middle classes of the towns and villages. The leaders came mostly from prosperous families. Once the revolt started, the majority of the population wanted nothing to do with it. As one writer describes the reaction:

> Not pitched battles, but paralyzed ignorance, treachery, flight, mutual invective, and desperate dreams of saving the situation dominated the Bulgarian cause in this one-sided affair. Bulgarian initiative, such as it was, almost immediately passed into the hands of conservative members of the community. These elements disavowed the rebels and denied that the Bulgarians had rebellion in their hearts.[3]

Despite its failure, the revolt was to become a major issue in European diplomacy because of the atrocities committed in its suppression. The Ottoman government at the time was hard pressed to deal with the problems facing it. The rebellion in the western Balkans was continuing. The empire had few regular troops on the scene and therefore used irregulars, called *bashi bozuks*, and Circassians to deal with the revolt. At the beginning the uprising had been accompanied by a massacre of Muslim civilians. In reply, the Ottoman irregulars used methods of the utmost violence. The figures on the number killed differ according to the source. The Bulgarian estimates range from 30,000 to 100,000; the Ottoman government admitted to over 3,000.

---

3 Thomas A. Meininger, "The Response of the Bulgarian People to the April Uprising," *Southeastern Europe* 4, no. 2 (1977):260.

The best estimates are probably the British and American, which are between 12,000 and 15,000.

The responsibility for the reprisals rests primarily on the Ottoman irregular forces and the Circassians, who were recent arrivals in the country and who had themselves undergone a tragic fate. After the Russian conquest of the Caucasus, a policy of compulsory resettlement had been adopted. Forced to leave their homeland, the majority of the people had emigrated to the Ottoman Empire. The government attempted to settle about 100,000 to 250,000 in Bulgaria. Integrating such a large group into a population that numbered under 4 million was difficult. They were not well received, and they lived in miserable conditions. In other words, many of the excesses were the acts of people who were themselves victims of atrocious treatment.

By June the revolution had been completely suppressed. The Bulgarian question would henceforth be handled by the great powers. It will be noted that the revolutionary activities just described were organized and carried through on Bulgarian initiative alone, with some help from individual Romanians. Neither the Russian government nor the Panslav committees had been involved, although many European diplomats laid the direct responsibility on the Russian organizations. The future of Bulgaria was discussed in the general negotiations carried on among the powers in 1876–1877, which had as their major problem a solution to the crisis that had arisen with the revolt in Bosnia and Hercegovina. The principal achievement of the April Uprising was that it forced the European governments to deal with conditions in the Bulgarian lands, as well as in the western Balkans.

BOSNIA AND HERCEGOVINA

In dealing with Bosnia and Hercegovina in the nineteenth century, the Ottoman government encountered many of the problems that were present in the previous period. Constituting about a third of the population, the Muslim element continued to dominate the region. The great majority of this group, it will be remembered, were Slavic in background and Serbo-Croatian in speech. Other Muslims of various ethnic origins had come to Bosnia as janissaries, sipahis, government officials, or refugees from Hungarian lands that had passed under Habsburg control. Since many of these men, particularly the janissaries and captains, were trained fighters, the central government had great difficulty in enforcing its desires on the provincial government. In the eighteenth century the Bosnian military elements had been in frequent conflict with the central government and occasionally with each other, and they were involved in the affairs of Montenegro and Albania. This condition was to continue until the middle of the nineteenth century.

Despite the Muslim control of Bosnia, the Porte had been unable to rely on the region for support against its adversaries. At the time of the Serbian revolt the Ottoman government had not received effective aid until 1813, when

Ali Pasha Derendelia was vezir. Soon thereafter a janissary uprising took place in Sarajevo. Although another governor, Ali Celăleddin Pasha, achieved some successes against these rebels, the Porte was not in a position to move effectively against them until 1829, after the Russo-Turkish War. Mahmud's abolition of the janissaries was naturally strongly resisted. The opposition became fully organized in 1831 when it was realized that the sultan really intended to implement the military reforms. The formation of a modern army struck directly at the privileges and position of the Bosnian military men. The Muslim landholders and the military joined together under a leader named Hüsein, a captain. Their political program strongly resembled that put forward by the Christians in other parts of the Balkans. They demanded autonomy for Bosnia and Hercegovina with an elected native ruler. They were willing to recognize the suzerainty of the sultan and to pay tribute. Hüsein was in touch with Mustafa Pasha Bushati of Shkodër, who was similarly resisting Ottoman central control. The Bosnian forces were on their way to join with Mustafa when the Albanians were defeated by an Ottoman army under the leadership of Mehmed Reshid Pasha. Meeting with Hüsein, Mehmed Reshid assured him that his demands would be met and that he could be vezir of Bosnia. When Hüsein returned home, he was faced by an uprising against his authority led by Ali Rizvanbegović and Smail Aga Čengić, both from Hercegovina. The Ottoman forces backed these men, and together they defeated Hüsein.

Hercegovina was at this point separated from Bosnia and placed as a reward under the rule of Ali Rizvanbegović. In 1834 a new administrative system was introduced into Bosnia; the province was divided into six sanjaks, 42 nahiyes, and many more communes. Officials appointed by the Porte were placed in charge of the major districts. In 1845 provincial councils were set up. All of these centralizing measures were strongly opposed by the local Muslim leaders. During the vezirate of Tapir Pasha, from 1847 to 1850, they again organized and rebelled against the central authority. The Ottoman government sent their best general, Ömer Pasha Latas, to subdue the uprising. A Serbian convert from Lika, Ömer Pasha had been in command of the Ottoman army of occupation in Wallachia in 1848 and 1849, and he had subsequently crushed a rebellion in the Vidin area. He arrived in Bosnia in 1850 with a strong army. He not only defeated the Bosnian rebels, but moved against Ali Rizvanbegović, who had also attempted to rule independently. By 1851 the Ottoman government was in full military control of both Bosnia and Hercegovina. About six thousand had been killed in the suppression of the Muslim defiance of central control. Ömer Pasha then turned to improving the conditions in the region. New administrative divisions were drawn with a military commander at the head of each. In 1853 Ömer launched an attack on Montenegro, but Austrian intervention with the Porte resulted in his recall and the end of what had been a highly successful campaign.

Events in this period in Bosnia, Hercegovina, Montenegro, and the Albanian lands were closely interwoven. In all of these regions the attempts of the Porte to centralize the government and to assert its direct authority over its lands were greatly resented by the local notables. Montenegro, as we have seen, was able to resist the Ottoman forces. The Muslims of Bosnia, Hercegovina, and Albania, where local rebellion was crushed, were becoming increasingly disillusioned with the Ottoman government. The centralizing reforms cut directly into their privileges and seemed to offer no compensating benefits. Influential Muslims throughout the empire objected to the increasing influence of the Christian great powers in Constantinople. Strong resentment remained directed against the changes that had been made in the administration and the military system. Similarly, the continued efforts made to reform the tax system and to aid the peasant struck at the interests of Muslim leadership. Not surprisingly therefore, during the Crimean War the central government received only minimal assistance from Bosnia.

Despite this opposition from the strongest element in Bosnian society, the Porte pressed the reform program. In the sixties, during the administration of Topal Osman Pasha, an effort was made at further internal improvements. Schools and roads were built; a railroad running from Banja Luka to Novi began operation in 1872. Nevertheless, Bosnia and Hercegovina remained among the most backward areas of the peninsula.

The Muslim landholding nobility and the military represented, of course, only a minority of the inhabitants, both Christian and Muslim. Largely excluded from political influence, the Christian population has been estimated at about 43 percent Orthodox or Serb and 22 percent Catholic or Croat. Since Bosnia was a border region, both groups had connections across the frontiers. The Croats were well aware of events in Zagreb. Some were acquainted with the supporters of the Illyrian program, with its espousal of cooperation between Serbs and Croats. The Franciscan order, the predominant Catholic institution in Bosnia, had a great deal of influence upon the Croatian society. The Orthodox hold on the Serbian population was, of course, equally strong.

As we have seen, both Bosnia and Hercegovina were among the first objectives of the Serbian national program. Should they be acquired, together with the Sanjak of Novi Pazar and the lands of Old Serbia, a compact Serbian state of a respectable territorial extent would be established. From the 1840s the Serbian leaders directed their attention westward. They assumed that the Muslim population was Serbian in ethnic background despite the religious difference, and they thus saw Bosnia and Hercegovina as Serbian national lands. The Montenegrin rulers were willing to cooperate. Montenegro kept its own territorial objectives, in particular access to the sea and an extension of the frontiers into Hercegovinian and Albanian lands, but the leaders felt that they were Serbs and they supported Serbian national objectives. During the reign of Michael, under Garašanin's direction, agents were sent into Bosnia and Hercegovina to establish a network of organizations that would support the Serbian cause.

The Serbian program, it is important to note, was national, not social. Garašanin's agents sought the unification of the provinces with Serbia, and they did not advocate radical agrarian reform. Yet this issue was the predominant one in the lives of the majority of the people. Peasant conditions, despite the reforms, remained bad. Constituting 90 percent of the population, the peasantry, both Christian and Muslim, were subject to heavy obligations. The fact that the landowners were of the same national background and language as those who worked their estates did nothing to improve matters. Throughout the century there were constant peasant uprisings caused by the bad agrarian conditions, but they were directed against local abuses, not against the central government. The situation was made worse by the Porte's difficulty in controlling the begs and agas who retained their local social and economic privileges even after the central administration was in the hands of officials appointed from Constantinople.

Agrarian relationships had changed little since the eighteenth century. There were still two principal types of estates, the agaliks and the begliks. On the first the peasants had certain rights to use the land; in 1859 these were guaranteed by law. The begliks, in contrast, were the full property of the landlord. The peasant worked the land on terms agreed upon with the owner. He paid a large percentage of his produce to the beg, and he owed labor dues. The peasants objected principally to the conditions of landholding on the agaliks and the labor obligations on the begliks. They were also injured by the high state taxes and the abuses of tax farming.[4] As part of the reform program the Porte tried to do something to alleviate the position of the Bosnian peasant. After 1851, with the rebellion crushed and its authority reestablished, the Ottoman government could take some measures. In 1858 the land was registered and classified. The next year the agaliks were recognized as the property of their holders, but the state guaranteed certain rights on them for the peasants. Neither the peasants nor the begs and agas liked these regulations. They were almost impossible to enforce, and they did not offer adequate protection for the peasant. The Muslim landholders naturally made every effort to turn the agaliks into begliks and thus avoid state interference.

The agrarian conditions within the Ottoman Empire had by the 1870s become the concern of the great powers. Their consuls throughout the Balkans reported regularly on these questions. Peasant groups also sent petitions concerning their grievances not only to the Porte, but to the foreign representatives. Any major rebellion would necessarily be a matter of European interest. In the Treaty of Paris of 1856 the European powers had declared themselves to be guarantors and protectors of the Christians, although what this meant had never been clearly defined. They did, however, have some rights of inter-

---

4 For the agrarian conditions in Bosnia and Hercegovina see Jozo Tomasevich, *Peasants, Politics, and Economic Change in Yugoslavia* (Stanford, Calif.: Stanford University Press, 1955), pp. 96–107.

vention in favor of the Balkan Christians if extremely dangerous or atrocious conditions arose. In the summer of 1875 a revolt broke out in Hercegovina and rapidly spread into Bosnia. The basic cause was the agrarian situation and the strained relations between the peasants and the landholders, both of whom, it will be remembered, were usually South Slavic in language and ethnic background, although they differed in religion. The movement was thus primarily social and economic, not national, in nature. The rebels were in a very strong position. They were backed by the armed mountain tribes inhabiting lands adjacent to Montenegro, who were experienced fighters, and aid was received from Dalmatia. The Porte was thus called upon to suppress a rebellion in a region where previously it had found military operations costly and impractical. This event was to reopen the Eastern Question and to lead to another Russo-Turkish War.

THE CRISIS OF 1875–1878

Although the Balkan lands continued to be a center of great-power concern, no major conflict erupted in the twenty years after 1856. The unification of the Principalities, followed by the accession of a foreign prince, and the revolts in Crete were settled by diplomatic means. One other major alteration occurred in the balance of forces in the region. During the Franco-Prussian War, which broke out in the summer of 1870, Russia adopted a policy of benevolent neutrality in favor of Prussia. When it became clear that this latter power would make enormous gains, the question of compensation for Russia arose. The objective was clear. Ever since the signing of the humiliating Treaty of Paris, the first goal of Russian foreign policy had been to break the terms of this peace, in particular the clauses pertaining to the neutralization of the Black Sea and the cession of southern Bessarabia. The opportunity had now arisen when positive action could be taken. At the end of October the Russian foreign minister, Alexander M. Gorchakov, denounced the Black Sea provisions in a circular note to the powers. His action caused particular consternation in London because this limitation had been the major British achievement in the Crimean War. Nevertheless, a conference of the signatory powers of the treaty was held in London. They accepted the Russian action, and some alterations were made in the conditions surrounding the closure of the Straits.

The Russian government was thus freed from the treaty restrictions preventing it from fortifying its southern coast and maintaining a Black Sea fleet. Although very few measures were taken in this direction, a major block to Russian action in the Balkans had been removed. The Russian leaders, however, had no intention of adopting adventurous policies. Instead, after the unification of Germany, they supported the rebuilding of the conservative alliance with Vienna and Berlin whose chief purpose was the preservation of the status quo. The new alignment, known as the Three Emperors' Alliance

(*Dreikaiserbund*), was based not on signed agreements, but rather on the close relations that were maintained among the three monarchs, Alexander II, Franz Joseph, and William I, and the frequent consultations of their ministers. The rulers exchanged visits, discussed questions of current importance, and cooperated in international affairs. As long as these three powers remained united, they formed the most powerful diplomatic combination in the world.

In the past the danger spot in the relations of these states had always been the Near East, because of the often contradictory interests of Russia and the Habsburg Empire. Austrian fears of Russian predominance in the Balkans were never laid at rest. The rebellions in Bosnia and Hercegovina produced exactly the type of situation that had caused conflict in the past. Moreover, influences were at work within Russia that could lead to friction between the two powers. Although both Gorchakov and the tsar, as well as most of their principal advisers, were in favor of continuing a policy of retrenchment in foreign affairs, other elements in Russian society were arguing for more positive action. Alexander II always allowed much divergence of opinion among his ministers, and he consulted different advisers on foreign policy matters. Gorchakov was in his late seventies and was often sick. The government was thus open to the pressure exerted upon it by the adherents of the Panslav doctrines, which had won increasing popularity after the Crimean War.

The Panslavs had no single program or spokesman. In general, they stood for the removal of all the Slavic people from foreign, that is, Ottoman or Habsburg, rule and their organization into a federation of states in which Russia would take the leading role. Their emphasis was on the Orthodox Slavs: the Serbs, Bulgarians, and Montenegrins. They certainly did not stand for the liberation of Polish territory from Russian rule; in fact, they regarded the Catholic Poles with extreme distrust and as traitors to their fellow Slavs. In foreign relations they tended to be more anti-Habsburg than anti-Ottoman. There was much talk about the road to Constantinople leading through Vienna. The central organization for the movement was the Slavic Benevolent Society, which was founded in 1858 in Moscow, with branches established later in other cities. It was this group that brought hundreds of Bulgarian and other Slavic students to study in Russia. The Panslavs had at their service a number of talented publicists and journalists, including Ivan Aksakov, M. N. Katkov, R. A. Fadeev, and N. I. Danilevsky. It is important to note that although they were proponents of radical action abroad, they were strongly conservative in domestic politics. Thus they fully supported Russian autocracy.

The Panslav ideas offered a great attraction to large elements of Russian society in the 1870s. Russia had been defeated in a major European conflict; the great reforms were not achieving their expected goals. A united Germany had been created, and although it was at present an ally, the unification marked a resurgence of German power. The Panslav program offered a plan for Russian and Slavic greatness in a period of apparent national weakness, and its doctrines attracted a large number of highly influential people. Both the empress and the heir to the throne, the future Alexander III, were to have a part in the movement. Ignatiev, the ambassador at Constantinople, was a Panslav, but, as we have seen, he was primarily interested in using the Slavic people for Russian aims. Panslavism was in fact a fad; its influence in foreign policy was not long-lasting. However, a protracted period of crisis that arose in the Balkans allowed its proponents to play an influential role in the formation of foreign policy.

When the Ottoman Empire was unable to suppress the uprising in Bosnia and Hercegovina, the members of the Three Emperors' Alliance consulted. At this time the Russian government recognized the priority of the Habsburg interests, because of the geographic location of the rebellion, and the lead in the negotiations was taken by the Habsburg foreign minister, Gyula Andrássy. In December 1875 the three powers offered a reform proposal, the Andrássy Note, as a basis of settlement. The terms were accepted by the Porte, but refused by the insurgents. In May 1876 another program, the Berlin Memorandum, was formulated, but it was rejected by the Ottoman government. By this time the crisis had intensified, with the outbreak of the Bulgarian revolt and the subsequent massacres.

Meanwhile, political conditions had deteriorated in Constantinople. A combination of conservatives, who wished to return to old ways, and liberals, who wanted to advance toward representative institutions, overthrew Abdul Aziz at the end of May. Murad V then came to the throne. Mentally impaired by the events surrounding him, the new sultan was never able to assume the duties of his office. The Ottoman government was thus in a state of confusion until August, when the stronger and more determined Abdul Hamid II came to power. During this period of Ottoman weakness, conditions in the Balkans worsened. With the continuation of the revolt and the increasing intervention of the great powers, the Montenegrin and Serbian governments found themselves under great pressure to take advantage of the situation.

In the past Montenegro had been deeply involved in the affairs of the neighboring lands. The government had designs on Hercegovinian territory and wanted to acquire an outlet on the Adriatic Sea. Negotiations had, as we have seen, been carried on with Serbia, particularly during the reign of Prince Michael Obrenović. After his death, the Serbian government had adopted a more passive attitude and had shown less interest in national expansion. Milan was still young; foreign policy was under the direction of Jovan Ristić, who was not in favor of bellicose policies. Despite the lack of official involvement, various groups continued the work of national organization and propaganda. This was still an age of romantic nationalism and revolutionary ardor. During the summer of 1875 there was naturally great pressure on both Milan and Prince Nicholas of Montenegro to support the insurgents and to exploit the Ottoman weakness. Nicholas was quite willing to take strong action, but

Milan hesitated. The elections had returned a majority that favored military action, but the prince recognized that the country was not ready for war. Moreover, all of the powers, including Russia, were urging restraint.

Although official Russia was thus attempting to prevent Serbia and Montenegro from moving, support for an opposite course of action came from the Panslav circles who had actively involved themselves in the affair. Money and volunteers poured into the area. In May 1876 General M. G. Cherniaev, who had been responsible for the great Russian victories in Central Asia, arrived in Belgrade to take command of the Morava section of the Serbian army. The combination of Serbian public pressure and Panslav enthusiasm was too strong for Milan. In July both Serbia and Montenegro were at war with the Porte. The belligerents hoped that another uprising would occur in Bulgaria and that help would come from the insurgents in Bosnia and Hercegovina. Nevertheless, the correctness of Milan's judgment on the unpreparedness of his forces was soon demonstrated. The Montenegrin army was quite successful, but Serbia faced disaster. Cherniaev proved a poor commander in this situation. There were few trained soldiers among the five thousand Russian volunteers, and they became the cause of friction and controversy. In contrast, the Ottoman army, strengthened by the reforms and with better equipment, was able to win a series of victories. When in October the road to Belgrade had been opened, the Russian government intervened, forcing the Porte to make an armistice at the beginning of November.

During this period the representatives of the Three Emperors' Alliance kept in close touch. After the commencement of the Balkan conflict, Gorchakov and Andrássy met in July in Reichstadt. Here they came to an understanding concerning their mutual interests in the crisis. Although there were to be important differences between the Austrian and the Russian version of the decisions reached, the statesmen agreed on a policy of cooperation and settled certain questions in connection with the war that was in progress. They decided that, should the Ottoman Empire win, the territorial status quo ante should be preserved. If, however, the Balkan states were victorious, a partition of the Ottoman possessions would be undertaken, but no large Slavic state would be created. Montenegro and Serbia would receive extensions of territory; Greece would be given Thessaly and Crete. The remaining Ottoman lands would be divided into three autonomous states – Bulgaria, Rumelia, and Albania – whose territorial extent was not specified. Constantinople was to become a free city. The two diplomats also provided for rewards for themselves. Russia was to receive back southern Bessarabia and an extension of the Russian boundary in the Caucasus area; Austria-Hungary was to obtain compensation in Bosnia and Hercegovina. It was on this point that the two governments were later to disagree on what had been decided at Reichstadt. The Habsburg representatives later were to claim the right to annex or to determine the fate of almost the entire area of the two provinces; the Russian government, in contrast, asserted that only "Turkish Croatia," a small area in northwest Bosnia adjacent to Dalmatia, had been assigned to Vienna. In any case, it was agreed that Serbia was not to gain its principal territorial objective.

When it became clear that the two Balkan states would be defeated, and when the full extent of the massacres in Bulgaria became known, a very strong public reaction against the Ottoman Empire occurred in both Britain and Russia, which was to affect the attitudes of both governments. In London the conservative cabinet of Benjamin Disraeli found its policy of supporting the Ottoman government severely hampered. Even more important, the Russian statesmen faced strong pressure from the Panslavs and those elements of Russian society who felt that support should be given to the Orthodox Slavic people in their struggle against Ottoman control. Serious preparations for war were commenced, but the responsible Russian statesmen still sought a peaceful solution. In an effort to achieve a settlement, representatives of all of the great powers met in Constantinople in December 1876. Here they drew up proposals and presented them to the Porte. The Ottoman government, however, took the occasion to issue a constitution, which it claimed gave full equality to all of the Ottoman citizens and made the intervention of the powers needless. The European suggestions were thus rejected, and the conference broke up. Despite this failure, further efforts to settle the crisis through diplomacy continued from January to April 1877.

With the failure of these negotiations, the Russian leaders had to face the probability of war. Their major fear was that the events of the Crimean War might be repeated, and they might find themselves fighting a European coalition. Austria-Hungary and Britain caused the most concern. Under these circumstances it was considered essential that Habsburg neutrality be assured. In January and March 1877 further agreements were made that achieved this aim and reaffirmed the general partition arrangements of Reichstadt. At the same time an agreement on the passage of troops was discussed with the Romanian government. Since a peaceful settlement seemed hopeless, the tsar in April reluctantly came to the conclusion that war could not be avoided. On April 16 the convention with Romania was signed; on April 24 the Russian troops crossed the Pruth River.

The Russian statesmen had wished to avoid a war because of both their uncertainty over the reaction of the other powers and their lack of confidence in their own military capabilities. The reforms begun in the 1860s had not been completed, and the Black Sea defenses were not in readiness. During the war the Ottoman navy commanded the Black Sea. The Russian leaders fully realized the great financial burdens which a war would entail and for which they were not prepared. The difficulties of the war justified many of their previous apprehensions. After passing through Romania, the army in June crossed the Danube and thereafter won a series of quick victories. Bulgarian volunteer units joined the Russian troops. In July, however, the adv-vance was stopped at Pleven (Plevna), and the Ottoman army succeeded in holding this city until December. With this serious check, it became clear that the war would not be won quickly. In this situation the attitude of the Balkan states became important. At the beginning of the campaign the Russian leaders had shunned their assistance, looking upon their participation as a nuisance and a hindrance. The Balkan governments also wanted arms and money, which the Russians could not easily provide. However, with the failure of Russia's first offensive, assistance from the Romanian, Serbian, and Greek armies took on another aspect. Each of these governments, facing a decision about entering the war, found it under the circumstances not an easy one to make. Montenegro was still technically at war with the Porte; Serbia had made peace in March; Greece was neutral. The Romanian position was perhaps the most complicated.

Although the Romanian government had signed the agreement concerning Russian passage, it had not immediately entered the war. In fact, the entire diplomatic situation caused great uneasiness in Bucharest. The Romanian leaders were concerned that the presence of the Russian army in the country would lead to a return of the conditions of the protectorate. They also, with justification, feared that Russia would take back southern Bessarabia. To protect themselves against the possibilities, they had insisted that the treaty on troop passage contain assurances about Romanian "territorial integrity and political rights." Once the hostilities commenced it was difficult for the Romanian government to remain passive, since nationalist public opinion pressed for action. On May 21 the senate and the chamber passed a resolution declaring the independence of the country, which the prince signed the next day. No great power recognized this act; it was chiefly significant for domestic politics.

Romanian policy was being decided at this time principally by Charles, in cooperation with the Liberal statesmen Ion Brătianu and Mihail Kogălniceanu. The prince, in particular, disliked Romanian neutrality. He wished to exploit the situation to make positive gains for his country. When after the Pleven defeat the Russian government requested Romanian participation, he was eager to agree, particularly when he was offered the command of the operations around this beleaguered city. Romanian troops thus went into action at Pleven and in the Vidin-Belgradchik area.

The Serbian decision was more difficult. The country was exhausted by the previous war. The government was also apprehensive about the territorial settlement that might follow the conflict. At the Constantinople conference the powers had agreed on the establishment of two autonomous Bulgarian states, with the line of division running from north to south. Areas claimed by Serbia, such as Niš and Skopje, had been assigned to Bulgarian authority. The Serbian leaders thus wanted both assurances on what they would receive at the peace and financial assistance before they would commit their country to war. Although they never received satisfactory assurances, they did enter the war on December 13, after the fall of Pleven. They feared that if Serbia did not fight, its claims would be ignored at the peace conference.

The Greek government was, if anything, in a worse position than the other two states. On the one hand, an opportunity had apparently arisen to gain more territory; on the other, the British government exerted constant pressure to prevent a Greek action. Even more dangerous, the Russian support would clearly be given to the Balkan Slavs, the Bulgarians in particular. Like the Habsburg, British, and Romanian governments, the Greek leaders opposed the creation of large Slavic states. They had been jolted by the decisions of the Constantinople conference, which had included territories they considered ethnically Greek in the Bulgarian provinces. The ardent nationalists were convinced that Macedonia, Epirus, Thessaly, and Thrace were solidly Greek in population. The question whether to enter the war or not caused a split in the government, which was also under pressure from a public enthusiastic for war. Finally, in early February 1878, Greek troops crossed into Ottoman territory. When it was learned that an armistice had been signed between Russia and the Ottoman Empire on January 31, this army had to withdraw back behind its own borders.

The victory had not been easy for the Russian forces to achieve. The advance had been stalled at Pleven until December, when the city was finally taken. Thereafter, the army had moved swiftly toward Constantinople. Facing a military disaster, the Ottoman government asked for peace, and on January 31 the armistice was concluded at Adrianople. Ottoman and Russian representatives then negotiated a treaty, which was signed at San Stefano on March 3. Although assurances were given that this agreement was "preliminary" and that the terms involving a change in European treaties would subsequently be reviewed by the powers, it caused consternation in the European capitals. The San Stefano settlement threatened to upset gravely the balance of power in the Near East, and it led to a protracted crisis.

The negotiations had been conducted chiefly by Ignatiev, and the terms reflected his concern for Russian interests. For the great powers the most disturbing sections of the agreement were those calling for the creation of a large Bulgarian state whose territories would include lands north and south of the Balkan Mountains, Macedonia, and a large section of Thrace (see Map 24). It could be assumed that this state would be a Russian satellite. The treaty provided for a two-year occupation by the Russian army and Russian participation in the organization of the government of the new autonomous state. The geographical extent of the country, together with the Russian military occupation, would have placed Constantinople under a permanent threat from the north. With full control of Macedonia, Bulgaria would also be the strongest Balkan power.

Other provisions of the treaty were also disturbing. Montenegro received a huge increase in territory; in fact, that state more than tripled in size. In

Map 24. The Treaty of San Stefano; the Treaty of Berlin

contrast, Serbia received only about 150 square miles of additional territory, much less than that assigned to Montenegro. Romania received even worse treatment. Despite the fact that the state had joined in the war and thus had become a Russian ally, the treaty required that southern Bessarabia be surrendered in return for the Danube Delta and Dobrudja. Greece and Austria-Hungary received nothing. Despite the secret treaties, the Habsburg interest in Bosnia and Hercegovina was not given recognition, and a large Slavic state had certainly been created.

The agreement was chiefly detrimental to British and Habsburg interests; both powers protested strongly. A British fleet entered the Straits. The Romanian, Greek, and Serbian governments also made their dissatisfaction clear. The Serbian position was particularly difficult. It was obvious that Russian patronage would henceforth be placed exclusively behind Bulgarian national aims. In fact, the Russian government told the Serbian representatives that they should look to Vienna for support. The Romanian government refused to accept the surrender of Bessarabia and appealed to the other governments. A period of extreme tension lasted through the spring months.

Facing this opposition and fearful that it might have to deal with a situation similar to the Crimean War, the Russian government backed down. In May it made an agreement with Britain whose chief provisions included the division of the large Bulgarian state. Austria-Hungary was given assurances that its desires would be taken into consideration in relation to Bosnia and Hercegovina. In addition, Russia agreed to attend a European conference that would take place in Berlin under the chairmanship of the German chancellor, Otto von Bismarck. Since the discussions would involve changes in existing European treaties, all of the great powers – Russia, Britain, France, Germany, Italy, Austria-Hungary, and the Ottoman Empire – were invited. There was to be no participation by the Balkan states, although their governments were allowed to send representatives to present their views at the sessions that concerned their interests. Their opinions, in fact, were to have little, if any, effect on the proceedings.

The Congress of Berlin opened on June 13, 1878, and lasted a month. Its principal achievement was a partitioning of a large part of the Ottoman Empire, which lost control over many of its remaining Balkan possessions (see Map 24). The large Bulgarian state was divided into three sections: Bulgaria, including the area to the north of the Balkan Mountains together with the Sofia region, was to become an autonomous tributary principality; Eastern Rumelia, the land between the Balkan and the Rhodope mountains, received a semiautonomous status with an Ottoman appointed Christian governor and was placed under great-power supervision; Macedonia and Thrace were returned to direct Ottoman rule. It was assumed that Russia would be the predominant power in the autonomous principality. To balance this Russian gain, Austria-Hungary received the right to occupy and administer Bosnia and Hercegovina. In addition, the monarchy was allowed to occupy the Sanjak of Novi Pazar, a strip of territory separating Serbia and Montenegro. This territorial arrangement was the principal bargain of the conference. As a result, Russia gained a strong position in the eastern half of the peninsula, with the Habsburg Empire assuming a similar position of dominance in the west, including a major influence in Serbia.

From the point of view of the Balkan states, the results of the conference were very disappointing. Romania, Montenegro, and Serbia were recognized as independent. Montenegro obtained a port on the Adriatic, but not as much territory as it wished. Serbia received only some additional land. Although Greek claims were still not met, Article XXIV of the treaty provided that the Greek government should enter into negotiations with the Porte; should the two states not come to an agreement on a territorial settlement, the great powers would mediate the dispute. Despite the protests of the Romanian representatives at the conference, their government was still required to surrender southern Bessarabia and to take in return the Danube Delta and Dobrudja. The recognition of Romanian independence was attached to changes in the status of the Jews in the state, conditions that were strongly resented in Bucharest. Therefore, although all of the Balkan governments received some compensation, the treaty in no way met their aspirations.

The major losses were suffered, of course, by the Ottoman Empire. In addition to the lands that went to the Balkan states, the Porte had to cede even more important areas to the great powers. Russia, besides southern Bessarabia, acquired Batum, Kars, and Ardahan. Even before the Berlin conference opened, Britain had compelled the Ottoman government to surrender control of the island of Cyprus, a majority of whose inhabitants were Greek. The greatest Ottoman resentment, however, was felt over the Habsburg occupation of Bosnia, Hercegovina, and the Sanjak. The monarchy had not defeated the Porte in a war, and the demand was totally unexpected.

This settlement marked the effective end of Ottoman power in the Balkan peninsula. Although Albania, Macedonia, as well as Thessaly and Epirus until 1881, were still under Ottoman administration, they could be held only with difficulty. An Albanian national movement had already taken shape. Both Bulgarian states, together with Bosnia, Hercegovina, and the Sanjak of Novi Pazar, were still technically a part of the empire, but the government held no illusions that they would ever be returned to full Ottoman control.

The peace was also very unpopular in Russia. It appeared to many Russians that their country had fought a costly war and received very little for its efforts. More than that, the government had been called to account by Europe and had been forced to agree to the partition of the large Bulgarian state, the one great achievement. It appeared that the real victors were Britain and the Habsburg Monarchy; they had gained Cyprus and Bosnia-Hercegovina. Although this judgment was certainly true in regard to Britain, who had indeed won a great diplomatic victory, the Habsburg gains were to become a heavy liability. The occupation of Bosnia and Hercegovina, with their Serb, Croat, and Muslim population, was simply to add another national problem to a state that was unable to handle the controversies it already had. World War I was to have its immediate origin in just these issues.

The closing of the Congress of Berlin in July 1878 did not mark the end of the territorial changes occasioned by the Russo-Turkish War. The Greek claims had to be discussed and new boundary lines drawn. Moreover, the frontiers of Montenegro and Albania had still to be settled. The Albanians were now compelled to organize to defend their national lands.

ALBANIA: THE LEAGUE OF PRIZREN

The treaties of San Stefano and Berlin both assigned Albanian-inhabited land to other states. The inability of the Porte to protect the interests of a region that was 70 percent Muslim and largely loyal forced the Albanian leaders not only to organize for their defense, but also to consider the establishment of an autonomous administration like those which Serbia and the Danubian Principalities had enjoyed. The revolt of the Albanians against both the great-power decisions and the Ottoman authority compelled the Porte once again to take action against this refractory Muslim population.

The Albanian lands had never been easy for the government to control. At the beginning of the century there had been two great pashaliks, which often acted independently of the central government. Ali Pasha of Janina, it will be remembered, alternated between cooperating with and defying Constantinople; the Bushati family in Shkodër adopted a similar position. After the death in 1796 of Kara Mahmud Bushati, who had resisted the Porte, his brother, Ibrahim Pasha, was appointed as his successor in the governorship. Opposed to the policies of Kara Mahmud, Ibrahim governed in cooperation with the Porte until his death in 1810. After a struggle over the governorship, Mustafa Pasha Bushati came to power in 1811. Although he too proved recalcitrant in his attitude, the Ottoman government did not move against him because of its primary concern with Ali Pasha. Mustafa was able to bring a large area under his control and to work with the mountain tribes.

In 1820, it will be remembered, Mahmud I decided to crush Ali Pasha. He first discharged him from his official posts and then summoned him to Constantinople. When Ali refused, he was sentenced to death and an army was sent to Janina. The fact that the Ottoman government chose to concentrate its strength against Janina allowed the Greek rebels the opportunity to gain their first victories in the Peloponnesus and Rumeli. Although most of Ali's local allies deserted him, he was able to put up a strong resistance from his fortress city. Finally, in January 1822, Ottoman agents had him assassinated and his head was sent to Constantinople. The Ottoman army was then free to deal with the Greek revolt. Mustafa Pasha supported the Ottoman military efforts against both Ali Pasha and the Greek rebels. In 1826 he took part in the victory at Misolonghi. Thereafter, he resumed his independent stance, but the war with Russia in 1828–1829 prevented the Porte from moving against this defiant vassal.

In 1830, however, the sultan was again free to act. He dispatched Mehmed Reshid Pasha to Albania. Here the Ottoman general invited the principal Albanian Muslim leaders to meet with him in Bitola in August 1830. Despite the safe-conducts that had been given, he massacred about five hundred of these men. The most prominent begs and agas were thus eliminated. Mehmed Reshid then turned to defeat Mustafa Pasha. He, however, surrendered and spent the rest of his life as an official in Constantinople. This decisive action by the central government ended the period of almost seventy-five years when the Albanian lands had been controlled by local leaders. The Albanian pashaliks had not been representative of a national movement. They were based on the power and influence of a strong leader, Ali Pasha, and of the Bushati family. Their loyalties and allegiances could shift radically. They fought both with and against the Ottoman army; they could cooperate with or fight their Greek and Slavic neighbors.

With the region back under its control, the Porte was able to introduce some reforms. Although the timars were abolished in 1832, this measure had little effect on the country. In most areas the large estates had already passed into the full possession of individual landholders. The Ottoman state too held huge tracts of land. The system of large estates with Muslim owners was to remain predominant, especially in the central lowland areas. In the mountains the tribal system was still in effect. Because of this situation the question of land reform or peasant rights was not to become a major issue until after

World War I. Rural conditions were bad. At this time, as before, there was a great deal of emigration. Large Albanian colonies existed in Romania, Egypt, Bulgaria, the United States, and Constantinople; the settlements in southern Italy have already been mentioned.

Albanian opposition to the Tanzimat reforms was to be expected. Like the Bosnians, the Albanian Muslim notables resented officials imported from Constantinople and preferred to be governed by their own begs. They similarly disliked the military reforms and the establishment of a modern army based on recruitment. Albanian military men had always fought for the Ottoman Empire, but they wished to retain traditional procedures and to follow their own leaders into battle. In Albania as in Bosnia, the Porte could not secure many soldiers for the Crimean War. In fact, it was difficult for the government to enforce any of its decrees in this Muslim society. Attempts to control the highland regions were abandoned. There the population continued to run its own affairs under its tribal leaders according to the local laws and customs.

Nevertheless, despite this widespread opposition, administrative changes were accomplished. New regional divisions were made, but at no time were the Albanian lands joined in a single political unit. In 1836 the region was divided into the eyalets of Janina and Rumelia, with Bitola as the center. In the reforms of 1865 three vilayets were created: Shkodër, Janina, and Bitola; a fourth, Kosovo, was added later. All had large populations of other nationalities. Although the Porte had by this time gained much experience in dealing with national problems, it did not look upon the Albanians as presenting a difficulty of this sort. Since they were Muslims, they were regarded as Ottomans despite their distinctive language and past history. Indeed, up to this time there had been no national movement comparable to those which we have seen in other Balkan regions. Some intellectuals had been aware of the issue, but there was no central organization and no real national program.

The negotiations among the powers in 1878 forced a radical change in the Albanian attitude. The Treaty of San Stefano, which assigned Albanian-inhabited territory to Serbia, Montenegro, and the Bulgarian provinces, virtually compelled a defensive action. In the spring of 1878 prominent Albanians in Constantinople organized a secret committee. The most important individual here was Abdul Frashëri, who was to remain the leading figure in the early stages of the Albanian national movement. In May this group decided to call a general meeting at Prizren that would be composed of representatives from all of the Albanian lands. The vital necessity of the formation of a central authority and the organization of an armed force was recognized.

On June 10 the conference opened at Prizren. It was attended by about eighty delegates from the four vilayets; the representatives were predominantly Muslim religious leaders, notables, and clan chiefs. They decided to set up a permanent organization with its headquarters in Prizren; it was to be under the direction of a central committee. A network of regional organizations in other areas of the country would be subordinate to this authority. The central committee would have the power to levy taxes and raise an army. During the meetings a division of opinion arose that was to be of fundamental importance at this stage of Albanian national development. The major issue to be settled was the attitude to be taken toward the Ottoman government. At first the Porte gave support to the Albanian actions. It, however, wanted the representatives to declare themselves Ottomans, not Albanians. Those who supported this position urged the new organization to emphasize its Muslim Ottoman composition and to direct its chief efforts toward defending all Muslim lands, including Bosnia. A second group, under the leadership of Frashëri, stressed the unity of all Albanians no matter what their religion. These men wished to concentrate on the achievement of predominantly Albanian goals and to seek to secure an autonomous administration. Since most of the delegates were conservative Muslims, the conference in the end supported the maintenance of Ottoman suzerainty.

Despite these differences of opinion, a central authority was established with a center at Prizren. Thereafter the League of Prizren, or the Albanian League, was to direct the efforts made to prevent the implementation of the treaties. Other centers also were established, of which the best known to the outside world was that at Shkodër. Here Catholics and Muslims worked together. Prenk Bib Doda, a Mirdite mountain captain, played a prominent role in events in this region.

One of the main tasks undertaken by the Prizren assembly was the dispatching of a memorandum to the Congress of Berlin. This appeal had no more effect on the great-power decisions than had those of any other Balkan nationality. In the Berlin treaty Montenegro was assigned the cities of Bar (Antivari) and Podgorica, together with the districts of Gusinje and Plav, which the Albanian leaders regarded as integral parts of their own lands. They were also concerned about the future territorial settlement with Greece. There was a strong internal reaction against the cessions to Montenegro and against the Porte, which had not defended the Albanian regions. Centers of resistance were established, in particular in the areas near the border, that is, Prizren and Shkodër in the north and Prevesa and Janina in the south. The Albanian defiance was aided by the fact that able fighting men were available for action. Like Montenegro, Albania had a large supply of armed men who regarded military valor as the highest virtue.

In August 1878, the powers, as provided for in the Treaty of Berlin, set up a commission to delineate the Turkish–Montenegrin border. They expected the Porte to enforce the decisions upon the local population, despite the fact that the Ottoman forces in the region were not strong enough to do so. Although it made some efforts to implement the treaty provisions, the Ottoman government could only benefit from Albanian resistance. It gave the rebels arms, and it approved their collection of taxes. In many areas where the Ottoman forces were obligated to withdraw by the peace agreements, the Albanians simply took control after the Turkish evacuation.

The Albanian forces, nevertheless, had to be prepared to fight both the Montenegrins and the Ottoman army. They were very successful against Montenegro. The Albanian reaction was so strong that the powers decided to switch the territories involved. Instead of Gusinje and Plav, they gave Montenegro the port of Ulcinj (Dulcigno). The Albanians firmly resisted the surrender of this city too. To force the transfer the European powers set up a naval blockade, and they pressed the Ottoman government to act.

Meanwhile, difficulties had arisen in the south. The Treaty of Berlin had directed Greece and the Ottoman Empire to enter into negotiations. In these the Porte naturally wished to give up as little territory as possible. At the same time Albanian committees were organized at Prevesa and Janina. They were willing to accept a cession to Greece of Thessaly, but not of Epirus, which they claimed was Albanian. Once again Ottoman authorities supported the resistance and provided arms. In May 1881 the powers decided that only the relatively small Arta district of Epirus should be given to Greece, which received also Thessaly.

The Ottoman government at this point faced a difficult choice. It was under strong pressure from the European powers to enforce the transfer of Ulcinj to Montenegro, and there were aspects of the Albanian movement that could bring a challenge to the Porte's authority in the region. As we have seen, many Albanian leaders, with a growing consciousness of their own national individuality, supported a program calling for the unification of the Albanian-inhabited lands into a single political unit with the capital at Bitola; Albanian was to be the language of government and education. They did not seek independence because they recognized that the country was too weak to stand alone. This attitude did not receive general acceptance. The division of opinion was shown in a meeting held by the League in July 1880 in Gjirokastër, which was attended by delegates from all the Albanian regions. Here Frashëri presented the arguments for an autonomous organization. According to his plan, the Porte would appoint a governor for Albania, tribute would be paid to the empire, and support would be given in war, but otherwise the country would administer its own affairs. At this congress and at another held at Dibër in October 1880, attended by about three hundred representatives, the conservative forces supporting a close union with the Ottoman Empire were stronger than those favoring a truly autonomous status.

The entire matter was to be settled by force. Although the Porte at first hesitated on the policy to follow, it finally determined, both from domestic and from international considerations, to suppress the League and deliver Ulcinj to Montenegro. A large army under Dervish Pasha was sent to Albania, where it received assistance from loyal Albanians. The League attempted to resist, but in April 1881 Prizren was taken and the movement collapsed. The resistance in Ulcinj was similarly crushed. The Ottoman officials did not take strong reprisals: The leaders were arrested and some were deported. Frashëri himself was captured, sentenced to death, and then to life imprisonment instead. He was released in 1885, but remained in exile until his death in 1892. The Ottoman government restored the centralized administrative system. Some Albanians were named to official posts, but no other moves were made toward political autonomy. Since the majority of the population was Muslim, the Porte continued to regard the Albanians primarily as Ottomans.

Despite the final failure, the League of Prizren had accomplished a great deal. Both Montenegro and Greece received significantly less Albanian territory than they would have gained without the organized protest. Moreover, the great powers were made aware of the existence and separate national interests of the Albanian people. The danger that Albanian lands would be partitioned among the neighboring Balkans states remained, but at least a first step had been taken in the direction of national organization.

BULGARIAN UNIFICATION, 1878–1887

The division of the Bulgarian state set up in the San Stefano treaty was naturally a bitter blow to the Bulgarian nationalists. They thereafter regarded the boundary drawn by this treaty as the state's correct border, and its attainment became the national goal. Despite this disappointment, much had been achieved. Two Bulgarian states were in existence, and it was generally expected that Eastern Rumelia would eventually join the autonomous principality (see Map 25). In addition, changes had occurred in the countryside that were to the advantage of the Bulgarian peasantry. During the war, the Bulgarians had seized Ottoman lands and personal property. Even more important, thousands of Muslims had fled southward toward Constantinople. During the centuries of Ottoman rule a large Muslim and Turkish population had settled in the territory south of the Balkan Mountains. Although the Treaty of Berlin confirmed the rights of these people, neither the Bulgarians nor the Russians intended to allow them to remain. In August 1878 a Russian order stipulated that a Muslim accused of crimes would be tried in a military court; some executions were carried out as a result of this measure. Other Muslim owners were victims of extreme harassment. Under these conditions most Muslims were afraid to return to or to stay in their former homes. In the end the Bulgarian peasants acquired the land after making a payment to the state, and some compensation was paid to the original owner. The land settlement resulting from the war was thus to accelerate the development of Bulgarian agriculture in the direction it had already taken. Like Serbia, Bulgaria was henceforth to be primarily a land of small peasant farms.

Because of the process by which Bulgarian autonomy had been won, there

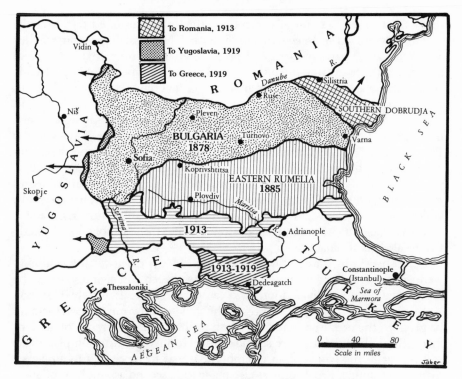

Map 25. Bulgarian territorial changes, 1878–1919

was in 1878 no recognized central authority. In the movements in other lands – in Montenegro, Serbia, Greece, and the Danubian Principalities – a national leadership had been formed before the state passed out of Ottoman control. Despite the fact that no similar development had occurred in Bulgaria, the people did have some administrative experience. They had held posts in the Ottoman administration, and the village communities had run their own affairs. As in other Balkan states, the change to an autonomous regime did not involve a social upheaval. Those who had run local affairs under Ottoman rule now began to direct the nation.

The organization of the first national government was made the responsibility of the Russian government. The Treaty of Berlin limited the Russian army occupation to nine months. Russia's major gain from the war was the creation of the autonomous Bulgarian state, and the Russian officials were determined to establish a strong and stable government that would be closely tied to Russia in the future. Although it was not stated in the treaty, all of the powers recognized Russian predominance in the area. As had been the case in regard to the Danubian Principalities after the war of 1828–1829, it was in the Russian interest to have Bulgaria become a model principality. Moreover, the Russian representatives wanted to set up an administration that would serve as a point of attraction to the Bulgarians of Eastern Rumelia and that would aid in an eventual unification. The Russian government thus accepted for Bulgaria modern and progressive institutions that were far in advance of those existing in Russia itself. It must be remembered that Russia at this time was an autocracy and had no national representative institutions whatsoever.

The Russian commissioner, Prince A. M. Dondukov-Korsakov, assumed in Bulgaria the tasks that had been undertaken previously by Kiselev in the Principalities. He and his assistants drew up a draft constitution, based on the Serbian and Romanian examples, that provided for a strong executive. It was sent to St. Petersburg and there examined by various committees. After it was returned to Bulgaria, it was considered by a constitutional assembly, which met at Tŭrnovo in February 1879. The Russian authorities made it clear that the draft was only a suggestion and that the assembly was perfectly free to alter its stipulations.

The constitutional assembly was attended by 231 delegates, of whom 89 were elected and the rest chosen from among church and civil notables. The representatives soon divided into two camps, the Liberals and the Conservatives. The basis of disagreement was the issue of how much power should be given to the executive, and how much to the legislative branch of government. Since the Liberals were stronger, the Tŭrnovo constitution placed the real power in the hands of an assembly that was to be elected by universal manhood suffrage. Provision was also made for a second assembly to be summoned only on special occasions, such as the confirmation of a new ruler, the amending of the constitution, or the discussion of questions regarding the disposition of Bulgarian territory. As in the neighboring countries, a centralized administrative system was introduced. The state was divided into departments and districts, whose officials were appointed by the central government. More power than in other Balkan states, however, was given to the local population on the lowest level of administration, the communes, in recognition of their historic role in Bulgarian life. Here an elected council chose the mayor.

Although a Bulgarian assembly was chiefly responsible for the constitution, the great powers chose the ruler. They named the twenty-two-year-old prince of Hesse, Alexander of Battenberg, to the position. He had the enormous advantage of being related to the British royal family as well as to the tsar, whose wife was the sister of Alexander's father. Bulgaria, like Greece and Romania, thus had a ruler from a European dynasty of considerable prestige. The prince was an extremely able man, but he had no background in Balkan affairs and, of course, no experience in dealing with the problems of constitutional government.

Meanwhile, the powers had supervised the establishment of an administration in Eastern Rumelia that represented the worst that can come from international collaboration. In April 1878 an Organic Statute was issued that was the product of a mixed commission, with the British, Italian, Habsburg, French, and Russian representatives each drafting a section. The result was a document of 495 articles that was much too complicated for the province. The mess thus created is illustrated by the comments of the British consul in Plovdiv on the French-sponsored administrative regulations:

> Before the war of 1877, the present Province of Eastern Rumelia was divided into two Sandjaks and fourteen Cazas. The two Prefects with the fourteen Baillis who then governed the Province were found more than sufficient. Now, then to the System with which the French delegate has endowed it, there are six Departments and twenty-eight Cantons, and consequently, six Préfets, six "Conseils généraux," six "Commissions permanentes," twenty-eight "Baillis," twenty-eight "Commandants de Gendarmerie," twenty-eight "Commissaires de Police" and so forth . . . Obscure Hamlets which before the War never saw an Official – except the tax collector – have now been erected into "Chef lieux de Cantons" with each of them a "Bailli" "Commandant de Gendarmerie" "Commissaire de Police" a "Juge de Canton" a "Percepteur de Finance" a "Caissier" a "Chef des Contributions indirectes" and a Brigade of Gendarmerie consisting of six or eight gendarmes . . . A province which contains at the utmost 800,000 inhabitants – the population of a City of the second rank – has been endowed with an Executive worthy of a Kingdom. Besides the Governor General, there is the Secretary General or Director of the Interior, Directors of Justice, Public Works, Education, and a Commander in Chief of Militia and Gendarmerie.[5]

The first governor was Aleko Pasha. He had associated with him an assembly of fifty-six members, of whom thirty-six were elected. Aleko soon won the disfavor of both the Russian and the Ottoman governments. When his term of office expired, he was replaced by Gavril Effendi Krustevich. As could be expected, from the beginning there was a strong desire for unification with Bulgaria. At first the Russian representatives supported any activity in this direction. Committees were organized and "gymnastic societies," whose members could be used for revolutionary activities, were founded. Local Rumelian officials too expected that union was only a matter of time.

The main Russian effort was made in Bulgaria proper. As they had done in the Principalities, the Russian agents expected to have a strong influence in the running of the government. The chief diplomatic representative was A. P. Davydov, the consul-general in Sofia. The real source of Russia's strength,

5 Quoted in Charles Jelavich, *Tsarist Russia and Balkan Nationalism: Russian Influence in the Internal Affairs of Bulgaria and Serbia, 1879–1886* (Berkeley: University of California Press, 1958), pp. 209–210.

however, lay in its control over the new Bulgarian army, which was in the process of formation. The minister of war for Bulgaria, General P. D. Parensov, was a Russian, as were all of the officers above the rank of captain. The Russian War Ministry expected to be consulted on all matters of importance. This arrangement gave the Russian government a military strongpoint in the heart of the Balkan peninsula and near Constantinople. It should also have assured it full political domination in the principality.

Three centers of political power emerged at this point: the prince, the political parties, and the Russian agents. The situation was further complicated by the fact that the Russian representatives did not agree. Instead, the diplomatic and military agents supported different parties. Alexander soon found that he could not govern with the constitution, which he thus wished to change. His position was supported by the Conservative party and by Davydov. In contrast, the Liberals and General Parensov opposed the move. In 1881 Tsar Alexander II was assassinated. He was succeeded by his son, Alexander III, who was extremely conservative in political orientation. Prince Alexander was thus able to obtain Russian support for the suspension of the constitution. Relations, however, were soon to become worse. The tsar and the prince, although cousins, did not get along well. Alexander III did not want to be treated as a relative, but as the ruler of a mighty empire to whom the Bulgarians owed gratitude and deference. Moreover, by this time increasing numbers of Bulgarians had become tired of Russian interference. By 1883 the situation developed to the point where the prince and the political parties joined together to form a common front against the Russian officials. In return for Liberal support, the prince restored the Tŭrnovo constitution. Faced with this opposition, the Russian diplomats changed their attitude toward the union of Bulgaria and Eastern Rumelia. Whereas previously they had favored the measure and had made it one of their major aims in foreign policy, they now sought to prevent an action that would increase the prestige and power of a prince whom they wished to replace.

Matters had nevertheless progressed too far in Eastern Rumelia. In September 1885 a revolt broke out in Plovdiv that was quickly successful. The leaders took control of the government and declared the union of the province with Bulgaria. The revolution placed Prince Alexander in a very difficult position. In the previous month he had met with the Russian foreign minister, N. K. Giers, and had given assurances that he would not promote a unification. The union was also in violation of the Treaty of Berlin and could not be accomplished without great-power approval. Russian opposition could be expected. Nevertheless, the prince was fully aware that, unless he retained the leadership of the Bulgarian national movement, he would lose his throne. He therefore accepted the situation and gave his full support to union. The Russian reaction was angry and immediate. All of the Russian officers were recalled, a move that was intended to leave Bulgaria defenseless.

Serbia, expecting Bulgaria to be weak as a result of the internal crisis, decided to take advantage of the situation. Until this time Milan's reign had not been much of a success. A personally unpopular ruler, he had achieved little in the national interest. His army had been defeated in the war with the Ottoman Empire in 1876. The territorial additions gained in the Treaty of Berlin were small compensation for the previous sacrifices and expectations. The Habsburg Monarchy was in occupation of exactly those lands which the Serbian nationalists had desired. Moreover, Milan had been forced to sign an agreement with Vienna that placed him under the domination of the monarchy. Russian favor and support had until the mid-1880s gone to the Bulgarians. The unification of the two Bulgarian states in 1885 did indeed upset the balance of power in the Balkans, and Milan felt that he could not allow this change without gaining compensation. To enforce this position, his government declared war in November and commenced an invasion of Bulgaria. To the surprise of most observers, the Serbian army was decisively beaten. Austria-Hungary was forced to intervene to protect its Balkan ally. Peace was made simply on the basis of the restoral of the prewar conditions.

Although the Bulgarian government gained no concrete rewards from the victory, the powers were compelled to recognize that the union would have to be accepted. The great problem was the enforcement of the terms of the Berlin treaty. As the suzerain power, the Porte would have to carry out any military measures taken, and no government wanted to allow the Ottoman army into the area. Moreover, the Bulgarian defiance of Russia changed the British attitude. The previous objection to a large Bulgaria had been based on the assumption that the state would be a Russian puppet and a permanent danger to Constantinople. Now that Prince Alexander was opposing his protector, the British reaction was favorable. The Habsburg attitude was similar. Given this situation, the Russian government had no practical means of blocking the unification. A compromise solution was therefore reached. The Porte recognized the personal union of the two states and appointed Alexander as governor of Eastern Rumelia for a five-year term. Despite this limitation, the prince proceeded to govern both areas as if they were one political unit. The two assemblies were immediately joined together.

These events naturally caused profound discontent in St. Petersburg. If union was to be accomplished, the Russian statesmen had wished it to be under their sponsorship and with the credit going to them rather than to the prince. As could be expected, they laid the blame for this awkward situation on Alexander. Most Russian officials were firmly convinced that the Bulgarian people were deeply pro-Russian and loyal to their leadership. Believing that their partisans would command popular support, they therefore cooperated in the organization of the opposition to the prince.

In Bulgaria at this time, as in every country, there were a number of discontented elements, including some army officers who felt that their talents had not been sufficiently rewarded. A conspiracy was organized with the knowledge of the tsar and of the Russian ministers of foreign affairs and war.

On the night of August 20–21, 1886, a group of officers seized the prince, forced him to sign an abdication, and escorted him out of the country. A revolutionary government was then set up. This military coup and the kidnapping of the prince had little popular backing. A counterrevolution under the direction of Stephen Stambolov, a Liberal politician, soon overturned the new regime. Alexander was then invited to return. After crossing the border into Bulgaria, the prince made a grave mistake. Hoping to win Russian support, he sent the tsar a telegram stating: "As Russia gave me my crown, I am prepared to give it back into the hands of its Sovereign," an offer that was promptly accepted.[6] This ill-judged action was resented by the Bulgarian patriots, who did not wish to remain in political subservience to St. Petersburg. Alexander had no other alternative than to abdicate. A regency was appointed and the prince left the country. Stambolov remained the most prominent national leader. When it became apparent that his government would retain a defiant attitude, the Russian government broke relations with the state on whose establishment so much effort had been expended.

A special assembly was summoned to choose a new Bulgarian ruler. The position of the country was very difficult. The powers had expected that Bulgaria would remain in the Russian sphere. Its break with St. Petersburg marked a significant alteration in the balance of power in the peninsula and the Black Sea region. The shift won the enthusiastic approval not only of Great Britain, but also of Austria-Hungary. Nevertheless, the Bulgarian leaders had a great deal of difficulty in finding another prince. No power had officially recognized the new situation or wished to defy Russia openly on the issue. Finally, Ferdinand of Saxe-Coburg accepted the office and became prince in August 1887.

Ferdinand's position was very precarious. He did not have great-power sanction. He could expect that conspiracies would be formed against him with Russian approval and assistance. At first he ruled in cooperation with Stambolov, but in 1894 disagreements forced the Bulgarian minister to resign. He was assassinated in 1895. By this time Ferdinand recognized that, because his own situation was so tenuous, regular relations would have to be restored with Russia. In addition, he and the other Bulgarian leaders were well aware that they could not attain their territorial objectives in Macedonia without great-power assistance, and this support could come only from Russia. The new tsar, Nicholas II, and the Russian diplomats also were in favor of a rapprochement. Regular relations were restored in 1896, and Russia and the other powers then recognized Ferdinand. The union had been accepted as permanent.

A united Bulgarian state under a foreign prince had thus been established. Although it was still in theory under the suzerainty of the Porte, that govern-

6 Quoted in C. Jelavich, *Tsarist Russia and Balkan Nationalism*, p. 258.

ment had no influence within the country. Great advances had been made. However, the nationalists still considered the Bulgaria defined by the Treaty of San Stefano as their goal. Events in Macedonia were followed with close attention. The Bulgarian unification and the deposition of Alexander had caused major international crises in the 1880s. Macedonia was to be the next center of conflict in the Balkans.

THE EASTERN QUESTION, 1887–1897: A DECADE OF RELATIVE QUIET

The predominant diplomatic alignment of the period before 1878 was, as we have seen, the Three Emperors' Alliance. The extreme Russian dissatisfaction with the meager results of the Russo-Turkish War was thereafter turned not against the outright opponent, Britain, but against the Russian allies, in particular Germany. Many Russian statesmen felt that the German government had not returned in kind the benevolent assistance that St. Petersburg had rendered during the period of German unification. When relations became particularly strained in 1879, Bismarck looked for alternate diplomatic combinations. The Three Emperors' Alliance of the 1870s had been an informal entente. In the future, in contrast, the international alignments were to be based on written engagements that specified the obligations of the partners. These were in theory secret, but their general contents were usually known. The Balkan states became associated with the alliances of the great powers either directly, through supplementary agreements, or indirectly, through some sort of special relationship with one of their members.

In the negotiations after 1878 the principal responsibility was taken by Bismarck. Germany, the strongest European state, stood at the center of the diplomatic stage. It will be noticed that Balkan issues played a key role in the formation of the alliances. The Dual Alliance, signed by Germany and Austria-Hungary in October 1879, was the first agreement made at this time. A defensive alliance directed against Russia, it obligated its members to go to war should either be attacked by Russia. The treaty was particularly significant because it involved Germany deeply in Balkan affairs and on the side of Vienna. Despite the distrust that had developed between Russia and the Habsburg Empire, Bismarck was able to bring all three courts together again in June 1881 when the Three Emperors' Alliance was revived, this time in the form of a written agreement. A general neutrality pact, this document had clauses directly affecting the Balkans. The signatories agreed that Bulgaria and Eastern Rumelia could unite at a propitious time and that the Habsburg Empire could annex Bosnia-Hercegovina under favorable circumstances. All three powers were to consult on any changes that occurred in the Balkans, and the Russian interpretation of the closure of the Straits was accepted.

A third agreement, the Triple Alliance, followed in May 1882. It linked

Germany, Italy, and Austria-Hungary. Although it was directed at first primarily against France, it too was to have great significance for Balkan affairs. Regarding their country as an equal great power, and dissatisfied with the failure to make gains at the Congress of Berlin, the Italian statesmen wished to share in influence in the Balkans. At each renewal of the pact, which occurred every five years, the Italian government pressed for the recognition of its position. The chief interest was shown in the fate of the Albanian regions, where Italy hoped to play a role similar to that of Russia in the eastern part of the peninsula and Austria-Hungary in the west.

By 1883 a pattern of alliances had thus been formed, with Germany at the center. This network included Serbia and Romania. After 1881 Serbia became associated with the Habsburg Empire through a series of agreements, and in 1883 the Romanian and Habsburg governments concluded a defensive alliance directed against Russia, to which Germany later adhered. Since these treaties were defensive in nature, their obligations did not conflict with those undertaken by Germany and Austria-Hungary in the Three Emperors' Alliance. They did, however, tie the Balkan states to Vienna and Berlin.

The weakest alignment was obviously that of the Three Emperors' Alliance. The basis of an understanding between Russia and the Habsburg Monarchy was an implicit division of the Balkans into two spheres of influence, with Russia predominant in Bulgaria. It was this balance that Alexander of Battenberg and then Ferdinand of Saxe-Coburg destroyed. Habsburg support of the Bulgarian actions made the renewal of the alliance in 1887 impossible. Since neither Russia nor Germany wished to break their partnership, another pact, the Reinsurance Treaty, was signed by these two powers. It was basically a neutrality agreement, but Germany assured the Russian government in a secret protocol that support would be given in securing a favorable regime in Bulgaria and in maintaining the closure of the Straits. As long as Russia did not have adequate coastal fortifications or a strong Black Sea fleet, its government wished to make certain that in case of war the British fleet could not enter the Black Sea; the two countries were in conflict in Central Asia and Afghanistan, as well as in the Near East.

Although Germany had apparently joined with Russia on the Bulgarian question, Bismark at the same time gave tacit approval to the formation of a counter-alignment, the Mediterranean Agreements. These informal understandings linked Britain, Italy, Austria-Hungary, and Spain against French expansion in northern Africa and in support of the status quo in the Mediterranean and Black Sea regions – language that implied backing for Ferdinand's rule in Bulgaria. This alignment made any Russian military action in Bulgaria almost impossible and led to St. Petersburg's eventual acceptance of the new regime.

This elaborate alliance system was upset when the German emperor, William II, in 1890 dropped the Reinsurance Treaty and accepted Bismarck's resignation. Both France and Russia were thus out of any diplomatic system. Neither could afford to remain isolated. In 1891 and 1894 they signed first a military agreement and then an alliance. The Continent was thus divided into two diplomatic camps. On one side stood Russia and France; on the other Germany and the Habsburg Empire were joined by the Dual Alliance, and Germany, Italy, and the monarchy by the Triple Alliance. Romania and Serbia were associated with what came to be known as the Central Powers by supplementary agreements. The break between Berlin and St. Petersburg in 1890, which was completely a German initiative, was to be extremely significant for Balkan affairs. German prestige and power were ultimately to be used to support the Habsburg interests and to contribute to a renewal of the Russian–Habsburg antagonism in the region. Britain, it will be noted, joined neither side, preferring to follow a policy of "splendid isolation."

After the passing of the crisis over Bulgaria, however, these alliances had little direct effect on events in the Balkans. In fact, the area was to enjoy a relatively long period of repose. The European powers wished to avoid another Eastern conflict, so they cooperated to maintain calm in the area. The Habsburg Monarchy was thoroughly occupied with its internal problems; it had to follow a cautious foreign policy. Russian attention was drawn increasingly to the Far East. Britain too no longer looked at Ottoman affairs in the same light. In 1882 a British army occupied Egypt. Thereafter the base for British Near Eastern policy became Egypt and Suez, not Constantinople and the Straits. The reluctance of the powers to become involved in another Ottoman crisis was clearly shown in the years 1894 to 1897. At this time a national movement very similar to those in the Balkans occurred in the Armenian provinces. Local revolts were repressed with massacres, which, like those in Bulgaria in 1876, were fully reported in the European press. However, this time the great powers did not organize the massive intervention that had occurred in the previous period.

Despite the existence of the two European alliance systems and the breakdown of the Three Emperors' Alliance, Russian and Habsburg interests in the Balkans were very close in this last decade of the century. Both wanted conditions of tranquility maintained in the region. In April 1897 Franz Joseph and his foreign minister, Agenor Goluchowski, traveled to St. Petersburg, where they signed an agreement with the Russian government stipulating that the two powers would cooperate in maintaining the status quo in the Balkans. For a decade thereafter the governments did work together to prevent any major crisis from developing that could reopen the Eastern Question. There were to be two major centers of disturbance in the Balkan peninsula. In 1897, as the result of another Cretan uprising, Greece and the Ottoman Empire went to war. The Greek army was defeated, but great-power pressure prevented the Porte from taking any Greek territory. Instead, a small indemnity was paid. Throughout this period there were also constant problems in

Macedonia. However, Russia and the Habsburg Empire were to cooperate to try to calm the situation. All of the great powers, with the exception of Austria-Hungary, were occupied with carving out empires for themselves in Asia and Africa. Russia was soon to become involved in a disastrous war with Japan. No power wished to be distracted by Balkan events.

Conclusion

The national movements: a century of accomplishment

BY 1887 THE MAJOR STEPS toward the formation of the Balkan national states had been taken. An independent Greece, Montenegro, Romania, and Serbia, and an autonomous Bulgaria, were in existence. A movement aiming at the unification of the Albanian lands had been organized. Although the Balkan people of the Habsburg Empire had suffered a political setback with the conclusion of the Ausgleich, Croatia enjoyed a restricted but nevertheless autonomous status. The Romanians, Serbs, and Slovenes had political organizations, usually closely identified with their churches.

The paths to national independence or autonomy had been varied. In Serbia and Greece local notables led armed peasants into battle against the Ottoman army. Although foreign intervention was in the end decisive in determining the final political status, the revolutionary forces did take control of national lands and establish governments. In contrast, the Danubian Principalities and Bulgaria, despite the fact that revolts occurred, owed their freedom from Ottoman control largely to shrewd diplomatic negotiations in Romania's case, and to a war waged by Russia in Bulgaria's.

The position of the nationalities inside the Habsburg Monarchy before 1867 was, of course, entirely different. They could not call in outside assistance or play the international diplomatic rivalries. There was, however, the possibility of utilizing the internal struggle between the imperial government in Vienna and the most self-confident and nationally conscious group in the empire, the Hungarians. Since the majority of the Habsburg Croats, Serbs, and Romanians lived within the boundaries of the lands of the crown of St. Stephen, their fate was closely tied to the results of this conflict. When the choice had to be made, the Romanian leadership sided with Vienna; the Croats at times supported the Hungarian position. With the conclusion of the Ausgleich both lost their gamble, and they were placed under the effective domination of a militant and aggressive Hungarian administration. The battle for power between the national groups and Budapest, and between that capital and the Habsburg imperial government, was to end only with the collapse of the monarchy in 1918.

A great deal has been said in this account about the role of the great powers. In the nineteenth century, not only were they influenced by their desire to maintain the balance of power in the Near East, but individual governments were often tempted to make use of their advantages to gain a controlling position either in a single region or in the entire area. The French interest and influence in the Egypt of Muhammad Ali and in the Principalities has been noted. At different periods Britain, France, and Russia contested for predominance in the councils of the sultan. All of the Balkan people at one time or another called for British, French, Habsburg, or Russian assistance. The temptation to answer the appeals and to exploit them was sometimes great. Much of the European intervention rested on treaties concluded by the Porte that gave the governments individually or collectively the right to interfere in Ottoman domestic affairs or limited the actions of Ottoman officials in their own territory. These agreements dealt with more than the affairs of the nationalities; as we have seen, capitulations and trade treaties gave special privileges to foreigners trading inside the empire. The treaties of Karlowitz and Kuchuk Kainarji were the first that allowed outside powers the right to speak in behalf of Ottoman Balkan subjects. Even more dangerous to the Porte were the agreements signed in the nineteenth century, such as the Convention of Akkerman in 1826, the Treaty of Adrianople of 1829, the Treaty of London of 1830, and the Treaty of Paris of 1856, all of which gave the great powers political protectorates over Balkan territories.

It should nevertheless be emphasized that intervention was a two-edged sword. The Balkan people often asked foreign governments for assistance; they expected this aid to be given freely and without political implications. When a European power attempted to gain repayment for its expenditures of money or lives, the Balkan governments usually reacted with horror and indignation. Russia, of course, was the state most affected by this circumstance. Its repeated wars with the Ottoman Empire had been the chief instrument securing autonomous rights in the Balkans. These efforts cost enormous amounts, which, considering the meager results gained for Russian national interests, could better have been spent at home. This dilemma was well expressed in a letter from A. G. Jomini, a close associate of Gorchakov, to N. K. Giers, who at the time was second to the foreign minister. Writing in the middle of the Russo-Turkish War of 1877–1878, Jomini took a pessimistic view of the outcome of the conflict, which was to be completely justified by subsequent events:

> Moreover, even if, in one way or another, we finish by achieving our object, it would still be impossible for me to see things through rose-tinted glasses! In that case first of all will come the settling of accounts. Once the gunsmoke and the clouds of glory have faded away the net result will remain; that is to say enormous losses, a deplorable financial situation, and what advantages? Our Slav brothers freed, who will astonish us with their ingratitude . . .
>
> This is the balance which I foresee if everything goes as well as

possible. I cannot find this situation a good one, or the policy which is drawing us towards it at the cost of the country's ruin an able one! I persist in thinking that instead of pursuing these Slav chimaeras, we should have done better to see to our own Slav Christians. If the Emperor would come down from the heights and from official splendours and play the role of Haroun al Rashid, if he would visit incognito the suburbs of Bucharest and those of his own capital, he would convince himself of all there is to be done to civilize, organize and develop his own country, and he would draw the conclusion that a crusade against drunkenness and syphilis was more necessary and more profitable to Russia than the ruinous crusade against the Turks for the profit of the Bulgars![1]

In addition to the direct intervention by the diplomats, there was, as has been demonstrated, a strong European influence over the political institutions adopted by the Balkan states. In every case, the governments came to be based on constitutions drawn after Western models. However, the extent of this outside influence can be overstated. Certainly, the form and language of European liberalism was used, but the Balkan societies did have precedents for representative institutions. The interests of the nobility and the notables had been defended in the councils of the medieval kingdoms; the divans in the Principalities had the same function. Peasant participation in administration during the Ottoman period was perhaps even more significant. The role of the communities has been discussed; there heads of peasant families had a major role in deciding local affairs. The institution of the skupština in Serbia, where the men of a region met to discuss major problems, played an important part in the evolution of the Serbian political system. Similar customs existed in primitive areas such as Montenegro. In fact, these traditional, democratically based institutions were to cause problems for all of the national regimes.

Although representative assemblies had a place in Balkan history, centralized, secular Christian administrative systems usually did not. With only a few exceptions, the Balkan people in the past had been governed indirectly through agents of the central power or by a local nobility that might rival in real authority the titular master of a region. Through most of the period of Ottoman rule, the Christian was under the direct authority of his millet and communal leaders, not the representatives of the Porte. In the Habsburg domains and the Danubian Principalities he was subject to the local noble, not to the monarch's officials. In the nineteenth century the convictions of most Balkan statesmen, as well as the influence of the great powers, led to

1 Jomini to Giers, September 1/13, 1877, in Charles Jelavich and Barbara Jelavich, eds., *Russia in the East, 1876–1880* (Leiden: Brill, 1959), pp. 59, 60; trans. in M. S. Anderson, ed., *The Great Powers and the Near East, 1774–1923* (New York: St. Martin's Press, 1970), pp. 96–98.

the adoption of centralized bureaucratic regimes. Here the aim was to extend the control of the central offices of the state over the citizenry without the intermediary of provincial or local institutions. Agents of the central government would thus deal directly with the individual. The Balkan governments adopted this system, because it was considered modern, progressive, and enlightened at the time. The Ottoman Tanzimat reforms, the Bach system in the Habsburg Empire, and the Hungarian administration in 1848–1849 and after 1867 were all based on the attempt to organize the lands in question on these principles. The result of this process, which is discussed in greater detail in Volume II, was the limitation of the political power of the peasantry and the growth in influence of a middle class composed primarily of those members of Balkan society who were able to acquire a higher education. The representative institutions granted in the constitutions were thus canceled out by the existence of a strong, centralized bureaucracy that, in control of the police and the electoral procedures, could manipulate and dominate the political process.

Although by 1887 much had been accomplished, many of the major goals of the national leadership had not yet been fully attained. The territorial unification of the states had not been achieved; the Albanian national movement in particular had far to go. Moreover, many South Slav and Romanian nationals lived in the Habsburg Empire, which at the beginning of the twentieth century remained a strong, functioning great power. The Ottoman Empire also still controlled much of the peninsula. In addition, although national regimes had been organized, these governments had to face severe economic and social problems. The tragedy of the two devastating world wars of the twentieth century, both of which caused great destruction in the Balkans, was to make their solution even more difficult. The accomplishment of the final formation of the modern Balkan states of Albania, Bulgaria, Greece, Romania, and Yugoslavia, and their subsequent efforts to secure economic advancement and to maintain their independence in an era of continuing great-power imperialism, will provide the major themes for the second volume of this narrative.

Bibliography

T HIS BIBLIOGRAPHY CONTAINS a selection of books in English designed to guide a reader who would like more information on the subjects covered in this volume. It does not, of course, include all of the excellent books concerning Balkan history that are available. Articles have been excluded, as well as works in other languages. For information on publications of these sorts and on studies on the Balkan area in all disciplines the reader is referred to Paul L. Horecky, ed., *Southeastern Europe: A Guide to Basic Publications* (Chicago: University of Chicago Press, 1969), and to the bibliographic essays in volumes V and VIII of *A History of East Central Europe*, edited by Peter F. Sugar and Donald W. Treadgold, cited herein. An examination of American scholarship in Balkan studies is to be found in Charles Jelavich, ed., *Language and Area Studies: East Central and Southeastern Europe* (Chicago: University of Chicago Press, 1969). Publications that appeared in the decade after the completion of that book are reviewed in the journal *Balkanistica* 4 (1977–1978), in an issue devoted to the question.

For a better understanding of Balkan life in this period, the reader is strongly advised to read some of the many travel accounts on the region. The majority of these are listed in Shirley Howard Weber, *Voyages and Travels in the Near East during the Nineteenth Century* (Princeton: American School of Classical Studies at Athens, 1952). Although this book does not cover the subject in detail, some surveys of Balkan literature are listed in the final section of the bibliography.

GENERAL HISTORIES OF THE BALKANS

Djordjevic, Dimitrije, and Stephen Fischer-Galati. *The Balkan Revolutionary Tradition*. New York: Columbia University Press, 1981.

Hösch, Edgar. *The Balkans: A Short History from Greek Times to the Present Day*. Translated by Tania Alexander. New York: Crane, Russak, 1972.

Jelavich, Charles, and Barbara Jelavich. *The Balkans*. Englewood Cliffs, N.J.: Prentice-Hall, 1965.

Jelavich, Charles, and Barbara Jelavich, eds. *The Balkans in Transition: Essays on the Development of Balkan Life and Politics since the Eighteenth Century*. Reprint ed., Hamden, Conn.: Archon Books, 1974.

Bibliography

Lampe, John R., and Marvin R. Jackson. *Balkan Economic History, 1550–1950*. Bloomington: Indiana University Press, 1982.

Ristelhueber, René. *A History of the Balkan Peoples*. Edited and translated by Sherman David Spector. New York: Twayne, 1971.

Schevill, Ferdinand. *The History of the Balkan Peninsula*. New York: Harcourt, Brace & Co., 1933.

Seton-Watson, Robert W. *The Rise of Nationality in the Balkans*. London: Constable, 1917.

Stavrianos, L. S. *The Balkans, 1815–1914*. New York: Holt, Rinehart & Winston, 1963.

The Balkans since 1453. New York: Rinehart, 1958.

Stoianovich, Traian. *A Study in Balkan Civilization*. New York: Knopf, 1967.

Sugar, Peter F., and Ivo J. Lederer, eds., *Nationalism in Eastern Europe*. Seattle: University of Washington Press, 1969.

Sugar, Peter F., and Donald W. Treadgold, eds. *A History of East Central Europe*. Seattle: University of Washington Press. Vol. V, *Southeastern Europe under Ottoman Rule, 1354–1804*, by Peter F. Sugar, 1977; vol. VIII, *The Establishment of the Balkan National States, 1804–1920*, by Charles Jelavich and Barbara Jelavich, 1977.

NATIONAL AND IMPERIAL HISTORIES

Balkan nationalities

ALBANIANS

Frasheri, Kristo. *The History of Albania*. Tirana: n. p., 1964.

Logoreci, Anton. *The Albanians: Europe's Forgotten Survivors*. Boulder, Colo.: Westview Press, 1977.

Marmullaku, Ramadan. *Albania and the Albanians*. Translated by Margot Milosavljević and Boško Milosavljević. London: Hurst, 1975.

Swire, Joseph. *Albania: The Rise of a Kingdom*. London: William & Norgate, 1929.

BULGARIANS

Kossev, D., H. Hristov, and D. Angelov. *A Short History of Bulgaria*. Sofia: Foreign Languages Press, 1963.

Macdermott, Mercia. *A History of Bulgaria, 1393–1885*. Allen & Unwin, 1962.

Michew, C. *The Bulgarians in the Past: Pages from the Bulgarian Cultural History*. Lausanne: Librairie Centrale des Nationalités, 1919.

GREEKS

Campbell, John, and Philip Sherrard. *Modern Greece*. London: Benn, 1968.

Clogg, Richard. *A Short History of Modern Greece*. Cambridge: Cambridge University Press, 1979.

Bibliography

Forster, Edward S. *A Short History of Modern Greece, 1821–1956*. London: Methuen, 1958.

Heurtley, W. A., H. C. Darby, C. W. Crawley, and C. M. Woodhouse. *A Short History of Greece*. Cambridge: Cambridge University Press, 1965.

Kousoulas, D. George. *Modern Greece: Profile of a Nation*. New York: Scribner, 1974.

Miller, William. *Greece*. New York: Scribner, 1928.

Sophocles, S. M. *A History of Greece*. Thessaloniki: Institute for Balkan Studies, 1961.

Woodhouse, C. M. *The Story of Modern Greece*. London: Faber & Faber, 1968.

ROMANIANS

Chirot, Daniel. *Social Change in a Peripheral Society: The Creation of a Balkan Colony*. New York: Academic Press, 1976.

Giurescu, Dinu C. *Illustrated History of the Romanian People*. Bucharest: Editura Sport-Turism, 1981.

Oţetea, Andrei, ed. *The History of the Romanian People*. New York: Twayne, 1970.

Seton-Watson, Robert W. *A History of the Roumanians from Roman Times to the Completion of Unity*. Cambridge: Cambridge University Press, 1934.

SERBS, CROATS, AND SLOVENES

Auty, Phyllis. *Yugoslavia*. New York: Walker, 1965.

Clissold, Stephen, ed. *A Short History of Yugoslavia from Early Times to 1966*. Cambridge: Cambridge University Press, 1966.

Dedijer, Vladimir, Ivan Božić, Sima Ćirković, and Milorad Ekmečić. *History of Yugoslavia*. Translated by Kordija Kveder. New York: McGraw-Hill, 1974.

Gazi, Stephen. *A History of Croatia*. New York: Philosophical Library, 1973.

Temperley, H. W. V. *History of Serbia*. New York: Fertig, 1969.

Tomasevich, Jozo. *Peasants, Politics, and Economic Change in Yugoslavia*. Stanford, Calif.: Stanford University Press, 1955.

The Ottoman Empire

Davison, Roderic H. *Turkey*. Englewood Cliffs, N.J.: Prentice-Hall, 1968.

Gibb, H. A. R., and Harold Bowen. *Islamic Society and the West: A Study of the Impact of Western Civilization on Moslem Culture in the Near East*. 1 vol., 2 pts. London: Oxford University Press, 1950, 1957.

Inalcik, Halil. *The Ottoman Empire: The Classical Age, 1300–1600*. Translated by Norman Itzkowitz and Colin Imber. New York: Praeger, 1973.

Itzkowitz, Norman. *Ottoman Empire and Islamic Tradition*. New York: Knopf, 1972.

383

Bibliography

Lewis, Bernard. *The Emergence of Modern Turkey*. London: Oxford University Press, 1961.

Miller, William. *The Ottoman Empire and Its Successor, 1801–1927*. Cambridge: Cambridge University Press, 1936.

Parry, V. J., H. Inalcik, A. N. Kurat, and J. S. Bromley. *A History of the Ottoman Empire to 1730: Chapters from "The Cambridge History of Islam" and "The New Cambridge Modern History"*. Cambridge: Cambridge University Press, 1976.

Shaw, Stanford, J., and Ezel Kural Shaw. *History of the Ottoman Empire and Modern Turkey*. 2 vols. Cambridge: Cambridge University Press, 1967, 1977.

Vucinich, Wayne S. *The Ottoman Empire: Its Record and Legacy*. Princeton, N.J.: Van Nostrand, 1965.

The Habsburg Empire

Kann, Robert A. *A History of the Habsburg Empire, 1526–1918*. Berkeley: University of California Press, 1974.

The Multinational Empire: Nationalism and National Reform in the Habsburg Monarchy, 1848–1918. 2 vols. New York: Columbia University Press, 1950.

Macartney, C. A. *The Habsburg Empire, 1790–1918*. London: Weidenfeld & Nicolson, 1968.

May, Arthur J. *The Habsburg Monarchy, 1867–1914*. New York: Norton Library, 1968.

Tapié, Victor. *The Rise and Fall of the Habsburg Monarchy*. Translated by Stephen Hardman. New York: Praeger, 1971.

Taylor, A. J. P. *The Habsburg Monarchy, 1809–1918*. New York: Harper Torchbooks, 1948.

SELECTED STUDIES: PRE–NINETEENTH CENTURY

Barker, Thomas M. *Double Eagle and Crescent: Vienna's Second Turkish Siege and Its Historical Setting*. Albany: State University of New York Press, 1967.

Cassels, Lavender. *The Struggle for the Ottoman Empire, 1717–1740*. London: Murray, 1966.

Fine, John V. A., Jr. *The Bosnian Church: A New Interpretation*. Boulder, Colo.: East European Quarterly, 1975.

McNeill, William H. *Venice: The Hinge of Europe, 1081–1797*. Chicago: University of Chicago Press, 1974.

Olson, Robert W. *The Siege of Mosul and Ottoman-Persian Relations, 1718– 1743*. Bloomington: Indiana University publications, 1975.

Bibliography

Roider, Karl A., Jr. *The Reluctant Ally: Austria's Policy in the Austro-Turkish War, 1737–1739.* Baton Rouge: Louisiana State University Press, 1972.

Rothenberg, Gunther Erich. *The Austrian Military Border in Croatia, 1522–1747.* Urbana: University of Illinois Press, 1960.

Runciman, Steven. *The Great Church in Captivity.* Cambridge: Cambridge University Press, 1968.

Sorel, Albert. *The Eastern Question in the Eighteenth Century.* New York: Fertig, 1969.

Vacalopoulos, Apostolos E. *The Greek Nation, 1453–1669: The Cultural and Economic Background of Modern Greek Society.* Translated by Ian Moles and Phania Moles. New Brunswick, N.J.: Rutgers University Press, 1976.

History of Macedonia, 1354–1833. Translated by Peter Megann. Thessaloniki: Institute for Balkan Studies, 1973.

Vryonis, Speros, Jr. *Byzantium and Europe.* New York: Harcourt, Brace & World, 1967.

Ware, Timothy. *The Orthodox Church.* Harmondsworth, Middlesex: Penguin Books, 1963.

THE NINETEENTH CENTURY: THE FORMATION OF THE NATIONAL STATES TO 1914

Economic Developments

Berend, Iván T., and György Ránki. *Economic Development in East-Central Europe in the Nineteenth and Twentieth Centuries.* New York: Columbia University Press, 1974.

Blaisdell, Donald. *European Financial Control in the Ottoman Empire: A Study of the Establishment, Activities, and Significance of the Administration of the Ottoman Public Debt.* New York: Columbia University Press, 1929.

Evans, Ifor L. *The Agrarian Revolution in Roumania.* Cambridge, Mass.: Harvard University Press (Belknap Press), 1962.

Feis, Herbert. *Europe the World's Banker, 1870–1914.* New York: Norton, 1965.

Hočevar, Toussaint. *The Structure of the Slovenian Economy, 1848–1963.* New York: Studia Slovenica, 1965.

Sugar, Peter F. *Industrialization of Bosnia-Hercegovina, 1878–1918.* Seattle: University of Washington Press, 1963.

Warriner, Doreen. *Contrasts in Emerging Societies: Readings in the Social and Economic History of South-Eastern Europe in the Nineteenth Century.* Bloomington: Indiana University Press, 1965.

General Studies on Diplomacy

Anastassoff, Christ. *The Tragic Peninsula: A History of the Macedonian Movement for Independence since 1878.* St. Louis: Blackwell & Wielandy, 1938.

Bibliography

Anderson, M. A. *The Eastern Question, 1774–1923*. New York: Macmillan, 1966.

Brailsford, H. N. *Macedonia: Its Races and Their Future*. London: Methuen, 1906.

Georgevitch, Tihomir R. *Macedonia*. London: Allen & Unwin, 1918.

Geshov, Ivan E. *The Balkan League*. Translated by Constantin C. Mincoff. London: Murray, 1915.

Helmreich, Ernst C. *The Diplomacy of the Balkan Wars, 1912–1913*. Cambridge, Mass.: Harvard University Press, 1938.

Jelavich, Barbara. *The Habsburg Empire in European Affairs, 1814–1918*. Reprint ed., Hamden, Conn.: Archon Books, 1975.

    The Ottoman Empire, the Great Powers, and the Straits Question, 1870–1887. Bloomington: Indiana University Press, 1973.

    St. Petersburg and Moscow: Tsarist and Soviet Foreign Policy, 1814–1974. Bloomington: Indiana University Press, 1974.

Jelavich, Charles, *Tsarist Russia and Balkan Nationalism: Russian Influence in the Internal Affairs of Bulgaria and Serbia, 1879–1886*. Berkeley: University of California Press, 1958.

Langer, William L. *European Alliances and Alignments, 1870–1890*. New York: Vintage Books, 1964.

Medlicott, William N. *The Congress of Berlin and After: A Diplomatic History of the Near Eastern Settlement, 1878–1880*. London: Methuen, 1938.

Petrovich, Michael B. *The Emergence of Russian Panslavism, 1856–1870*. New York: Columbia University Press, 1956.

Puryear, Vernon J. *England, Russia and the Straits Question, 1844–1856*. Berkeley: University of California Press, 1931.

Stavrianos, Leften S. *Balkan Federation: A History of the Movement toward Balkan Unity in Modern Times*. Northhampton, Mass.: Smith College Studies in History, 1944.

Stojanović, Mihailo D. *The Great Powers and the Balkans, 1875–1878*. Cambridge: Cambridge University Press, 1939.

Sumner, B. H. *Russia and the Balkans, 1870–1880*. Oxford: Oxford University Press, 1937.

Temperley, H. W. V. *England and the Near East: The Crimea*. Reprint ed., Hamden, Conn.: Archon Books, 1964.

Wilkinson, H. R. *Maps and Politics: A Review of the Ethnographic Cartography of Macedonia*. Liverpool: University Press of Liverpool, 1951.

National Development

ALBANIANS

Great Britain, Office of the Admiralty, Naval Intelligence Division. *Albania: Basic Handbook*. 2 pts., 1943–1944.

Skendi, Stavro. *The Albanian National Awakening, 1878–1912*. Princeton, N.J.: Princeton University Press, 1967.

n, M. A. *The Eastern Question, 1774–1923*. New York: Macmillan, 1966.

d, H. N. *Macedonia: Its Races and Their Future*. London: Methuen

itch, Tihomir R. *Macedonia*. London: Allen & Unwin, 1918.

Ivan E. *The Balkan League*. Translated by Constantin C. Mincoff
don: Murray, 1915.

ch, Ernst C. *The Diplomacy of the Balkan Wars, 1912–1913*. Cambridge.
s.: Harvard University Press, 1938.

Barbara. *The Habsburg Empire in European Affairs, 1814–1918*. Reprint
Hamden, Conn.: Archon Books, 1975.

ttoman Empire, the Great Powers, and the Straits Question, 1870–1887.
mington: Indiana University Press, 1973.

tersburg and Moscow: Tsarist and Soviet Foreign Policy, 1814–1974.
mington: Indiana University Press, 1974.

Charles, *Tsarist Russia and Balkan Nationalism: Russian Influence in
nternal Affairs of Bulgaria and Serbia, 1879–1886*. Berkeley: University
alifornia Press, 1958.

William L. *European Alliances and Alignments, 1870–1890*. New York:
age Books, 1964.

t, William N. *The Congress of Berlin and After: A Diplomatic History
e Near Eastern Settlement, 1878–1880*. London: Methuen, 1938.

, Michael B. *The Emergence of Russian Panslavism, 1856–1870*. New
: Columbia University Press, 1956.

Vernon J. *England, Russia and the Straits Question, 1844–1856*. Berke-
University of California Press, 1931.

s, Leften S. *Balkan Federation: A History of the Movement toward
an Unity in Modern Times*. Northhampton, Mass.: Smith College
ies in History, 1944.

ić, Mihailo D. *The Great Powers and the Balkans, 1875–1878*. Cam-
ge: Cambridge University Press, 1939.

B. H. *Russia and the Balkans, 1870–1880*. Oxford: Oxford University
s, 1937.

y, H. W. V. *England and the Near East: The Crimea*. Reprint ed.,
den, Conn.: Archon Books, 1964.

n, H. R. *Maps and Politics: A Review of the Ethnographic Cartography
acedonia*. Liverpool: University Press of Liverpool, 1951.

National Development

ALBANIANS

tain, Office of the Admiralty, Naval Intelligence Division. *Albania:
Handbook*. 2 pts., 1943–1944.

tavro. *The Albanian National Awakening, 1878–1912*. Princeton, N.J.:
ceton University Press, 1967.

Forster, Edward S. *A Short History of Modern Greece, 1821–1956*. London: Methuen, 1958.

Heurtley, W. A., H. C. Darby, C. W. Crawley, and C. M. Woodhouse. *A Short
History of Greece*. Cambridge: Cambridge University Press, 1965.

Kousoulas, D. George. *Modern Greece: Profile of a Nation*. New York: Scribner, 1974.

Miller, William. *Greece*. New York: Scribner, 1928.

Sophocles, S. M. *A History of Greece*. Thessaloniki: Institute for Balkan Studies, 1961.

Woodhouse, C. M. *The Story of Modern Greece*. London: Faber & Faber, 1968.

ROMANIANS

Chirot, Daniel. *Social Change in a Peripheral Society: The Creation of a Balkan
Colony*. New York: Academic Press, 1976.

Giurescu, Dinu C. *Illustrated History of the Romanian People*. Bucharest: Editura Sport-Turism, 1981.

Oţetea, Andrei, ed. *The History of the Romanian People*. New York: Twayne,
1970.

Seton-Watson, Robert W. *A History of the Roumanians from Roman Times to
the Completion of Unity*. Cambridge: Cambridge University Press, 1934.

SERBS, CROATS, AND SLOVENES

Auty, Phyllis. *Yugoslavia*. New York: Walker, 1965.

Clissold, Stephen, ed. *A Short History of Yugoslavia from Early Times to 1966*.
Cambridge: Cambridge University Press, 1966.

Dedijer, Vladimir, Ivan Božić, Sima Ćirković, and Milorad Ekmečić. *History
of Yugoslavia*. Translated by Kordija Kveder. New York: McGraw-Hill,
1974.

Gazi, Stephen. *A History of Croatia*. New York: Philosophical Library, 1973.

Temperley, H. W. V. *History of Serbia*. New York: Fertig, 1969.

Tomasevich, Jozo. *Peasants, Politics, and Economic Change in Yugoslavia*. Stanford, Calif.: Stanford University Press, 1955.

The Ottoman Empire

Davison, Roderic H. *Turkey*. Englewood Cliffs, N.J.: Prentice-Hall, 1968.

Gibb, H. A. R., and Harold Bowen. *Islamic Society and the West: A Study of
the Impact of Western Civilization on Moslem Culture in the Near East*. 1
vol., 2 pts. London: Oxford University Press, 1950, 1957.

Inalcik, Halil. *The Ottoman Empire: The Classical Age, 1300–1600*. Translated by
Norman Itzkowitz and Colin Imber. New York: Praeger, 1973.

Itzkowitz, Norman. *Ottoman Empire and Islamic Tradition*. New York: Knopf,
1972.

Lewis, Bernard. *The Emergence of Modern Turkey*. London: Oxford University Press, 1961.

Miller, William. *The Ottoman Empire and Its Successor, 1801–1927*. Cambridge: Cambridge University Press, 1936.

Parry, V. J., H. Inalcik, A. N. Kurat, and J. S. Bromley. *A History of the Ottoman Empire to 1730: Chapters from "The Cambridge History of Islam" and "The New Cambridge Modern History"*. Cambridge: Cambridge University Press, 1976.

Shaw, Stanford, J., and Ezel Kural Shaw. *History of the Ottoman Empire and Modern Turkey*. 2 vols. Cambridge: Cambridge University Press, 1967, 1977.

Vucinich, Wayne S. *The Ottoman Empire: Its Record and Legacy*. Princeton, N.J.: Van Nostrand, 1965.

The Habsburg Empire

Kann, Robert A. *A History of the Habsburg Empire, 1526–1918*. Berkeley: University of California Press, 1974.

The Multinational Empire: Nationalism and National Reform in the Habsburg Monarchy, 1848–1918. 2 vols. New York: Columbia University Press, 1950.

Macartney, C. A. *The Habsburg Empire, 1790–1918*. London: Weidenfeld & Nicolson, 1968.

May, Arthur J. *The Habsburg Monarchy, 1867–1914*. New York: Norton Library, 1968.

Tapié, Victor. *The Rise and Fall of the Habsburg Monarchy*. Translated by Stephen Hardman. New York: Praeger, 1971.

Taylor, A. J. P. *The Habsburg Monarchy, 1809–1918*. New York: Harper Torchbooks, 1948.

SELECTED STUDIES: PRE–NINETEENTH CENTURY

Barker, Thomas M. *Double Eagle and Crescent: Vienna's Second Turkish Siege and Its Historical Setting*. Albany: State University of New York Press, 1967.

Cassels, Lavender. *The Struggle for the Ottoman Empire, 1717–1740*. London: Murray, 1966.

Fine, John V. A., Jr. *The Bosnian Church: A New Interpretation*. Boulder, Colo.: East European Quarterly, 1975.

McNeill, William H. *Venice: The Hinge of Europe, 1081–1797*. Chicago: University of Chicago Press, 1974.

Olson, Robert W. *The Siege of Mosul and Ottoman-Persian Relations, 1718–1743*. Bloomington: Indiana University publications, 1975.

Roider, Karl A., Jr. *The Reluctant Ally: Austri… War, 1737–1739*. Baton Rouge: Louisiana Sta…

Rothenberg, Gunther Erich. *The Austrian Mil… 1747*. Urbana: University of Illinois Press, …

Runciman, Steven. *The Great Church in Capt… University Press, 1968.

Sorel, Albert. *The Eastern Question in the Eighte… tig, 1969.

Vacalopoulos, Apostolos E. *The Greek Nation… Economic Background of Modern Greek Soc… and Phania Moles. New Brunswick, N.J.: R… History of Macedonia, 1354–1833*. Translated by… Institute for Balkan Studies, 1973.

Vryonis, Speros, Jr. *Byzantium and Europe*. … World, 1967.

Ware, Timothy. *The Orthodox Church*. Harmo… Books, 1963.

THE NINETEENTH CEN… FORMATION OF THE NATION…

Economic Developm…

Berend, Iván T., and György Ránki. *Econom… Europe in the Nineteenth and Twentieth … University Press, 1974.

Blaisdell, Donald. *European Financial Control… of the Establishment, Activities, and Signif… Ottoman Public Debt*. New York: Colum…

Evans, Ifor L. *The Agrarian Revolution in… Harvard University Press (Belknap Pres…

Feis, Herbert. *Europe the World's Banker, 1870…

Hočevar, Toussaint. *The Structure of the Sl… York: Studia Slovenica, 1965.

Sugar, Peter F. *Industrialization of Bosnia-He… versity of Washington Press, 1963.

Warriner, Doreen. *Contrasts in Emerging So… Economic History of South-Eastern Eu… Bloomington: Indiana University Press…

General Studies on I…

Anastassoff, Christ. *The Tragic Peninsula: A… ment for Independence since 1878*. St. Lou…

Bibliography

BULGARIANS

Beaman, A. Hulme. *M. Stambuloff*. London: Bliss, Sands & Foster, 1895.

Black, C. E. *The Establishment of Constitutional Government in Bulgaria*. Princeton, N.J.: Princeton University Press, 1943.

Clarke, James F. *Bible Societies, American Missionaries, and the National Revival of Bulgaria*. New York: Arno Press, 1971.

Corti, Egon Caesar Conte. *Alexander von Battenberg*. Translated by E. M. Hodgson. London: Cassell, 1954.

Hall, William W. *Puritans in the Balkans: The American Board Mission in Bulgaria, 1878–1918*. Sofia: Cultura Printing House, 1938.

Harris, David. *Britain and the Bulgarian Horrors of 1876*. Chicago: University of Chicago Press, 1939.

MacDermott, Marcia. *The Apostle of Freedom: A Portrait of Vasil Levsky against a Background of Nineteenth Century Bulgaria*. London: Allen & Unwin, 1967.

Madol, Hans Roger. *Ferdinand of Bulgaria: The Dream of Byzantium*. Translated by Kenneth Kirkness. London: Hurst & Blackett, 1933.

Meininger, Thomas A. *Ignatiev and the Establishment of the Bulgarian Exarchate, 1864–1872: A Study in Personal Diplomacy*. Madison: State Historical Society of Wisconsin, 1970.

GREEKS

Augustinos, Gerasimos. *Consciousness and History: Nationalist Critics of Greek Society, 1897–1914*. Boulder, Colo.: East European Quarterly, 1977.

Chaconas, Stephen G. *Adamantios Korais: A Study in Greek Nationalism*. New York: Columbia University Press, 1942.

Clogg, Richard, ed. and trans. *The Movement for Greek Independence, 1770–1821: A Collection of Documents*. London: Macmillan Press, 1976.

Clogg, Richard, ed. *The Struggle for Greek Independence: Essays to Mark the 150th Anniversary of the Greek War of Independence*. Hamden, Conn.: Archon Books, 1973.

Couloumbis, T. A., J. A. Petropulos, and H. J. Psomiades. *Foreign Interference in Greek Politics: An Historical Perspective*. New York: Pella, 1976.

Crawley, C. W. *The Question of Greek Independence: A Study of British Policy in the Near East, 1821–1833*. Cambridge: Cambridge University Press, 1930.

Dakin, Douglas, *The Greek Struggle for Independence, 1821–1833*. London: Batsford, 1973.

The Greek Struggle in Macedonia, 1897–1913. Thessaloniki: Institute for Balkan Studies, 1966.

The Unification of Greece, 1770–1923. London: Benn, 1972.

Diamandouros, Nikiforos P., and John P. Anton, John A. Petropulos, and Peter Topping, eds. *Hellenism and the First Greek War of Liberation (1821–*

1830): Continunity and Change. Thessaloniki: Institute for Balkan Studies, 1976.

Dontas, Domna N. *Greece and the Great Powers, 1863–1875*. Thessaloniki: Institute for Balkan Studies, 1966.

Finlay, George. *History of the Greek Revolution and of the Reign of King Otho*. 2 vols. in 1. London: Zeno, 1971.

Frazee, Charles A. *The Orthodox Church and Independent Greece, 1821–1852*. Cambridge: Cambridge University Press, 1969.

Henderson, G. P. *The Revival of Greek Thought, 1620–1830*. Albany: State University of New York Press, 1970.

Jelavich, Barbara. *Russia and Greece during the Regency of King Othon, 1832–1835*. Thessaloniki: Institute for Balkan Studies, 1962.

Russia and the Greek Revolution of 1843. Munich: Oldenbourg, 1966.

Kaldis, William P. *John Capodistrias and the Modern Greek State*. Madison: State Historical Society of Wisconsin, 1963.

Kaltchas, Nicholas S. *Introduction to the Constitutional History of Modern Greece*. New York: Columbia University Press, 1940.

Kofos, Evangelos. *Greece and the Eastern Crisis, 1875–1878*. Thessaloniki: Institute for Balkan Studies, 1975.

Kolokotrones, Theodoros. *Memoirs from the Greek War of Independence*. Translated and edited by E. M. Edmonds. Chicago: Argonaut, 1969.

Koumoulides, John T. A. *Greece in Transition: Essays in the History of Modern Greece, 1821–1974*. London: Zeno, 1977.

Levandis, John A. *The Greek Foreign Debt and the Great Powers, 1821–1898*. New York: Columbia University Press, 1944.

Makriyannis, Ioannes. *Makriyannis: The Memoirs of General Makriyannis, 1797–1864*. Translated and edited by H. A. Lidderdale. London: Oxford University Press, 1966.

Papacosma, S. Victor. *The Military in Greek Politics: The 1909 Coup d'état*. Kent, Ohio: Kent State University Press, 1977.

Petropulos, John Anthony. *Politics and Statecraft in the Kingdom of Greece, 1833–1843*. Princeton, N.J.: Princeton University Press, 1968.

Prevelakis, Eleutherios. *British Policy towards the Change of Dynasty in Greece, 1862–1863*. Athens: n.p., 1953.

Woodhouse, C. M. *Capodistria: The Founder of Greek Independence*. London: Oxford University Press, 1973.

The Battle of Navarino. London: Hodder & Stoughton, 1965.

The Greek War of Independence: Its Historical Setting. London: Hutchinson's University Library, 1952.

ROMANIANS

Bodea, Cornelia. *The Romanians' Struggle for Unification, 1834–1849*. Translated by Liliana Teodoreanu. Bucharest: Academy of the Socialist Republic of Romania, 1970.

Bibliography

Bobango, Gerald. *The Emergence of the Romanian National State*. Boulder, Colo.: East European Quarterly, 1979.

Constantinescu, Miron, et al., eds. *Unification of the Romanian National State: The Union of Transylvania with Old Romania*. Bucharest: Academy of the Socialist Republic of Romania, 1971.

East, William G. *The Union of Moldavia and Wallachia, 1859*. Cambridge: Cambridge University Press, 1929.

Eidelberg, Philip Gabriel. *The Great Rumanian Peasant Revolt of 1907: Origins of a Modern Jacquerie*. Leiden: Brill, 1974.

Florescu, Radu R. N. *The Struggle against Russia in the Roumanian Principalities, 1821–1854*. Munich: Societas Academica Dacoromana, 1962.

Georgescu, Vlad. *Political Ideas and the Enlightenment in the Romanian Principalities, 1750–1831*. Boulder, Colo. East European Quarterly, 1971.

Hitchins, Keith. *Orthodoxy and Nationality: Andreiu Şaguna and the Rumanians of Transylvania, 1846–1873*. Cambridge, Mass.: Harvard University Press, 1977.

The Rumanian National Movement in Translyvania, 1780–1849. Cambridge, Mass.: Harvard University Press, 1969.

Jelavich, Barbara. *Russia and the Formation of the Romanian National State, 1821–1878*. Cambridge: Cambridge University Press, 1983.

Russia and the Rumanian National Cause, 1858–1859. Reprint ed., Hamden, Conn.: Archon Books, 1974.

Jelavich, Charles, and Barbara Jelavich, eds. *The Education of a Russian Statesman: The Memoirs of Nicholas Karlovich Giers*. Berkeley: University of California Press, 1962.

Jowitt, Kenneth. ed. *Social Change in Romania, 1860–1940*. Berkeley: Institute of International Studies, 1978.

Oldson, William O. *The Historical and Nationalistic Thought of Nicolae Iorga*. Boulder, Colo.: East European Quarterly, 1973.

Riker, T. W. *The Making of Roumania: A Study of an International Problem, 1856–1866*. Oxford: Oxford University Press, 1931.

SERBS, CROATS, AND SLOVENES

Despalatović, Elinor Murray. *Ljudevit Gaj and the Illyrian Movement*. Boulder, Colo.: East European Quarterly, 1975.

Djilas, Milovan. *Njegoš*. Introduced and translated by Michael B. Petrovich. New York: Harcourt, Brace & World, 1966.

Edwards, Lovett F., trans. and ed. *The Memoirs of Prota Matija Nenadović*. Oxford: Oxford University Press (Clarendon Press), 1969.

McClellan, Woodford D. *Svetozar Marković and the Origins of Balkan Socialism*. Princeton, N.J.: Princeton University Press, 1964.

MacKenzie, David. *The Serbs and Russian Panslavism, 1875–1878*. Ithaca, N.Y.: Cornell University Press, 1967.

Bibliography

Noyes, George R., trans. and ed. *The Life and Adventures of Dimitrije Obra-dović*. Berkeley: University of California Press, 1953.

Pavlowitch, Stevan K. *Anglo-Russian Rivalry in Serbia, 1837–1839: The Mission of Colonel Hodges*. Paris: Mouton, 1961.

Petrovich, Michael Boro. *A History of Modern Serbia, 1804–1918*. 2 vols. New York: Harcourt Brace Jovanovich, 1976.

Ranke, Leopold von. *The History of Servia and the Servian Revolution*. Translated by Mrs. Alexander Kerr. London: Bohn, 1853.

Rogel, Carole. *The Slovenes and Yugoslavism, 1890–1914*. Boulder, Colo.: East European Quarterly, 1977.

Rothenberg, Gunther E. *The Military Border in Croatia, 1740–1881: A Study of an Imperial Institution*. Chicago: University of Chicago Press, 1966.

Seton-Watson, Robert W. *The Southern Slav Question and the Habsburg Monarchy*. London: Constable, 1911.

Stokes, Gale. *Legitimacy through Liberalism: Vladimir Jovanović and the Transformation of Serbian Politics*. Seattle: University of Washington Press, 1975.

Wilson, Duncan. *The Life and Times of Vuk Stefanović Karadzić, 1787–1864: Literacy, Literature, and National Independence in Serbia*. Oxford: Oxford University Press (Clarendon Press), 1970.

The Ottoman Empire

Bailey, F. E. *British Policy and the Turkish Reform Movements: A Study in Anglo-Turkish Relations, 1826–1853*. Cambridge, Mass.: Harvard University Press, 1942.

Berkes, Niyazi. *The Development of Secularism in Turkey*. Montreal: McGill University Press, 1964.

Davison, Roderic H. *Reform in the Ottoman Empire, 1856–1876*. Princeton, N.J.: Princeton University Press, 1963.

Devereux, Robert. *The First Ottoman Constitutional Period: A Study of the Midhat Constitution and Parliament*. Baltimore: Johns Hopkins Press, 1963.

Karpat, Kemal. *An Inquiry into the Social Foundations of Nationalism in the Ottoman State: From Social Estates to Classes, from Millets to Nations*. Research Monograph no. 39. Princeton, N.J.: Princeton University, Center for International Studies, 1973.

Karpat, Kemal, ed. *Social Change and Politics in Turkey: A Structural-Historical Analysis*. Leiden: Brill, 1973.

Mardin, Şerif. *The Genesis of Young Ottoman Thought: A Study in the Modernization of Turkish Political Ideas*. Princeton, N.J.: Princeton University Press, 1962.

Ramsaur, Ernest E. *The Young Turks: Prelude to the Revolution of 1908*. Princeton, N.J.: Princeton University Press, 1957.

Bibliography

HISTORIES OF BALKAN LITERATURE

Barac, Antun. *A History of Yugoslav Literature*. Translated by Peter Mijuš-ković. Ann Arbor: Michigan Slavic Publications, 1973.

Dimaras, C. Th. *A History of Modern Greek Literature*. Translated by Mary P. Gianos. Albany: State University of New York Press, 1972.

Mann, Stuart E. *Albanian Literature: An Outline of Prose, Poetry, and Drama*. London: Quaritch, 1955.

Moser, Charles A. *A History of Bulgarian Literature, 865–1944*. The Hague: Mouton, 1972.

Munteano, Basil. *Modern Romanian Literature*. Bucharest: Editura Cuvântul, 1943.

Index

In addition to the material normally contained in an index, the reader will find here a listing of most of the foreign words, usually Turkish, used in the text. The page or pages cited contain a translation or a definition of the term. This index thus also serves as a glossary.

Index

Boris, Bulgarian ruler, 15–16
Boris II, Bulgarian emperor, 17
Bosnia: administration of, 349; and Austria-Hungary, 355, 360; captains in, 88, 90; Christian population of, 89, 350; conversions to Islam in, 36, 88; and Dalmatia, 25; and devshirme, 41; and Dubica War, 90; early history of, 25; 1875–1876 revolt in, 287, 346, 352; and Habsburg Empire, 89, 90; under jurisdiction of Patriarchate, 91; landholding in, 88–89; and Muslims, 88, 89–90, 348–350; and Načertanije, 331; notables in, 90; Orthodox church in, 89; under Ottomans, 32, 88–90, 331, 348–352, 361; peasants in, 89, 351; and Serbia, 333, 334, 350; society of, 88
Bosphorus, see Straits
Botev, Khristo, 346, 347
Brač, 121
Brăila, 69, 105, 265
Branković, George, 31
Braşov, 150, 152, 182, 212, 322
Brătianu, Dumitru, 272, 274
Brătianu, Ion, 272, 274, 295, 296, 357
Bratislava, 139, 304
Brda, 85, 87, 248, 250
Brîncoveanu, Constantine, 66, 101
Bucharest, 235, 294
Bucharest, Treaty of (1812), 118, 164; Article VIII of, 189, 201–202, 203, 239
Buda, 64, 91, 139, 304, 308; see also Budapest
Budapest, 212, 313; see also Buda, Pest
Budva, 121
Bug River, 69, 112
Bukovina, 66, 70, 160, 290
Bulgarian Benevolent Society, 346
Bulgarian Exarchate, 344
Bulgarians and Bulgaria: and April uprising, 347–348; centers of political power of, 370; and constitutional assembly at Tŭrnovo, 368, 370; and cultural revival, 335, 337; early history of, 15–18; and 1875–1876 revolt, 287; and First Bulgarian Empire, 16; Greek influence on, 56, 57, 97; and Greek Project, 71; and Helleno-Bulgarian schools, 337; and landholding, 338–339, 342; and local self-government, 339; and Muslims, 95, 366; and national movement, 335–348, 366–373; and Orthodox church, 12, 95, 97; under Ottoman Empire, 95–97, 331, 339; and Panslav influence, 338; and peasants, 339–340, 341; and revolt in Plovdiv, 370; and Russia, 337–338, 341, 343, 344, 345–346, 359, 367–372; and San Stefano, 358; and Serbia, 246, 341, 371; and Stara Zagora revolt, 346; and taxation, 340–341; and trade, 338–339

Bulgars, 10, 15, 19
Burebista, Dacian king, 9
Bushati, Ibrahim Pasha, 362
Bushati, Kara Mahmud, 84, 87, 123, 124, 125, 362
Bushati, Mehmed Pasha, 84
Bushati, Mustafa Pasha, 349, 362
Byron, Lord, 224–225
Byzantine Empire, 10–13, 21–23, 56; decline and collapse of, 18, 22–23, 31, 32; emperor in, 11; ethnic composition of, 11; Greek language in, 11; influence on Balkan civilization of, 13, 29; religion in, 12–13; temporary resurgences of, 15, 17–18, 23; and Venice, 22–23; see also Roman Empire
Byzantium (city), see Constantinople
Byzantium (empire), see Byzantine Empire

Callatis, 7
Callimachi, Scarlat, 208
Campo Formio, Treaty of (1797), 119, 162
Canning, Robert, 223
Cantacuzino, Constantine, 273
Cantacuzino, George, 105
Cantemir, Dimitrie, 66, 101
capitulations, 180, 236, 378
Capodistrias, Avgoustinos, 223, 228
Capodistrias, Ioannis, 205, 206, 207, 211, 221, 222, 223, 228, 254, 255, 260
Caracalla, Roman emperor, 11
Caragea, Ioan, 208
Carpathian Mountains, 1
Castlereagh, Viscount, 223
Catargiu, Lascar, 296, 297
Catargiu, Marie, 246
Catherine the Great, 68–72, 78, 86, 90, 112, 119, 121, 157
Catholic church, 10, 53, 77, 81, 89, 91, 137; see also Christian churches, Papacy, Uniate church
Čengić, Smail Aga, 349
Certa Puncta, 157
Cetinje, 36, 85, 247, 248, 253
Charlemagne, 22, 128
Charles V, Habsburg emperor, 34
Charles VI, Habsburg emperor, 129, 133, 134, 143
Charles X, king of France, 226
Charles XII, king of Sweden, 66, 101
Charles of Hohenzollern-Sigmaringen, 295–297, 330, 333, 357
Charles of Lorraine, 64
Cherniaev, M. G., 355
Chernishevsky, N. G., 338
Chesme, 69
chetas (defined), 345
chiftliks (defined), 59–60
Chios, 69, 217
chorbazhi, see archon

Index

Index

Mahmud II, Ottoman sultan, 125–126, 201, 216, 219, 227, 277, 278, 279, 281, 282, 341
Mahmud Nedim, 287
Makrigiannis, Ioannis, 231–232
manorial land, 132, 163
Manzikert, battle of (1071), 22
Marashli Ali Pasha, 203
March Laws of 1848, 313
Marko, Krali *or* Kraljević, *see* Mark, Prince
Maria Theresa, Habsburg empress, 68, 70, 129, 134–136, 142, 147, 156, 167, 301
Marie Antoinette, queen of France, 161
Maritsa River, battle of (1371), 31
Mark, Prince, 175
Marković, Nicholas, 86
Marseilles, 54
Maurer, Ludwig von, 254, 255, 256, 258
Mavrocordat, Constantine, 105, 106, 107, 108, 167
Mavrocordat, Nicolae, 107
Mavrokordatos, Aiexander, 55, 220, 221, 222, 260, 261, 262
Mavrokordatos, Ioannis, 55
Mavromichalis, Petrobey, 206
Maximian, Roman emperor, 9
Mazeppa, Ivan Stepanovich, 66
mazili (defined), 107
Mažuranić, Ivan, 319
Mecelle, 282
Mediterranean Agreements, 374
Medjumurje, 317
Megali Idea (Great Idea), 56, 262, 331
Mehmed I, Ottoman sultan, 31
Mehmed the Conqueror, Ottoman sultan, 32, 46, 49
Mehmed III, Ottoman sultan, 45–46
Mehmed Pasha Kukavica, 90
Mehmed Reshid Pasha, 349, 362
Menshikov, Prince Alexander, 283
Mesembria, 7
Metaxas, Andreas, 260
Methodius, 16
Metternich, Prince Clemens von, 163, 192, 211, 223, 301–302, 309
Michael VIII Palaeologus, Byzantine emperor, 23
Michael the Brave, prince of Wallachia, 35
Mickiewicz, A., 175
Midhat Pasha, 282, 340
Milaković, D., 250
Military Frontier, 139, 140, 143, 145–148, 157–158, 161
Miliutin, Serbian ruler, 19
millet (defined), 48–53
millet bashi (defined), 50
Minchiaki, *see* Minciaky, Matei Leovich
Minciaky, Matei Leovich, 266, 269

Mircea the Old, Wallachian ruler, 31
miri (defined), 59
Misolonghi, 217, 219, 224, 277, 362
Mohács, battle of (1526), 34, 128
Moldavia: autonomy of, 99; centers of power in, 100–101; first prince in, 21; Organic Statutes in, 266–269; under Ottomans, 35, 36, 99–101; peasants in, 109; and Russia, 68, 101–105, 110–112, 123, 264–274; *see also* Danubian Principalities, Romanians and Romania
Moltke, Helmut von, 281
Monastir, *see* Bitola
Mongols, 10
Montenegro: and Albania, 87, 365; attack on, by Ömer Pasha, 349; attempts at central administration of, 248–254; autonomous government in, 331; characteristics of, 247; and Congress of Berlin, 360, 364; dual offices in, 247, 249; emigration from, 247; and Habsburg Empire, 87; justice in, 248–249; and the Načertanije, 331; nineteenth century population of, 248; Orthodox church in, 56, 85; and Ottoman Empire, 36, 84, 87, 252–254, 355–361; revolt in, 85, 251; and Russia, 66, 85–87, 120–121, 249–250, 252, 253; and San Stefano, 358–359; and Serbian national objectives, 350; taxation in, 84; and Venice, 85
Morava River and valley, 1, 3, 4
Moravia, 16
Morosini, Francesco, 77
Moruzzi, Alexander, 122
Mostar, 88, 248
*mufti*s (defined), 43
Muhammad Ali, 219, 223, 227, 274, 277, 278, 281, 285, 378
mülk (defined), 59
Münnich, General, 68, 105
Murad I, Ottoman sultan, 31
Murad II, Ottoman sultan, 31, 34
Murad IV, Ottoman sultan, 64
Murad V, Ottoman sultan, 354
Mustafa Bayraktar Pasha, 125, 126
Mustafa Reshid Pasha, 282
Mustafa III, Ottoman sultan, 116
Mustafa IV, Ottoman sultan, 125, 126, 201
Müteferrika, Ibrahim, 115
mütevelli (defined), 59
Mycenae, 4

Načertanije, 244–245, 331, 333
Nagodba, 320, 327
nahije, see nahiye
nahiye (defined), 57, 93, 285
Naissus, *see* Niš
Naples, Kingdom of, 35

Index

Index

Index

Straits, Convention of the (1841), 281–282
Stroganov, G. A., 213
Strossmayer, Bishop Josip, 319, 320, 328, 333
Struma River and valley, 1, 3
Sturdza, Ion, 214
Sturdza, Mihail, 268, 270, 272
Sublime Porte, *see* Ottoman Empire
Suleiman the Magnificent, Ottoman sultan, 32, 34, 36, 39, 45, 64
Suleiman Pasha, 273
Suleiman II, Ottoman sultan, 46
Suleiman III, Ottoman sultan, 65
Suleiman Usküplü, 202, 203
Suli, 73, 80, 83
Şuluţiu, Alexander, 326
Šumadija, 94, 196
Šupljikac, Stephen, 316
Supplex Libellus Valachorum, 159–160
Suţu, Alecu, 209, 210
Suţu, Alexander, 208
Suţu, Mihai, 208, 209
Suvorov, Alexander, 71, 112
Sviatoslav, tsar of Russia, 17
Sweden, 66, 71, 80
Sylva, Carmen, *see* Elizabeth of Wied
Szatmár, Peace of (1711), 140
Széchenyi, Stephen, 303
Szeklers (defined), 21; *see also* Transylvania, Szeklers in

Tamerlane, 31
Tanzimat, 282, 286, 287, 340
Tapir Pasha, 349
Tartars, 19, 66, 69
Tatich, Vladislav, 345
Temesvar, *see* Banat of Temesvar
Teofil, metropolitan, 154
Thebes, 4, 5
Theiss River, *see* Tisza River
Theodosius, Roman emperor, 12
Thessaloniki, 3, 30, 31, 95, 97, 182
Thessaly, 19, 26, 73, 217, 331, 334, 355, 361, 365
Thracians and Thrace, 3, 4, 73, 95–97, 331, 360
Three Emperors' Alliance, 297, 352, 354, 355, 373, 374
Tilsit, Treaty of (1807), 121, 122, 199
timar land, 42, 59–60
Timişoara, *see* Banat of Temesvar
Tîrgovişte, 212
Tiryns, 4
Tisza River, 1
Titograd, *see* Podgorica
Tomis, *see* Constanţa
Tomislav, king of Croatia, 23
Topal Osman Pasha, 350
Tosks, 83

Tott, Baron de, 117
Trajan, Roman emperor, 9
Trandifilov, Alexander, 270
Transleithania, *see* Austria-Hungary
Transylvania: and Aulic Council, 153; autonomy of, 34, 150, 152–153; under Habsburg Empire, 65, 101, 150–160, 304, 321, 332; Hungarians in, 150–153, 321, 322–323, 324, 326; and Hungary, 20, 21, 151, 152, 323–327, 332; National Assembly of, 323–324; "nations" and religions of, 150–153, 321; under Ottoman Empire, 35, 36, 150, 152; peasants in, 156–158, 323; political structure of, 151–152, 158–159, 321; population of, 156–157, 321; revolt in, 157–158; and Romanian language, 321–322; Romanians in, 152, 321–324, 325–327; Saxons in, 150–152, 153, 321, 323, 325, 326; Szeklers in, 150, 152, 153, 321, 322, 324, 325, 326; *see also* Romanians and Romania
Transylvanian School, 155
Travnik, 88, 89, 248
Triavna, 337
Triple Alliance, 373–374
Tripolis, *see* Tripolitza
Tripolitza, 78, 217
Triune Kingdom, 25, 317, 318
Trogir, *see* Trogurium
Trogurium, 7
Tsakalov, Athanasios, 205
Tsintsars, 15, 62
Tuhutum, 156
Tulip Period, 114–115
Turkish Constitution, 242, 243
"Turkish Croatia," 355–356
Tŭrnovo, 27, 31
Turnu Severin, 265
Tvrtko, Stephen, 25
Two Sicilies, Kingdom of the, 54, 192
Tzimisces, John, Byzantine emperor, 17

Ulcinj, 365, 366
ulema (defined), 40, 43, 113
Ulm, 120
Uniate church, 153–155
Unionists, *see* Croato-Hungarian Party (Croatia)
United Principalities of Wallachia and Moldavia, *see* Romanians and Romania
Unkiar Iskelessi, Treaty of (1833), 279, 281, 282
urbarial land, *see* manorial land
Urbarium of 1756, for Slavonia, 144
Urbarium of 1769, for Transylvania, *see* Certa Puncta
Urbarium of 1780, for Croatia, 144
Üsküb, *see* Skopje

Index

vakif (defined), 59
valide sultan (defined), 46
Varaždin, 146
Vardar River, 1; 3
Varna, 7, 344
Varna, battle of (1444), 32
Venice: and Byzantine Empire, 22–23; and Dalmatia, 23, 25, 65, 68, 77, 85; as enemy of patriarch and Porte, 53; and France, 87; and Fourth Crusade, 23; and Genoa, 30; and Greece, 76–77; and Greek Project, 70; Greeks in, 54; maritime empire of, 3, 22; and Montenegro, 85; and Treaty of Karlowitz, 65, 77, 85; and Treaty of Passarowitz, 77, 89; and war with Ottoman Empire (1645–1664), 81, (1714–1718), 68, 85, 105; *see also* Holy League
Via Egnatia, 3
Victoria, queen, 263
Vidin, 124, 338, 340, 349, 357
Vienna, 34, 54, 64, 309–310
Vienna, Treaty of (1815), 163–164, 186
vilayet (defined), 57, 285
Villafranca, Truce of (1859), 332
Villehardouin, Geoffrey de, 23
Vis, 7
Vlachs, 15
Vlach Statutes, *see* Statuta Valachorum
Vladimirescu, Tudor, 204, 208, 209–210, 211–213, 231
Vladislav, king of Poland and Hungary, 31, 32
vojvoda (defined), 146, 316
Vojvodina, 3, 242, 316, 318, 326
Volksgeist (defined), 172, 173
Voulgaris, Dimitrios, 263, 264
Vučićević, Matija, 249–250
Vučić-Perišić, Toma, 241, 243
Vukotić, Ivan, 120, 121, 249–250

Wallachia: autonomy of, 99; boyars in, 107–110; as center of Bulgarian revolutionary activity, 345; centers of power in, 100–101; 1848 revolution in, 272–274; first prince in, 21; Habsburg rule in, 105; Organic Statutes in, 266–269; under Ottomans, 35, 36, 99–101; and Pasvanoglu, 122; peasants in, 107–110; and Russia, 101–105, 110–112, 264–274; taxation in, 107–110; *see also* Danubian Principalities, Romanians and Romania
War of Austrian Succession, 68, 133
War of the League of Augsburg, 65
War of the First Coalition, 162
War of the Second Coalition, 162
War of the Third Coalition, 162
Wellington, Duke of, 226
William I, German emperor, 353
William II, German emperor, 374
William George, prince of Denmark, *see* George I, king of Greece

Xanthos, Emmanuel, 205

Yenikale, 69
Ypsilanti, Alexander, 107
Ypsilanti, Constantine, 122, 125, 206
Ypsilantis, Alexander, 206–207, 209, 210, 211–213, 216, 220
Ypsilantis, Dimitrios, 220

Žabljak, 252
Zadar, 23
zadruga (defined), 91
Zagreb, 27, 90, 140–141, 142, 307, 308, 316, 317
Zaimis, Thrasyvoulos, 264
Zara, *see* Zadar
Zeta, 18
ziamet (defined), 42
Žiča, 19
Zrinski, Peter, 141
župan (defined), 18
Zvonimir, king of Croatia, 24

SUPPLEMENTARY PLATES

1. View of the Dardanelles
2. The Seraglio Point
3. Port Constantinople
4. Yeniköy on the Bosphorus
5. The Bosphorus (opposite the Genoese Castle)
6. Entrance to the Black Sea (from the Giant's Grave)
7. Ruse. (The Danube)
8. The plains of Lower Wallachia. (The Danube, from the Castle of Sistova)